Financial Modeling and Reporting with Microsoft Power BI

Build models, KPIs, and modern finance reports in Power BI from scratch

Andy Clark
Tom Gough
Shailan Chudasama

<packt>

Financial Modeling and Reporting with Microsoft Power BI

Portfolio Director: Pavan Ramchandani
Relationship Lead: Mohd Riyan Khan
Content Engineer: Rounak Kulkarni
Technical Editor: Vidhisha Patidar
Copy Editor: Safis Editing
Indexer: Pratik Shirodkar
Production Designer: Vijay Kamble
Growth Lead: Nivedita Singh

First published: April 2026

Production reference: 1290426

Published by Packt Publishing Ltd.
Grosvenor House
11 St Paul's Square
Birmingham
B3 1RB, UK.

ISBN 978-1-83588-026-5
https://www.packtpub.com

Foreword

As finance professionals, we operate in an era of overwhelming data but limited clarity. Teams spend countless hours sourcing, mapping, and uniting data from multiple systems – often in Excel – just to produce a single version of the truth. In larger organizations, consolidation upon consolidation erodes value, while centralized control over BI reporting can create bottlenecks that slow decision-making. Numbers keep shifting with late journals and restatements, and tracing a figure from the P&L to its source transaction can feel nearly impossible amidst overlapping reports and unclear ownership.

At **Unity Advisory**, our people have seen these challenges first-hand across many businesses. We've also seen how tools like Power BI can change the game. Power BI unifies disparate data sources into a single, coherent view and, with the right governance, enables end users to build reports that meet their own needs. Its AI capabilities bring additional power—automating commentary, detecting anomalies, and highlighting key insights—while ensuring that access remains secure and data remains trusted.

When embedded into everyday tools like Microsoft Teams or Dynamics, Power BI helps finance teams move beyond static reporting to deliver real-time, shared insight at the speed of business. It enables finance to shift focus from collecting numbers to interpreting what they mean—and to drive action.

Financial Modeling and Reporting with Microsoft Power BI provides a practical foundation for making that shift. In an era of AI-driven change, the ability to build trusted, scalable, well-governed data models is not just a technical advantage – it is a strategic one. Finance professionals who invest in these skills will be better placed to lead, not merely respond. Andy, Tom, and Shailan bring years of hard-won experience to these pages. I have no doubt this book will serve as an authoritative and practical guide for any finance professional ready to harness what Power BI makes possible.

Marissa Thomas, CEO, Unity Advisory

Contributors

About the authors

Andy Clark is a Power BI and Data Analytics consultant with a career focused on ERP, CRM, and Business intelligence. He is the CEO of Clearly Solutions LLC, based in Houston, TX, which is a specialist consultancy with a focus on digital transformation using the Microsoft Power Platform. Andy also runs the Greater Houston Power BI User Group and regularly delivers Microsoft Fabric and Power BI training to the Houston data community.

I'd like to thank everyone who's been part of this book, starting with my co-authors, Tom and Shailan. Our wonderful technical reviewers, Deedee, Anuja, Brad, and Adam. Marissa, for an inspiring foreword. The team at Packt, especially Rounak and Riyan, for their guidance and support throughout this process.

Outside of the immediate contributors to the book, I'd like to thank our clients and our communities. Every day, you bring new data challenges to be solved that make us grow as people and professionals. This book is a reflection of solving those challenges together, and it wouldn't exist without you.

Finally, I'd like to thank my Power BI partner-in-crime, Helen Wall, for all the fun in building the Houston Power BI community, but most of all, for being a bloody good friend.

Tom Gough is a data management and analytics professional with over 25 years of industry experience, working on BI solutions across a range of industries, specializing in Power BI in all areas of business, especially in finance. Tom is based in the UK and is the Technical Director at Clearly Cloudy Ltd. In 2015, he delivered one of the first publicly available Power BI courses in the UK, and in 2018, established the first Power BI user group in Birmingham, UK.

First of all, I need to thank my wife, Sue, for putting up with all the weekends I have spent on this project. Also, to my family for not minding the time I have spent on this book instead of with them. Finally, to my friends Hollie and Sofia for listening to my self-doubts, and to my community here in North Wales - diolch yn fawr iawn!

Shailan Chudasama is a business professional with over 25 years of experience in business intelligence and data analytics. He has successfully delivered national and global multi-faceted projects with Microsoft, including Microsoft BI and Microsoft Dynamics. He has a background in Finance and Accounting and is a principal who has architected large-scale data and analytics solutions with the latest Microsoft offerings. A pragmatic business leader, he helped establish Clearly Cloudy Limited in 2015. Shailan is based in the South East, UK. In his spare time, if he has any, he is a qualified firefighter.

About the reviewers

Brad Wilson is a **Certified Public Accountant** (**CPA**) in North Carolina with more than 20 years of experience working with both public and privately held companies. Throughout his career, he has focused on financial reporting and the use of modern analytics platforms, including Power BI, to present financial information in clear and meaningful ways.

His experience spans a variety of industries and business environments, with a strong interest in helping organizations make better use of their financial data to improve operational efficiency.

Anuja Nair is a results-driven data professional specializing in building ETL and business intelligence solutions. She holds certifications as an Azure Data Engineer Associate, Power BI Data Analyst Associate, and Fabric Analytics/Data Engineer Associate, and is committed to continuous learning.

Anuja actively contributes to the data community by participating in events like SQL Saturday. She supports the event's operations and engages with speakers and attendees, fostering a collaborative environment. She is also an artist and enjoys reading books.

Deedee Atsumi-Sarno is a finance executive and digital transformation leader with 25+ years of experience. She specializes in using Power BI and the Microsoft Power Platform to replace manual tasks with automated workflows, driving accuracy and efficiency across multinational organizations.

At TotalEnergies, she led Power BI training for 100+ professionals and implemented Dataverse solutions that slashed reporting man-hours. In Morocco, her Power BI initiatives boosted financial control KPIs by 50%.

Deedee holds an MS in Multinational Commerce from Boston University and a Harvard Business School Corporate Director certificate. An active member of the Houston Power BI community, she brings a global perspective to finance transformation.

Adam Stoltenberg is a finance leader with deep expertise in financial planning, transformation, and data analytics. He has led cross-functional finance initiatives across FP&A, accounting, and operations, with a focus on improving cash flow visibility, forecasting accuracy, and decision-making. Adam has extensive experience working with enterprise systems, including SAP, Oracle, and Hyperion, and has been at the forefront of leveraging Power BI to modernize reporting and drive actionable insights across organizations. His work has helped finance teams move beyond static reporting toward dynamic, KPI-driven performance management.

Table of Contents

Preface xvii

Free benefits with your book xxv

Chapter 1: Identifying Your Reporting Needs and Data Sources 1

Setting project scope 2

Setting clear goals and objectives • 4

Detailed scoping – list of reports to create • 4

Report standards • 7

Security and access • 8

Data sources • 8

Stakeholder identification and engagement • 9

Risk management • 10

Resource planning and time management • 10

Change control process • 11

Test plan • 12

Training plan • 13

Communication plan • 13

Documentation and sign-off • 14

Who needs to use your reports? 14

Identifying your data sources 18

Planning for self-service 21

Summary 23

Chapter 2: The Basic Model for Financial Reporting 25

Creating the core entities 26

Getting familiar with common terminology • 26

Database • 26

Table • 27

Entity • 27

Relationships • 29

Facts and dimensions • 30

Schema • 31

The common structure of financial applications • 33

Calendar • 34

Chart of Accounts • 36

Totaling accounts • 38

Transactions • 41

Managing relationships in Power BI 42

Filter direction • 46

Active versus inactive relationships • 46

Modeling across multiple companies or legal entities 46

Approach 1 – linking the company to the chart of accounts • 47

Approach 2 – linking to the transaction • 49

Considerations for foreign exchange 51

Pitfalls of calculating foreign exchange in the data model • 52

Summary 53

Chapter 3: Creating a Trial Balance and Income Statement 55

Technical requirements 56

Introduction to DAX calculations 56

Understanding measures and calculated columns 57

Understanding the basics: SUM, MIN, MAX, and AVERAGE • 58

Adding measures to the data model 61

Adding our credit and debit totals • 64

Creating an income statement 69

Creating a trial balance 77

Steps to create our Trial Balance • 78

Summary 82

Chapter 4: Common DAX Measures 83

Technical requirements 84
Introducing CALCULATE 84
Revenue • 86
Percentages 87
Time intelligence 89
Period to date – the easy way • 89
Period to date – the hard(er) way • 90
Period-on-period calculations • 91
Foreign exchange 93
Summary 99

Chapter 5: Handling Manual Journal Entries 101

Technical requirements 102
Understanding the value of including manual journal entries 103
Exploring the structure of manual journal entries • 105
Deriving facts and dimensions from the manual journals 109
Linking manual journal entry data to the GL transaction 111
Summary 120

Chapter 6: Streamlining with Power Query 123

Technical requirements 124
What is Power Query? 124
Using Power Query to reduce datasets 128
Only importing the required tables or entities • 129
Removing columns you don't need • 129
Removing rows you don't need • 131
Common data transformations 134
Changing data types • 134
Adding conditional and custom columns • 135
Conditional columns • 135

Custom columns • 137

Merging data • 138

Pivoting and unpivoting columns • 140

Changing column names using AI to be readable by humans • 141

Correcting opening balances • 142

Summary **147**

Chapter 7: Incorporating Budgets and Targets 149

Technical requirements **149**

Creating a budget table **150**

Handling differences in granularity **153**

Budgeting monthly • 154

Budgeting daily • 157

Seeing the details with drill-through **160**

Visuals to consider for analyzing budgets **163**

Working with multiple budget models or scenarios **165**

Maintaining a common structure • 166

Using Power Query to incorporate your budgets into one table **166**

Managing multiple budgeting methods • 167

Managing budget revisions • 167

Managing multiple budgets in your model • 168

Summary **169**

Chapter 8: Managing Inventory Data 171

Technical requirements **171**

Introducing inventory data **172**

Working with inventory snapshot data **172**

Measures for snapshot reporting • 174

SUM or SUMX • 174

CALCULATE • 174

Period-on-period calculations • 175

Working with transactional inventory data **177**

Inventory-specific dimensions • 179

Creating inventory measures 180

The basics • 180

Summary 187

Chapter 9: Creating a Suite of Financial Reports 189

Technical requirements 189

Designing a suite of reports 190

Your numbers are accurate • 190

Data is secure and appropriate for the user • 191

The reports are responsive • 191

The report has a clear purpose or answers a defined question • 192

Report layout and design are consistent, clean, and well considered • 193

Avoid garish colors • 195

Subtle, rounded boundaries • 196

Use negative space • 197

Corporate color schemes • 198

Key visuals for financial reporting 199

Magnitude • 199

Change over time • 201

Part to whole • 202

Tables • 206

Matrices • 206

Cards • 208

Building reports 208

Profit and Loss report • 208

Step 1: Creating the category groups • 209

Step 2: Adding a table to the report • 210

Step 3: Filtering the page for only P&L items • 211

Step 4: Adding a column chart • 213

Step 5: Adding the details in a matrix • 213

Step 6: Adding the gross margin • 216

Step 7: The headline figures • 217

Step 8: Adding a gross margin gauge • 218

Step 9: Adding slicers • 219

Step 10: Adding a title • 220

Budget variance report • 221

Step 1: Adding a table to show budget, total revenue, and variance by account • 222

Step 2: Adding a matrix • 225

Step 3: Adding the headline figures • 226

Step 4: Showing change over time • 227

Step 5: Adding slicers • 228

Summary 230

Chapter 10: Testing and Fine-Tuning Your Data 233

Technical requirements 234

What is incorrect data? 234

Using the trial balance to test your data 235

Common checks for the trial balance • 235

Creating a transaction-level reconciliation 238

Before you start • 238

What to do • 238

What to do, and what to look out for • 241

Cleansing data in Power Query and Power BI 242

Non-functional testing 243

Summary 245

Chapter 11: Printable Financial Statements with Power BI Paginated 247

Technical requirements 248

Understanding when paginated reports are useful 248

Using Power BI Report Builder 249

Creating a printable income statement 252

Creating the trial balance report 262

Summary 263

Chapter 12: Financial Reporting in an AI-Driven World 265

What is AI? 266

Foundations of AI • 266

Looking at the current trends • 266

Where do you start with an AI project? • 267

Start with a business need • 267

A technical method to solve the problem • 268

Using Power BI and AI together 268

Simplify the data schema • 271

Verified answers • 272

Add AI instructions • 274

Short and medium-term data planning and storage • 277

Long-term considerations for AI projects 279

Think about how you develop AI capabilities • 280

Working with Microsoft Fabric 283

Storage • 284

Data warehouse and data lakehouse • 284

Data factory and data engineering • 285

Data science • 285

Real-time intelligence • 286

Power BI • 286

Understanding the risks of AI 287

Maintainability • 288

Accuracy • 288

Security • 288

Managing and mitigating the risk • 289

Summary 289

Chapter 13: Evolving and Maintaining Your Reports 291

User access and publishing to the web 292

Admin portal and publishing to the web • 292
Workspaces • 294
Publishing reports • 297
From Power BI Desktop • 297
Within the service • 297
Workspace planning 297
Deployment pipelines • 298
Sharing reports 298
Workspace versus app sharing • 299
Row-level security • 300
Data refreshes 301
Change control 303
Bug or change • 303
Planning and implementation changes • 304
Monitoring • 305
Maintenance and retirement of reports • 306
Summary 306

Chapter 14: Unlock Your Exclusive Benefits 309

Unlock this book's free benefits in 3 easy steps 310

Other Books You May Enjoy 314

Index 317

Preface

Power BI has been good to us. Tom, Shailan, and I (Andy) have carved out successful and enjoyable careers and for the past 10 years, Power BI has been a large part of that. We all had the good fortune, or maybe good luck, to start riding the Power BI wave early, working with the product as it evolved and developed. To support this, we all work with many datasources and business systems across a broad range of clients and industries. To say no two days are alike is an understatement.

Tom's roots are as a SQL database admin and Shailan and I worked with ERP providers (Navision and SAP), then Microsoft.

Now, we all ply our trade as consultants in the UK and USA and a large part of that is working with Power BI and finance data. You know why we work with Power BI, but why do we work with so much finance data? Well, most of the use of Power BI is in the financial arena so if you're going to dedicate yourself to this product, you'll inevitably spend a reasonable proportion of your time working with financial data.

The intersection of the worlds of Power BI and finance means this book has scratched an itch for the three of us. That is, to write a book dedicated to Power BI from the perspective of the finance user. We've seen every experience of finance users starting to use this tool and we've all had a long desire to write the handbook that could get them up to speed quicker.

Most Power BI books are written for developers, not users – which I hasten to add, isn't a criticism. We own many of those books and are friends with some of the authors. The Power BI and data community is a relatively small and definitely friendly group and we all intend to be part of this for much longer. We wanted to add something to the large volume of Power BI books that does something slightly different.

That's a few words on us and how we got here, so let's move on to the reason you're here, which is the book.

This is mainly a technical book and we know from our own use of technical books, they're rarely read in a linear fashion. We don't expect too many people to start with *Chapter 1* then work through to the end of *Chapter 13*, page after page. If you want to, that's great, and we've written it so anyone can do exactly that, but we've also worked hard to make chapters reasonably self-contained. For example, if you need to pick up the book to help you with your budgeting processes, please go straight to *Chapter 7*. You don't have to read chapters 1 to 6 first, but you can. There may even be chapters or sections that don't support your work. Finance is a broad topic so we had to make some difficult decisions about content from the outset. Put succinctly, please use the resource to support your requirements.

At the start of the book, the examples are rudimentary and we have step-by-step guides. But, we pick up the pace quickly as the book progresses, so we had to assume you have some training in Power BI and Power Query. If you're coming to the book cold, we recommend taking some structured Power BI training, even if it's binge watching YouTube videos. There are so many great books, videos, in-person, and online courses that we didn't want to replicate, so we can focus these pages on the intersection of Power BI and finance.

From the outset we wanted to use examples the reader could follow. So, we gave ourselves the extra task of building a demonstration dataset. Credit where credit's due, Tom built the dataset and did an amazing job to build an imaginary entity called Clearly Clothing that you see in these pages. Building a dataset is not a quick and simple task and many weekends were spent working on this.

We have to store this data somewhere our readers can easily find it and we chose GitHub. As finance users, GitHub may be new so a quick explanation for GitHub is it's Microsoft's online platform for developers to store and manage code. We use it in a pretty rudimentary way, as a file share to store the Power BI and source Excel files we use for the examples in the book. More on this later.

That's a little about us, why we did this and how we designed the book. From here we hope this book helps you to develop your Power BI skills and maybe solves a few challenges you had in using Power BI.

-Andy Clark

Who this book is for

This book is for finance professionals, accountants, financial analysts, and BI developers who want to leverage Power BI to improve, automate, and future-proof their financial reporting. Whether consolidating data from ERPs, building reports across entities, or exploring advanced Power BI features, this book equips readers with practical skills and strategic insight.

What this book covers

Chapter 1, Identifying Your Reporting Needs and Data Sources, provides an introduction and overview of what you need to consider when embarking on a Power BI project and how to identify specific needs.

Chapter 2, The Basic Model for Financial Reporting, introduces the basic concepts for creating a data model for financial reporting.

Chapter 3, Creating a Trial Balance and Income Statement, shows how to create two of the most basic and fundamental reports in any financial suite – the Trial Balance and Income Statement. This chapter introduces some basic DAX and data visualization techniques.

Chapter 4, Common DAX Measures, expands on the use of DAX to more complex measures. It introduces the ideas of time intelligence and some considerations for handling foreign exchange calculations.

Chapter 5, Handling Manual Journal Entries, introduces some more advanced data modeling techniques such as the snowflake schema and role-playing dimensions. While this chapter uses manual journal entries as an example, the concept is applicable beyond this.

Chapter 6, Streamlining with Power Query, demonstrates how to manage data sizes and improve report performance by controlling what is being imported and helping to keep focus on what is important.

Chapter 7, Incorporating Budgets and Targets, shows how budgets and targets can be incorporated into the data model to measure performance. Here we also look at how to handle variations in the granularity of different data sets.

Chapter 8, Managing Inventory Data, expands on data modeling techniques to show additional context to the financial reporting suite and demonstrates how to deal with data that is very different in nature from the core financial data sets.

Chapter 9, Creating a Suite of Financial Reports, builds on the techniques demonstrated up to this point to build a more comprehensive set of financial reports, expanding beyond the basics to produce engaging visuals for a variety of reports across data sets.

Chapter 10, Testing and Fine-Tuning Your Data, addresses the issue of ensuring the accuracy of reports and non-functional testing to make sure that reports are both accurate and usable, and that the user base will continue to use the reports in the long term.

Chapter 11, Printable Financial Statements with Power BI Paginated, introduces Power BI Paginated for creating printable and other types of fixed-format reports.

Chapter 12, Financial Reporting in an AI-Driven World, provides an overview of the hottest topic of today – AI. This chapter covers how to use AI features in Power BI, when and why to use AI, and how to structure data to facilitate future use of AI.

Chapter 13, Evolving and Maintaining Your Reports, shows how to manage the reporting suite, from defining security, to capturing bugs, and new requirements, through to the end of the lifecycle of a report – its final retirement.

To get the most out of this book

At the start of each chapter with examples, we have a link to the GitHub folder that stores the Power BI files for the chapter so you can download and follow along if you like. There are 2 components to make this work: the **Power BI PBIX** files and the **Excel** source data files. For most chapters, you'll only need the Power BI PBIX file. For *Chapter 6*, where we have tips and tricks for streamlining your data with Power Query, you'll also need the Excel files. And, if you want to freestyle a little and explore the data on your own, we recommend downloading the files and connecting the Power BI PBIX file to the Excel source data. To do this, please follow these steps:

1. Starting with the Core Data Model, follow this link: `https://github.com/PacktPublishing/Financial-Modeling-with-Power-BI_Packt/tree/main/Chapter2`. You'll see the *Chapter2* contents as follows:

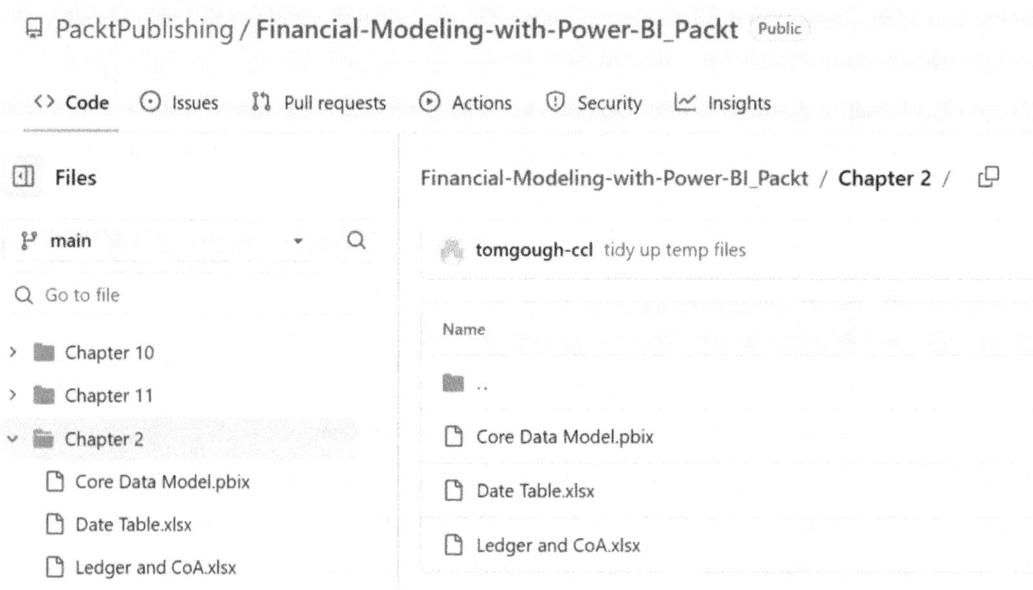

Figure 0.1: GitHub repository

2. Click on each file and download:

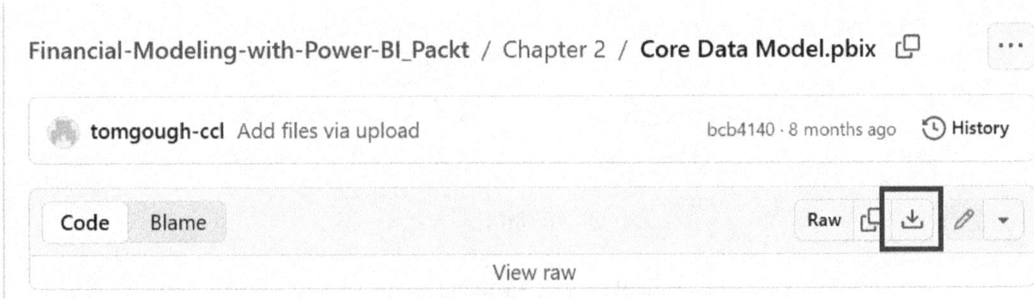

Figure 0.2: Download icon

For this example, in *Chapter 2*, you'll download 3 files:

1. `Core Data Model.pbix`
2. `Date Table.xlsx`
3. `Ledger and CoA.xlsx`

Store them somewhere on your PC. We usually create a folder to store all three files.

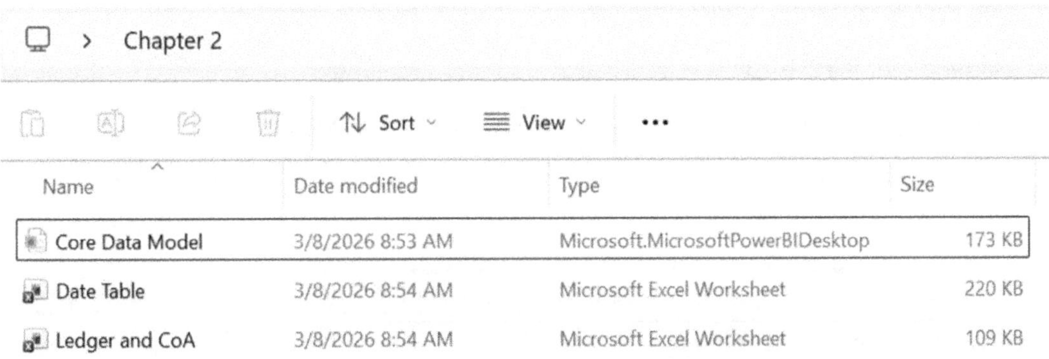

Figure 0.3: Storing files in a local folder

3. Open the `Core Data Model.pbix` file. From the **Home** tab, click the dropdown chevron icon on **Transform data** and then select **Data source settings**. Quick warning: if you click the icon you'll open Power Query, so be sure to click on the bottom half of the icon.

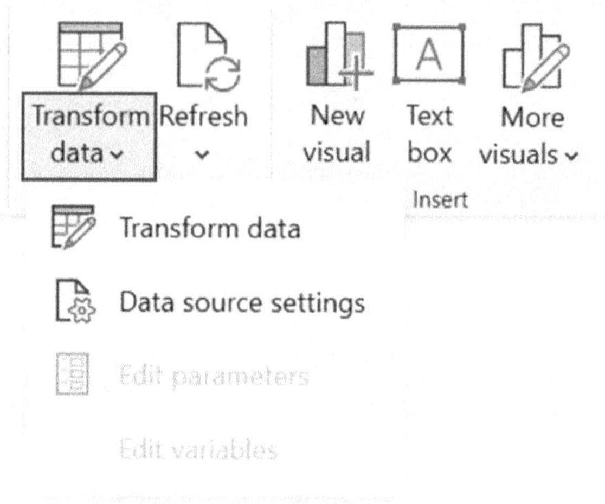

Figure 0.4: Transform data option

When you click **Data source settings**, you'll see the following dialog box.

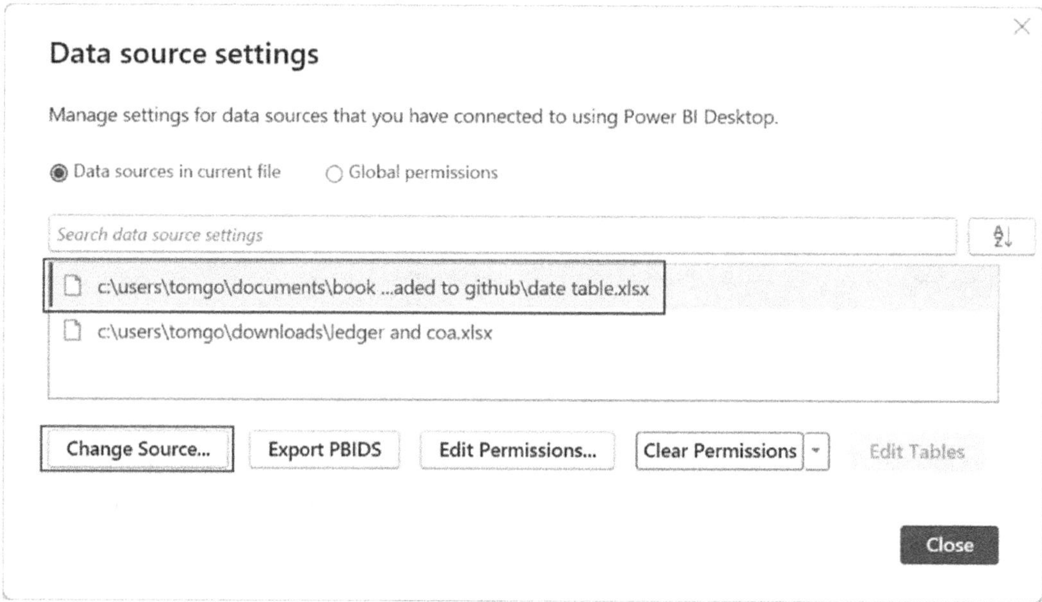

Figure 0.5: Data source settings window

4. Next, click **Change Source...**

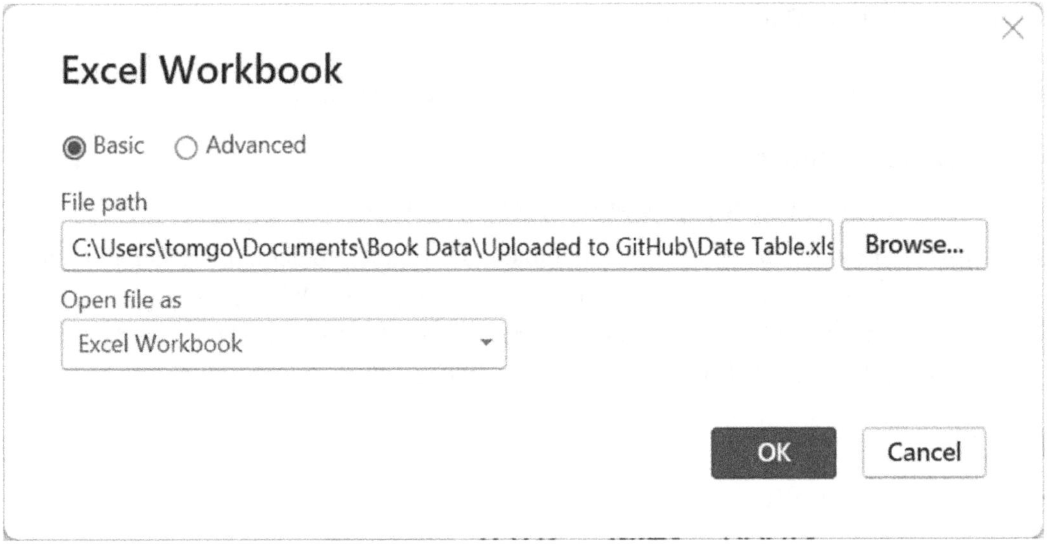

Figure 0.6: Selecting the Excel Workbook

This opens the source for the data file. As you can see from our screen images, the Power BI file is set to Tom's PC, so unless you're using Tom's PC (which he may not be happy with), click **Browse**, locate the folder with the downloaded files on your PC and click on the `Date Table.xlsx` option, then click **OK**.

Repeat the process for the `Ledger` and `CoA.xlsx` files and your Power BI Desktop file will be connected to the Excel files on your PC. This means when you open Power Query (from the Transform Data button), you'll be able to use the tools within Power Query.

Within the examples, Tom builds various models that represent different business scenario's or concepts. At the start of each chapter that has examples there'll be a link to the model you need and the accompanying files will be in the same GitHub folder.

Of course, you may prefer to use your own data to practice the examples; just be aware the formulas may not match your data, so you'll need to amend them to work.

Download the example code files

The code bundle for the book is hosted on GitHub at `https://github.com/PacktPublishing/Financial-Modeling-with-Power-BI_Packt`. We also have other code bundles from our rich catalog of books and videos available at `https://github.com/PacktPublishing`. Check them out!

Download the color images

We also provide a PDF file that has color images of the screenshots/diagrams used in this book. You can download it here:`https://packt.link/gbp/9781835880265`.

Conventions used

There are a number of text conventions used throughout this book.

`CodeInText`: Indicates code words in text, database table names, folder names, filenames, file extensions, pathnames, dummy URLs, user input, and Twitter handles. For example: "In Notepad, delete the text `['=Table.Unpivot('` from the start of the pasted text and `'"Attribute", "Value")]'` from the end of the pasted text."

A block of code is set as follows:

```
Opening Balance =
SUMX(
    FILTER(
        ALL('Calendar'[Full Date]),
        'Calendar'[Full Date]< MIN('Calendar'[Full Date])
    ),
    [Total Amount]
)
```

When we wish to draw your attention to a particular part of a code block, the relevant lines or items are set in bold:

```
Total Revenue = CALCULATE(
    [Total amount],
    FILTER(
      'Chart of Account',
      'Chart of Account' [AccountCategory]="SALE" ||
             'Chart of Account' [AccountCategory]="OTHER1NC"
    )
)*-1
```

Bold: Indicates a new term, an important word, or words that you see on the screen. For instance, words in menus or dialog boxes appear in the text like this. For example: "Power Query is accessed from the **Transform data** button on the ribbon."

Note

Warnings or important notes appear like this.

Tip

Tips and tricks appear like this.

Get in touch

Feedback from our readers is always welcome.

General feedback: If you have questions about any aspect of this book or have any general feedback, please email us at `customercare@packt.com` and mention the book's title in the subject of your message.

Errata: Although we have taken every care to ensure the accuracy of our content, mistakes do happen. If you have found a mistake in this book, we would be grateful if you reported this to us. Please visit `http://www.packt.com/submit-errata`, click **Submit Errata**, and fill in the form.

Piracy: If you come across any illegal copies of our works in any form on the internet, we would be grateful if you would provide us with the location address or website name. Please contact us at `copyright@packt.com` with a link to the material.

If you are interested in becoming an author: If there is a topic that you have expertise in and you are interested in either writing or contributing to a book, please visit `http://authors.packt.com/`.

Free benefits with your book

This book comes with free benefits to support your learning. Activate them now for instant access (see the "*How to Unlock*" section for instructions).

Here's a quick overview of what you can instantly unlock with your purchase:

Complete Code Bundle

Download the full source code for this book's examples and projects.

DRM-Free PDF Version

Download DRM-free PDF and ePub copies of this book.

7-Day Packt Library Access

Get 7-day unlimited access to 8,000+ books and videos. No credit card required.

Available for first-time Packt+ trial users only.

Next-Gen Reader Access

Read this book on Packt Reader with progress sync, dark mode and note-taking.

How to unlock

Scan the QR code (or go to `https://www.packtpub.com/unlock`). Search for this book by name, confirm the edition, and then follow the steps on the page.

UNLOCK NOW

Note: Keep your invoice handy. Purchases made directly from Packt don't require one.

Share your thoughts

Once you've read *Financial Modeling and Reporting with Microsoft Power BI*, we'd love to hear your thoughts! Scan the QR code below to go straight to the Amazon review page for this book and share your feedback.

`https://packt.link/r/1835880274`

Your review is important to us and the tech community and will help us make sure we're delivering excellent quality content.

1

Identifying Your Reporting Needs and Data Sources

The landscape of financial reporting is undergoing a rapid transformation, fueled by modern analytics tools such as Power BI. The reason for the shift is due to both the adoption of new technology and the embracing of smarter ways of using data. As organizations move from static, two-dimensional reporting to interactive advanced analytics, knowing how to manage the transition is crucial for success.

In this chapter, you'll learn how to structure a Power BI project from the ground up, ensuring smooth implementation. We'll also cover the importance of understanding your audience, identifying key stakeholders for your reports and insights, and how to identify the data sources that power your analytics models. Finally, we'll discuss best practices for enabling self-service analytics, empowering your team to make informed decisions independently.

By the end of this chapter, you will have learned about the following topics:

- Structuring a comprehensive project scoping document for successful implementation
- Segmenting your audience to deliver the right data to the right people
- Identifying and assessing the data sources that underpin your Power BI models
- Exploring strategies to enable effective self-service analytics across your organization

The starting point should be a proper project scoping exercise where a process is followed to set the organization up for a successful implementation. We cover that next.

> Note
>
> **Your purchase includes a free PDF copy + exclusive extras**
>
> Your purchase includes a DRM-free PDF copy of this book, 7-day trial to the Packt+ library (no credit card required), and additional exclusive extras. See the *Free benefits*

> *with your book* section in the *Preface* to unlock them instantly and maximize your learning.

Setting project scope

Setting project scope is fundamental to the success of any project; a Power BI implementation is no different. A project's scope is far bigger than the list of reports you want to produce; it defines every aspect of the project. A good project scope should set a budget, a timeframe, and resources, and then be communicated to and agreed upon by the project team. Once signed off, the project scope should be the operating manual for the project. Yes, it'll more than likely change as the project progresses, and scope change needs to be part of the project scope.

To put this in context, let's look at a common path of Power BI adoption to understand why project scope is important.

The start of many Power BI projects is a curious employee with a business problem, data, and a free Power BI Desktop download. There's a particular report that needs to be produced, or the individual wants to impress their manager. Fast-forward via ad hoc online learning, some attractive interactive visuals, and an excited data-oriented executive, and interest is sparked in an organization. Power BI is the "thing" to use, and one curious employee will become many curious employees as they dip their toes into the water of this new and exciting tool. Many Power BI fires will be lit around the organization, and PBIX files will be frequently emailed around it.

This is a common form of adoption. Everyone is excited and wants to be on board. Many people are using Power BI, albeit in a self-learned and uncoordinated manner.

Then, reports start to show cracks, there are issues with incorrect data, and no one is certain about which **Power BI file** (**PBIX**) in their inbox is current. Confidence starts to wane, and Power BI falls into limited use. To be safe, many users return to their tried and trusted best friend, Excel.

There are common elements to this form of technical adoption that cause issues:

- Untrained/self-trained employees using a complex product and introducing errors.
- A lack of understanding of how to deploy Power BI via the Power BI Service, treating it like any other file-based application. Therefore, reporting is distributed via email or OneDrive/SharePoint/file shares.
- No version control garners uncertainty about which file to use. The organization has many versions, many of which are, generally imperceptibly, slightly different from each other.

In some organizations, the Power BI project may be saved by an experienced member of the IT team who has been here before, recognizes the signs, and realizes that a properly formed project will save the day. There's nothing wrong with the technology and its capability to meet once-heady expectations. If the organization follows the basics of IT project management, the technology will deliver.

In other cases, cognitive dissonance sets in as people within the organization wrestle with the contradiction that the tool that promised so much is not delivering on once-elevated expectations.

It won't surprise you that we don't recommend the approach outlined, as we often work with organizations that have been through a variant of the aforementioned situation. That said, it sometimes takes a curious employee to introduce new thinking into some organizations, so we can't pretend to be completely opposed. In reality, the reasons that drove the organization to Power BI are all completely valid; the technology is capable of everything first envisaged, and in most cases, much more.

As mentioned in the previous section, Power BI involves a mix of disciplines and processes, and the start of any well-executed project is proper scoping. Even if the genesis of the project is the curious employee, it's important for the organization to take control of the implementation and adoption process.

Proper scoping follows a process to understand and structure the reporting requirements within the finance function. Power BI projects are inherently complex with multiple moving parts, and a project scope is far more than a list of required reports. It's an articulation of all aspects of the project that should inform anyone new to the project about the requirements, purpose, and process to deliver success, including a definition of what success looks like.

There's an abundance of material available on IT project scoping that we don't want to repeat here, as the length of the book will quickly grow, but we wanted to document a concise scoping process that's focused on a successful Power BI project within a finance function.

We urge all organizations to have some level of education on Power BI to understand its capabilities. Power BI, like all products, has strengths and weaknesses, so it's useful to understand the product, its features, and what best practice use looks like in a few similar organizations. This will set the tone for the project scoping and stop requests for capabilities outside of Power BI's functionality.

This can be completed in a half-day workshop with a consultant expert in Power BI who has relevant expertise and the ability to explain the concepts to a lay audience.

After an education session, here's a simple checklist you can work through to scope your Power BI project.

Setting clear goals and objectives

You should agree, in simple terms, on the purpose of the project, with some clear goals and objectives. This is more specific than "Implement Power BI in Finance," although that could be an overall name for the project. Your goals will be broad intentions, and your objectives should be specific and measurable. It's common to link goals and objectives, so there's a clear correlation between the broad intention of the goal and the specifics of the objective. Here are some examples:

- **Goal**: Enhance financial reporting efficiency
  Objectives:
    - Within 6 months, all standard finance reports will be capable of being run daily without the need for human intervention.
    - Create Power BI dashboards that cover key financial metrics such as revenue, expenses, and profit margins within the next six months.
- **Goal**: Improve stakeholder satisfaction with the quality of financial reporting
  Objectives:
    - 80% satisfaction rating from report stakeholders based on a standard qualitative and quantitative survey to be run every 3 months.
    - Scores less than 80% to be investigated with corrective plans implemented to maintain an over 80% score.

A half-to-one-day workshop with the project team's core members is a great way to brainstorm through goals. We recommend an experienced facilitator who can guide the team through the process, avoiding the inevitable rabbit-holes that are often entered during the discussions and consume valuable hours. It's important to get the goals and objectives written and circulated quickly for agreement.

Goals and objectives should be easily understood, using clear and concise language that is common parlance for the culture of the organization.

Detailed scoping – list of reports to create

Part of the evaluation is an inventory of the reports you currently have in place and why they're not providing the insights you need. This will help identify the gaps in functionality and what needs to be developed. You'll likely see common themes with the gaps, such as a lack of flexibility, missing information, and having to export to Excel to provide the detail required by the organization.

With the inventory of standard reports, you'll likely see three trends:

- Standard accounting reports that may/may not need reproducing in Power BI: We don't always suggest that a client reproduces everything in Power BI. Reporting in most financial applications generally has value and many reports should continue to be used, especially detailed transactional reports that are refreshed each time they are run (real-time transactional reporting is not the best use of Power BI).
- Reports provided by the accounting application that are not meeting the needs of the business, and are generally exported and manipulated.
- Reports required by the organization, identified by the goals and objectives, missing from currently available reports. These may be currently generated through manual effort.

Against this backdrop, also consider the reporting capabilities you want from Power BI, such as slicers – allowing users to interactively filter data, drillthrough – giving access to the details that underly the measures, and buttons – to aid navigation, to name a few. The specification of a report should be about much more than data; think of your reports as applications with functionality to help improve interactivity with the users.

Once you have a list of reports, we recommend that you prioritize report development. The delivery of new reports can take some time, and the start of a Power BI project will see an organization with demand akin to drinking from a fire hydrant. It's impossible to meet all demand on day 1, and whoever shouts the loudest isn't a good method to determine the order of development. A useful tool in this prioritization is the MoSCoW method:

Figure 1.1: The MoSCoW prioritization method

The MoSCoW method is a commonly used technique to prioritize requirements or tasks in project management and software development. It also works well for Power BI during the scoping phase. It helps stakeholders understand the importance and urgency of each item to ensure that the most critical tasks are completed first. The acronym MoSCoW stands for the following:

1. Must have:
   - These are the most critical reports that are non-negotiable to deliver the goals and objectives set in the previous exercise. These may not be the reports that form statutory reporting or deliver basic accounting processes, such as trial balance, as these may come from your accounting application, and you may choose to maintain them there.
2. Should have:
   - These are important reports that will add significant value but may not meet the project's goals. These reports can be assigned to phase 2 of the project, after the must-have reports have been delivered.
3. Could have:
   - These are desirable but not necessary reports. They are considered nice-to-haves and can be included if time and resources permit or possibly pushed back to a long-term maintenance project.
4. Won't have (this time):
   - These are reports that have been agreed to be postponed or left out of the project's scope. They are worth capturing as they may be considered for future releases or projects.

MoSCoW sessions are often run as brainstorms where the project team lists everything, then categorizes the results of the brainstorm into the four buckets. This isn't always easy, especially for should-have and could-have reports, as the differences between them may cause disagreement.

When working on Power BI implementations, we generally work to a 90/10 rule. 90% of our time is spent building data models, and 10% of our time is spent on the reports and visualizations our users interact with daily. That sometimes seems strange when we first introduce the concept to our customers. Why is so little time spent on the part users interact with daily? The reason is simple: when we get the data model structure and measures correct, and we know the list of reports required, the visuals are relatively easy. That's why the report list prepared in this section is so important. It means we know what the data model(s) need to contain to support the required reports.

It's worth consulting with your Power BI developers once the MoSCoW prioritization has been completed, as some should-have or could-have reports may be derivatives of the must-have reports and could be easily accommodated because of the work scheduled to deliver them. Developers are especially prone to the negative effects of task switching, and an extra hour to build measures for a should-have report while engaged on the model can easily turn into 2-3 hours if asked to break the workflow for a few weeks or months. We appreciate that this may contradict some of our advice for prioritization, as you could end up delivering a could-have report before a should-have, but you may choose to be practical and cost-effective with resources.

Report standards

As Power BI allows users to be creative with report design, we advise that standards are set for all reports at an early stage, so reports have a common user interface. A Power BI project shouldn't be an opportunity for the free artistic expression of each report developer. It's a business project, not an art class. Standards make it easier for users to work with the reports as they'll conform to a common look and feel. Users will understand new reports, and new employees will be able to quickly learn corporate standards. We advise that you consider the following:

- **Layout of your reports**: Adopt a consistent layout with user interface elements. To some extent, Power BI reports should be considered similar to apps, as there are capabilities that provide functionality such as filtering and drillthrough. It's important to use these consistently so users know what to look for and where in the report. The layout of a report should not be governed by the person who built the report, as you'll end up with a myriad of different report styles that'll confuse your users.
- **Color scheme and branding**: Our general advice is to use corporate branding color schemes for your reporting. Assign colors to user interface elements so they are consistent and easy to recognize by your users.
- **Naming conventions**: Names should be obvious and descriptive for the end user.

We've seen many examples where one organization's Power BI reports have very different styles that detract from usability. It's common for many Power BI report developers to work on one project, and we recommend a review of correct processes on all reports, so they meet the standards described previously.

Security and access

Plan which users or roles need access to which reports. Understand the sensitivity of your data and who should see what data. You have granularity of access to reports and data with Power BI, with two main security methods:

- Workspaces and apps where reports reside in folders and users are granted access to the folders. To clarify, reports are saved to workspaces, then published to apps.
- Row-level security, where data is filtered according to the user. All users see the same report, but different data. We often deploy this where organizations are broken down into operating companies or subsidiaries, and each subsidiary has its own finance manager who needs to see the company they are responsible for. Row-level security allows you to deploy a single report where each finance manager just sees the organizations they are responsible for. This topic is covered in more detail in *Chapter 13, Evolving and Maintaining Your Report*.

Workspaces/apps and row-level security work together. Therefore, a report will reside in a workspace/app, and users are granted access to the workspace/app. Furthermore, the users may be subject to row-level security that governs the data they view in the workspace/app. It's important to note that row-level security is optional; workspaces are not.

To make user management easier, you can use Microsoft 365 security groups, so you add the security group to the workspace, and the users that belong to the security group will be added. As users are added to and removed from security groups, they will gain and lose access to the workspaces.

Data sources

It's important to list your potential data sources for the project with organizational owners included as project stakeholders (discussed later, in the *Identifying your data sources* section). Understand what access you need from which system and communicate with the system owners to set expectations about the need to access the data and to understand considerations of accessing the data. To provide an example, some organizations use the payroll capabilities of their ERP application. Payroll records are treated with the highest confidentiality by most organizations, for obvious reasons. So, if the project team needs to access the database tables for finance, should they be able to see payroll data? If the answer is no, user access roles will be required for the team to see finance tables, but not payroll tables.

Another important consideration with data sources is the effect of data refresh on the source application. If the application is hosted on-premise or in a data center with fixed compute resources, Power BI refreshes at scale may degrade application responsiveness to core users. You may want to consider a data warehouse architecture where necessary tables are copied to a separate server overnight or when a few users are using the application, so performance issues are not an issue.

The other major consideration that would drive a Power BI project is the need to consolidate data from multiple different systems; for example, if there is a need to report across a group of companies that use different financial recording systems. In this case, the "standard" reports are effectively negated anyway. While a trial balance is broadly the same across all applications, the specifics of the format will be different, and even the calendars and chart of accounts may vary. In these cases, a further piece of work needs to be considered in the project scoping: how to map between these different datasets. This will be covered in more detail in the chapters looking at how to implement a model, but this is an area that will need engagement from the appropriate subject matter experts within the business.

Stakeholder identification and engagement

Your stakeholders are people involved and impacted by the project. We've provided the following list of some common stakeholders that we see in the projects we serve. The list is role-based, so one individual could fill multiple roles, and we recommend that all roles are considered, even if you initially feel that not all roles are relevant. For example, if you don't have a data security function within your organization, this should be a good reason to assign someone to understand the risk of data leakage and methods to mitigate the risks.

- **Project sponsor**:
    - For Power BI and finance projects, usually the CFO, but it can also be the CEO
    - Has the authority to approve budgets, changes, and key project decisions
- **Project manager**:
    - Responsible for planning, executing, and closing the project
    - Manages the project team, resources, schedule, and scope
- **Project team**:
    - Includes all the individuals working to deliver the reports for the project, ensuring they're in line with the standards set in the project scope
    - The project team can include data architects, report developers, and end users, led by the project manager
- **IT department**:
    - Many of the Power BI finance projects we work on are led by the finance function, with the IT department as an important stakeholder
    - Provides technical expertise, support, and provisioning of the technical and licensing infrastructure

- **End users and data owners**:
    - The individuals or groups who will use the final reports
    - Provide valuable feedback on functionality, speed, design, and usability
- **Stakeholders from other departments**:
    - Representatives from departments that will be affected by the project, such as marketing, finance, HR, or operations
    - They provide input on requirements and ensure the reporting outputs align with departmental needs
- **Security team**:
    - Ensures that the project adheres to security policies and best practices
    - Identifies potential security risks and implements measures to mitigate them

It's important to set expectations with stakeholders of their role(s) and purpose early in the project. We also recommend that stakeholders have time allocated to execute project tasks, such as testing reports, so the project isn't held back by stakeholders being "too busy."

Risk management

Identify potential risks early and develop mitigation strategies. Include a risk management plan in the project scope. Common risks during a Power BI project are as follows:

- Resource availability with competing business priorities. Hearing that something hasn't been done because something else more important came up is common. You'll need a plan to avoid this from the start.
- The technical risk of getting information from diverse systems is frequently an issue. We recommend a proof of concept for all aspects to understand where issues are likely to arise.
- Scope creep (despite this exercise) is a factor with all projects and should be listed.

The risk management plan should be revisited on a frequent basis to monitor mitigation actions and record new risks as they arise, with their own mitigation plans. As with all the project documentation we describe, please consider them live documents that are updated as the project progresses.

Resource planning and time management

Identify the resources (human, financial, technical) required for the project. Ensure resource availability and allocation are planned and signed off. One of the most common challenges for a Power BI project is resource availability, as we've mentioned previously.

Develop a project timeline with realistic deadlines. We generally deliver based on an agile methodology through project sprints where the work is divided into one- or two-week (generally two) sprints. At the end of each sprint, completed work is reviewed, and the project is course-corrected for the next sprint as lessons are learned. The benefit of this method is quick and frequent delivery of reports and report updates. For most finance organizations, a pure agile methodology is not required, and we recommend a mix of project planning methods to help set expectations for budget and timeframes.

> Note
>
> **Agile versus waterfall methodology, and sprints**
>
> Waterfall methodologies are generally the more "traditional" project methodologies – in a waterfall methodology, all aspects of the project are built, tested, and then released to the users all in one go.
>
> Agile methodologies, by contrast, break the work up into smaller parcels that can be released piece by piece over a period of time. Using such methods, it is possible to release elements of a project much earlier and start gaining a return on investment much sooner.
>
> Sprints are the basic unit of work that an agile project is broken into. Typically, they consist of 2-week periods at the end of which there is normally a release of the work done within that sprint.

Using a hybrid methodology, you'll plan the overall delivery timeframe and phases using a waterfall methodology. This will help you understand the overall timeframes of the project and allow you to plan when resources will be required for certain phases. Testing and training are good examples where you'll need certain people within the organization to plan time to be available.

In execution, you can get the best of the Agile methodology through sprints by having daily standups, feedback through retrospective meetings, and incremental releases that keep the desire for continual delivery satiated.

Change control process

Establish a change control process to handle scope changes. Your scope will change throughout your project, and this should be expected and managed. We've seen too many instances of users directly asking developers for changes without consideration of how the change affects the overall scope or conflicts with other requirements. Change requests need to be submitted to the project team and signed off on a frequent basis to allow developers to maintain their workflow.

Change control should include the following as a minimum:

- A request form completed to log the change request. This can be a Power App, a SharePoint list, or a DevOps or Jira case.
- A method of dealing with change requests. This can be an individual or a change control board that meets frequently to discuss and accept/decline change requests.
- Adding the accepted change request to the schedule of work or sprints to assess the impact on the project.
- The incorporation of agreed changes into the test plan.

Remember that all changes have an impact on the timeframe and cost of the project. These can be positive and negative, as change sometimes means cutting functionality that isn't required.

Test plan

Testing is an essential part of a Power BI project to help you deliver quality reports, so we've devoted *Chapter 10, Testing and Fine-Tuning Your Data,* to this subject. This section briefly describes how to incorporate testing into your project scope.

Testing has two interesting distinctions in Power BI projects. The first is that most users think it's optional, and the second is that most users expect the developers to deliver perfect, accurate reports.

Here's some friendly advice, italicized for dramatic impact:

Testing your reports is a business task. Do not expect your developers to do it.

For the purposes of the scoping document, each report needs to have at least one tester assigned to the report who will sign it off as being correct. If it's not correct, they will work with the developer until the report is correct. You'll need definitions of what is being tested and signed off on, with functional aspects:

- Accuracy of data
- Working slicers
- Speed

There are also non-functional aspects:

- Adherence to design guidelines
- Correct use of color

- Neatness of layout
- Accessibility

We recommend building a checklist that can be used as a guide for the testers to check off as they test and record any issues.

Training plan

As Power BI has capabilities that most people in your organization won't have experienced, comprehensive training is essential for users to understand the new tool and to get the best from it.

In our training, we seek to conceptualize how Power BI is different from standard application reports in terms of functionality and how you can interact with data. We also train users on the flexibility of Power BI and how measures can easily be added to help understand and analyze data. If users are exporting Power BI data to Excel, you have a training problem.

For the purposes of the project scope, the training plan should identify the purpose of the training, who will deliver it, and the users who will be trained. We segment users, described in the section – *Who needs to use your reports?*

Think about users in two ways:

- Where they sit functionally in the organization. Finance is obvious, but you'll also have many users of financial reports outside of the finance function, such as operations, management, or purchasing.
- Their skill level or desired skill level with Power BI. The majority of your users will be consumers of the Power BI data. Some will want to create reports based on validated data models, and a subset may even have the skills to become developers. All these groups will need a different level of training.

The training plan needs to reflect your potential users in both functional and skill requirements. You'll also need to plan to train users over time who join and move within your organization, so make sure you plan for repeatability of the material.

Communication plan

Develop a communications plan that articulates the who, what, frequency, and channel.

- Who will be your project team, project stakeholders, and the wider organization, as many people will interact with Power BI at some point, even if it's presented at a meeting?
- What is the purpose of communication? Projects generate lots of detailed information, so identification of different types of information is essential to decide who needs to see it. For example, users probably don't need to see how many change requests have

been generated in a week, but will want to understand functional changes that will affect them.

- What is the frequency of communication? We recommend communicating at set times/days of the week or month so recipients of the communications know what to expect and when to expect it.

The communications channel is also important. We have many options within organizations, such as Teams and Slack, and most of them allow *@mentions*. People still use email, although we don't recommend spamming people with project updates, as they won't get read. Use whatever works in your organization so people can easily find the information when required. Plan to be clear and concise with your communications and follow a standard format.

Documentation and sign-off

Document all aspects of the project scope and obtain sign-off from key stakeholders. This ensures alignment and commitment.

The project scope is a living document. As changes happen to the project, the scope needs to be updated to document the changes. We recommend storing the document somewhere that everyone required can see it, but only a few people can change it. Like any document that changes frequently, don't distribute it by email, as you'll encounter versioning issues with many people working on outdated versions on their hard drives or email inboxes.

Depending on the size and complexity of your project, you may choose to skip some of this list. Conversely, you may need to expand certain aspects to suit specific circumstances. Having to make some architectural changes, such as implementing a data warehouse, may necessitate a section on the implications of this architectural requirement. Whatever you choose to exclude, include, or expand upon, we strongly recommend a good scope as the guide for the rest of the project.

You may not need everything in the requirements of project scoping that we've described here, but we ask that you consider everything. Power BI projects are complex, with many moving parts. The purpose of a detailed project scope and plan is to help you navigate the occasional bump in the road, as they will occur. Thorough planning rarely has downsides, especially if there are issues and you can quickly deal with them. And if everything goes to plan, you just did your job well.

Who needs to use your reports?

While the focus of this book is the finance department, the data models produced will have information useful for many users across the organization. When built correctly, Power BI provides a single version of the truth, and its flexible reporting capabilities allow for reports that suit many users in their own visual style and language. Departments outside of Finance can therefore have reports to suit their own needs, using different visuals or layouts. If language and measures are used consistently, it's a powerful capability. Put another way, if you use the term "Net Sales" against a measure, then always use that term for that measure. Conversely, ensure measures across multiple models called "Net Sales" are calculated using an identical formula so they produce consistent results.

A common example is building data models that link transactions in the sales ledger to the salesperson responsible for the customer or territory that originated the sale. The finance department may not need this level of detail or data linkage, but the sales department certainly will. Based on the 90/10 rule discussed earlier, it's not a huge amount of work when building data models to accommodate the other departments.

We mentioned the identification of stakeholders in the previous section as an important part of your project scoping exercise. For the purpose of who needs to use your reports, we think of these stakeholders in two ways:

- Users from other departments could benefit from the reporting, especially when repurposed for their specific needs.
- Users across the organization with specific skillsets may need or want to take advantage of Power BI's self-service capabilities. We discuss the concept of self-service in more detail in the next section, but we will introduce the concept of user types here.

Starting with departmental users, here are some common examples where financial data can benefit:

- **Sales**: The most obvious department that would have a use for financial reporting would be sales. For example, analysis of revenue data will provide key insights into sales KPIs. This is especially true if this data can be linked to information about the customers sold to and the products sold. Typically, Sales will be interested in trends and the relationship between revenue KPIs and product and customer information. This will need consideration of how the data model can support drill-through to lower levels of data and provide interactive visuals. Other finance measures, such as margins and aged debt, will also be useful to the sales team.
- **Purchasing**: The purchasing department will be interested in understanding the spend by category and vendor, minimizing the costs, and increasing the stock turnover. They will therefore, in addition to **Cost of Goods Sold** (**COGS**) measures, be interested in analyses of the best performing products – in this requirement, there is an overlap with the Sales department.
- **Stock control**: One of the core interests of stock control in financial reporting is to reduce poorly performing inventory. Here, the need is to see the stock turn measure, and how that is improving – or not – over time. This would allow a stock control

manager to identify poor-performing stock that can be discounted by Sales or not purchased again.

- **Finance analysts**: The core target of this book is expected to use most of the reports in the suite. In standard reports, there would be analyses used to produce monthly or quarterly board packs. There would be reports that facilitate the day-to-day working of the department, and others to simplify the operation of month- and year-end processes. Finally, other reports would help provide for ad hoc requests from other departments.
- **The executive board**: Headline figures from other departments would, inevitably, feed dashboards for the executive board. While periodic board packs remain important, executives expect faster-paced updates and more timely data when making decisions. At the top level, the data presented to the board will tend to be less granular, skipping detail, but that detail will be expected to be available at the touch of a button.

Across these users, also identify the Power BI user types across four categories:

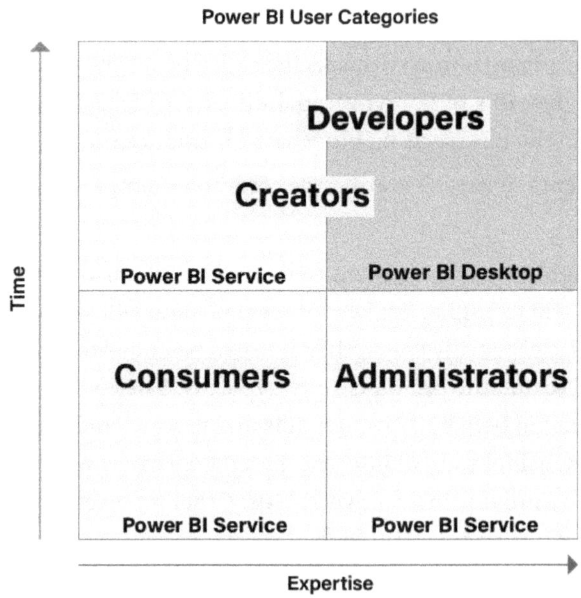

Figure 1.2: Power BI user types

1. **Consumers**: Most of the users in most organizations will be consumers of the data, and in some organizations, all users are consumers as reporting standards are enforced. They consume data by viewing reports and filter visuals. Power BI is an integral part of their job, so they've usually got a browser window open at all times with Power BI available. They have no interest or desire to build their own reports and certainly no

ambition to write a single line of **Data Analysis eXtensions** (**DAX**) – the main language used for calculations in Power BI. Most of your reporting is built for these users.

2. **Creators**: A smaller subset of users will be creators. These users will consume the reports already built and want a blank canvas to work with the data models to build their own visuals and reports. They have a curiosity to analyze data on their own terms and want to build their own visuals to see data according to their specific needs. Yes, they can work with a report developer to specify a report and have the developer build the report but there's something in the process of experimentation with the data that scratches an itch to create. Some of our clients have policies that Power BI reporting will only cater to consumers, as they want verified sign-off reports in the organization (creators generally don't develop reports in line with the reporting standards), and they'll often find creators downloading data to analyze in Excel. Creators may work on both the Power BI service and Power BI Desktop, although we always warn about the risks of many users working with Power BI Desktop due to file sharing and versioning. The Power BI service and Power BI Desktop have feature parity for building visuals and reports, so pushing creators to the Power BI service is advisable.
3. **Developers**: You may find some of your users have the desire or aptitude to become Power BI developers. We generally warn organizations of the risks of many untrained or unmanaged developers because that can introduce reporting anarchy, as described at the start of the book. But, for many organizations, a few employees who can be trained to support the ongoing management of Power BI models can be extremely cost-effective. Another valuable contribution of the developer can be to work with users to help train them or provide daily support when questions arise due to their understanding of the core workings of Power BI. However, you decide to use these users, they generally exist in most organizations and when deployed alongside experienced consultants, can provide a cost-effective and flexible support resource.
4. **Administrators**: As Power BI deployments have become more complex over time, the role of Administrator has become more important. The Administrator fulfills several functions within the organization. Generally, these are as follows:
    a. Deployment/removal of users to/from workspaces and row-level security filters if appropriate
    b. Checking licensed employees
    c. Enabling new features
    d. Checking reports are working correctly

In most cases, your users will change over time, alongside your usage of Power BI. Again, in most cases, that generally means more users alongside more functionality, so this is an area that's important to manage carefully.

The next step in identification that's just as important as your users is your data sources, which is the subject we cover next.

Identifying your data sources

One of the many benefits of Power BI is the ability to take data from many sources and present mashed-up data transparently to your users. The data may be from multiple sources, but it's woven to tell a coherent story, with your users blissfully unaware. Choosing and working with many data sources requires some thought and planning.

At its core, the data model will take data from the financial recording system – this could be a system aimed at the SME market, such as Xero or QuickBooks, or it could be a large enterprise-scale system such as Microsoft Dynamics, SAP, or Oracle.

It is also likely that in larger organizations, there will be more than one instance of the accounting or ERP system or multiple accounting and ERP systems. Even where only one system is in use, there may well be multiple legal entities with independent ledgers configured in use. As you can see, this world gets complex fast. Add separate financial planning and budgeting applications or spreadsheets, and you have many moving parts required to build your data models and reports.

Here's a list of considerations with your data sources:

- What data do you need from the source? Taking an example from the more complex end of the spectrum, a normal SAP enterprise implementation will have somewhere between 80,000 and 100,000 tables. Tables then have a varying number of columns, with complex tables (more than likely the ones you'll need) having hundreds of columns. Just to make life more complex, the table and field names are generally 5- or 6-character codes, taken from German. You certainly won't need all of those tables and fields, and in the case of SAP, it's well documented online, so finding the tables and key fields is not quite as daunting as the preceding description.
- When you have your data, how do you need to filter it? Financial applications generally store all transactions, even if you think they've been deleted or deactivated. In most cases, a "delete" is actually a soft "delete" where transactions remain, but users don't see them. However, when you connect Power BI to the data, you will see all of those "deleted" transactions, so you'll need to filter them out. Then you'll need to think about credit memos, debit memos, accruals, and reversals. They'll all be included within the

data you've just downloaded, so if you simply `SUM` the `Amount` field, you'll not get the number you expected. Filtering is your friend.

- Is there any data within the data source that's confidential, such as payroll? In most cases, you'll need a profile set up for Power BI to access the data. Profiles give certain rights and privileges over what data can be viewed and whether data can be created, read, updated, or deleted (CRUD). Generally, users will just require read privileges, but you may need to also restrict data based on sensitivity or confidentiality.
- Depending on the location of your data source, you may need to consider the effects of Power BI demand on the server(s). If you have an on-premise production environment that's near capacity and users are complaining about response times from the application, Power BI will become another demand that could potentially cause further performance degradation. You therefore need to consider upgrading the server, a data warehouse, or being very specific about when data is refreshed. As so many accounting and ERP systems are cloud-hosted, these issues may not present a problem to most normal-sized businesses, but you'll still have to plan for them.

If you have concerns about any of the preceding, a **Proof of Concept** (**POC**) exercise is generally a good way to derisk your project with minimal impact on time and budget. In a POC, you'll quickly build an environment to service your Power BI needs based on 1 or 2 must-have reports, allowing you to test any specific unknowns. We regularly advise clients on the wisdom of a POC at the early stages of a project to identify any issues that could derail progress if uncovered at a later stage.

Returning to the specifics of your financial reporting, cases where there is consolidation across different ledgers, there will need to be, at a minimum, a mechanism to map between different charts of accounts and calendars. Even if the different entities currently use the same calendars and chart of accounts, it's always possible for them to diverge at some point in the future when changes are made to the finance application. While it's possible to address this when the issue arises, that would turn a relatively simple change in the finance system into a much more complex change that impacts the whole reporting estate. It's far better to address this from the outset. We will look at ways of doing this in the next chapter, but at the inception of the project, you should establish the following:

- The format of this dataset
- How the data will be stored
- Who will be responsible for maintaining it
- What the mechanism for maintaining it will be

Beyond the core financial system, the sources of data will depend a lot on the audiences identified for the reports. Here are some examples:

- Product information that would be useful to sales and purchasing
- Inventory information for the stock controllers
- Sales order information
- Purchase order data
- Budgets and forecasts

In this book, we concentrate on how inventory and budget information can be included in the financial data model, since these tend to be trickier to handle, but the general principle remains the same.

In larger organizations, it would be expected that inventory data would be brought in from the main ERP system, but equally, it would not be unusual for there to be additional warehouse management systems in play too. For SMEs, the more common pattern would be for there to be one or more warehouse management systems in use that reside separately from the financial management data. In these cases, there needs to be consideration of how this data is linked to the financial transactions taken from the financial management system. Consideration needs to be given to the following:

- How are stock movements posted to the general ledger?
- What is the mapping between inventory transactions and ledger accounts?
- What level of detail is needed (warehouse level, location level, etc.)?
- Does product information also get recorded in the general ledger?
- What is the inventory costing model?

Budgeting modules are frequently included in financial management packages – and almost always available in larger ERP systems. Those modules are, however, often not well used. It is frequently the case that budgets are managed on various spreadsheets, as this makes it easier for budget planners to try out different scenarios and see the effects of changes quickly, without complex import procedures or time-consuming data entry. We need to consider the following:

- Where is the budget being stored?
- How is that controlled?
- What is the update schedule?
- How is the quality of that data enforced?

We generally recommend that a list of data sources with access details be stored somewhere for updates and future reference. Your list of sources will expand and change over time, so keeping track is essential when personnel and technology change. Service accounts instead of user accounts will help maintain continuity and mitigate against the risk of personnel changes.

As you can see, identification and management of data sources is critically important for the success of your Power BI project. Users need accurate data delivered securely, and the organization has to make sure its interests are being protected through proper management of sensitive data. This management of data is especially important when considering and planning for employee self-service of data sources, which is becoming a growing trend.

Planning for self-service

Self-service business intelligence provides non-technical users with access to data and tools, allowing them to build their own reports and visuals, rather than relying on technical resources to build for them. In many ways, users have had a form of self-service business intelligence through exporting to Excel, with self-service becoming a method to formalize that approach through proper management of data and tools, avoiding the problems that have come with exporting to Excel.

There are varying shades of self-service reporting, as the meaning behind the term has become a gray area. At its heart, it's the concept that users of reports are not reliant on central delivery, but can access the data they need, when they need it. There are, however, different levels of reporting that can all be described as self-service.

At its most unstructured, nothing is provided centrally, and all reporting is left in the hands of the consumers of the reports. That means no datasets, no models, no calculations, and certainly no reports. The report consumers would be given access to the data and left to their own devices. Where the requirement is for ad hoc, one-off analyses, this can be useful, but it requires a group of highly skilled analysts and is a high-risk strategy since there would be no shared single source of truth. This form of self-service is therefore very rare, and almost always supplemented by a less extreme form. You may gather from the tone of our language that we certainly don't recommend this approach, as in many ways, many organizations have had this approach through exporting to Excel. The main downsides are as follows:

- Time taken for inexperienced users to build their own reports
- Risk of incorrect analysis and calculations caused by a lack of expertise
- Lack of definition of standard concepts in the organization, such as net sales
- Duplication of reports due to a lack of coordinated planning

Next would be a semi-structured model whereby datasets, models, and calculations are provided, and report consumers are left to create their own reports and augment the models.

This has the advantage of allowing every report user to build the reports they need while maintaining trusted datasets. The downside, of course, is that there would be no consistent reporting format, which makes collaboration more difficult.

A structured or balanced approach to self-service allows for models, calculations, and many standard reports to be built with the tools to build new reports on validated datasets, given to trained users. Experience tells us that, in most organizations, most users have little interest in building their own reports and will generally gravitate towards a report that's been built by an experienced developer. There is generally a subset of users who have the desire and capability to build their own reports based on validated datasets. This changes from function to function and organization to organization, and we certainly see instances where there's a thirst for data and a desire to work with the data to experiment, build inferences, and draw conclusions. But the norm is pre-built reports for most people and self-service for a few.

Although not self-service, there is a model where all reports are provided centrally, and users don't have the capability to build their own reports. This is certainly a valid approach for certain organizations where data precision or security is paramount. It's certainly not self-service, although we include it for completeness.

So, is self-service for you? Some form is almost bound to be, few organizations want to manage a totally top-down approach where a department produces and distributes all reports. Those organizations that do so frequently find a proliferation of spreadsheets as users circumvent that restriction. At the very minimum, it is best practice to allow some form of self-service, and likely some sort of hybrid of the preceding.

Consider the following: the CEO wants to quickly check in on monthly revenues. They want to be able to do this each day and do not want to have to do much more than click a button to get there. For the CEO, all they really want is the most restrictive form of self-service: pre-built reports that can be run on demand. In the same organization, a management accountant may need a report that contains data from the trial balance but is focused on a restricted time period and for only a limited number of account codes. They may wish to use an existing data model to create a bespoke report to meet that need. Finally, a financial analyst may be asked to produce a custom report that is not met by any existing modeling. They will need access to the data sources so they can produce that report from the ground up. So here, for three different audiences, we have three different self-service models, all within the same organization.

There is also a significant downside of self-service (and any form of "citizen" developer, data scientist, or analyst): it takes people away from their day job to go and create reports (or apps, etc.). In planning for self-service, it is important to consider how much time an individual is expected to spend self-serving, where that time could be spent on their day job, and balance that against the value they can get from some level of self-service as opposed to waiting on a central IT department producing a report for them.

Once again, how to do this will come down to the different audiences and skillset in the organization:

- How much time do you want an individual to spend creating a report?
- Will this distract from the job they are actually employed to do?
- Could a greater degree of autonomy make them more effective?
- Is there a risk that greater autonomy could undermine trust in data?
- Does the individual have the skills to self-serve?

Self-service reporting will, at least for the foreseeable future, be a part of all corporate reporting solutions. As such, it needs to be considered as part of a Power BI project from the very beginning. From the start of implementation, we need to develop with consideration of the following:

- Who will use self-service?
- What skills do they have?
- How will they self-serve?

Tailor the data model accordingly.

Summary

In this chapter, we discussed the key factors that contribute to the success of a Power BI project. In particular, we explored how to define the project scope and the factors that influence the specific reports to be built. We also covered the importance of planning effective resource allocation, implementing a proper test plan, and ensuring adequate training and communication for report users.

In the chapters that follow, we get into the details of how you'll build your Power BI reports and how you engage with your users and roll out to the organization. Success in a Power BI project is much more than clean DAX and the fastest-loading reports. It's about engaging and working with your organization to cater to their needs, and taking them on a journey about how Power BI can transform your organization.

Get this book's PDF version and more

Scan the QR code (or go to `https://www.packtpub.com/unlock`). Search for this book by name, confirm the edition, and then follow the steps on the page.

UNLOCK NOW

Note: Keep your invoice handy. Purchases made directly from Packt don't require an invoice.

2

The Basic Model for Financial Reporting

In the previous chapter, we described how to plan your Power BI project. Adoption of Power BI is high across organizations as its popularity has become almost viral. Proper project management disciplines are required to successfully implement the product and use it to its full potential. A project scope alongside an understanding of your user base and data sources will prepare your organization for the long term when considering self-service business intelligence and AI.

In this chapter, we start to look at the **data model**, or **semantic model** in Power BI terminology. Your semantic model defines how data is composed, its relationships, and how you can present it in Power BI. The art of data modeling is a critical skill when working with Power BI, and we'll discuss some best practices related to modeling data for financial reporting.

When using Power BI, a well-structured semantic model is critical to the accuracy and speed of your reporting. Most of the work for any set of reports is based on shaping, filtering, calculating, and cleaning the data that supports the visualizations your users interact with. We generally work to a 90/10 rule when working with Power BI, which means 90% of our time is data modeling and 10% building visuals. So, if you thought Power BI is all about building eye-catching visuals for corporate reporting and presentations, then, of course, you're right. How you allocate your time to get there is the important part.

By the end of the chapter, you will understand the following:

- How to create the core data entities, such as transactions and the chart of accounts, in the Power BI data model
- How to create relationships between the core entities

- The different approaches to modeling data across multiple companies or legal entities
- The considerations needed when working across multiple currencies, and the pitfalls that can come with calculating foreign exchange in the reporting model

Let's start with creating the core entities.

Creating the core entities

When working with financial reporting, the basic structure consists of three elements or entities, which are the calendar, transactions, and chart of accounts. In this chapter, we describe all three and what you need to consider when working with your own financial data. At the end of this section, we start to look at our accompanying working example, so you have a model that you can use to help your own financial modeling.

Getting familiar with common terminology

Before we dive into how to create your core entities, there are some key terms we need to explain first to help you understand how to structure your data properly, as follows:

- Database
- Table
- Entity
- Relationships
- Facts and dimensions
- Schema

Let's take a detailed look at each of these.

Database

The data for your financial application will be held in a database, which is the digital storage and management of your data, allowing new data to be written and existing data to be stored and manipulated. You may have interacted with Microsoft Access as a database or even used a SharePoint list, which is a basic form of a database. Databases have many features that provide peace of mind for the storage and safeguarding of your data, which are outside the scope of this book. One important database structural element is a table, which we explain next.

Table

A database is comprised of many tables that store data. A table provides a structure for a specific record, which will be composed of rows and columns. Each row is a specific record (e.g., a Sales Order line) and each column will represent a different variable or attribute, such as date, quantity, price, and customer. A database has many tables to break down the information stored for efficiency. Therefore, the sales order will generally have a `Sales Order` header and Sales Order line items as separate tables. The `Sales Order` header will contain a customer ID, so the Sales Order line items don't have to; they just have a link to the `Sales Order` header record. In turn, the `Sales Order` header won't have all the details of the customer, such as ship-to and bill-to addresses, as that'll be stored in the `Customer` table. Your Sales Order lines may only include a product ID, because that will link to the `Product` table. This is in the name of efficiency, so records are only stored once. When dealing with millions of records and finite computing power, efficiency matters.

You'll notice that we referred to a `Product` table in the singular, then both the `Sales Order Header` table and the `Sales Order Item` table as a combination that makes up the overall concept of a sales order. In database terms, we refer to both `Product` and `Sales Order` as entities, which is the concept we'll tackle next.

Entity

An entity represents a real-world object or concept. Therefore, customers and products are entities, and in the context of this chapter, the calendar, general ledger, and chart of accounts are also entities. Within your database, many tables will be entities, such as your `Customer` table, but there will also be tables that aren't entities. `Customer Order` is a common table used in financial applications to store the relationship between a customer and a product that's been ordered. It defines a relationship between entities but isn't an entity in itself. This is highlighted in *Figure 2.1*, where we depict how a single table can be an entity in the case of the `Product` table; however, in the case of the `Sales Order` and `Sales Order Line` tables, both are required to become a single entity.

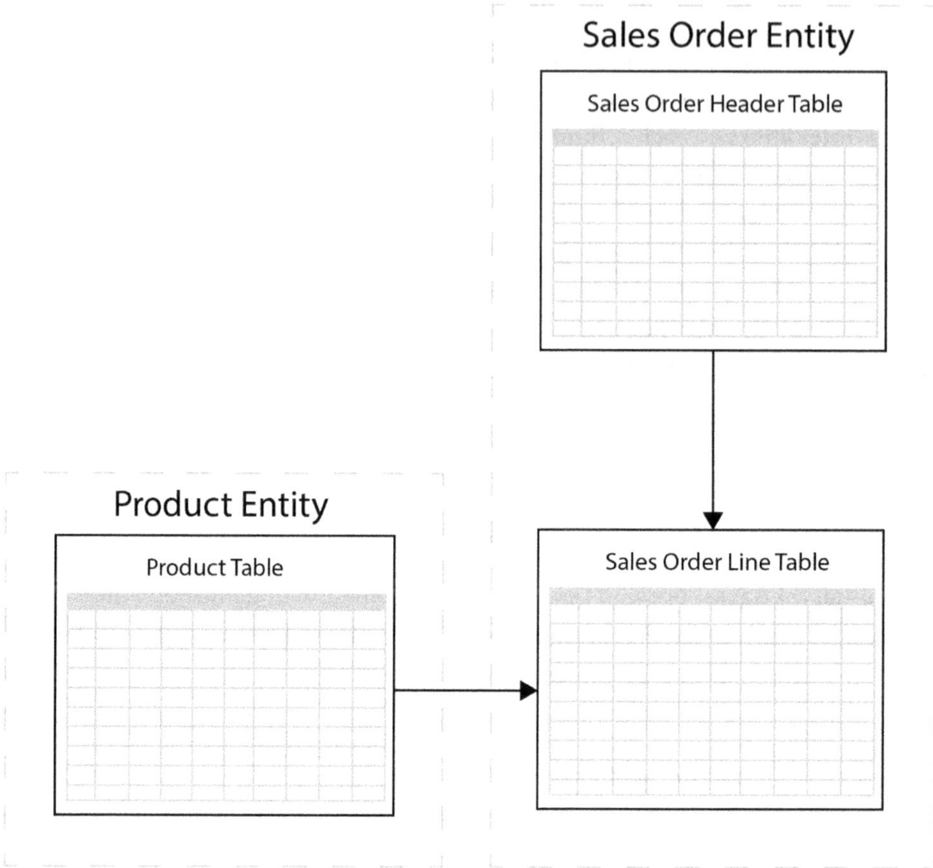

Figure 2.1: The difference between tables and entities

When working with database tables and Power BI, the term *entities* isn't used that frequently, although certain data sources will provide data in the form of entities rather than source tables, so it's important to understand the concept and the separation that can happen between entities and tables when working with data. Both tables and entities are important when considering relationships.

Relationships

We connect the tables from our database according to related entities to form relationships between the tables. In some regards, relationships work a little like VLOOKUP in Excel, only more powerful since a relationship can be defined once and then reused in different ways across a whole Power BI file. This is important for the efficiency of our data processing, as we tell the database how the tables relate to each other. Relationships should be based on **unique identifiers (IDs)**, or in database terms, primary keys. For example, each product will have an ID that is unique. When specifying a product in a Sales Order line, the row for the Sales Order line will use the product ID, not the name or any other characteristic. Within the `Product` table, the IDs will be unique for each product, and each product will only exist once within the table. However, on the `Sales Order Line` table, we may sell the same product many times to the same or different customers, so one product may exist many times. When we join the `Product` table to the `Sales Order Line` table, we connect the product IDs, and this becomes a one-to-many (from the Product table to the Sales Order Line table) relationship. In Power BI, relationships can be the following:

- One-to-one
- One-to-many
- Many-to-many

One-to-one is unusual, as it could be argued that a one-to-one relationship should actually be a single table. One-to-many is the norm, and many-to-many should be avoided. There are multiple reasons why many-to-many should be avoided; the main reasons are performance and data integrity. When we see many-to-many relationships, there are frequently records on either table that don't exist in the other table. When you attempt to filter your data between your tables in calculations, you can't be certain the filter will work as intended, potentially leading to incorrect results. In instances where you see a many-to-many relationship, a bridging table is recommended. A bridging table is a single table that contains the unique IDs from the two tables involved in the many-to-many relationship. Each of the original tables can then be related to the bridging table via a one-to-many relationship. In this way, you can remove the explicit many-to-many relationship, improving the readability and performance of the overall data model.

Now that we have entities and relationships, we start to define our data in terms of facts and dimensions.

Facts and dimensions

In the data analytics world, we have two key concepts when describing our data: facts and dimensions. When explaining how to create the core entities you'll need for your financial reporting, the concepts of facts and dimensions will be critical to understand how to properly structure your data.

In your finance application, you'll have transactions such as sales orders, purchase orders, and journals. To take the sales order, you'll sell *X* amount of a product at price *Y* to a customer with a fulfillment date. The sales order is initially a method to log and manage the transaction, then it becomes a long-term record of the event for your financial reporting to show what was sold and when. When aggregated, your sales orders allow you to understand and account for revenue to the business.

In data analytics terms, facts are transactions, such as sales orders. They're specific events and can be quantified. To take a sales order (and to be reasonably generic), it'll have a product or service, a quantity, a price, and dates for fulfillment. The product, customer, and date components of the sales order are all dimensions and provide context to the facts of the sales order; they provide the descriptive framework in which the data resides. Dimensions have several characteristics in that they describe and categorize the facts. Typically, dimensions are relatively short tables (few rows) but often wide (many columns). Conversely, facts tend to be longer but narrower. They can also provide a hierarchy, such as date (think year, quarter, month, and day). In *Figure 2.2*, we show how fact and dimension tables can connect to each other using one-to-many relationships. Between the `Sales Order Header` and `Sales Order Lines` tables, we're connecting the `Customer`, `Product`, and `Date` dimension tables to the `Sales Order Line/Header` fact tables.

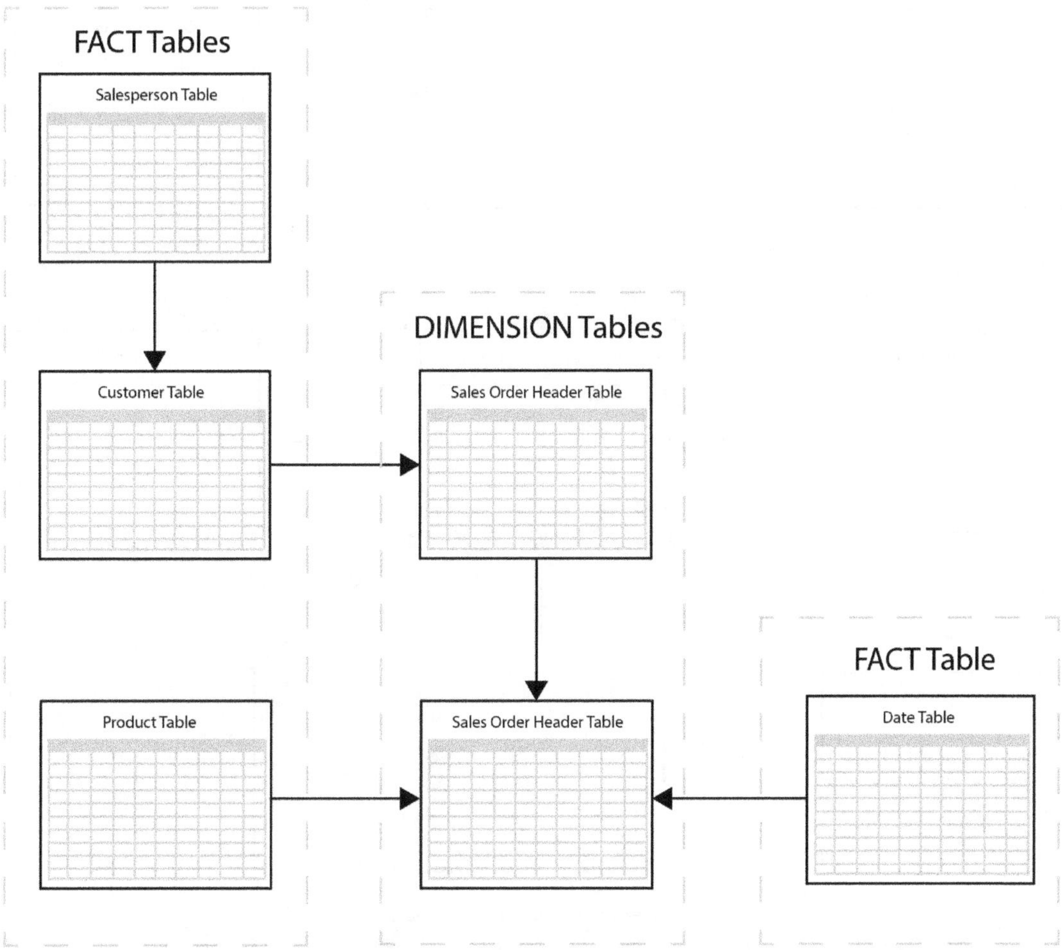

Figure 2.2: Fact and dimension tables

With entities, tables, relationships, facts, and dimensions in place, we start to consider how these concepts build the big picture of our data model, which is known as a schema.

Schema

The relationships just described, between your tables and the types of tables, will form a schema. The basic schema for your tables is a star, where you'll have a central fact table with dimension tables surrounding it. The dimension tables allow you to filter the transactions in the fact table, allowing you to perform calculations on your data. In *Figure 2.3*, we show a typical star schema, where you'll see the visual metaphorical reference with a center table of fact data surrounded by tables of dimension data.

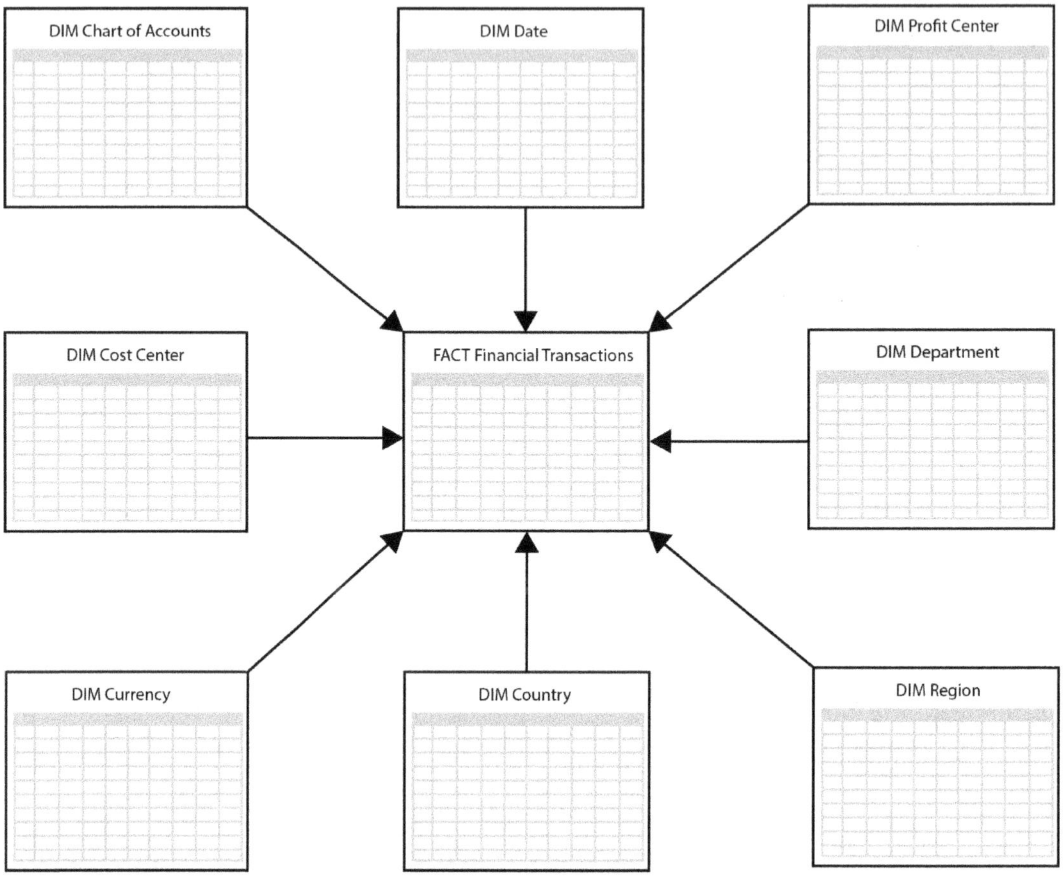

Figure 2.3: Star schema example

You may need to add complexity to your data model through additional tables that are linked to your fact tables. When you do this, your star schema becomes a snowflake schema, another visual metaphor. Star and snowflake schemas are designed for the efficiency of data structures that support our reporting. It means the `Sales Order` table can contain a single reference, such as a product, without containing all the characteristics of the product, such as cost, color, or weight. There are times, however, when we'll want to combine tables to simplify the structure and make our reporting easier. We call this practice **flattening the tables**, or to use the more official database term, **denormalization**. We discuss this in reference to totaling accounts later in the chapter.

In this section, we've briefly explained the main terminology and concepts in analytics modeling, which are databases, tables, entities, relationships, facts, dimensions and schemas. We consider these to be the essentials that will help you through the sections that follow and prepare you for other texts on this topic. With these new terms, let's start applying them to the world of financial modeling.

The common structure of financial applications

While financial systems may have unique table structures, the way transactions are recorded is fundamentally the same across all accounting systems. This consistency allows for the creation of a common structure within one or many Power BI semantic models to house all ledger transactions, whether from single or multiple systems. This becomes particularly valuable when working with clients who use multiple financial applications across different companies, as it enables consolidated financial reporting. Although this process can be complex, it is achievable. We won't delve into that level of detail in this book, but it's important to know that it's possible.

At the heart of the financial semantic model, we consider three entities that may be contained in multiple tables: the calendar, the chart of accounts, and transactions. On top of this, it's possible to extend the model in various directions – we will be looking in future chapters specifically at journal entries, inventory, and budget, but the same ideas can extend into sales, purchasing, manufacturing, and more.

In the GitHub repository of this book (`https://github.com/PacktPublishing/Financial-Modeling-with-Power-BI_Packt`), we have Power BI models you can download and use to follow our examples. We must start with a warning: the actual structure of your finance system will differ, and it'll certainly be more complex, but the basic structure will be the same, just as the basic measures and visualizations will be the same. Of the three entities we explain, you'll need to create one yourself (calendar), and the other two (transactions and chart of accounts) will come from the finance application. Creating a `Calendar` table is a core skill for working with Power BI, and we explain why and how to do it in the next section.

The upcoming sections explain these entities, and then we have the working example you can load into Power BI from the sample files.

> Note
>
> **Clearly Clothing**
>
> Throughout this book, we will be using examples from a fictional clothing retailer, *Clearly Clothing*. We will walk through creating a full suite of financial reports using this company, adding complexity as we go. Initially, however, we will start with a simple model using just one legal entity. Later in this chapter, we will add additional legal entities to report across the whole group.

Calendar

Starting with the `Calendar` table, possibly the first question is why you need such a table; surely transactions have dates? Of course, transactions do have dates, often many dates, but what they don't have is structure beyond numerical day, month, and year. The requirements for date reporting, or **time intelligence**, vary from organization to organization, but most will need month names, some want to see the long name (e.g., January), and others will just want the short name (e.g., Jan).

Many organizations have fiscal calendars in addition to a Gregorian calendar (1st January to 31st December) that need to be catered for. For example, the Microsoft fiscal calendar runs from July 1st to June 30th. Most often, this means a different start and end date to the year, but sometimes, fiscal periods do not map exactly to calendar months – for example, in a `4-4-5` pattern. To deal with this complexity, we add some "helper" fields to the `Calendar` table that help us map fiscal periods to ordinary periods.

All of this, and more, is accommodated by a `Calendar` table.

A common structure for a `Calendar` table follows in *Table 2.1*:

Field name	Description
`Full Date`	This represents the unique identifier – or primary key – for the table
`Day Name`	The day name
`Day of Week`	The day number in the week; this will be used for sorting days
`Calendar Week Name`	A name for the calendar week (e.g., Week 3)
`Calendar Week Sort`	The number of the week within the year; if the year starts partway through a week, you may wish to number from 0
`Calendar Month Name`	The name of the month
`Calendar Month Sort`	The number of the month in the year

Field name	Description
`Calendar Quarter Name`	A name for the quarter (e.g., Quarter 2)
`Calendar Quarter Sort`	The number indicating the quarter in the year
`Calendar Year Name`	The name of the year, although this would normally just be a numerical value, such as 2024
`Calendar Year Sort`	The sort order for the year, if the year name is not numerical
`Calendar Day of month`	(Optional) number indicating the day of the month
`Calendar Day of Quarter`	(Optional) number indicating the day of the quarter
`Calendar Day of Year`	(Optional) number indicating the day of the year
`Fiscal Week Name`	Name of the fiscal week; it is good practice to give this a name distinct from the calendar version
`Fiscal Week sort`	Number indicating the week in the year
`Fiscal Period Name`	The name of the fiscal period – ignore opening and closing periods for now
`Fiscal Period Sort`	The sort order for the period
`Fiscal Quarter Name`	The name of the fiscal quarter

Field name	Description
`Fiscal Quarter Sort`	The sort order for the quarter
`Fiscal Year Name`	The name of the fiscal year (e.g., 2024/5)
`Fiscal Year Sort`	The order – since the fiscal year is likely to be a text name, this will be needed

Table 2.1: Common fields for a Calendar table

In addition to these, there may be other calendars that need to be added, based on organizational needs. For example, an education establishment may need to add details of the academic year and include additional fields, such as semesters and terms. Whilst it is possible to build most of this from data stored in the systems of record, it is often expedient to build much of this data in a spreadsheet and import it into your semantic model. This is especially true where there are a lot of custom fields involved or more complex helper fields for sorting are needed.

With a `Calendar` table, each row will represent a day, so the table will be a reasonable size, although certainly not large by Power BI's capabilities. As with all things in the data world, it's sensible to keep the table as small as is functional to provide the best performance. At a minimum, however, the dates must go back at least as far as the history to be imported into the model, and probably a few years into the future. The shorter the future import, the more maintenance will be required in the long term, but the model will be more performant. Managing data is full of trade-offs.

In addition to the `Calendar` table, you may also consider a `Periods` table – this would just handle fiscal periods and is especially useful when handling opening and closing periods (P0 and P13) that should not be included in "normal" periods.

Once we have a `Calendar` table in place, we'll find it far easier to manage and visualize our transactional data. In the following sections, we'll discuss our main dimension table, `Chart of Accounts`, followed by the **general ledger** (**GL**) transactions table, which is a fact table.

Chart of Accounts

The Chart of Accounts is a critical component that categorizes transactions into their various accounts and types. This is also the place where you can consolidate different charts of accounts from different systems in one centralized table and map different accounts together. The basis of your chart of accounts table should look something like this:

Field name	Description
Account ID	Either the account number for the account, or a sequential ID – the latter is useful if you are mapping accounts from different systems
Account Number	The account number from the source system
Account Name	The human-readable name for the account
Account Type	High-level type of account (e.g., Balance Sheet or Profit and Loss)
Account Category	A more detailed category (e.g., Revenue or COGS)

Table 2.2: Chart of Accounts basic table structure

These fields will (usually) create a basic hierarchy, from `Account Type` -> `Account Category` -> `Account Number/Name`. Please see *Figure 2.4* for a visual example. The purpose of the hierarchy is to enable Power BI to calculate totals based on the various levels. In computing, we talk about parent-child relationships where one (e.g., mother) can have many children, but one child can only have one (biological) mother. When we explained relationships earlier in the chapter, the one-to-many relationship is also a parent-child relationship.

There may also be other hierarchies and relationships to consider, for example, parent-child relationships in the chart of accounts, or accounts being grouped together into totaling accounts, which are accounts used for the summation of other accounts (discussed next).

Power BI does not offer a direct way to handle parent-child relationships, but it does contain the tools to manage them. In doing so, we make explicit all the levels of the hierarchy. Consider this: Logically, the parent-child relationships we have in our accounts form a hierarchy. To translate to a format that Power BI can readily understand, we transform the data into a tabular structure where we take the hierarchical data structure and build a single table. The unique values in the table will be at the lowest level of the hierarchy, and each row will contain the entire structure. The data from your financial application will usually be represented in a parent-child structure, where you will have separate tables for each level of the hierarchy. In this case, we would have tables for `Account Type`, `Account Category`, and `Account Number`. Using the tools in Power Query (sometimes also referred to as **Transform Data** after the name of the button that launches it), we're able to merge these tables into one. In database terms, the exercise is called denormalization, and it's a common exercise when taking structured data and using it for analytics purposes.

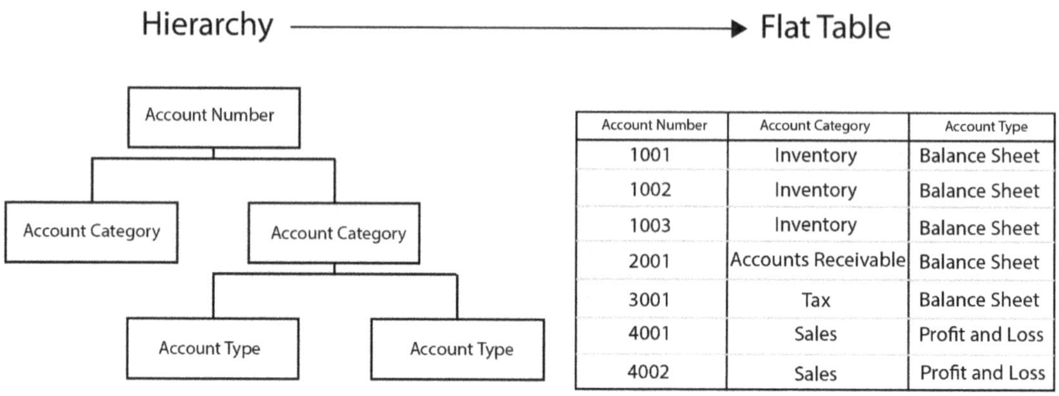

Account Number	Account Category	Account Type
1001	Inventory	Balance Sheet
1002	Inventory	Balance Sheet
1003	Inventory	Balance Sheet
2001	Accounts Receivable	Balance Sheet
3001	Tax	Balance Sheet
4001	Sales	Profit and Loss
4002	Sales	Profit and Loss

Figure 2.4: Chart of Accounts hierarchy

Next, we cover totaling accounts as a subset of the chart of accounts. Not all financial applications use this concept, but enough do to justify its incorporation in this book. If you don't think your finance application uses these, then feel free to skip the next section.

Totaling accounts

Certain applications, such as **QuickBooks**, use totaling accounts, so you may or may not encounter them. If your financial application uses totaling accounts, you won't see direct postings against them; instead, you'll see other accounts post to them. Take the following example:

Account Number	**Account Name**
`4001`	Shirt sales revenue
`4002`	Trousers sales revenue
`4003`	Hat sales revenue
`4010`	Total clothing revenue

Table 2.3: Totaling account example

In this case, account number `4010` will total accounts `4001` to `4003` and have no direct postings itself. The most flexible way to deal with this pattern is to add a mapping table, where each account is represented as totaling itself, along with the totaling accounts and the children they sum up, as follows:

Account Number	**Totaling Account**	**Totaling Account Name**
`4001`	`4001`	Shirt sales revenue
`4002`	`4002`	Trousers sales revenue
`4003`	`4003`	Hat sales revenue
`4001`	`4010`	Total clothing revenue
`4002`	`4010`	Total clothing revenue
`4003`	`4010`	Total clothing revenue

Table 2.4: Totaling account posting structure

This allows you to create a table containing the accounts and amounts themselves alongside the totaling accounts.

If you want to look at the core data model from the GitHub site (`https://github.com/PacktPublishing/Financial-Modeling-with-Power-BI_Packt/tree/main/Chapter2`), you'll see the following example for totaling accounts:

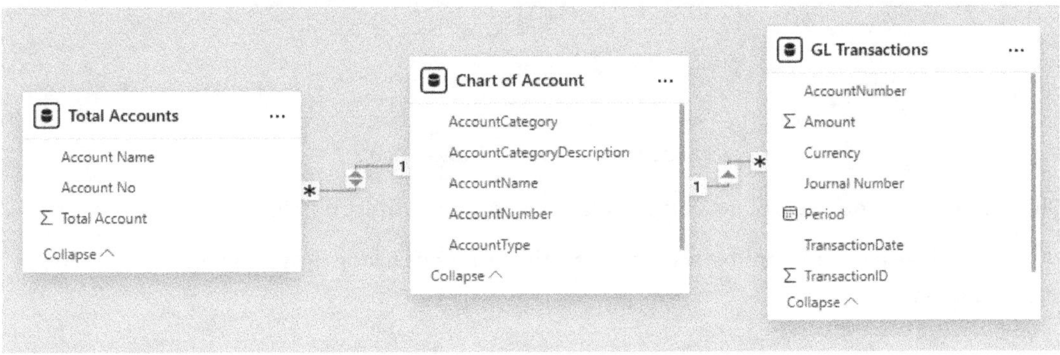

Figure 2.5: Totaling Accounts tables and relationships

When we look at the data tables in the core data model, you'll see `GL Transactions`, `Chart of Account`, and `Total Accounts`. There's a two-way or bidirectional relationship between the `Total Accounts` and `Chart of Accounts`, which allows the `Total Accounts` table to filter the `Chart of Accounts` table. Generally, the side of the "one" table filters the "many" table, which is the standard one-to-many relationship. In this case, we've implemented a bidirectional relationship so the "many" side can filter the "one" side. We generally advise against bidirectional relationships as they can cause calculation and performance issues with your data model, but in this case, the filtering table, `Total Accounts`, is not connected to any other tables. We will examine this in more detail in the next section. When you look at the Power BI visuals, you'll see the following table:

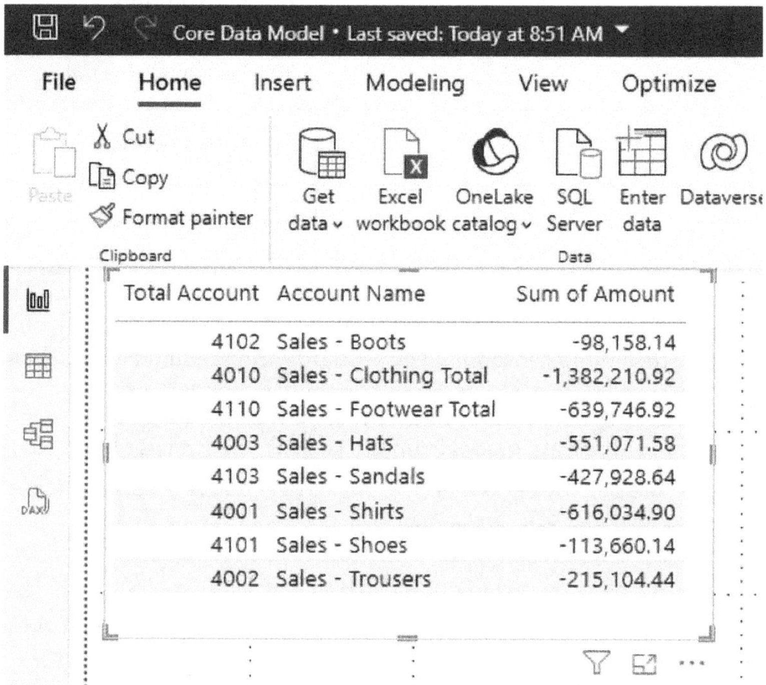

Figure 2.6: Postings from Total Accounts

This allows us to total sets of accounts even if they have no direct postings.

Now that we've covered totaling accounts, it's time to move a step down the hierarchy to look at transactions.

Transactions

Finally, we can consider the transactions. In our data model, we create a table to hold basic transaction details that will represent your GL. In your finance application, you'll probably have one, possibly two tables that will act as a central repository for your GL transactions. The transaction table is a type of table known as a fact table, as we described earlier in the *Facts and dimensions* section. Typically, fact tables should be narrow (few columns) but contain many rows, and you may have to remove unwanted or unused columns that are part of the tables. It's typical to have many columns within the tables of commercial finance applications that are unrelated to your implementation, so please remove them using **Choose Columns** in Power Query (this is covered in the next chapter). You'll find that this will also make your life easier when navigating the data. The context of the transaction is provided by the dimension tables (such as `Calendar` and `Chart of Accounts`), which were described previously. These dimension tables should have a few rows, but can typically have many columns (as we have seen in the `Calendar` table).

The pattern for a ledger transaction table could resemble the following example, in *Table 2.5*:

Field name	Description
Transaction ID	ID for the transaction taken from the source system.
Source System ID	(Optional) Good practice when taking data from multiple source systems.
Date	Transaction date, used to link to the `Calendar` table.
Period	Accounting period, used to link to the `Periods` table.
Account No	Links to the chart of accounts.
Currency	(Optional) Needed if working in multiple currencies.
Debit (transaction currency)	(Optional) Debit amount in the transaction currency.
Credit (transaction currency)	(Optional) Credit amount in the transaction currency.

Field name	Description
Total (transaction currency)	Total amount in the transaction currency. Even if the source does not have this explicitly, calculate it! It will make your life so much easier.
Debit (Accounting currency)	(Optional) Only needed in multi-currency, the debit amount in the accounting currency.
Credit (accounting currency)	(Optional) Only needed in multi-currency, the credit amount in the accounting currency.
Total (accounting currency)	(Optional) Only needed in multi-currency, the total amount in the accounting currency.

Table 2.5: GL transactions example table

Now that we've covered the core entities that you'll use for your financial reporting, it's time to roll up our sleeves and look at how we manage and manipulate this data in Power BI.

Managing relationships in Power BI

To help you start working with Power BI quickly, we've included the files used in the examples we've used for this book. For this section, please refer to the `Core Data Model.pbix` file.

The first item to check is how Power BI relates the data tables that are loaded. As a default setting (which can be changed in **Options and Settings**), Power BI will automatically attempt to relate key columns within the tables as they are loaded. This can be based on identical column names and data types, with a preference for one-to-many relationships. For example, `CustomerID` on the `Customer` table will automatically be related to `CustomerID` on the `Sales Orders` table. Please note, Power BI doesn't always get this correct, as column names aren't always named consistently, so it may be the case that `CustomerID` on the `Customer` table needs to be linked to `CustomerName` on the `Sales Order` table.

To look at the example file, navigate to the data model view, and you'll see the example in *Figure 2.7*:

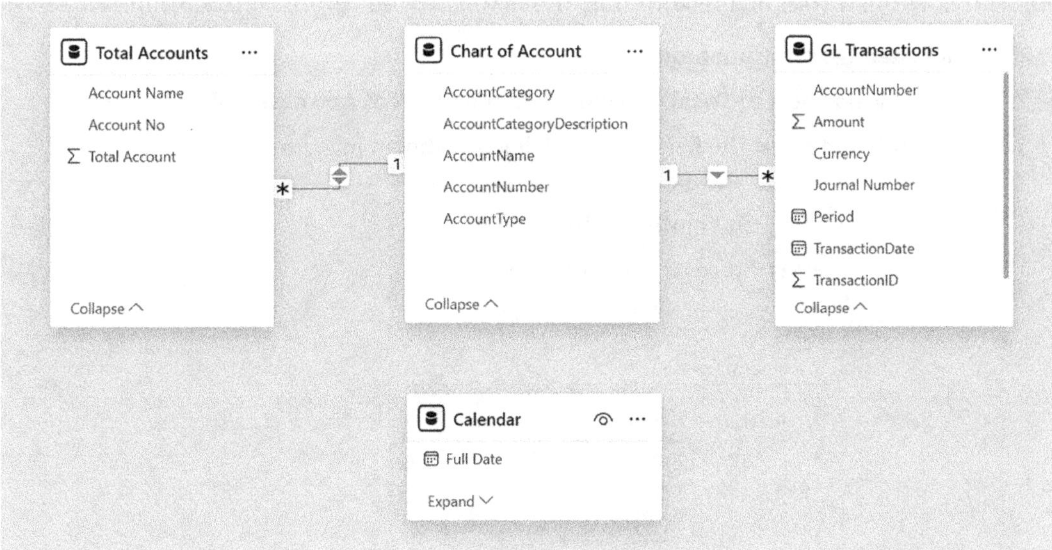

Figure 2.7: Initial load of tables

Accounts and transactions have connected correctly, but the `Calendar` table hasn't connected at all. First, we need to confirm that the relationships that have been created are correct, so we go to **Manage relationships**.

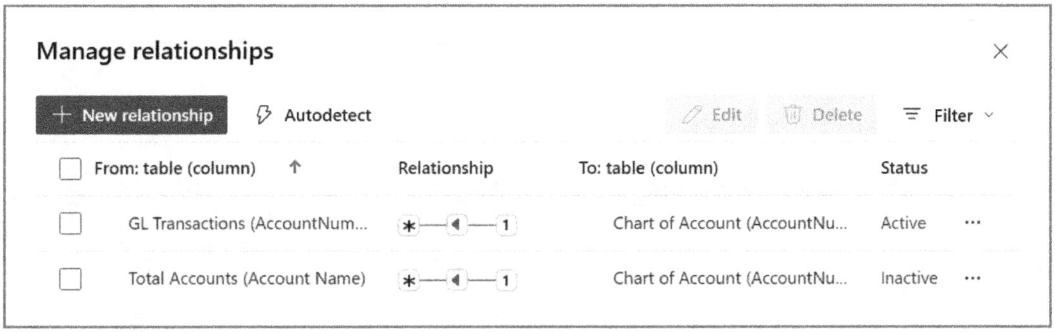

Figure 2.8: Power BI Manage relationships

Here, we can see that the link between our `Chart of Accounts` and `GL Transactions` tables looks good, but the relationship between `Total Accounts` and `Chart of Account` has been created by name and not by account number. This is important because, typically, the account number must be unique, but the account name may not be (although best practice would suggest that you should make the account names unique as well – otherwise, there is likely to be a lot of confusion).

From here, we can correct that relationship, which we do by editing the relationship as follows:

1. Click **Manage relationships**.
2. Check the box next to **Total Accounts** and the **Chart of Account** options.
3. Click **Edit** and select the fields in the dialog box shown in *Figure 2.9*.

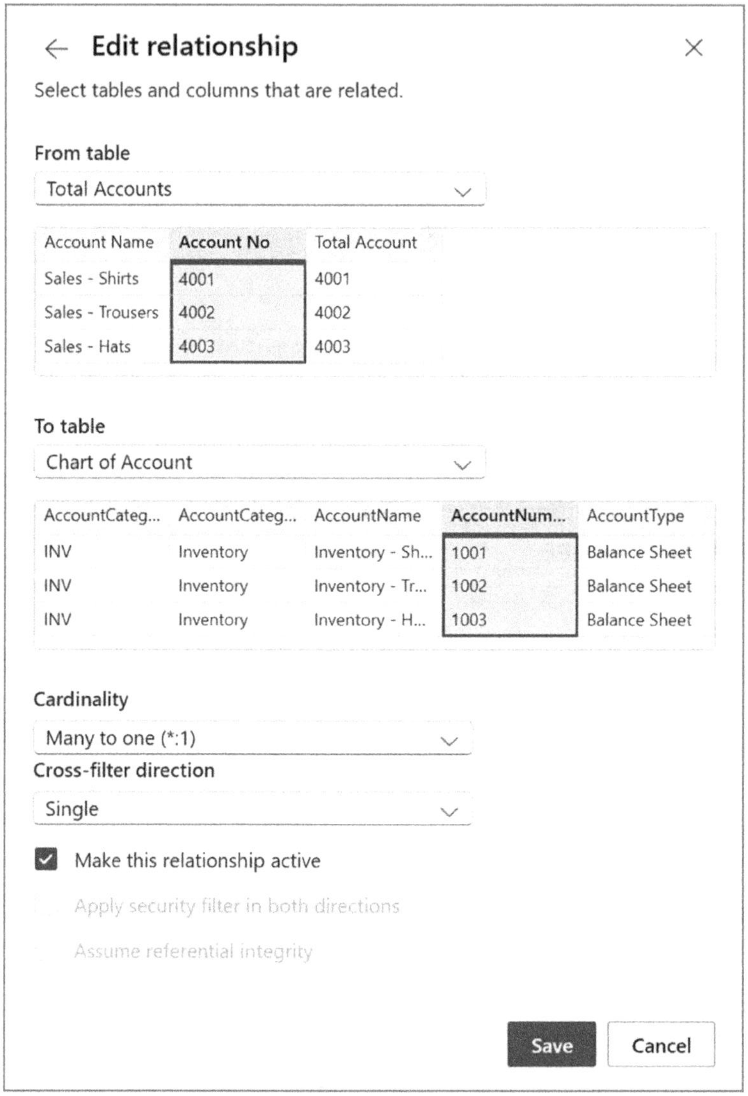

Figure 2.9: Creating the relationship to Total Accounts

Similarly, we can create the missing relationship that could not be detected, as the field names were different:

1. Again, select **Manage relationships**.
2. Click **New relationship**.
3. **From table** is the `Calendar` table, and **To table** is the `GL Transactions` table.
4. As shown in *Figure 2.10*, select `Full Date` from the `Calendar` table and `TransactionDate` from the `GL Transactions` table.
5. Click **Save** and watch Power BI form the relationship.

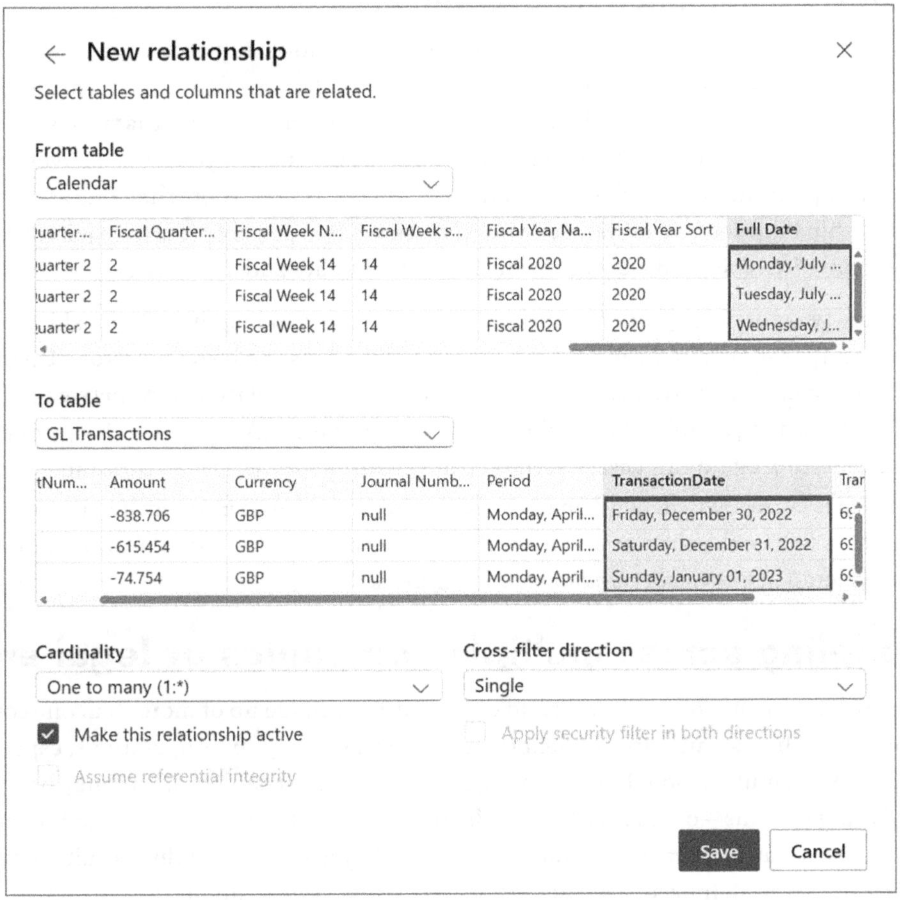

Figure 2.10: Creating the relationship to the Calendar table

Congratulations, you've fixed and generated relationships in Power BI. This is a core skill that you'll be using over and over again, and you're off to a great start.

We've talked about relationships earlier in the chapter, but didn't cover filter direction, which we'll cover next.

Filter direction

Normally, we expect filters to be single-directional, from the *one* side to the *many* side; you can't filter from *many* to *one*. There are times when relationships need to be in both directions – such as to make our totals accounts work since the total account needs to filter the `Chart of Accounts` table. Finally, it follows that any one-to-one relationships must flow in both directions – again driving the question of whether these are truly separate objects.

Active versus inactive relationships

Between any two tables, there can only be one active relationship at any time – this is the default means by which data selected in one table can filter another. If that wasn't the case, the application of filtering as described previously would be ambiguous – that is to say that there are two paths via which the filter could be applied. Sometimes, if you try to activate an inactive relationship, the interface will not let you, as that would create more than one active relationship between two tables. So, what if there are two possible routes to join things? Say we have an invoice table, and we want to have an invoice date and a due date.

There are two possible approaches here. The first is to use an inactive relationship. An inactive relationship is shown in the interface by a dotted line. This can be referred to in DAX functions that allow you to roll up the calculations based on different relationships between the tables. The second is to use a role-playing dimension that involves taking a second copy of the table you are filtering by (in this case, `Calendar`) and creating two active relationships. Which approach is correct will depend on the specific circumstances, but typically, the role-playing dimension will be the simpler and more flexible method. We look at role-playing dimensions in more detail in *Chapter 5, Handling Journal Entries*.

Modeling across multiple companies or legal entities

There will frequently be cases where an organization is made up of more than one company or legal entity. This can arise from a deliberate separation of a group's operations, especially common with multinationals, or from acquisitions. Since these companies may have different accounting systems – or at least different instances of the same system – consolidated reporting can cause a challenge, and this is often a key driver for building a suite of financial reports in Power BI. Indeed, even where an accounting system supports multiple companies, differences in the calendars and chart of accounts can render many built-in consolidations difficult or meaningless. In our example scenario, we have successfully piloted Power BI in the UK and now want to onboard the US trading entity.

As a result, we need to look at how we can add the data of multiple companies into the data model. There are broadly two approaches:

- **Approach 1**, where we link the company details to the Chart of Accounts and, therefore, to the transactions, or link the company to the transactions directly. This approach will tend to lead to a simpler structure for the Chart of Accounts, but can make consolidation difficult.
- **Approach 2**, where we link the company code directly to the transaction, which will be more performant, but will make the Chart of Accounts structure more complicated and harder to add new companies later; however, it will make consolidations easier.

First, we need to add a company table; regardless of the final approach we use, the essential fields are in *Table 2.6*.

Field name	Description
Company ID	Unique ID for the company
Company Name	The display name of the company
Accounting Currency	(Optional) If different companies use different currencies

Table 2.6: Essential fields for the company

Let's look at each approach in a bit more detail.

Approach 1 – linking the company to the chart of accounts

Here, we need to add a Company ID field to the chart of accounts. At the same time, we must ensure that every account ID in the chart of accounts is unique. Therefore, if two or more companies have the same account numbers (account ID), the solution is either to use a surrogate key that is looked up during the import process (this is typically the case when importing from a data warehouse, although it can be generated in Power Query) or, more commonly, creating a compound key by concatenating the company ID with the account number and some sort of separator. You will also need to add columns for the consolidated account structure.

Here, the `Chart of Accounts` table should resemble *Figure 2.11*:

AccountNumber	AccountName	AccountType	AccountCategory	AccountCategoryDescription
1001	Inventory - Shirts	Balance Sheet	INV	Inventory
1002	Inventory - Trousers	Balance Sheet	INV	Inventory
1003	Inventory - Hats	Balance Sheet	INV	Inventory
1101	Inventory - Shoes	Balance Sheet	INV	Inventory
1102	Inventory - Boots	Balance Sheet	INV	Inventory
1103	Inventory - Sandals	Balance Sheet	INV	Inventory
2001	AR Control	Balance Sheet	AR	Accounts Receivable
3001	Tax Control	Balance Sheet	TAX	Tax
4001	Sales - Shirts	Profit and Loss	SALES	Sales
4002	Sales - Trousers	Profit and Loss	SALES	Sales
4003	Sales - Hats	Profit and Loss	SALES	Sales
4101	Sales - Shoes	Profit and Loss	SALES	Sales
4102	Sales - Boots	Profit and Loss	SALES	Sales
4103	Sales - Sandals	Profit and Loss	SALES	Sales
5001	COGS - Shirts	Profit and Loss	COGS	Cost of Goods Sold
5002	COGS - Trousers	Profit and Loss	COGS	Cost of Goods Sold
5003	COGS - Hats	Profit and Loss	COGS	Cost of Goods Sold
5101	COGS - Shoes	Profit and Loss	COGS	Cost of Goods Sold
5102	COGS - Boots	Profit and Loss	COGS	Cost of Goods Sold
5103	COGS - Sandals	Profit and Loss	COGS	Cost of Goods Sold
6001	Salaries - Shop	Profit and Loss	SALEXP	Salary Expenses
6002	Salaries - Warehouse	Profit and Loss	SALEXP	Salary Expenses
6003	Salaries - Office	Profit and Loss	SALEXP	Salary Expenses
6101	Rent	Profit and Loss	PROPEXP	Property Expenses
6102	Building Maintenance	Profit and Loss	PROPEXP	Property Expenses
3101	Salaries Control	Balance Sheet	SALC	Salary Control
3201	Buildings Cost control	Balance Sheet	BUILC	Building Cost Control

Figure 2.11: Chart of Accounts table in Power BI

And the tables would be joined into the data model as shown in *Figure 2.12* (notice that * is at the "many" end, and **1** is at the "one" end):

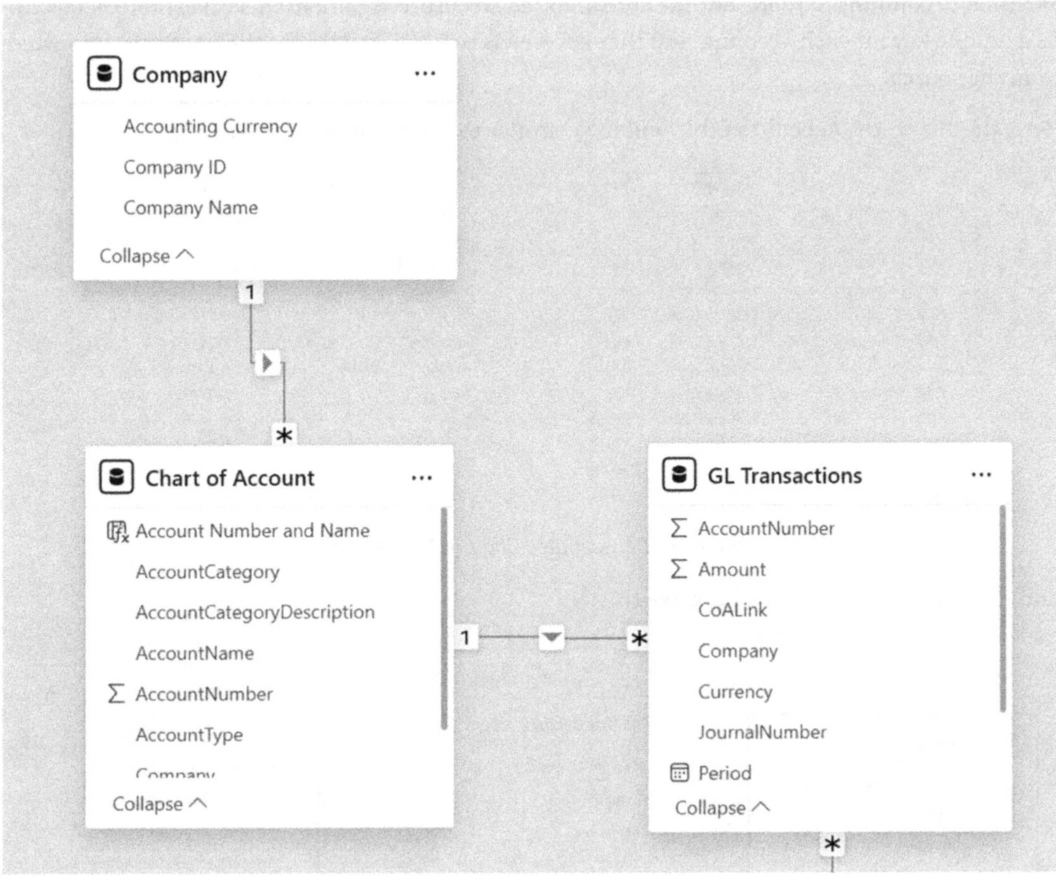

Figure 2.12: Joined tables for Approach 1

It's important to consider the advantages and disadvantages, as listed here:

- **Advantages**:
    - Simpler table structure, especially with a large number of companies
    - Easier to add new companies
- **Disadvantages**:
    - Harder to see the mapping between two different companies' Chart of Accounts
    - Can be slower

Approach 2 – linking to the transaction

Here, we need to add the company ID to the `Transactions` table. In addition, we need to add fields to the `Chart of Accounts` table to represent the Charts of Accounts of each company, and a set of columns to represent the consolidated structure. Again, in this case, there needs to be a unique key for each account, and that key needs to be looked up for each account imported from the source.

Here, the `Chart of Accounts` table will look similar to the example in *Figure 2.13*:

AccountNumber	AccountName	AccountType	AccountCategory	AccountCategoryDescription	Account Number and Name
1001	Inventory - Shirts	Balance Sheet	INV	Inventory	1001-Inventory - Shirts
1002	Inventory - Trousers	Balance Sheet	INV	Inventory	1002-Inventory - Trousers
1003	Inventory - Hats	Balance Sheet	INV	Inventory	1003-Inventory - Hats
1101	Inventory - Shoes	Balance Sheet	INV	Inventory	1101-Inventory - Shoes
1102	Inventory - Boots	Balance Sheet	INV	Inventory	1102-Inventory - Boots
1103	Inventory - Sandals	Balance Sheet	INV	Inventory	1103-Inventory - Sandals
2001	AR Control	Balance Sheet	AR	Accounts Receivable	2001-AR Control
3001	Tax Control	Balance Sheet	TAX	Tax	3001-Tax Control
4001	Sales - Shirts	Profit and Loss	SALES	Sales	4001-Sales - Shirts
4002	Sales - Trousers	Profit and Loss	SALES	Sales	4002-Sales - Trousers
4003	Sales - Hats	Profit and Loss	SALES	Sales	4003-Sales - Hats
4101	Sales - Shoes	Profit and Loss	SALES	Sales	4101-Sales - Shoes

Figure 2.13 – Consolidated Chart of Accounts table

And the data model will now look like this:

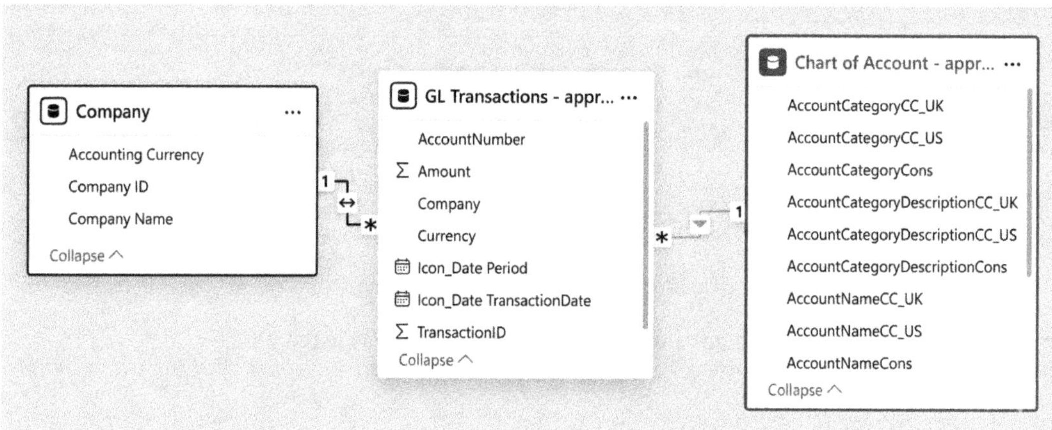

Figure 2.14: Tables for Approach 2

The advantages and disadvantages of Approach 2 are as follows:

- **Advantages**:
  - It is easy to see the mapping between different companies
  - Queries are generally faster
- **Disadvantages**:
  - Each time a new account structure is added, the Chart of Accounts gets wider

- It is unwieldy in complex organizations
- Problems can arise with consolidations

A potential "halfway house" exists where there may be two or three structures used by many companies, so the `Chart of Accounts` table would only need a few mapping columns. For the remainder of the book, we will use Approach 1 since this is the most flexible way of modeling data for the widest range of organizations.

Considerations for foreign exchange

Ideally, if there is a need for handling foreign exchange, this should be handled in the accounting systems and not in an ad hoc way in the reporting system. If a legal entity transacts in many currencies, it would be common practice for the accounting system to hold transaction amounts in at least the transaction currency and the accounting currency for that legal entity. Furthermore, if an accounting system supports multiple legal entities using different accounting currencies, it would be common practice (although not universal) to store a third reporting currency. In all of these cases, the best course of action is almost always to use the values stored in the accounting system. This means that there is no possibility of discrepancy between the reports and the accounting system. And after all, the accounting system is the system of record and is supposed to be definitive.

But what about other situations where this is not possible? Consider an organization where there are multiple legal entities using different systems. They may well have different accounting currencies and are not guaranteed to have the facility for an additional reporting currency, or, for historical reasons, such as acquisitions, they may use different reporting currencies. In any case, to create a consolidated reporting suite, all the currencies need to be converted into a single currency.

The first step is to get exchange rate data; in an ideal world, this would be sourced from an accounting system. If this is not the case, you will need to source data from elsewhere. Most likely, this will be from a web service – these come in free and paid variants. The price is generally set by the number of API calls allowed and the speed of updates. Typically, for most accounting systems, an update cadence of once per day is sufficient, since that is the normal granularity of posting to the general ledger. Most web APIs at all pricing tiers offer more than enough calls for updates to financial reporting.

Once the exchange rate data is available, the next step is to consider the strategy for converting and displaying the data. There are two basic approaches: static or dynamic. By far the easiest approach is static, and a dynamic approach should only be used if there is a clear need to display the values in different currencies at the touch of a button. This is a rare situation and should be avoided as it adds unnecessary complexity and maintenance costs. We will look in more detail in a future chapter at the calculations needed to use a dynamic approach.

Taking a static approach, the conversion can be done either during data load or by using calculated columns in DAX. The way to do this will depend on how exactly you intend to use the exchange rate data. If you are using daily spot rates, then it is almost certainly going to be more efficient to do the calculation during data load.

If, on the other hand, you need to use an average rate – for example, a 30-day moving average, or an average over the current period – then it is usually easier to handle this using calculated columns. We will examine this further in *Chapter 4, Common DAX Measures*.

Pitfalls of calculating foreign exchange in the data model

It must be noted that there are significant downsides to calculating foreign exchange in the data model, rather than the accounting system. Most obvious is the fact that it will mean that values in the converted currency will almost certainly not match properly or add up as expected. If the currencies we are converting between are relatively stable, this is not a big issue, as the variation is usually <1% of the overall transaction value. If the relative values are more volatile, though, there may be a more significant problem.

But how does this occur? Essentially, the mechanism is changing exchange rates between related transactions. Suppose we raise an invoice for 100 GBP, and on the day we raise it, the exchange rate makes that 120 USD. In our transactional system, we debit 100 GBP to the Accounts Receivable control account, and in the report, we convert that to 120 USD. A month later, we receive payment, so we credit the AR control with 100 GBP. All good, the accounting system and the report show a balance of 0 for that on the AR control. However, if the exchange rate has changed – let's say that 100 GBP is now worth 119 USD – the report will show a credit of 119 USD, leaving a debit balance of 1 USD. That means that there will be a contradiction between the base currency and the converted currency. In an accounting system, exchange rate variations between accounting and transaction currencies can be handled via postings to the realised loss/gain to exchange rate accounts. Reporting systems do not create their own transactions, so they are unable to handle this in this way. As such, converted values in the reports need to carry a health warning.

The other big issue is processing – the more calculated currencies you need, and the more complex the logic behind the calculation, the slower things will be. If you are tied to doing this in the reporting layer, you will also be tied to a service to provide those rates. And if you change providers, be prepared to have to re-engineer all reports using that.

Given the complexity, the limitations, and the downsides mentioned previously, think very carefully about whether the value that calculating exchange rates in the reporting is really worth it. Usually, that investment is better used to improve the source system.

Summary

In this chapter, we've started our journey in financial modeling for Power BI by focusing on how the core entities are either created or located within your financial application. Learning some important terms along the way, we then explained how the basic structure of financial systems follows a similar pattern, so you'll be well prepared to apply it using your own financial data. We looked at totaling accounts, which you may need, and finished by considering the complexities of multi-company and foreign transactions. We have to say that the last two examples are complex, but you'll now have a basic idea of how to deal with them.

We now have a basic model to start working with. In the next chapter, we'll start to apply some of Power BI's core language, **Data Analysis eXpressions** (**DAX**).

Get this book's PDF version and more

3

Creating a Trial Balance and Income Statement

In *Chapter 2, The Basic Model for Financial Reporting*, we began work on our Power BI model by loading and relating the tables, starting the process of building a semantic model. This gave Power BI information on the context between the tables, providing the basis to relate the various elements of data. Good practices in data modeling are the foundation of Power BI. However, so far, we haven't visualized anything, and we're sure that many of you will be keen to see something tangible.

Before we can visualize our data, we need to do some further enrichment of our data model. Unless we do this, we'll be limited as to what we can do beyond simple aggregations, and since every balance will add up to zero, what would be the point? We'll need some calculations for items such as revenue, costs, opening and closing balances, and the difference between them.

To do this, we'll use Power BI to add some calculations. As a foundation for this book, we've assumed some prior Power BI knowledge and recommended basic training if you haven't worked with Power BI. From this point, we'll assume you have some knowledge as we introduce **Data Analysis eXpressions (DAX)**.

By the end of the chapter, you will be able to demonstrate the following competencies:

- Understand and work with fundamental DAX calculations and apply them to a semantic model populated with sample finance data
- Know how to build visuals for a Trial Balance and Income Statement
- Understand the value of adding slicers to the model to help analyze visuals

Technical requirements

To follow the worked examples in this chapter and beyond, you'll need a Windows PC with an internet connection, and you'll also need to download **Power BI Desktop**.

For more details, we suggest you access the following link, where Microsoft details the download process for Power BI Desktop and the PC hardware requirements: `https://learn.microsoft.com/en-us/power-bi/fundamentals/desktop-get-the-desktop`.

You will also need the resources from the `Chapter3` folder in the GitHub repository:

`https://github.com/PacktPublishing/Financial-Modeling-with-Power-BI_Packt/tree/main/Chapter3`.

Introduction to DAX calculations

DAX is the language that allows us to work with our data in Power BI, enabling us to add measures, columns, and tables, and then create advanced and complex formulas. It's designed to be capable of dealing with very large datasets and is an immensely powerful component of Power BI. Understanding how to use DAX properly is essential for developing good habits as your skills progress. Don't worry – we'll start with basic examples that you'll be able to immediately employ in your everyday work.

We've mentioned before, and it's worth repeating, that initial impressions could suggest that DAX is identical to the formula language in Excel. In some instances, that may be the case, but please don't make this assumption; it can behave differently, even when a function has an identical name. `IF` is a good illustration. In Excel, an `IF` statement works row by row on cell values directly, whereas an identical `IF` statement in DAX can work with columns and measures and may produce different results based on the filter context being applied to the data model. An Excel and DAX `IF` statement with identical data can produce different results.

For this chapter, we'll keep it simple to ease you into DAX for your financial reporting. We'll cover DAX in more detail in *Chapter 4, Common DAX Measures*. In this chapter, we'll work through examples that create the trial balance and income statements, and we'll show you how to calculate the following:

- Opening balance
- Closing balance
- Debits
- Credits

- Totals filtered by **Chart of Accounts** (**CoA**) properties
- Calculations based on the aforementioned points

Understanding measures and calculated columns

To start, let's look at your first decision when writing DAX, which is whether you're creating a measure or a calculated column (defined next). What's the difference, and why is it important to start with this decision? First and foremost, you must make this decision one way or the other, so this seems like a good starting point. Calculated columns are perhaps easier to conceptualize as you can see them in your data as they extend an existing data table. You won't immediately see a measure until you apply it to a visualization on the canvas within Power BI Desktop.

Calculated columns are columns of data that extend your data tables within Power BI. They don't change or extend the table in your source financial system; they just do this within the Power BI model. Therefore, if I have columns for sales quantity and unit price, I may want to extend my table with a *sales quantity x unit price* calculation so that I can see the total for the row.

Measures are calculated aggregations of data from the tables within your semantic model. They exist for the purposes of a visual and the evaluation changes based on filtering and user interactions. They do not extend your data model. So, why not just create calculated columns?

There are two reasons:

- As data models grow, efficiency is critical to the speed of operation. More data means more processing, and more processing can mean slower reporting. Adding columns means more processing.
- In many cases, creating a calculated column is not helpful. If I want to calculate the sum of a list of numbers, a column doesn't help as it'll contain the total of the entire column, in every row. It's nonsensical to the objective.

In contrast to columns, measures don't extend tables as they provide a calculation that exists for the purposes of the visualization. Take the following example in *Figure 3.1*:

ID	Date	Product	Quantity	Unit Price	Item Total	SUM as a Calculated Column
1001	1/1/2025	A	10	$50.00	$500.00	$3,500.00
1002	1/1/2025	B	20	$40.00	$800.00	$3,500.00
1003	1/1/2025	C	30	$30.00	$900.00	$3,500.00
1004	1/1/2025	D	40	$20.00	$800.00	$3,500.00
1005	1/1/2025	E	50	$10.00	$500.00	$3,500.00

SUM as a measure → SUM([Item Total]) = $3,500.00

Figure 3.1: Calculated columns and measures

In this case, we want to know the sum of the values in our `Item Total` column. If we add a simple measure, the calculation will exist for the purpose of the visualization and not extend our data model. However, if we add `SUM` as a calculated column, the data model is extended, but not in a helpful way, as Power BI will provide the sum of the values in the `Item Total` column, but in every row.

Measures versus calculated columns is a basic but essential consideration when working with data in your Power BI model. Generally, try to use measures where possible, as calculated columns will have a performance impact on your model and, in many cases, will be the wrong choice.

When you're building your own semantic models, you'll need to make these choices. In certain instances, it can be a gray area as both could meet your needs. If you can use a measure, then please do; otherwise, use a calculated column.

Understanding the basics: SUM, MIN, MAX, and AVERAGE

Once you've made the decision between a measure and a calculated column, you'll start writing DAX.

At its simplest, most measures for financial reporting can be worked out from the general ledger by aggregating figures based on data in the CoA, using `SUM` as a measure. Less used, but also useful, are the `MIN`, `MAX`, and `AVERAGE` functions. The `MIN` and `MAX` functions provide the minimum or maximum numbers in a column of data, and we will mostly use them for modifying the behavior of other measures, in particular, in conjunction with `CALCULATE`, which we'll deal with more thoroughly in *Chapter 4*, *Common DAX Measures*. The `AVERAGE` function tends to be less used since, in most use cases, it's desirable to have base measures for the numerator and denominator, so explicitly dividing one by the other is a common approach.

Let's take a basic example:

```
Total Amount = SUM('GL Transactions'[Amount])
```

This calculation is the most basic form of DAX. It's a measure that asks Power BI to add up the numbers in a column, and when we begin work on a semantic model, it'll almost always be our starting point.

In Power BI, we also have the `SUMX` function, which differs from `SUM` in that it performs a row-by-row calculation and then sums the results. We use `SUMX` when we need to calculate across multiple columns because it iterates across each row, performs the calculation, stores the result, and then sums each row's result to provide the overall result. The `SUM` function works straight down each row in the column to add up the numbers and provide a result. *Figure 3.2* illustrates this:

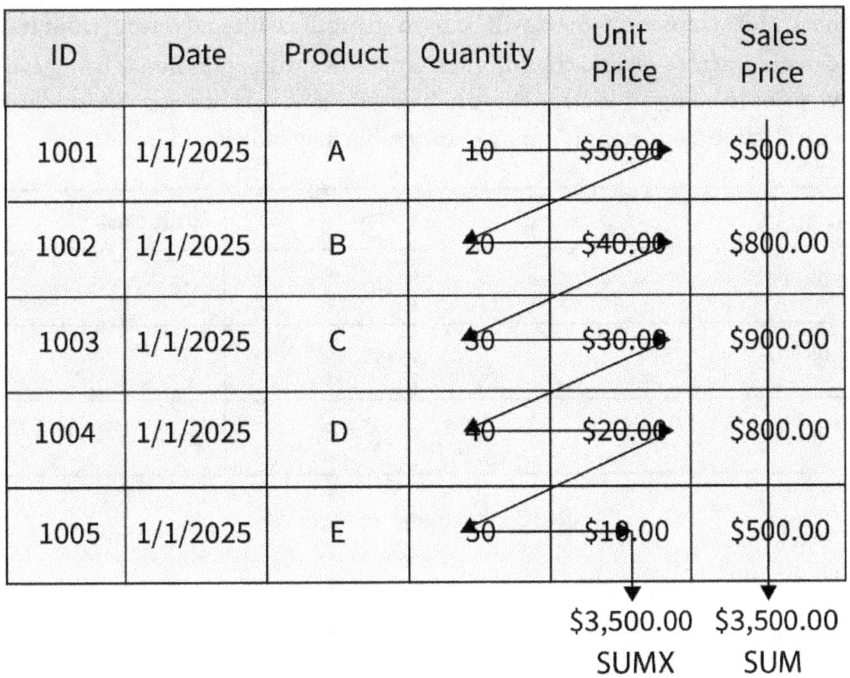

Figure 3.2: The difference between SUM and SUMX

If you have row totals in your table and purely want to add all the numbers, use `SUM`. It's more efficient and faster than `SUMX`. When you don't have row totals but have the basis of the calculation, you'll need to use `SUMX`.

The `SUMX` function also allows us to add filters to the row-by-row calculation, which can be used to create total credit and debit measures that allow us to create a trial balance:

```
Total Debit =
SUMX(
    FILTER(
        'GL Transactions',
        'GL Transactions'[Amount] > 0
    ),
    'GL Transactions'[Amount]
)
```

In this example, we calculated the sum of `Amount` from the `GL Transactions` table, applying a filter to only consider values greater than 0. We also used the `GL Transactions'[Amount]` field instead of the `Total Amount` measure, which we did for clarity to explain the calculation (you can use either). Most commonly, `SUMX` will be used to produce filtered outputs, but it can also be used to calculate across several columns in a table since the expression is being evaluated for each row, prior to being added up. This can be useful if a table has quantity and unit values but not the total value. For example, an inventory table may look like this:

SKU Code	Qty	Unit Cost
`FrmlSh-bk-06`	10	30
`FrmlSh-bk-07`	13	31
`FrmlSh-bk-08`	38	32

Table 3.1: Inventory transactions

We can calculate the total value as follows:

```
Total Value =
SUMX(
    'Inventory',
```

```
    'Inventory'[Qty] * 'Inventory'[Unit Cost]
)
```

We'll dive deeper into managing your inventory data in *Chapter 8, Managing Inventory Data.*

The `MIN`, `MAX`, and `AVERAGE` functions all work broadly the way you would expect (similar to Excel), returning the minimum value of a column, the maximum value of a column, and the arithmetic mean of the numerical values in a column. All three also have an "*X*" variation and behave much like how `SUMX` works. They also have "*A*" variations – `MINA`, `MAXA`, and `AVERAGEA`. These versions in general only work on numerical columns and ignore blank values, and their usefulness tends to be limited; they are mentioned here only for completeness.

From these functions, we can now start to create some measures that we'll want to use across our financial reports. Please remember that this is not an exhaustive list, merely a sample based on common requirements.

Adding measures to the data model

Now that you know some basics about calculated columns and measures, let's continue to build out our data model.

We'll start with the core data model, which is stored in this book's GitHub repo at `https://github.com/PacktPublishing/Financial-Modeling-with-Power-BI_Packt`. Download the Power BI model called `Core Model.pbix`. We have also included a Power BI model called `Chapter 3 Final.pbix`, which is a version with all the examples used within this chapter. If you get stuck at any point, this model is a great reference.

Our first task is to create a place to store our measures. A common practice in Power BI is to separate your measures from data tables within their own dedicated table. This helps you quickly and easily differentiate and find measures that have been written for the model. It's not essential; you can store measures within your data tables, but all our examples work based on a separate table for measures. Let's start by creating that table to store our measures:

1. From the **Modeling** tab, click **New table** as shown in *Figure 3.3*:

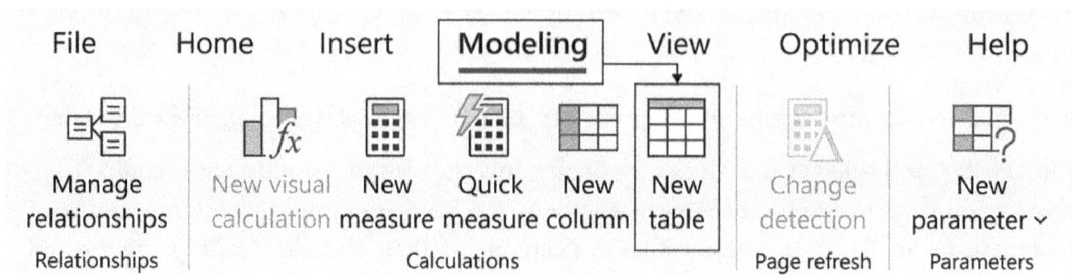

Figure 3.3: Creating a new table in Power BI Desktop

2. After creating the new table, you'll see that a command line is available with the text `Table =`, which will be highlighted. Replace that text with `List of Measures =` and hit *Enter*. You'll notice on the right that the new table is created, shown in *Figure 3.4*. Note that we've enhanced and copied the text so that it's easier to read.

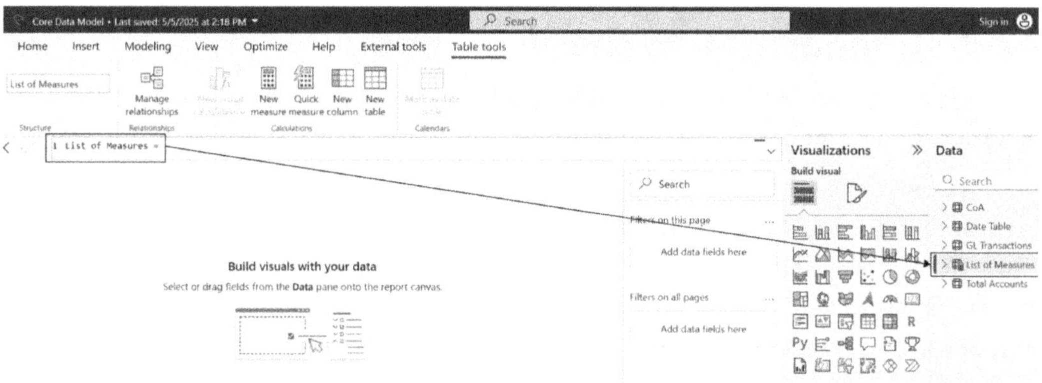

Figure 3.4: Creating a List of Measures table

To use our example model, there's a column in the `GL Transactions` table called `Amount` that provides the total value of each line item. We will go through each of the steps to add this measure. For the measures that follow, please revisit these steps.

From the new `List of Measures` table, click on the ellipsis and select **New Measure**. In the command line, type the following:

```
Total Amount = SUM('GL Transactions'[Amount])
```

In the command line of Power BI Desktop, it'll look like *Figure 3.5*. We've magnified the text for readability.

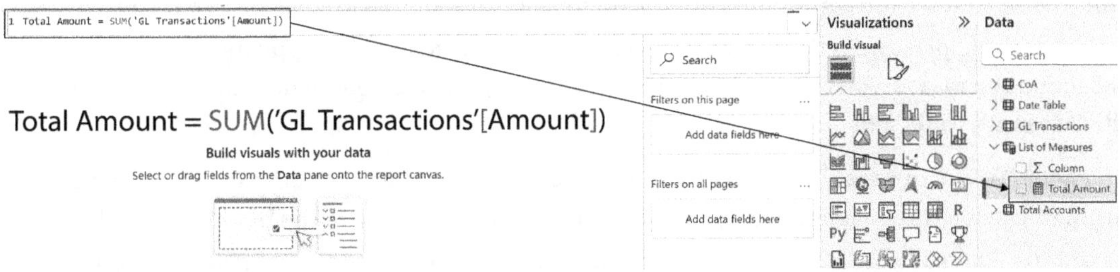

Figure 3.5: Adding the SUM measure

This will provide the sum of values in the `Amount` column from the `GL Transactions` table. If we show this total in Power BI, the sum of all line items will be `0` because the general ledger transactions table needs to balance. To provide some context, we could apply our `Total Amount` measure to the `AccountCategoryDescription` column within a table visual, as shown in *Figure 3.6*:

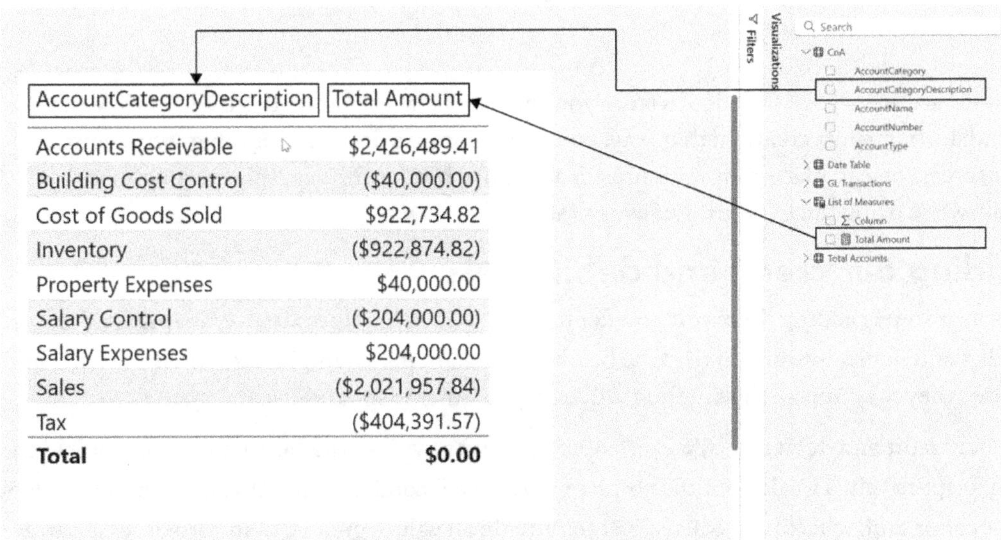

Figure 3.6: Using our SUM measure

To do this, follow these steps:

1. Select the table visual icon from the **Visualizations** pane.
2. Drag the `AccountCategoryDescription` field from the CoA table into the new table visual.
3. Also, drag the `Total Amount` measure into the table visual.

You'll note that we formatted the `Total Amount` measure to 2 decimal places, so if you see too many decimal places, set the decimal places in the **Measure** tab that appears. This is done by selecting the measure in the **Data** panel, then choosing the number of decimal places under the **Measure tools** tab.

In *Figure 3.6*, we can see that Power BI automatically breaks down our measure based on items from the `AccountCategoryDescription` field. It does this because of the link between the `Chart of Account` and `GL Transactions` tables that we created in the previous chapter.

You'll also notice this simple example has provided a basic trial balance.

The `SUM` function is just one aggregation we could have applied, and just like Excel, we could have also used `MIN`, `MAX`, `AVERAGE`, and `COUNT` against the column of data as follows:

```
Minimum Amount = MIN('GL Transactions'[Amount])
Maximum Amount = MAX('GL Transactions'[Amount])
Average Amount = AVERAGE('GL Transactions'[Amount])
Count of Values = COUNT('GL Transactions'[Amount])
```

To reiterate, it's a good practice to store your measures in a separate table where they can be found during report creation; that way, you won't confuse data in your tables with your measures. You can place your measures in any table, but for the examples throughout this book, we're using the `List of Measures` table.

Adding our credit and debit totals

Our next step is adding the credit and debit totals, which involves `SUMX`. We separate the credits and debits to work on the trial balance visual. In our example, the values balance, but in reality, they may not, so this method will help you quickly spot issues.

For our credit and debit totals, we use `SUMX` as we want values that are greater than or less than zero, respectively. To calculate the correct values, we'll combine the `FILTER` command with our `SUMX` command, where we ask Power BI to provide all values greater than zero or less than zero and add them up. The `Total Debit` measure looks like this:

```
Total Debit =
SUMX(
    FILTER(
        'GL Transactions',
        'GL Transactions'[Amount] > 0
    ),
```

```
        'GL Transactions'[Amount]
)
```

You'll notice that Power BI tries to help you with the syntax of the measure as you type it; this is a code completion aid called IntelliSense.

`SUMX` is an iterator function that calculates row by row and iterates down the data table. If you're unsure about how it works, please skip back to *Figure 3.2*. It starts at the top row of the table and checks whether the `GL Transactions` amount is greater than zero. If yes, it gets added to the total; if no, it gets ignored.

In a similar way, we can write a measure for `Total Credit` by reversing the greater-than sign:

```
Total Credit =
SUMX(
    FILTER(
        'GL Transactions',
        'GL Transactions'[Amount] < 0
    ),
    'GL Transactions'[Amount]
)
```

Both the `Total Debit` and `Total Credit` measures will ignore transactions that equal `0`, which, of course, will not impact the total.

Now that we have some basic measures, we can use them as the foundation for further calculations. It's important to note the benefit of DAX in using calculations as the basis for other calculations; think of one DAX measure as a building block for other DAX measures. The minimum measures needed to create an income statement are for revenue and expenses of various kinds. In our example CoA, we've kept revenue very simple – that is, retail sales. Many organizations have many income streams, and you'll want to customize your calculations to that. We provide a few examples here to get you started, and we're sure you'll develop many more of your own as your skills develop.

We can now combine our `Total Amount` measure with `SUMX` to write measures that calculate sales revenue, **cost of goods sold** (**COGS**), salary expenses, and building lease expenses.

Starting with sales revenue, we'll filter our `Total Amount` measure using the `Sales` category from `AccountCategoryDescription` in the `Chart of Account` table. Because the `Chart of`

`Account` table and the `GL Transactions` tables are linked, Power BI will be able to do this as follows:

```
Sales Revenue =
SUMX(
    FILTER(
        'Chart of Account',
        'Chart of Account'[AccountCategory] = "SALES"
    ),
    [Total Amount]
) * -1
```

> **Note**
>
> We multiply by -1 as the normal posting here will be a credit, but we want to show a positive number on the income statement.

Similarly, COGS is calculated thus:

```
COGS =
SUMX(
    FILTER(
        'Chart of Account'
,
        'Chart of Account'[AccountCategory] = "COGS"
    ),
    [Total Amount]
)
```

COGS is not the only expense we have as an organization. Again, to keep it simple, we're going to look at two other types of expenses with slightly different approaches to handling them – salaries and rents:

```
Salary Expenses =
SUMX(
    FILTER(
        'Chart of Account'
,
        'Chart of Account'
[AccountCategory] = "SALEXP"
```

```
    ),
    [Total Amount]
)
```

In our `Chart of Account` table, `Rent` has an ID within the `AccountNumber` field of `6101`. It also shares `PROPEX` as an `AccountCategory` value and `Property Maintenance` as an `AccountCategoryDescription` value with the `AccountName` value of `Building Maintenance`. In an ideal world, you would change this data to be more convenient, but we're going to assume it's not feasible, so we have to work around it. In this case, we'll filter based on the specific `Account Number` column from the `Chart of Account` table:

```
Rent Expense =
SUMX(
    FILTER(
        'Chart of Account'
,
        'Chart of Account'
[AccountNumber] = 6101
    ),
    [Total Amount]
)
```

Now, we can create the final measures we will need for our income statement so that we can show the total revenue, total expense, and net income. We'll start by calculating a measure for total revenue. In our example, our total revenue is equal to sales revenue:

```
Total Revenue = [Sales Revenue]
```

Then, we do the same for total expense:

```
Total Expenses = [COGS]+[Rent Expense]+[Salary Expenses]
```

Finally, we create a measure for net income:

```
Net Income = [Revenue]-[Expenses]
```

Note

Please note that this is not an exhaustive list of measures needed to prepare a complete income statement. The exact measures you will require will depend on the nature of your organization, business needs, and the jurisdiction in which you operate.

Finally, we need opening and closing balances for the Trial Balance. We'll start with the opening balance:

```
Opening Balance =
SUMX(
    FILTER(
        ALL('Calendar'[Full Date]),
        'Calendar'[Full Date] < MIN('Calendar'[Full Date])
    ),
    [Total Amount]
)
```

Then, we'll deal with the closing balance:

```
Closing Balance =
SUMX(
    FILTER(
        ALL('Calendar'[Full Date]),
        'Calendar'[Full Date] < MAX('Calendar'[Full Date])
    ),
    [Total Amount]
)
```

The `MIN` and `MAX` dates here, coupled with the `ALL` function, will return all transactions prior to that point. If a report is filtered for a year, the `MAX` date will return the end of the year, and the `MIN` date will return the start of the year. Depending on the postings that go into non-operating periods as the year is rolled over, these might need to be more complicated, either to exclude those periods or to only allow the calculation to look into the current financial year.

In this section, we started the DAX journey by creating a `List of Measures` table in Power BI Desktop. Then, we populated our `List of Measures` table with several measures that we'll need for our income statement. In the next section, we'll show you how to create that income statement.

Creating an income statement

Now that we have our measures, we can build our income statement. The income statement is one of the simplest financial statements, dealing with the profit and loss accounts. In our version, we'll limit the number of income and expense categories for simplicity, but the basic idea of building the report remains the same, no matter how many categories you have. Within the standard Power BI visuals, there's no income statement template, so we'll walk you through the process of building one.

We'll start in the report designer view, and on a blank canvas, we'll select the **Matrix** visual, as shown in *Figure 3.7*:

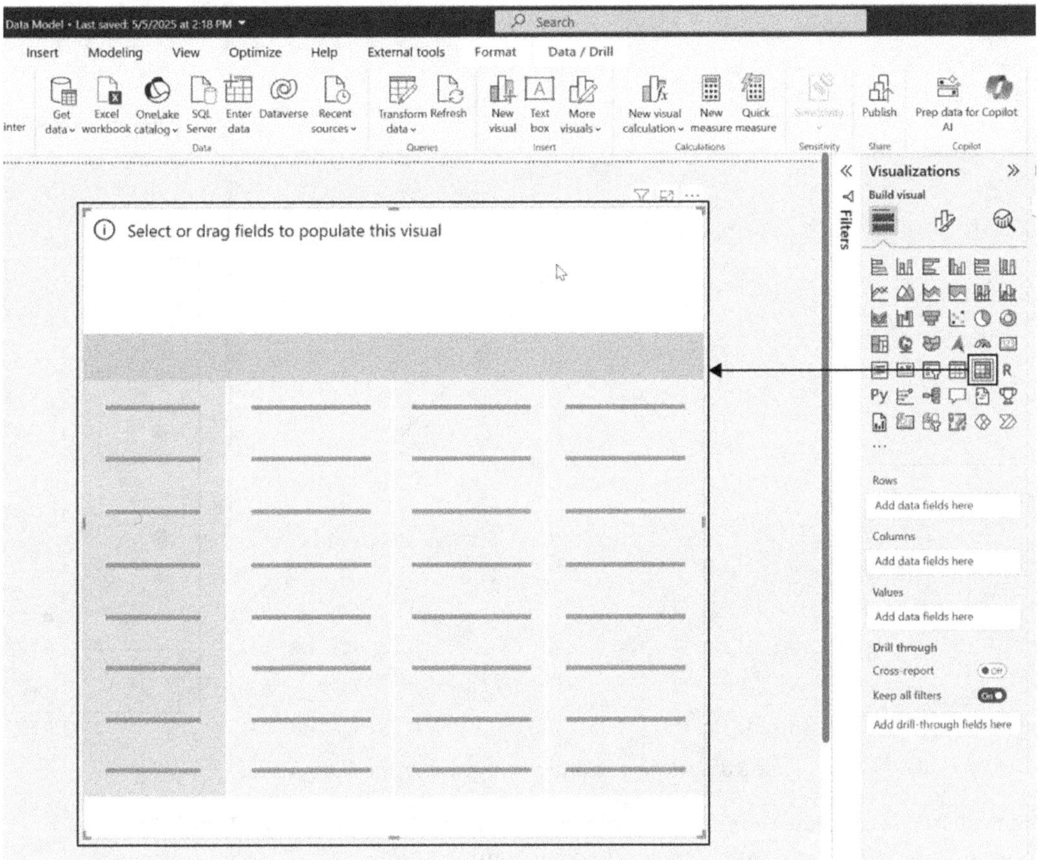

Figure 3.7: Creating a Matrix visual

We'll start by adding our expense accounts. Select `COGS`, `Rent Expenses`, and `Salary Expenses` from the `List of Measures` table. You can either check the box next to the measure or drag the item to the visual.

Your matrix will show the measure text and values as columns, so we need to switch them to rows as follows (you can also see an example in *Figure 3.7*):

1. From the **Visualizations** pane, click **Format your Visual**.
2. While on the **Visualizations** pane, select the **Visual** tab.
3. Select **Values**, then **Options**.
4. Under **Options**, select **Switch values to rows**.

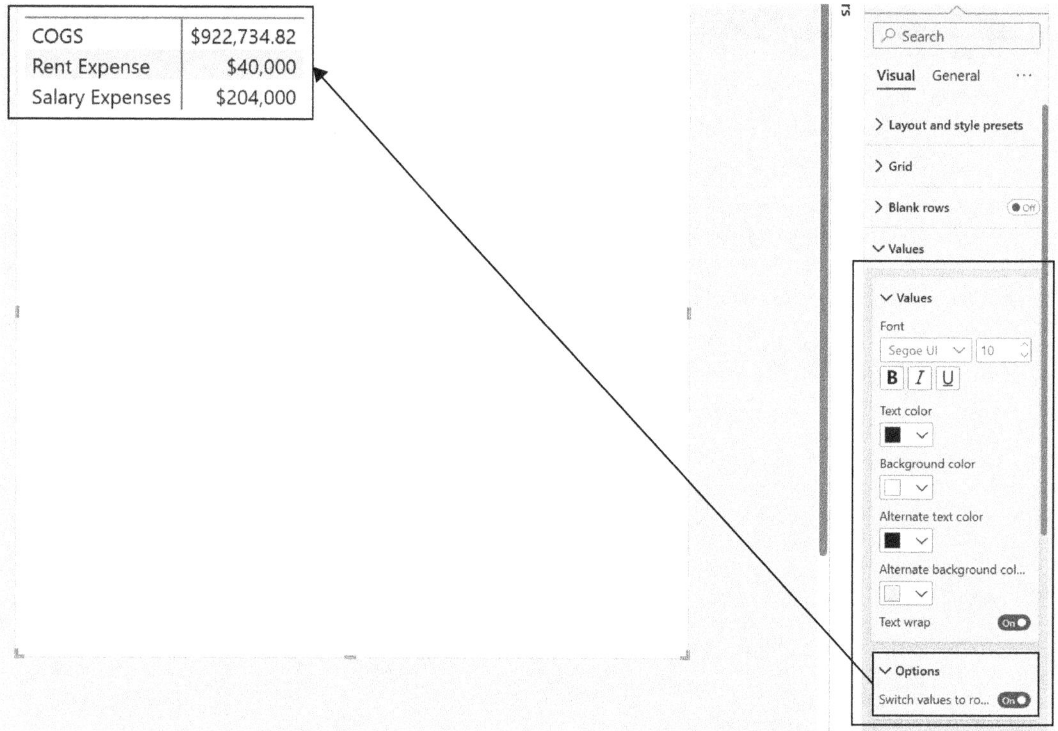

Figure 3.8: Switching columns to rows within the Matrix visual

The next step is to create four identical matrices to show `Sales Revenue`, `Total Revenue`, `Total Expenses`, and `Net Revenue`. To do this, we'll create one, then use copy and paste to create the others.

Start by creating another matrix and add a `Sales Revenue` measure. You'll then need to create a new measure called `Blank` as follows:

```
Blank = BLANK()
```

Then, add the `Blank` measure to the matrix, which will look like this:

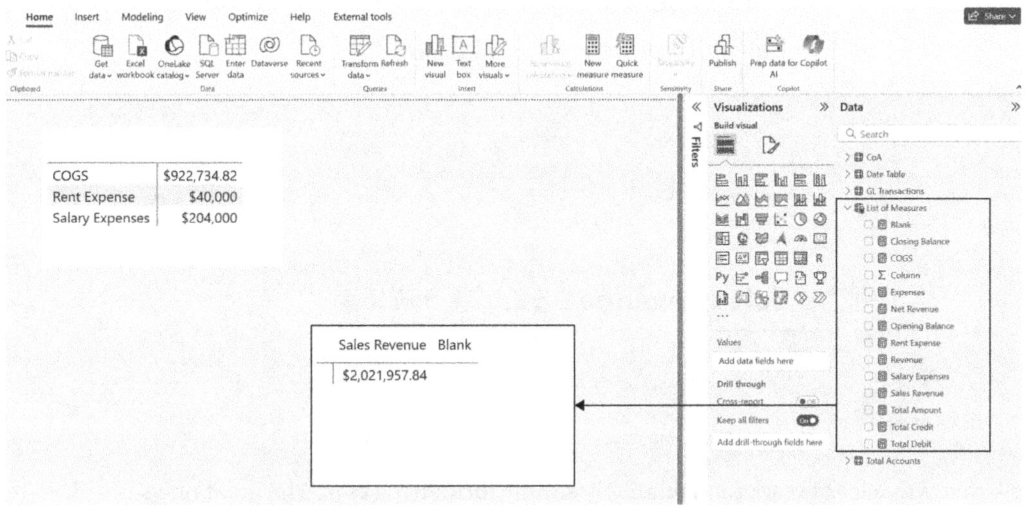

Figure 3.9: Adding the Blank measure

The purpose of the `Blank` measure is to allow us to switch values to rows as we did in the previous step. Without the `Blank` measure, Power BI won't allow us to do this as it only has one row. From this point, follow these steps from the **Visualizations** pane | **Visual** tab):

1. Go to **Values** | **Options**, then select **Switch values to rows**.
2. Go to **Layout and style presets** | **Style**, then select **None** from the dropdown. This removes formatting from the matrix.
3. Go to **Grid** | **Border**, then make the color white to remove the visible grid lines.
4. Go to **Specific column** | **Apply settings to** | **Series**, set this to **Blank**, set **Apply to header** to **On**, and set the color for **Values Text** to white. This will make the text color of the work white (blank) so that you can't see it.
5. Go to **Row headers** | **Text**, then toggle the bold formatting option to **On**. This will make the words `Sales Revenue` bold.
6. Go to **Values** | **Values**, then toggle the bold formatting option to **On**. This will make the numerical value for `Sales Revenue` bold.

Your matrix will look like the example in *Figure 3.10*:

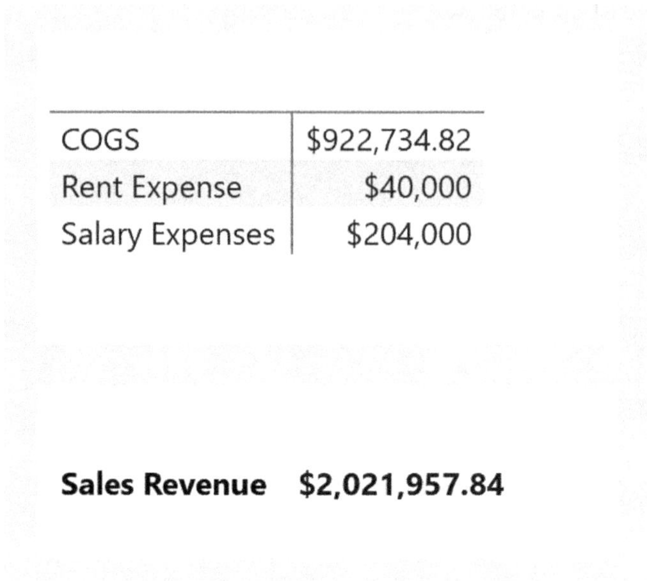

Figure 3.10: The formatted matrix

Yes – that was a lot of work for a relatively simple formatting task. The great news is we're going to copy and paste for the next three matrices we require. The next steps are as follows:

1. Copy the matrix we just created, then paste it three times.
2. Take the first pasted matrix and replace the `Sales Revenue` measure with the `Total Revenue` measure.
3. Take the second pasted matrix and replace the `Sales Revenue` measure with the `Total Expenses` measure.
4. Take the third pasted matrix and replace the `Sales Revenue` measure with the `Net Revenue` measure.

Your Power BI canvas should now look like *Figure 3.11*:

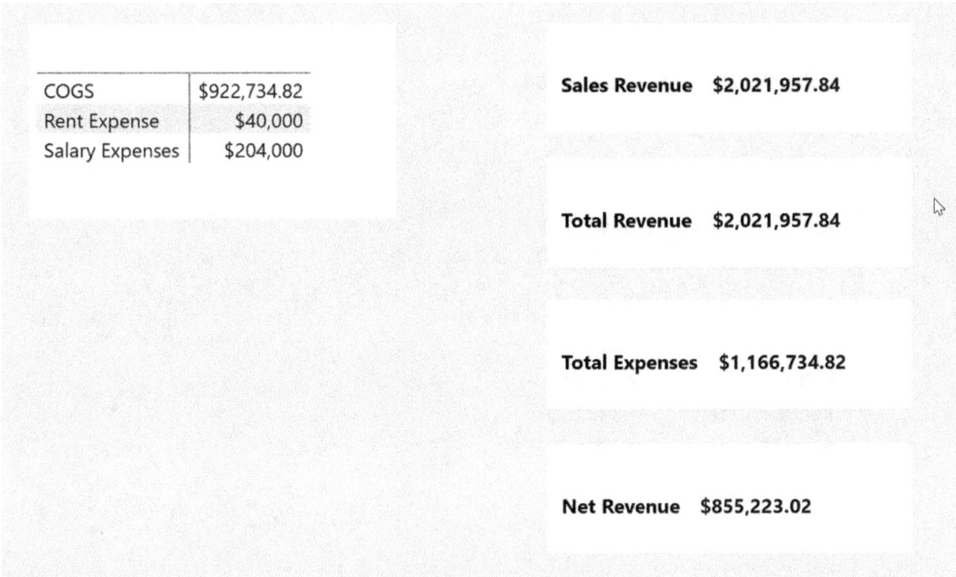

Figure 3.11: Our four matrices

> **Note**
>
> Note that in our sample data, the only revenue posted is sales revenue, so this is not broken down in the same way as expenses. If you have other revenue lines, then you will need to follow similar steps for revenue as we have for expenses.

The next step is to arrange the four matrices to follow the format of an income statement. Use the grab points on each of the matrices to resize them and use the grab points within the matrices to adjust the column widths. In the next screenshot, we've deliberately added a light gray to the canvas background so that you can see the outlines of the individual matrices:

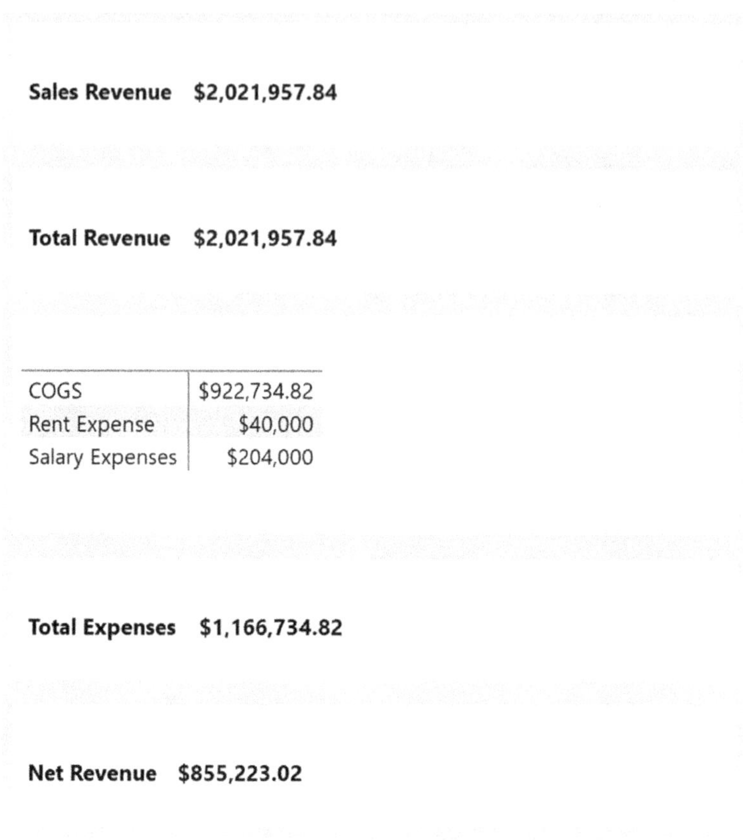

Figure 3.12: Positioning our matrices

The final step for the look and feel of a traditional income statement is the lines between the sections. For this, we'll add a line from the **Shapes** menu option as follows:

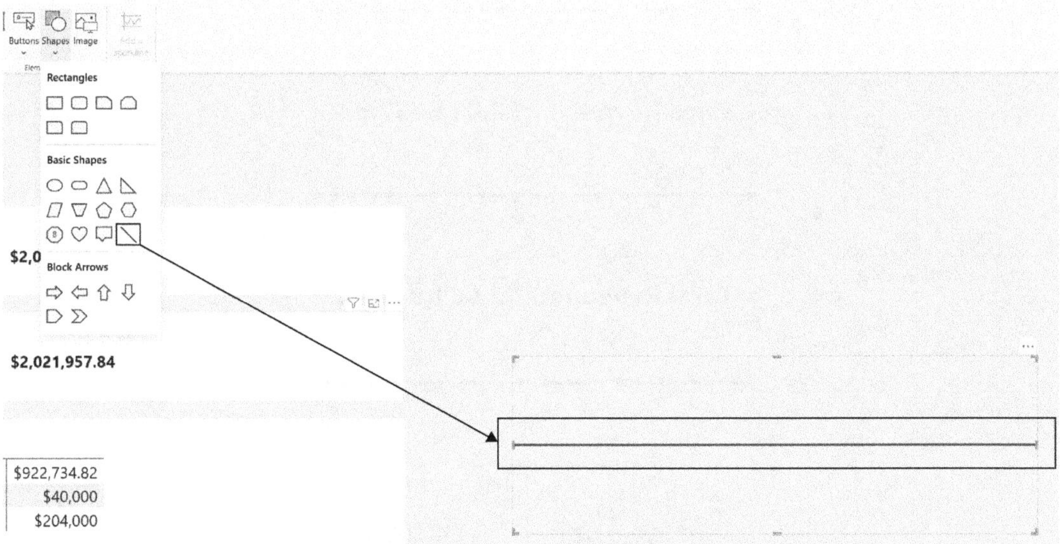

Figure 3.13: Adding line separators to our matrices

The default color is blue, so we'll change that to black by navigating to the **Visualizations** pane | **Shape** | **Style** | **Border** | **Color**, and changing to black on the color picker.

Again, the default shape has a selection box that's higher than we need, so use a grab point on the top or bottom of the shape to reduce the height all the way so that you just see a line with a minimal box around it, shown in *Figure 3.14*

Figure 3.14: Formatting our line separators

Now, copy the line and paste it five times. Take the total of six lines and arrange them as dividers between the sections. You may need to change the width to match the width of your line items. The final result should look like *Figure 3.15*:

Sales Revenue $2,021,957.84

Total Revenue $2,021,957.84

COGS	$922,734.82
Rent Expense	$40,000
Salary Expenses	$204,000

Total Expenses $1,166,734.82

Net Revenue $855,223.02

Figure 3.15: Our finished income statement

As your measures are summing all transactions, the minimum you'll need for this income statement is a date slicer to filter the correct reporting period. We'll cover this in more detail in *Chapter 9, Creating a Suite of Financial Reports*. As before, please note that these are just sample metrics and not a complete representation of everything you might need to include in your income statement.

In this example, we've built a very traditional and simple income statement. You may choose to use the **Matrix** visual in Power BI so that you can have more interactivity. There are many versions on this theme, so please feel free to experiment with the examples in the book to better suit your organization.

In this section, we got started with DAX measures and visualizations to build our income statement. In the next section, we're going to extend our Power BI skills by building a trial balance.

Creating a trial balance

Now that we have an income statement, the next foundation in financial reporting is a Trial Balance. This is a report that will exist in all accounting systems, so we might well pose the question, *Why create this ourselves?* There are reasons why we might want to create a Trial Balance report in Power BI:

- We're consolidating across different systems, and each system will have its own Trial Balance. One way to get an organization-wide Trial Balance is to create one ourselves.
- We're reconciling our semantic model in Power BI back to the accounting system. If the trial balance in Power BI and the Trial Balance in our accounting system match, we have high confidence in the integrity of our data.
- It enables us to carry out an accuracy check to ensure that total debits equal total credits, helping to identify errors in the ledger.
- It helps with error detection to aid in pinpointing discrepancies or mistakes in journal entries and accounts.
- It serves as a preliminary step in preparing financial statements, providing a summary of account balances.
- It facilitates the auditing process by providing a clear overview of account balances.
- It serves as a management tool to assist management in assessing the overall financial position and performance of the organization.
- It helps identify accounts that need adjustments before finalizing financial statements.

A trial balance report is essential for ensuring the accuracy of financial records, as it helps identify discrepancies and confirms that total debits equal total credits, thereby supporting the integrity of the accounting process.

Creating a trial balance itself is easier than creating an income statement, since we use the **Matrix** visual to show the four basic measures we need:

- `Opening Balance`
- `Debit`
- `Credit`
- `Closing Balance`

These can then be used directly in the matrix and grouped by account code.

Steps to create our Trial Balance

Our first step is to create a new calculated column in our model that shows both `Account Number` and `Account Name`. We do this for readability and are going to select the `Chart of Account` table. Click on **New Calculated Column**, and use the following DAX, as shown in *Figure 3.16*:

```
Account Number and Name = 'Chart of Account'[AccountNumber]&"-"&'Chart of Account'[AccountName]
```

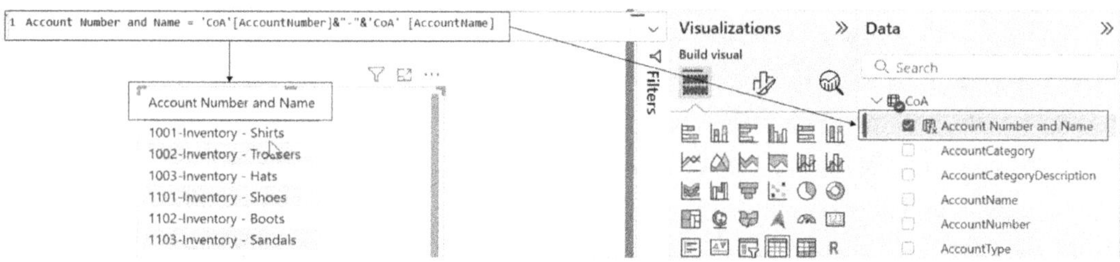

Figure 3.16: Starting our trial balance visual

Note that we create the column in the `Chart of Account` table rather than the `List of Measures` table. We do this because we're extending the table.

Now, we can add a **Matrix** visual and add this new column to the rows, as shown in *Figure 3.17*:

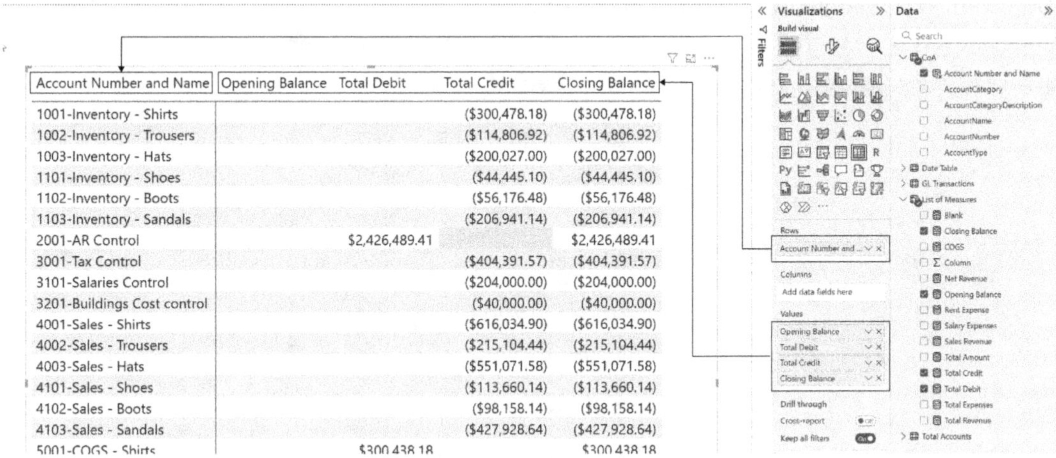

Figure 3.17: Building the trial balance visual

Adding our measures to the values gives us our basic trial balance, but because we have no date filtering, the `Opening Balance` column is empty. Therefore, the next step is to add date slicers to our visualization to help us make better sense of the data. We'll create slicers for year, quarter, and period. In our model, the period is a month.

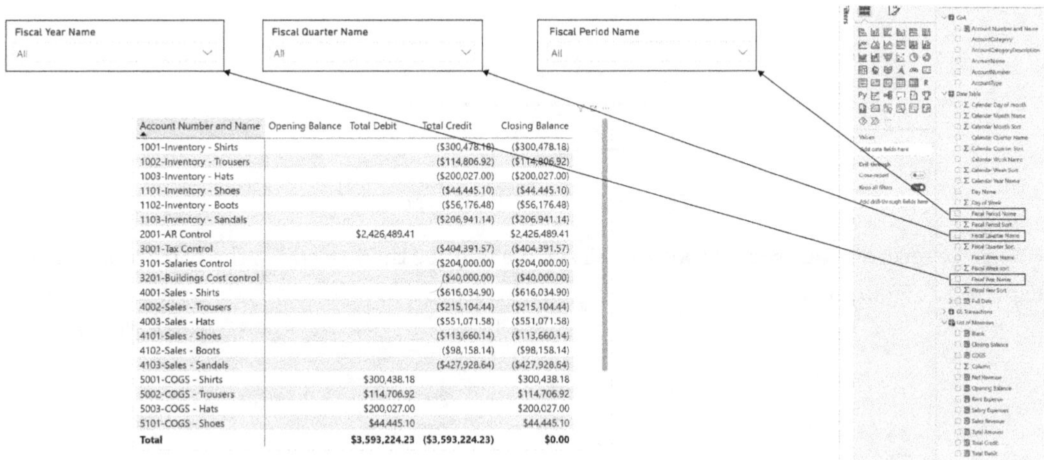

Figure 3.18: Adding date slicers to our visual

To create slicers, choose the **Slicer** visual and click three times to create three slicers. Populate them with the `Fiscal Year Name`, `Fiscal Quarter Name`, and `Fiscal Period Name` fields from our `Calendar` table, as shown in *Figure 3.18*.

You'll notice the periods are not ordered correctly, so we need to address this. Go to the **Data** panel and navigate to the `Calendar` table. Then, select the `Fiscal Period Name` column and choose **Sort By Column**. Now, choose **Fiscal Period Sort**.

Figure 3.19: Sorting by fiscal period

Now, if we return to our slicer in **Report View**, we will see the periods in the correct order, as displayed in *Figure 3.20*:

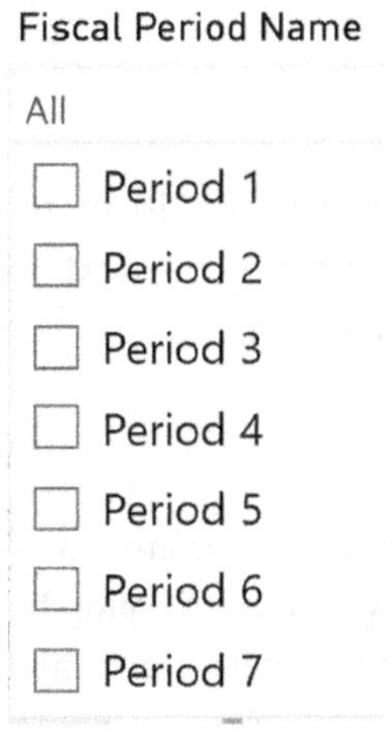

Figure 3.20: The correct fiscal period sort

We can also add other slicers, such as account category, account type, or other analytical dimensions, such as product group or cost center. We can also add extra features to our matrix. A common choice here would be `Account Type` so that we can separate our views of balance sheet and profit and loss (and any other segments configured in the CoA):

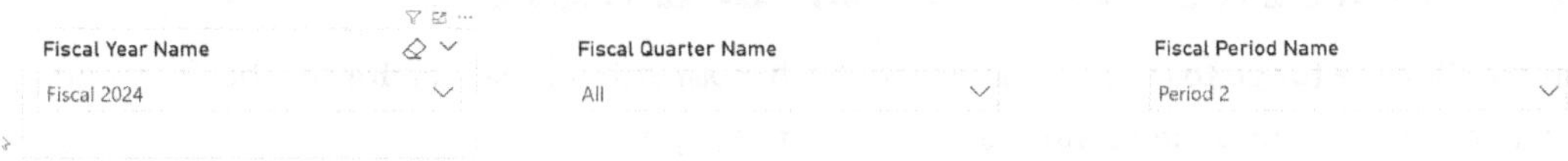

AccountType	Opening Balance	Total Debit	Total Credit	Closing Balance
Balance Sheet	**$488,746.76**	**$205,678.82**	**($131,849.43)**	**$576,128.07**
1001-Inventory - Shirts	($180,873.93)		($27,537.64)	($208,411.57)
1002-Inventory - Trousers	($70,498.65)		($9,873.77)	($80,372.42)
1003-Inventory - Hats	($120,010.19)		($19,057.69)	($139,067.88)
1101-Inventory - Shoes	($22,222.55)		($3,539.49)	($25,762.04)
1102-Inventory - Boots	($33,205.59)		($6,046.71)	($39,252.30)
1103-Inventory - Sandals	($106,964.37)		($14,514.33)	($120,950.62)
2001-AR Control	$1,393,812.45	$205,678.82		$1,594,719.88
3001-Tax Control	($232,290.41)		($34,279.80)	($265,774.98)
3101-Salaries Control	($119,000.00)		($17,000.00)	($119,000.00)
3201-Buildings Cost control	($20,000.00)			($20,000.00)
Profit and Loss	**($488,746.76)**	**$97,569.63**	**($171,399.02)**	**($576,128.07)**
Total	**$0.00**	**$303,248.45**	**($303,248.45)**	**$0.00**

Figure 3.21: Our finished trial balance

At this point, we have our first two reports and the basic foundations of a comprehensive suite of financial reports. Moving on from here, we will need to start building on the base model to add more calculations so that we can track some basic financial metrics.

This report can now be used with slicers and filters to enable dynamic analysis, allowing users to easily drill down into specific accounts and periods for a more detailed understanding of financial performance.

The final state of this report can be found in the GitHub repository, in the Power BI file named `Chapter 3 - Final.pbix`: `https://github.com/PacktPublishing/Financial-Modeling-with-Power-BI_Packt/tree/main/Chapter3`.

Summary

In this chapter, we continued to work on the semantic model from the previous chapter by building DAX measures and Power BI visuals to develop basic income statement and trial balance reports. You learned the difference between a calculated column and a measure and where to use both. Then, we added essential DAX measures into the semantic model to support the production of financial reports. Finally, we saw how to use some of the visual components of Power BI for financial reporting.

In the next chapter, we will help to expand your use of DAX by explaining some common DAX measures used in financial reporting.

Get this book's PDF version and more

4

Common DAX Measures

In *Chapter 3*, we started to apply DAX to populate visualizations for the Trial Balance and Income Statement reports. In this chapter, we're going to build on that work by introducing some of the most common DAX measures that finance professionals use. The intention is to maintain the momentum of the previous chapter by going deeper into the DAX language to develop your skills through the applied use of DAX.

We started gently in *Chapter 3*, with a few step-by-step examples. As we're working on the basis that readers of this book already have some DAX knowledge, we're going to pick up the pace and focus on how to write and use DAX without step-by-step guides. By now, you know how to add measures and write DAX, so you'll be able to apply our examples.

We'll start by introducing the `CALCULATE` function. After that, we'll cover percentages and time intelligence, and end with DAX functions for foreign exchange. We also recommend using one of the many DAX guides available to understand these functions in depth to accompany this chapter. Our intention is to introduce these concepts in the context of financial reporting as opposed to being a lengthy or definitive guide, so please supplement this chapter as required with additional resources to deeply understand how the DAX commands work.

By the end of the chapter, you will do the following:

- Appreciate the importance of `Calculate` as a DAX function and begin to understand the importance of `Calculate` within financial reporting and more broadly
- Understand how to use DAX for the calculation of percentages within your financial reports
- Learn how to use DAX for time-based comparisons such as month-on-month and year-on-year, including comparisons for non-standard reporting calendars such as 4-4-5
- Understand how to apply DAX to foreign exchange calculations

Technical requirements

If you wish to follow along with the calculations in this chapter, start with the `Chapter3 - Final.pbix` file in the *Chapter3* folder of the GitHub repository: `https://github.com/PacktPublishing/Financial-Modeling-with-Power-BI_Packt/tree/main/Chapter3`.

The final state of the model at the end of this chapter can be found in the *Chapter 4* folder, called `Chapter4 -Final.pbix`: `https://github.com/PacktPublishing/Financial-Modeling-with-Power-BI_Packt/tree/main/Chapter4`.

Introducing CALCULATE

The `CALCULATE` function is one of the most powerful and versatile functions in DAX. It plays a pivotal role in crafting financial calculations and enabling users to redefine the filter context dynamically within a calculation.

OK, what does that mean, especially the "filter context" part?

When we discuss "filter context" in DAX, we generally refer to how we use filters to show subsets of data. In *Chapter 3, Creating a Trial Balance and Income Statement*, we added slicers to the `Trial Balance` report for `Year`, `Quarter`, and `Period`. Slicers are filters that allow users to interact with reports and show subsets of data, such as data for a particular fiscal period, such as June 2024. Filtering report data can be performed onscreen through **Slicers** or on the **Filter** panel. We can also build filters directly into our DAX. We did this in *Chapter 3, Creating a Trial Balance and Income Statement*, where we used `SUMX` and `FILTER` together.

There are times when you don't want users to use onscreen filters for certain data. For instance, we often want visuals in Power BI reports to be specific. For example, we may have a metric for sales of shirts in the USA, labeled onscreen as **Sales of Shirts in the USA**. For the integrity of the metric, we don't want users to be able to apply a filter that adds, for example, hat sales to that metric. Therefore, we need a method to maintain the context of that filter, or the filter context. `CALCULATE` allows us to do this.

While `CALCULATE` is often categorized as an advanced DAX function and is typically introduced later in DAX tutorials, its importance to financial reporting means we need to cover it early in this book.

To further illustrate this concept, let's consider a gross margin example. In our financial model, we have the `CoA` table linked to the `GL Transactions` table via a one-to-many relationship on the `AccountNumber` field. This setup allows us to perform calculations and aggregations that respect the relationships between tables, as shown in *Figure 4.1*.

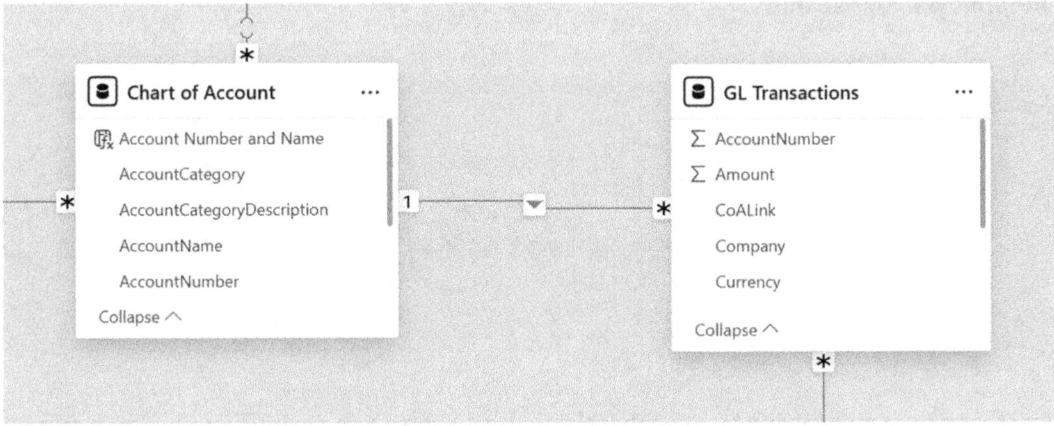

Figure 4.1: The link between the CoA and GL Transactions tables

Remember, the `Account Category` field isn't included on the `GL Transactions` table, but that's not an issue, as we've linked the tables so Power BI understands how `Account Category` relates to the rows in the `GL Transactions` table. If we need a calculation for, say, **gross margin,** we'll want to use `AccountCategory`, as that field includes `COGS` and `Sales` as categories, because we deduct COGS from sales to get gross margin.

As COGS is recorded as a debit and sales are recorded as credits, the sum of the categories will provide the gross margin.

To isolate COGS and sales to provide our gross margin amount, we use `CALCULATE` to take the `SUM` of the `GL Transactions Amount` column and filter by the `COGS` and `Sales` categories from the CoA `Account Category Description` field. We can do this because we've told Power BI how the tables are connected, so Power BI understands how to apply the filter to provide the correct answer.

Our `CALCULATE` formula will take the `Total Amount` measure we created in *Chapter 3, Creating a Trial Balance and Income Statement*: `(Total Amount = SUM('GL Transactions'[Amount])` and then modify the measure by filtering just for COGS and sales.

The formula looks like this:

```
Gross Margin =
CALCULATE(
    [Total Amount],
    FILTER(
        'Chart of Account',
        'Chart of Account' [AccountCategory] = "SALES" ||
              'Chart of Account' [AccountCategory] = "COGS"
)
)*-1
```

Note that we are multiplying by `-1` so that the figure is shown as a positive number for clarity in visuals.

In this case, the `CALCULATE` formula is reasonably simple and straightforward to read. Let's dissect it further:

- It asks Power BI to calculate the total amount, but only show the data for sales and COGS
- The || symbol tells Power BI that the calculation is "or" rather than "and"

Here, the result is a measure that calculates gross margin dynamically, respecting any filters applied to the report, such as date ranges, regions, or product categories. There may be times when we need to ignore the filters; we'll look at a few examples later.

To take another example, let's look at revenue.

Revenue

We briefly looked at revenue in *Chapter 3, Creating a Trial Balance and Income Statement*, when we created the total sales revenue. In that example, we only had one category in our chart of accounts. We may have other income streams, such as shipping and handling.

There are two ways to approach this – either to create measures for each income category and add them up, or we can create a measure that incorporates more categories into our revenue measure, like this:

```
Total Revenue = CALCULATE(
    [Total amount],
    FILTER(
        'Chart of Account',
        'Chart of Account' [AccountCategory]="SALES" ||
              'Chart of Account' [AccountCategory]="OTHERINC"
```

```
    )
)*-1
```

Again, we use the || symbol, meaning "or," so this measure filters the total amount where the account category is "`Sales`" or "`OTHERINC`". Of course, if you want to see both categories separately on your income statement, you will want to calculate each separately and add them in a further measure.

This section has been a concise and relatively gentle introduction to the use of `CALCULATE`. Its application can be far more complex, and often is. Later, in the *Time intelligence* sub-section, we have some similar, easy-to-digest examples of `CALCULATE` to help introduce the command. A comprehensive examination of the `CALCULATE` function is beyond the scope of this book. Its importance to DAX cannot be underestimated, and we encourage you to explore its application within your own DAX models.

We're going to now cover a subject that should be familiar to most of you, percentages and the `DIVIDE` function.

Percentages

Percentages and ratios are fundamental in financial analysis, serving as a universal language for expressing the financial health of an organization. Whether evaluating profitability, efficiency, or liquidity, these metrics provide a standardized way to compare performance across periods, departments, or companies.

The basis of percentages can be calculated very simply by dividing one number by another and formatting the measure as a percentage in Power BI. For example, gross margin can be calculated as follows:

```
Gross Margin % =

(
    ([Total Revenue] - [COGS]) / [Total Revenue]
)
```

Let's break down this formula:

- The numerator, `[([Total Revenue] - [COGS])]`, represents gross profit
- The denominator, `[[Total Revenue]]`, ensures the result is expressed as a proportion of total revenue

We can choose to multiply the measure by 100 at the end of the formula to provide the percentage, or we can format our measure as a percentage within Power BI.

We generally choose to format the percentage in Power BI since we can use this measure within other measures, so it's disadvantageous to include the multiplication by 100.

When calculating percentages, in most circumstances, a simple divide (/) will work, although we can experience problems if total sales revenue is 0, as we're asking Power BI to divide by 0, which will generate an error.

Generally, this is unlikely, but it does happen, and we advise taking some steps to make the formula more robust so users don't experience errors in the event of a divide by 0.

The first method is to use the `DIVIDE` function in DAX, which is a "safe" divide as it avoids errors if the denominator is blank or zero.

```
Gross Margin % =
DIVIDE(
    [Total Revenue] - [COGS],
    [Total Revenue],
    0
)
```

In this case, if the value of the denominator is 0, then the last value will be returned instead of an error message – in this case, 0.

In some cases, you may want to use DAX to raise an error message because you want to identify data issues. In this case, use the `[IF]` and `[ERROR]` functions, such as in the following DAX example:

```
Gross Margin % =
IF(
    [Total Revenue] = 0,
    ERROR("Not defined - total revenue is 0 within this filter"),
    ([Total Revenue] - [COGS]) / [Total Revenue]
)
```

Here, if the total sales revenue in the current context of the report is 0, then the error message will be returned; otherwise, the calculation will be used.

For the remainder of this book, to maintain brevity, we will use the `DIVIDE` function for all ratio and percentage measures.

Percentages are at the core of our financial calculations. The next essential function we'll cover is time intelligence. We've already looked at some basic time-based aspects of our semantic model, such as the calendar table and date slicers. We'll explore them in more detail in the next section by showing you how to do time-based comparative calculations.

Time intelligence

In order to track how financial metrics are changing, we need to track our data over time, by using Power BI's time intelligence functions.

We will focus our attention on two ideas: period-to-date and period-on-period change. The ideas behind these can be extended to more use cases. The examples here will use revenue, but again, you can substitute any measure into these, such as accounts receivable or inventory.

Before we start, we use the words "easy" and "hard" deliberately. Power BI has a full set of time intelligence features that work with our standard calendars. If your organization uses standard calendars, Power BI's functions make time intelligence very easy. That can extend to offset fiscal years, such as starting the fiscal year in July, instead of January. We must make some adjustments to the calendar table, but it's still straightforward, fitting into the "easy" category.

The "hard" way is necessary when using alternate financial calendars, such as 4-4-5 quarters, as they don't use standard months. Accommodating these calendars takes more work, but it's achievable, and we document methods to do this.

Period to date – the easy way

If your financial calendar aligns with the regular (Gregorian) calendar, Power BI's built-in time intelligence functions are probably the easiest way to build period-to-date (and by extension, quarter-to-date, and year-to-date) calculations. Here, we will see how to use the `TOTALMTD` function to calculate month-to-date revenue. Here's a DAX example:

```
Revenue MTD =
TOTALMTD(
    [Total Revenue],
    'Calendar'[Full Date],
    ALL('Calendar')
)
```

Let's break down this measure:

- We start with the DAX function `TOTALMTD`, which means total month to date
- The second component is the amount, and we use the measure we created earlier, which is `Total Revenue`

- We then need to provide the time component, which is the `Full Date` column from our calendar table, which provides the full date for each day, row by row
- Finally, we add the `ALL` function as a filter to the calculation that removes or ignores any other date filters

The `ALL` function has the effect of removing any applied date filters from Power BI.

Why do this?

We add this as a safeguard against users applying filters that are less than one month, which can provide misleading data. If `TOTALMTD` is applied to, for example, a single day, Power BI will return what appears to be a month-to-date result for that single day. Most users would like to avoid this, so we add `ALL` to remove this risk.

DAX also includes quarter and year-to-date in the form of `TOTALQTD` and `TOTALYTD` functions. Both work in a similar manner, although `TOTALYTD` has a fourth parameter, which is the year-end date.

Period to date – the hard(er) way

Some users may find that the default `TOTALMTD` function does not cater to their corporate financial calendar; this is especially true if you use a 4-4-5 style financial calendar. In this case, we have to derive our own rolled-up functions based on our actual calendar. Here, we will look at how we can calculate month-to-date revenue using `CALCULATE` and some filters.

```
Revenue MTD =
CALCULATE(
[Total Revenue],
FILTER(
ALL('Calendar'),
'Calendar'[Full Date] <= MAX('Calendar'[Full Date]) &&
'Calendar'[Fiscal Period Sort] = MAX('Calendar'[Fiscal Period Sort]) &&
'Calendar'[Fiscal Year Sort] = MAX('Calendar'[Fiscal Year Sort])
)
)
```

At first glance, this calculation might seem unusual, so let's break it down, step by step:

1. Once again, the `CALCULATE` function is used to adjust the behavior of the `Total Revenue` measure.

2. The `FILTER` function determines the specific subset of dates over which the `Total Revenue` measure is calculated, focusing on the dates within the current month.
3. To ensure other filters on the calendar table don't interfere, we use the `ALL` function to temporarily remove any existing filters. This gives us full control over the filtering logic.

The rest of the `FILTER` function allows us to define custom fiscal periods and years using the `Fiscal Period Sort` and `Fiscal Year Sort` columns from the calendar table. We use these fields within the calculation, but the important field where fiscal periods are set is `Fiscal Period Name`, which is a row-by-row mapping of fiscal period to a specific day of the year. That's how we align our `4-4-5` reporting calendar, or other calendar options your organization may use.

This customization ensures that the calculation aligns with our fiscal calendar rather than the standard Gregorian calendar.

The inclusion of the `MAX` function ensures that all dates up to and including the current date are captured in the calculation. This is especially useful for creating dynamic, time-sensitive reports.

This approach provides flexibility by letting us categorize and view data based on fiscal periods and years. Additionally, since our calendar table includes a `Fiscal Quarter Sort` column, we can easily adapt the calculation to analyze data by fiscal quarters as well.

Period-on-period calculations

Again, we have easy and hard ways to do this, and again, your approach will depend on the alignment of your financial calendar with the regular calendar. Before we can get as far as showing the calculation, we need to establish current versus prior period actuals. In this context, we consider "current" to be the month we have currently selected in our report, and prior to be the period immediately before that.

Once again, we will start the easy way. The first part is to get the prior period revenue, and for this, we can use the `PARALELLPERIOD` function as follows:

```
Revenue (Prior Period) =
CALCULATE(
    [Total Revenue],
    PARALLELPERIOD(
        'Calendar'[Full Date],
        -1,
        MONTH
```

```
    )
)
```

Note that we don't have an `ALL` function here, as this time we will rely on the actual selected date. The calculation again takes our `Total Revenue` measure and modifies it. We use `PARALLELPERIOD` to look at the `Full Date` column in our calendar table and calculate the `Total Revenue` based on the prior month, hence the `-1, MONTH` component of the calculation, which asks Power BI to calculate based on the current month -1. The -1 could be -12 for the same month in the prior year, and `MONTH` could be `YEAR`.

We then use the following measure to calculate the net difference between periods.

```
Revenue Growth = [Total Revenue]-[Revenue (Prior Period)]
```

This method works well when your fiscal periods and years match the standard calendar. However, if your fiscal periods and years differ from the standard calendar, you'll need to adopt the following approach.

For this, we can build on the `Revenue MTD` measure from before. We use the `CALCULATE` function to modify `Revenue MTD`, then use `DATEADD` as a filter to shift the dates back 1 month for the calculation:

```
Revenue (Prior Month to Date) =
CALCULATE(
    [Revenue MTD],
    DATEADD(
        'Calendar'[Full Date],
        -1,
        MONTH
    )
)
```

Now we can calculate `Revenue Growth` as follows:

```
Revenue Growth = [Revenue MTD]-[Revenue (prior month to date)]
```

When this is applied to complete months, the comparison will be between two complete months. When applied to incomplete months, we will see a comparison of similar periods. This same technique can be applied to weeks, quarters, and years by changing the specific details.

Finally, if you are using a 4-4-5 accounting period pattern, this technique will not work. There are potential ways of getting comparisons, but we have chosen not to cover that here, as in that period structure, 2 out of 3 comparisons will be between a 4-week and a 5-week period, rendering the calculation meaningless. In those cases, you should look to measure growth on a weekly, quarterly, and yearly basis only.

We have kept the focus here on the most common forms of time intelligence – that is to say, period to date and period on period. In calculating period-on-period, we also covered a third common pattern – that of the time shift as we calculated the prior period (noting that all these calculations can be adapted to any type of period).

Now that we have seen the basic calculations and some time intelligence, you can build on these to create more complex and specific measures for your organization.

In the next section, we'll cover an area that will affect some of you – foreign exchange calculations.

Foreign exchange

In *Chapter 2, The Basic Model for Financial Reporting*, we looked at methods to manage foreign exchange in our data model and how it may be undesirable to use calculations in a data model that could differ from the calculations in your finance system(s). That said, it's often necessary to do some foreign exchange calculations, so we'll explain some methods.

To follow the examples in this chapter, you'll need the **Exchange Rate** tab of the `Ledger and CoA.xlsx` file in the `Chapter3` folder of this book's GitHub repository referenced at the start of this chapter.

In this section, we explain three methods for calculating foreign exchange using Power BI. Please use the method that matches your specific use case. The three methods are as follows:

1. Conversions based on a daily exchange rate where you're converting one currency to another
2. Conversions based on a calculated average of the exchange rate for a month, again based on a simple model of converting one currency to another
3. Dynamic conversions where the currency changes on a transaction-by-transaction basis, so DAX needs to identify the currency and apply the correct conversion rate

Of the three methods, the easiest approach is method 1, where we work out spot rates for each day with a fixed or single target currency. Let's assume that we have an exchange rate table in our model like this:

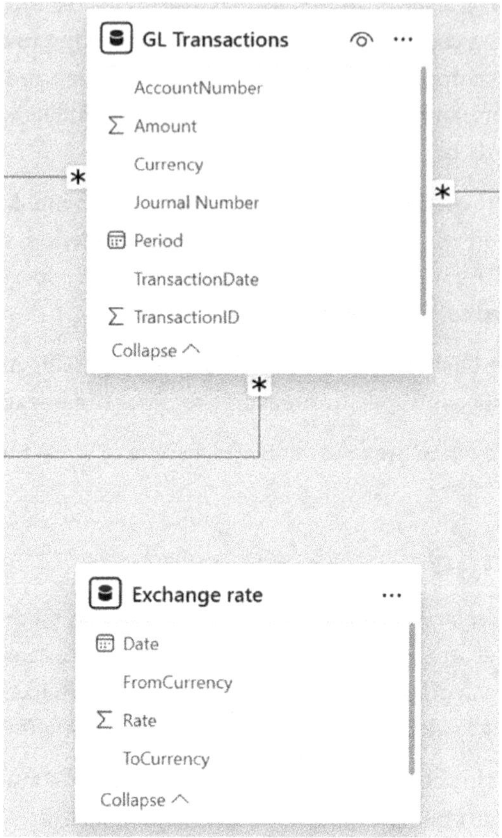

Figure 4.2: Disconnected exchange rate table

You can see we've imported the `Exchange Rate` table, which is on `the Exchange rate` tab on the ledger and `CoA.xlsx` file. In our example, we're converting GBP amounts to USD, which is a simple example, and we choose not to connect the `Exchange rate` table to other tables in our model. This is for simplicity, as we can easily use `LOOKUPVALUE` to find the correct conversion rate for the day, using a calculated column that's added to the `GL Transactions` table as follows:

```
Amount in USD =
DIVIDE(
    'GL Transactions'[Amount],
    LOOKUPVALUE(
        'Exchange rate'[Rate],
        'Exchange rate'[Date], 'GL Transactions'[TransactionDate],
```

```
            'Exchange rate'[FromCurrency], "USD"
        )
    )
```

We are dividing here because we are converting from USD to GBP. If you convert from GBP to USD, you will multiply. The `LOOKUPVALUE` function is like `VLOOKUP` in Excel, but more powerful:

- The first argument represents the value we want to return – in this case, the exchange rate.
- The next four values come in pairs; these are our conditions. The first pair is the column we are searching in, and the second is the value we are searching for.

The expression is asking to "return the exchange rate where the date matches the transaction date on the current row, and the `FromCurrency` field is USD."

When you add converted amounts, you'll want to duplicate any measures previously created, clearly marking the converted currency. In this example, we create a USD version:

```
Total Debit (USD) =
SUMX(
    FILTER(
        'GL Transactions',
        'GL Transactions'[Amount] > 0
    ),
    'GL Transactions'[Amount in USD]
)
```

Our second example uses average rates. This can be an effective method to buffer against some of the reporting challenges discussed in *Chapter 2, The Basic Model for Financial Reporting*, where the finance application and Power BI reporting may have some differences. In this case, we would apply the same rate to all transactions in each month, so if an invoice is raised and paid in a month, all the offsets for that exchange would, in fact, balance back to the finance application.

This time, we need to join the exchange rate into the model via the calendar table, connecting the `Full Date` column from the `Calendar` table to the `Date` column of the `Exchange rate` table:

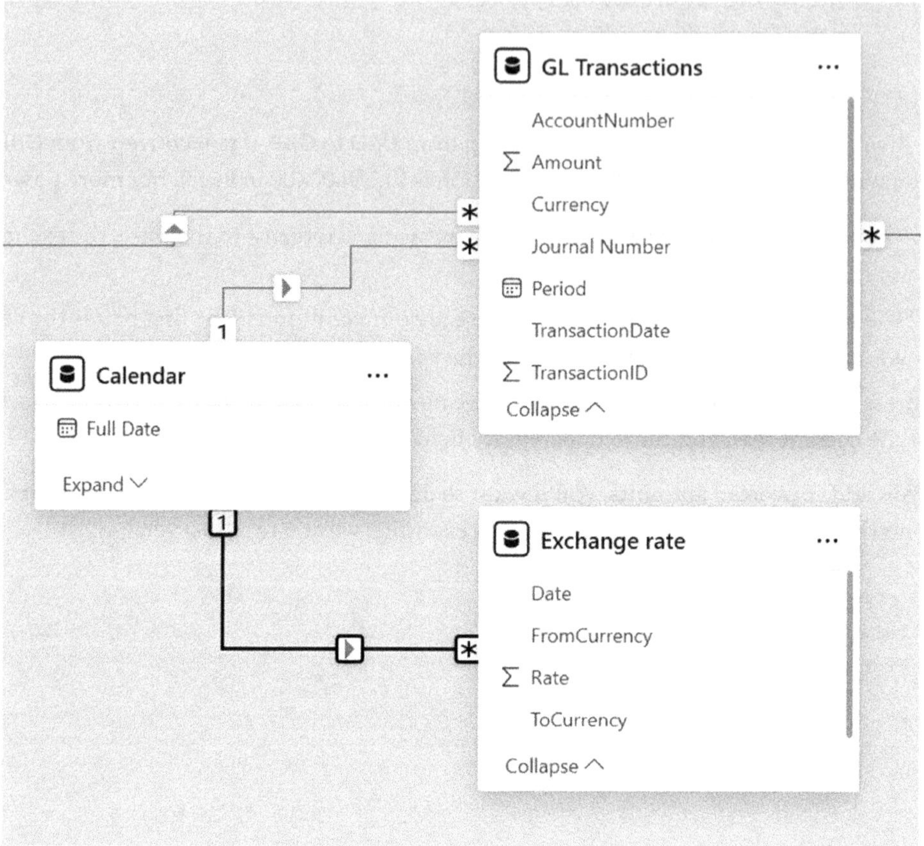

Figure 4.3: Connect Exchange rate table

We will add a calculated column to the `GL Transactions` table to look up the `Fiscal Period Name` from the `Calendar` table:

```
Fiscal Period = RELATED('Calendar'[Fiscal Period Name])
```

Now, we can use this to create an average exchange rate for the period:

```
Avg Exch Rate =
AVERAGEX(
FILTER(
'Exchange rate',
RELATED('Calendar'[Fiscal Period Name]) = 'GL Transactions'[Period]
),
```

```
'Exchange rate'[Rate]
)
```

And finally, we can add the USD amount:

```
Amount (USD) = 'GL Transactions'[Amount]/'GL Transactions'[Avg Exch Rate]
```

This gives us the following output, where we can see the calculated columns we have added to our `GL Transactions` model:

TransactionID	AccountNumber	TransactionDate	Period	Currency	Amount	Fiscal Period	Avg Exch Rate	Amount (USD)
601	3001	01 April 2023		GBP	-1485.618	Period 1	0.809	-1836.36341161928
602	3001	02 April 2023		GBP	-1742.986	Period 1	0.809	-2154.49443757726
603	3001	03 April 2023		GBP	-312.094	Period 1	0.809	-385.777503090235
604	3001	04 April 2023		GBP	-1284.938	Period 1	0.809	-1588.30407911001
605	3001	05 April 2023		GBP	-289.436	Period 1	0.809	-357.770086526576
606	3001	06 April 2023		GBP	-1283.03	Period 1	0.809	-1585.9456118665
607	3001	06 April 2023		GBP	-785.906	Period 1	0.809	-971.453646477132

Figure 4.4: FX transactions

While it is possible to combine all of these calculations into one calculated column, it is advisable not to do so since splitting the steps makes it easier to see the calculations and, therefore, easier to debug in the event of any issues.

The third approach is dynamic, where you may have a table of transactions that have different currencies, and you need to convert them into a single currency. In order to take this dynamic approach, we need to model our data, as shown in *Figure 4.5*, joining `Calendar` to both `Exchange rate` and `GL Transactions`.

Now we create a calculation for the exchange rate:

```
Amount in selected currency = SUMX('GL Transactions',
    VAR ExchRate=
        LOOKUPVALUE(
            'Exchange rate'[Rate],
            'Exchange rate'[FromCurrency],
            'GL Transactions'[Currency],
            'Exchange rate'[ToCurrency],
            SELECTEDVALUE('Exchange rate'[ToCurrency]),
            'Exchange rate'[Date],
            'GL Transactions'[TransactionDate]
        )
    RETURN
```

```
        'GL Transactions'[Amount]*ExchRate
)
```

The key point to note is the `LOOKUPVALUE()` function. This is being used to define a variable called `ExchRate` that can then be used to convert the values for each transaction. Breaking down the function further, the first parameter is the value we want to return – in this case, the exchange rate. The next set of parameters work in pairs – the first in the pair being the column we want to look up, and the second being the value we are looking up.

When using this data in a visual, please note you'll need to add a slicer to choose the reporting currency; otherwise, the visual won't show any data.

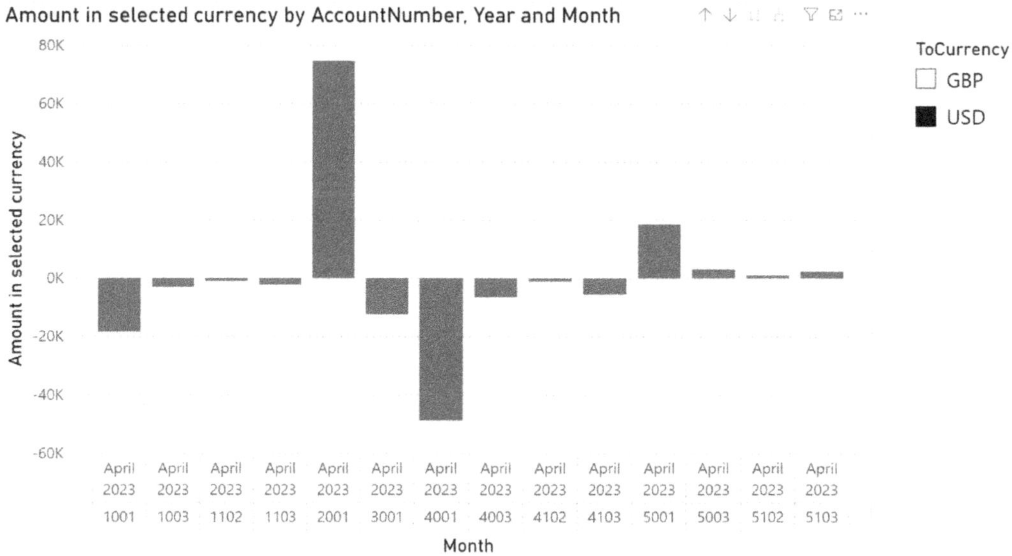

Figure 4.5: Adding the currency slicer now shows data

We'd like to make the point that reporting foreign currency conversions can be complex, and you may see inconsistencies between your finance application and Power BI. In this case, please experiment with methods to provide accurate reporting and always try to use converted data from the finance application where possible.

Summary

In this chapter, we continued our journey into the DAX language with a specific focus on the needs of the finance professional. We covered the differences between measures and calculated columns, took a more detailed look at the basic aggregations that we introduced in *Chapter 3, Creating a Trial Balance and Income Statement*, and took a first look at the `CALCULATE` function and how that can be used to control filtering. We then looked at the best ways to handle percentages and introduced the concept of time intelligence. Finally, we expanded on the considerations we covered in *Chapter 2, The Basic Model for Financial Reporting*, to show how we can handle foreign exchange where that is necessary.

In the next chapter, we're going to focus on the very specific area of the considerations around dealing with journals.

5

Handling Manual Journal Entries

In the last chapter, we furthered our understanding of DAX by focusing on some applied areas in finance. In this chapter, we're going to be even more applied, by looking at manual journal entries and how to deal with them, the data we can derive from them, and how we can include them in our data model.

Although we use the term *manual journals* in this chapter, the principles apply to many manual adjustments you may need to apply to your financial reporting.

Manual journal entries are manually-entered transactions that don't fit neatly into the "normal" transactions generated by the finance system during the normal course of business. They can be adjustments, corrections, or special entries that are entered to provide a complete picture of financial and business operations. Businesses don't run perfectly, and manual journal entries allow you to deal with imperfections. Manual journal entries in an **Enterprise Resource Planning (ERP)** system are user-entered financial transactions that allow businesses to record adjustments, corrections, or non-standard entries directly into the general ledger, ensuring accurate and customized financial reporting.

To be clear, we differentiate manual journal entries from the normal business transactions that are automatically created by financial management applications, such as transactions that are created for non-routine reasons or are unique. They sit outside of normal logic and are, hence, important to control and track.

While the examples in this chapter focus on manual journal entries, it also applies to any other non-standard data in the data model, such as invoicing details, purchase and sales orders, or production orders in a manufacturing environment. Moreover, it allows us to cover some important topics in Power BI – in particular, that of role-playing dimensions.

When manual journals are created, **General Ledger** (**GL**) transactions will also be posted, which raises the question about the need to include manual journal entries separately. In some

Power BI implementations, we haven't included manual journals as a subset of the GL transactions, and that's a valid approach. In other implementations, we've included manual journals due to the additional contextual information they provide when analyzing financial data. We have to say, the more common approach is to include manual journal entries as a specific subset of the GL, and both approaches are valid – both include a full picture of a company's finances.

We'll first consider why they are important and the reasons for including them, and the reasons we may decide they're unnecessary. We'll also discuss the difference between journal headers and lines, and why you may/may not want to include journal lines. From there, we'll consider the sort of data, both descriptive and numerical, we can get from the manual journals and how that maps into the idea of *fact and dimension* data. Finally, we'll look at how we can join that to our existing data model, and the potential impacts and pitfalls from it.

By the end of the chapter, you will understand the following:

- When to include manual journal entries
- How to add new objects to the data model
- How to use role-playing dimensions

Technical requirements

To follow the worked examples in this chapter and beyond, you'll need a Windows PC with an internet connection, and you'll also need to download **Power BI Desktop**.

For more details, we suggest you access the following link, where Microsoft details the download process for Power BI Desktop and the PC hardware requirements: `https://learn.microsoft.com/en-us/power-bi/fundamentals/desktop-get-the-desktop`.

The model picks up from where *Chapter 4, Common DAX Measures*, left off with the `Chapter 4 - Final.pbix` file, which can be found in the GitHub repository at `https://github.com/PacktPublishing/Financial-Modeling-with-Power-BI_Packt/tree/main/Chapter4`.

The sample data we use, and the final point we reach in the chapter, is the `Chapter 5-Final.pbix` file, which can be found in the GitHub repository at `https://github.com/PacktPublishing/Financial-Modeling-with-Power-BI_Packt/tree/main/Chapter5`.

Understanding the value of including manual journal entries

In all our financial implementations, we discuss how we include manual journal entries into the data that will be presented in visualizations. The choices are as follows:

- Do we include manual journal data, separate from the GL transactions?
- Do we just include manual journal header data or header and line?

To be clear, manual journal data is always included as it's part of the GL transaction data. The debate is centered around the amount of detail required when analyzing the data and what journal header and line-item data can add.

There's a school of thought that Power BI is an analytics tool that aggregates and calculates large volumes of data and, therefore, isn't a good tool for reporting on individual transactions. To some extent, that's true, but in almost every implementation of Power BI, we include drill-through capability to allow users to see the details of a transaction, so they don't need to refer to the financial application to understand those details. As manual journals are generally corrections, it may or may not be important to see the data via drill-through in Power BI.

Next, let's look at the reasons to include/exclude manual journal data.

Here are the main reasons for including manual journal entries:

- **Improves the accuracy of insights**:
  - Manual journal entries correct errors, allocate costs, and adjust accruals, which are necessary for accurate financial reporting
  - Excluding their details may hinder a user's ability to gain detailed insights that may be lacking from their corresponding GL record
- **Supports compliance and auditability**:
  - Manual journal entries are often created to meet regulatory requirements, such as **Generally Accepted Accounting Principles** (**GAAP**) and **International Financial Reporting Standards** (**IFRS**)
  - Including them in Power BI ensures that compliance-related adjustments are reflected in reports, helping maintain transparency, completeness, and audit readiness

- **Facilitates period-end analysis**:
  - End-of-period adjustments (e.g., depreciation and accruals) are crucial for understanding true profitability and financial performance
  - Including these ensures an accurate analysis of financial outcomes for decision-making
- **Provides granular detail**:
  - Manual journal entries often include detailed narratives and context about adjustments
  - These details can add value in BI by providing explanatory power behind financial movements
- **Enables scenario planning**:
  - Manual journal entries often represent discretionary adjustments
  - Including them allows Power BI to model scenarios, such as the impact of strategic adjustments or management overrides

Here are the main reasons for excluding manual journals:

- **Potential for overwriting automated insights**:
  - Manual journal entries often adjust or override automated data
  - If your semantic model is not built correctly, this could distort original trends or metrics in BI, making it harder to analyze the base data accurately
- **Complexity in data integration**:
  - Manual journal entries often require additional work to ensure they are correctly mapped into the BI system
- **Increased maintenance**:
  - Manual journal entries can vary in structure and purpose, possibly requiring updates to **Extract, Transform, and Load** (**ETL**) processes

- **Limited predictive value**:
    - Manual journal entries often represent unique, one-time adjustments
    - Their inclusion might skew predictive analytics or trend analysis in BI systems, as they may not represent recurring business behavior
- **Audit and security concerns**:
    - Including manual journal entries requires additional controls to ensure sensitive adjustments are handled securely
    - Without robust governance, there is a risk of exposing sensitive financial data or unapproved adjustments

There are valid reasons to include or exclude manual journal entries as a separate part of your reporting environment, and each business needs to make that decision; in many cases, it's contextual to the nature of the business. In some cases, you may not need them to be considered for special attention, and in some cases, you may. Our objective is to highlight the fact that every implementation process should consider the question of inclusion or exclusion.

So, with that in mind, let's consider the general structure of a manual journal, how it maps to the GL transaction, and what useful information can be gleaned from it.

Exploring the structure of manual journal entries

Typically, manual journal entries in a finance system will be split across two tables (this can vary): a header table containing information about the journal itself, and a line-item table that details the financial movements that it will trigger. A typical journal header will contain information such as the following:

Column	Description
Journal Entry Number	A unique ID for the journal
Journal Entry Type	What type of movement is represented here?
Description	Typically, there will be some sort of free-text description.
Created By	Who created the journal entry?
Created On	When was it created?
Approved By	Who approved it?
Approved on	When was it approved?

Column	Description
Posted	Has the journal entry been posted to the GL?
Posted by	Who posted the journal?
Posted on	When was it posted?

Table 5.1: Journal header

Journal lines will typically look something like this:

Column	Description
Journal Entry Number	To link to the header
Line number	Together with the journal number, this is a unique ID
Line Description	What this line is for
Transaction date	May or may not be present – sometimes Posting date is used
Amount	The amount for the transaction
Account`	The account to post to
Offset	The account to offset to

Table 5.2: Journal lines

When a manual journal entry is posted, it will generate transactions in the GL transactions table. Usually, we will see two lines posted in the GL for every line in the journal transactions, one for the account and the other with a reversed sign, in the offset account. Once again, systems may operate differently, and you may find there are processes behind the scenes that can add complexity to this, but the fundamental concept is the same across the board.

For clarity, let's see how this might work in reality. We'll create a manual journal entry to write off some stock.

Here is an example header posting:

Journal Number	ST-123
Journal Type	Stock
Description	Write off damaged stock
Created By	TG123
Created On	1/06/2023
Approved By	AC456
Approved On	2/6/2026
Posted	Y
Posted By	SC789
Posted On	3/6/2023

Table 5.3: Example journal header posting

Here is an example line posting:

Journal Number	ST-123	ST-123
Line Number	1	2
Line Description	Write off damaged shirts	Write off damaged gloves
Transaction Date	Write off damaged shirts	Write off damaged shirts
Amount	-20	-50
Account	1001	1002
Offset	2001	2001

Table 5.4: Example journal line posting

Once posted, this will generate transactions as follows:

Journal #	Account #	Transaction Date	Currency	Amount
ST-123	1001	1/06/2023	GBP	-20
ST-123	2001	1/06/2023	GBP	20
ST-123	1002	1/06/2023	GBP	-50
ST-123	2001	1/06/2023	GBP	50

Table 5.5: Example journal transactions on the GL transactions table

In our example, we have a journal entry number appearing on the GL, which is essential if we're going to link this data. It may be that this is not directly available through the GL tables in your system, and in that case, there may be a voucher number used to link back via other tables to the journal entry number. If no such route exists, it may well be impossible to link this data up, but that would be a very rare circumstance.

You will note the created by, approved by, and posted by fields are in the form of usernames, rather than actual names – this is typical for most systems. To make this data usable, we are going to want to create a `Users` table as well, so we can map this data:

User ID	User Full Name
TG123	Tom Gough
AC456	Andy Clark
SC789	Shailan Chudasama

Table 5.6: Users table

Now that we have identified what is in our manual journals, we can turn our attention to how we need to structure them to help us perform analyses and provide more context for our figures.

Deriving facts and dimensions from the manual journals

The most common use of manual journal entry data is to add descriptive context to the GL transactions. This is important as it will often link to who created a manual journal, who approved it, explanations of why it was done, and other related narrative data.

Typically, journal entries are linked to the GL at the journal entry header and not the line, so any descriptions at a line level may be lost unless the table containing the lines is imported and connected to the headers.

Here, we have our second decision, which is whether to include journal entry lines.

The decision is always based on the context of the business and the requirements for reporting. If journal entries are extensively used, users may benefit from the contextual and descriptive data from the lines. If the use of journal entries is limited or follows a common pattern, we may not need the additional data from the lines. For the rest of this chapter, we'll assume you're importing journal lines with the headers, but please remember it's a choice.

Our basic journal dimension will look something like this:

Column	**Description**
Journal Entry Number	A unique ID for the journal entry
Journal Entry Type	What type of movement is represented here?
Created By	Who created the journal entry?
Created On	When was it created?
Approved By	Who approved it?
Approved on	When was it approved?
Posted by	Who posted the journal?
Posted on	When was it posted?

Table 5.7: Journal dimension table

Note, we're dropping the free text description. Such fields are generally not useful for structured data analysis since they could contain anything and would not be suitable for use in categories on a visual. That is not to say they have no value at all; you may still want to include them for a drill-down or for use by data science tools. As the information will be available in the source system, you can retrieve it at a later date.

In addition to dimensional data from the journal entries, we'll generally need to add more measures. Adding measures to include the total value of the journal can be useful when looking to categorize and understand the purpose. Other measures you could derive from the journal entries could include the following:

- Time to approve
- Number of journal entries created per user
- Average lines per journal

As manual journal entries can fit outside of business norms, the number of journal entries, who created them, and when they were approved can be important to track.

There are two broad approaches you can take at this point:

- One is to import journal lines and calculate your measures over those
- The other is to create a summarized table of your journal lines (*Table 5.8*)

Column	Description
Journal Number	The unique ID for the journal
Number of lines	Total number of lines in the journal
Total Value	Note that once rolled up, this will hide individual credits and debits
Time to approve	Days from creation to approval
Time to post	Days from approval to posting

Table 5.8: Summarized table of journal lines

These can be added to the journal header table to make the model simpler or left as a separate table if preferred.

This works well if you're only bringing in posted journal entries, but if you intend to bring in unposted journal entries too, it's a good idea to include all lines, since a summary of an unposted journal will tell you little of any real value. In this case, measures of total value and number of lines will be better handled in DAX, and time to approve and time to post will be added to the journal dimension.

Now that we understand what we want to bring into our data model, we can look at how to link it together.

Linking manual journal entry data to the GL transaction

To demonstrate the most complete method for linking journal data, we will assume the following:

- We're interested in both posted and unposted journal entries
- We require the journal lines
- We need to analyze who creates, approves, and posts journal entries

The first step is to add the journal number column to the `GL Transactions` table. Check whether the `journal ID` is on the `GL Transactions` table and make sure it's clearly identified. You may need to change the name of the column in Power Query if the name used is unclear or cryptic. If you still don't have the journal ID, it may be the case that you're looking at a restricted column view, so you'll need to speak to someone responsible for the data you're receiving from the financial application or data warehouse. Note that not every transaction will necessarily have a journal number attached; this is especially true if most postings are automatic, although again, this varies by system.

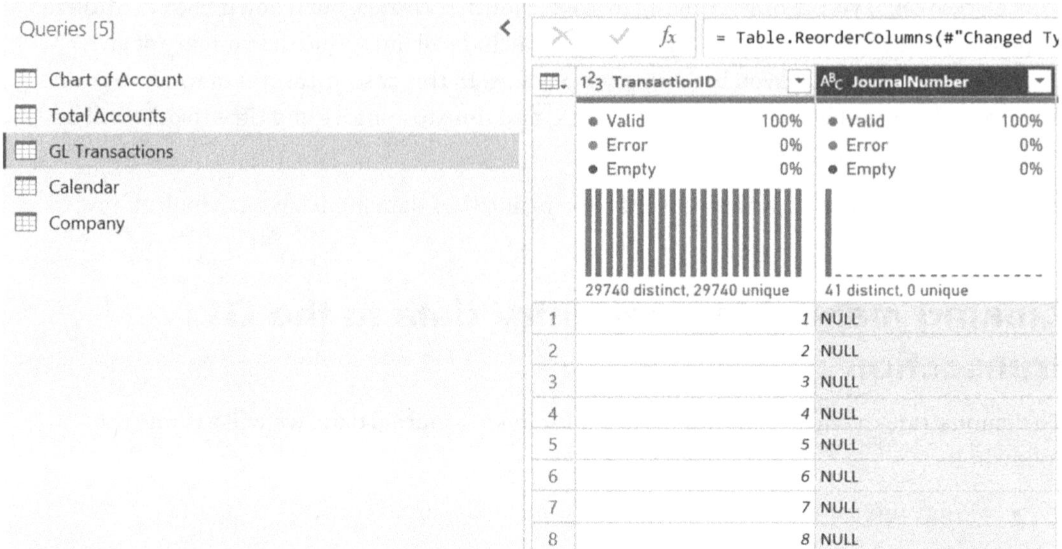

Figure 5.1: Exposing the journal ID in Power Query

Now that we have the journal ID, we can import our actual journal data. In our example, we're importing both the `Journal Header` and `Journal Lines` tables. There are two ways to do this, but both take you to essentially the same place:

- Use the **Get Data** button in Power BI
- Click **Transform Data** to launch Power Query, then select **New Source**

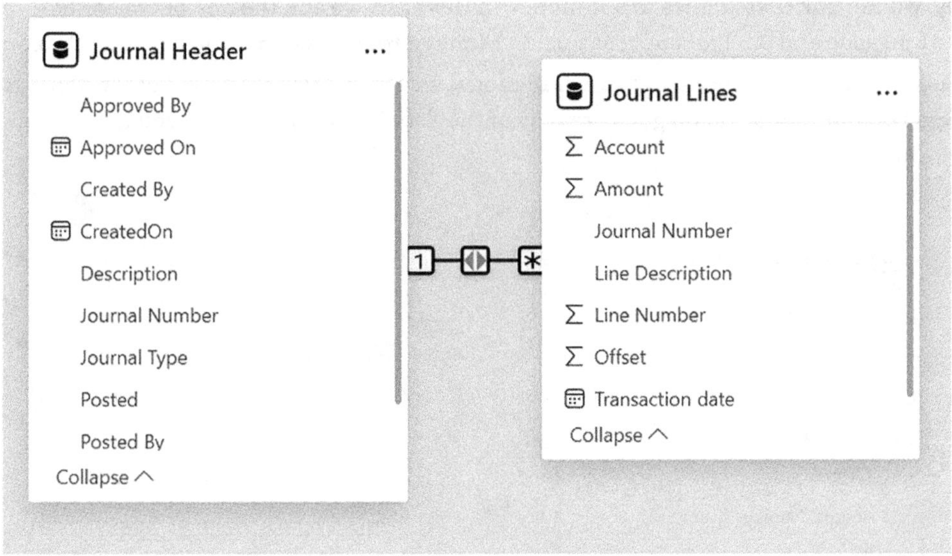

Figure 5.2: Linking Journal Header to Journal Lines

Using the data from our worked example, Power BI has automatically detected the data in both tables and linked the tables together when they were imported into the data model. It's worth noting that relying on Power BI to get this link correct is not guaranteed, and you should always check that the relationship has been created successfully on the fields you expect. You can do this using the **Manage relationships** option:

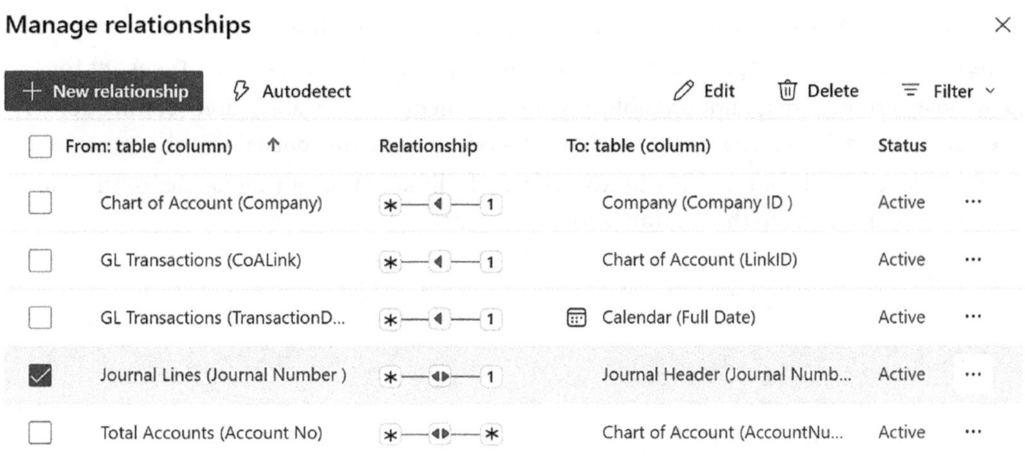

Figure 5.3: Using Manage relationships to check relationships

Finally, we can link these tables to our model. In this case, we add the link between the `Journal Header` and `GL Transactions` using **Manage relationships**. You can drag the correct columns between the tables in the Power BI model view using your mouse, but we prefer to use **Manage relationships,** as you get a preview of the data in the columns, so you have certainty that the link is correct.

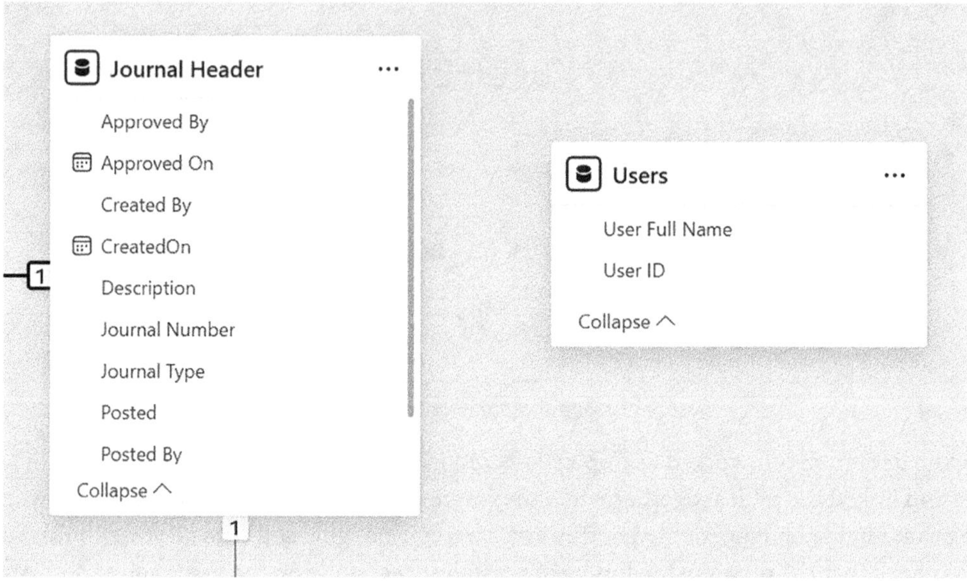

Figure 5.4: Joining Journal Header to GL Transactions

Note that we join `Journal Number` into the `GL Transactions` table and `Journal Header` into `Journal Lines`. We do not generally want to join from `Journal Lines` to `GL Transactions`, and in most systems, this is not possible. If your system does facilitate a direct connection of these, for example, by `GL Transactions` having a reference to the journal line that created it, you may wish to build your model slightly differently, linking the journal header to the journal line and the journal line to the GL transaction, like this:

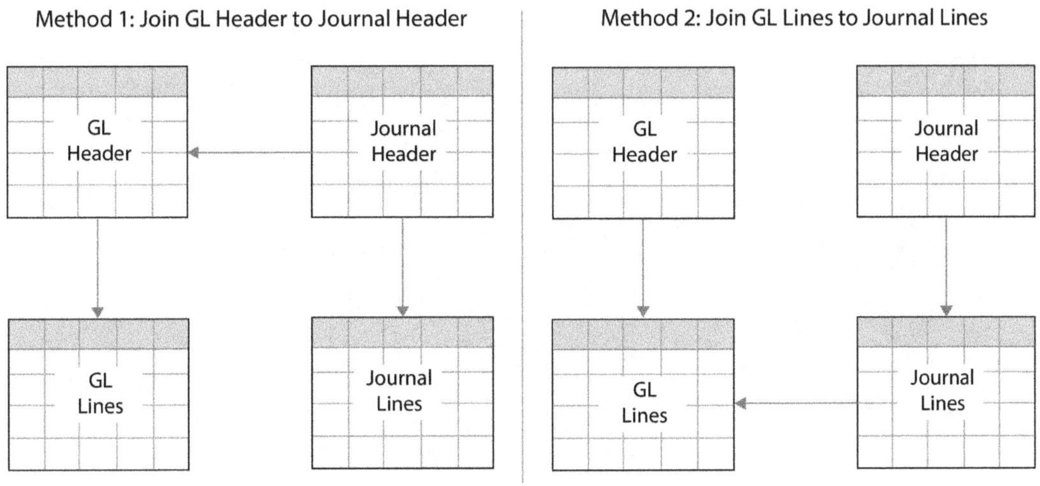

Figure 5.5: Methods of joining GL and journal data

For the remainder of this chapter, we'll assume the journal header is the common link between the GL transaction since this will most likely be the method for your solution.

At this point, we have enough information to satisfy our first two requirements, which were to view all journal entries, posted and unposted, with lines. The third requirement was to identify the users who created the manual journal entries. With our current dataset, we can do this through user IDs that are contained in the `Journal Header` table and our `Users` table, where we have full names:

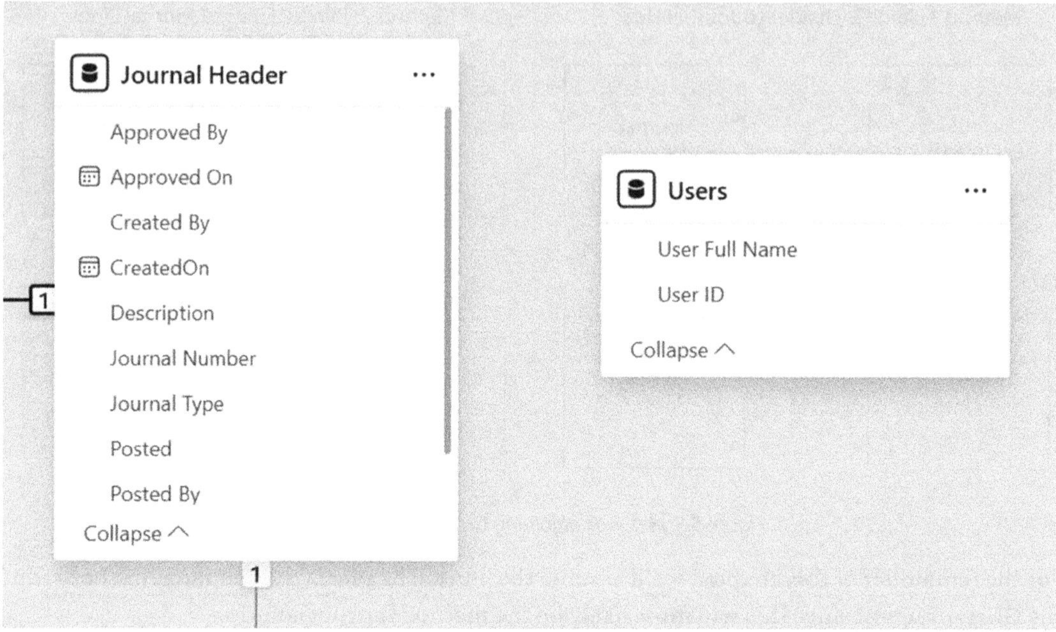

Figure 5.6: The Users table in the Power BI semantic model

The `Users` table is linked to the `Journal Header` table by the `User ID` column on the `Users` table and the `Created By`, `Posted By`, or `Approved By` columns on the `Journal Header` table. When we link these tables, we're able to use the users' full names when filtering and analyzing our data.

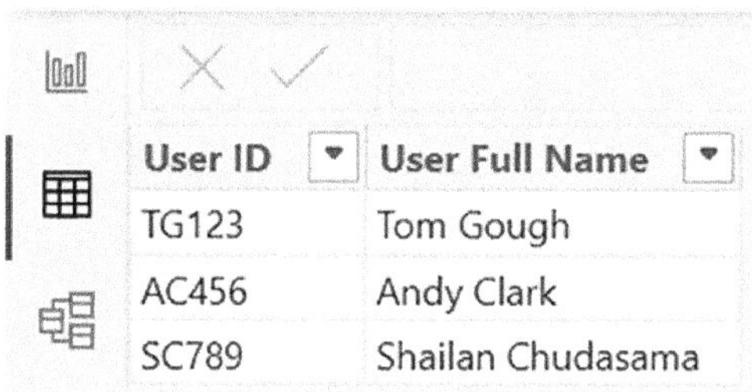

User ID	User Full Name
TG123	Tom Gough
AC456	Andy Clark
SC789	Shailan Chudasama

Figure 5.7: The Users table in Power BI

Then, we can join that into the model:

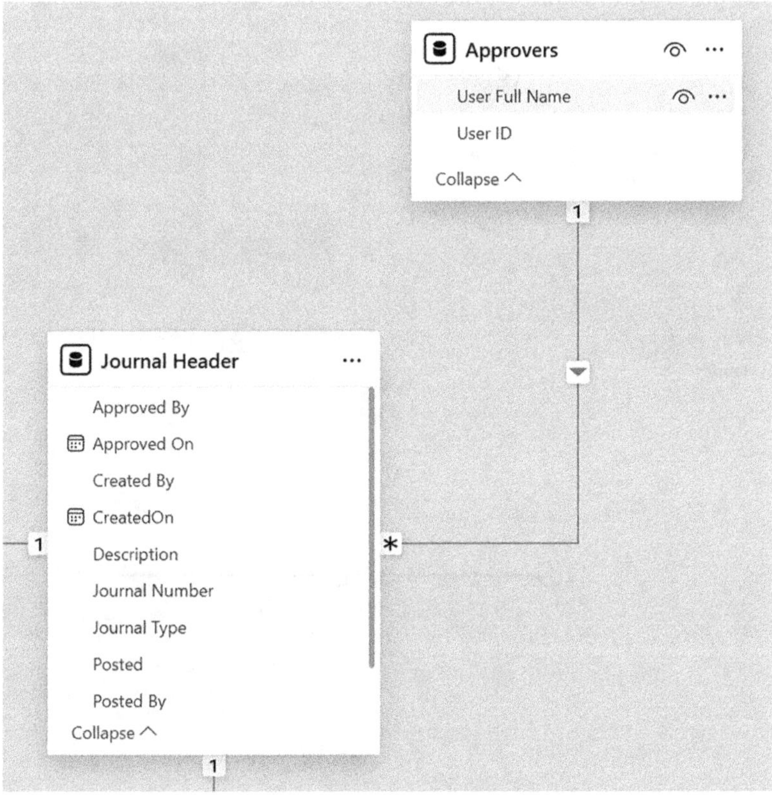

Figure 5.8: The Users table joined in Power BI

Now, repeat this process for `Creators` and `Posters`. These are role-playing dimensions. While the three tables are based on the same underlying data, each copy plays a different role, allowing us to filter by creator, poster, or approver.

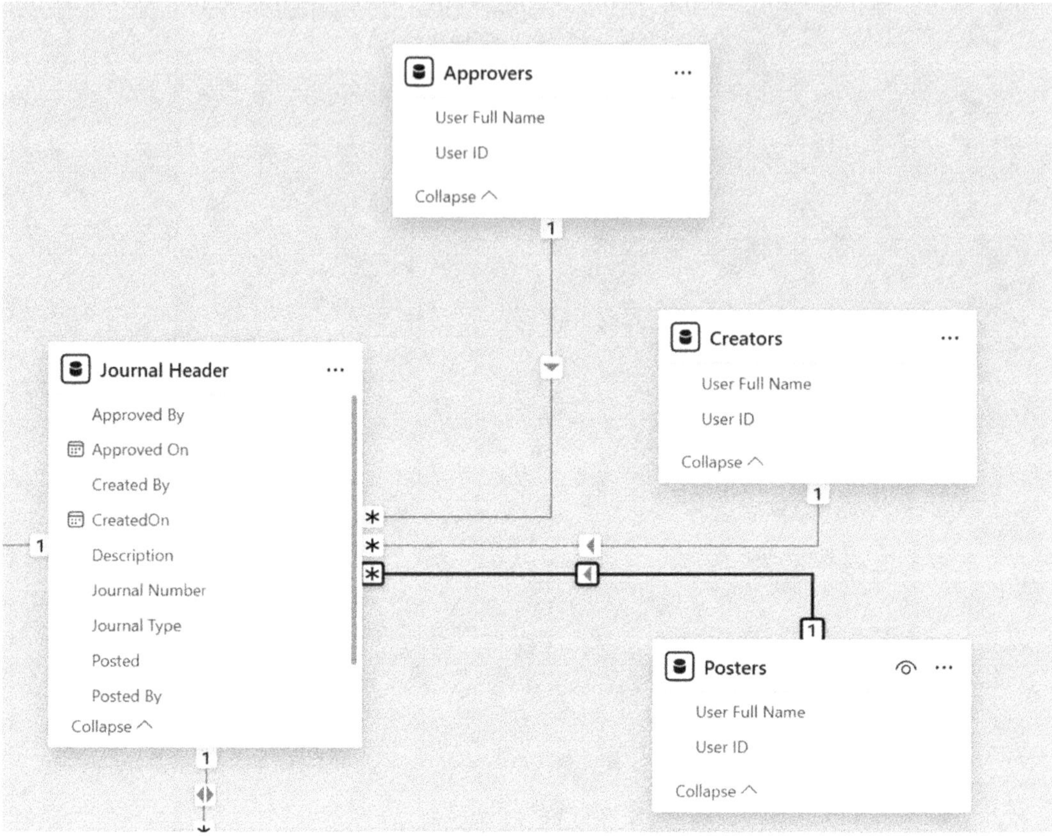

Figure 5.9: Role-playing dimensions

Now that we've completed the modeling, we can add our DAX measures.

This is not an exhaustive list of every measure that could be created from the journal data; instead, it is a few examples to provide a foundation for measures you may need in your project.

First, there's the question of speed in the journal approval process, by creating a measure to tell us how long it takes for manual journal entries to be processed. We'll start with the average time to post using the average number of days between the journal being created and the journal being posted.

```
Average time to post = AVERAGEX('Journal Header',DATEDIFF('Journal
Header'[Created On],'Journal Header'[Created By],DAY))
```

In a similar way, we can look at average time to approve, or average time from approval to posting, depending on what we want to try to improve or manage.

Next, we can look at the average number of lines in a journal. The more lines, the more items that have been adjusted, which can help show where problems are and what can be done to address them. As ever, there are several ways to tackle this; we'll look at two of them.

First, we add a calculated column to the `Journal Header` table to count the number of rows in the related table, `Journal Lines`:

```
Lines = COUNTROWS(
    RELATEDTABLE('Journal Lines')
)
```

Then, we can simply add a measure to calculate the average of the new `Lines` column:

```
Average Journal lines = AVERAGE('Journal Header'[Lines])
```

This approach, although needing two calculations, can be more transparent than doing it all in one, and is certainly easier to debug. However, if you prefer to do it all in one, then the **AVERAGEX** function comes to our aid again:

```
Average Journal Lines = AVERAGEX(
    'Journal Header',
    COUNTROWS(
        RELATEDTABLE(
            'Journal Lines'
        )
    )
)
```

The final example will be to look at journal values, which can tell us how large the adjustments are and help in controlling the scale of the adjustments needed. The average journal value can be created as follows (for an all-in-one calculation):

`Journal Avg Value = AVERAGEX(`

```
    'Journal Header',
    SUMX(
        RELATEDTABLE(
            'Journal Lines'
        ),
```

```
            'Journal Lines'[Amount]
        )
    )
```

If you prefer to create this as a two-part calculation, then the column is calculated as follows:

```
Journal Value = SUMX(
            RELATEDTABLE(
                'Journal Lines'
            ),
            'Journal Lines'[Amount]
        )
```

These calculations give some of the basic ideas of what can be calculated from the journal data. Building on these patterns, you can expand to measure what is relevant to your project or organization.

Summary

In this chapter, we looked at manual journal entries. It's a specific and important part of a Power BI implementation for some organizations. To start, we explained why manual journal entries are important to some organizations with a list of reasons that you may like to apply to your organization to help you decide.

We then looked at the considerations when including journal lines and why you may or may not choose to use them.

We then walked through the process of adding the `Journal Header` and `Journal Lines` tables to the Power BI semantic model with some DAX measures to help you get the most out of your data.

In the next chapter, we turn to the important task of data modeling. A good data model will make your calculations and visualizations faster and more accurate, so we're going to walk through the essential tasks you'll need to consider when importing data into your semantic model.

Get this book's PDF version and more

Scan the QR code (or go to `http://packtpub.com/unlock`). Search for this book by name, confirm the edition, and then follow the steps on the page.

UNLOCK NOW

Note: Keep your invoice handy. Purchases made directly from Packt don't require an invoice.

6

Streamlining with Power Query

In the previous chapter, we focused on an applied area when working with finance data: manual journal entries. In this chapter, we're going to change direction by focusing on some of our standard practices when shaping and managing the data we use for our semantic models.

When we think of Power BI, we need to think of two tools, not one. Power BI comprises Power BI and Power Query; the latter is launched by clicking the **Transform data** button from the Power BI ribbon and is used every time we work with Power BI. We're certain there will be some readers who haven't clicked **Home** | **Transform Data** to see what lies behind the button, and that's why we wrote this chapter to walk you through the basics of Power Query.

Power Query is an integral part of the Power BI process as an ETL tool.

Great – another acronym, and what does it mean? **ETL** stands for **E**xtract, **T**ransform, **L**oad, and is a common term in the data world that's certainly not unique to Power Query. There are many ETL tools available, and Power Query is the one built into Power BI; it's also built into Excel. The three components of ETL are described next:

- **Extract** allows us to connect to numerous data sources, from Excel files to databases to online services, and extract the data from the data source. Common examples are the capability to connect to your budgets in Excel, the data within your finance application, and an online FX conversion tool.
- **Transform** helps us clean up, reduce, and reshape our data so that it's more useful for consumption within Power BI. There's a maxim that applies to the data world: *Only carry what you need to survive.* Power Query helps us do just that.
- **Load** takes the transformed data and loads it into Power BI.

The size of financial data is often large in terms of the number of rows and columns, but in most cases, you won't need all of it. Less data means quicker queries, and it's also easier to manage. In this chapter, we'll look at what Power Query is, how we can use it to manage and reduce the amount of data we handle, and how it can transform and enrich the data we're working with. We also have a trick for working with AI tools to help with your column naming.

By the end of the chapter, you will be able to master the following:

- The need to use Power Query to streamline data
- The functions and tools offered by Power Query
- Some practical patterns that can be used in the real world

Technical requirements

To follow the worked examples in this chapter and beyond, you'll need a Windows PC with an internet connection, and you'll also need to download Power BI Desktop.

For more details, we suggest you access the following link, where Microsoft details the download process for Power BI Desktop and the PC hardware requirements: `https://learn.microsoft.com/en-us/power-bi/fundamentals/desktop-get-the-desktop`.

The examples outlined in this chapter can be tried out in the `Chapter 6.pbix` model. A fully worked example from the *Correcting opening balances* section is found in the `Chapter 6 - Opening Balances.pbix` file. Both files can be found in the GitHub repository here: `https://github.com/PacktPublishing/Financial-Modeling-with-Power-BI_Packt/tree/main/Chapter6`.

What is Power Query?

Power Query is a tool that's capable of a wide range of data transformations. At its most basic, it can filter out rows and remove columns. In more complex scenarios, it can be used to create new columns, split columns into their constituent parts, and do **time intelligence** (**TI**) calculations. In financial modeling, we generally use Power Query to do the following:

- Remove unnecessary columns to make our data tables easier to manage
- Remove rows to focus on the data we need
- Rename columns, assisted by AI tools
- Unpivot data in matrices
- Split columns into constituent parts

There is a significant overlap between what we can do in Power Query and what we can do in DAX. The creation of calculated columns is a great example, and there is usually no standard or best practice method of dealing with these situations. You need to create a calculated column, and you know you can create it in both tools, so which one do you choose? One thing to consider is creating a column in Power BI; using DAX means you won't see it in Power Query – only in the Power BI report. As a result, you cannot use it as part of the data transformation process. If, however, you create that column in Power Query, you'll see it in both Power Query and Power BI and indeed be able to use that column as part of the data transformation process. So, just create them all in Power Query? Depending on what you're trying to achieve, creating the column in Power Query may not be possible, as both tools have different capabilities. If you need an element of your data model (such as a relationship), then you must use DAX; beyond that, it's mostly your choice. That said, it's a good idea to set a policy and stick to it; otherwise, you'll create confusion and leave a situation where your data model is hard to maintain because there's no clear place to look for specific calculations.

To the developers among us, Power Query uses a language called **M**, which is a functional *mashup* language, having similarities to **F#**, though sufficiently different that an F Sharp programmer would still have a learning curve to transition. Please don't let that put you off. Almost everything you'll need to do in Power Query is accessible via clicks, so it's unlikely you'll need to write any code. Yes, it can be a complex tool, but it's been made relatively easy to navigate.

Power Query is accessed from the **Transform data** button on the ribbon, as shown in *Figure 6.1*:

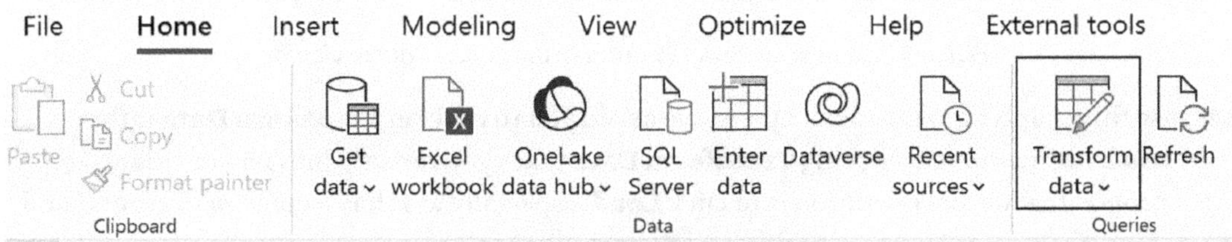

Figure 6.1: Launching Power Query

Alternatively, you can access it by clicking **Transform Data** in the **Import Data** navigator in *Figure 6.2*:

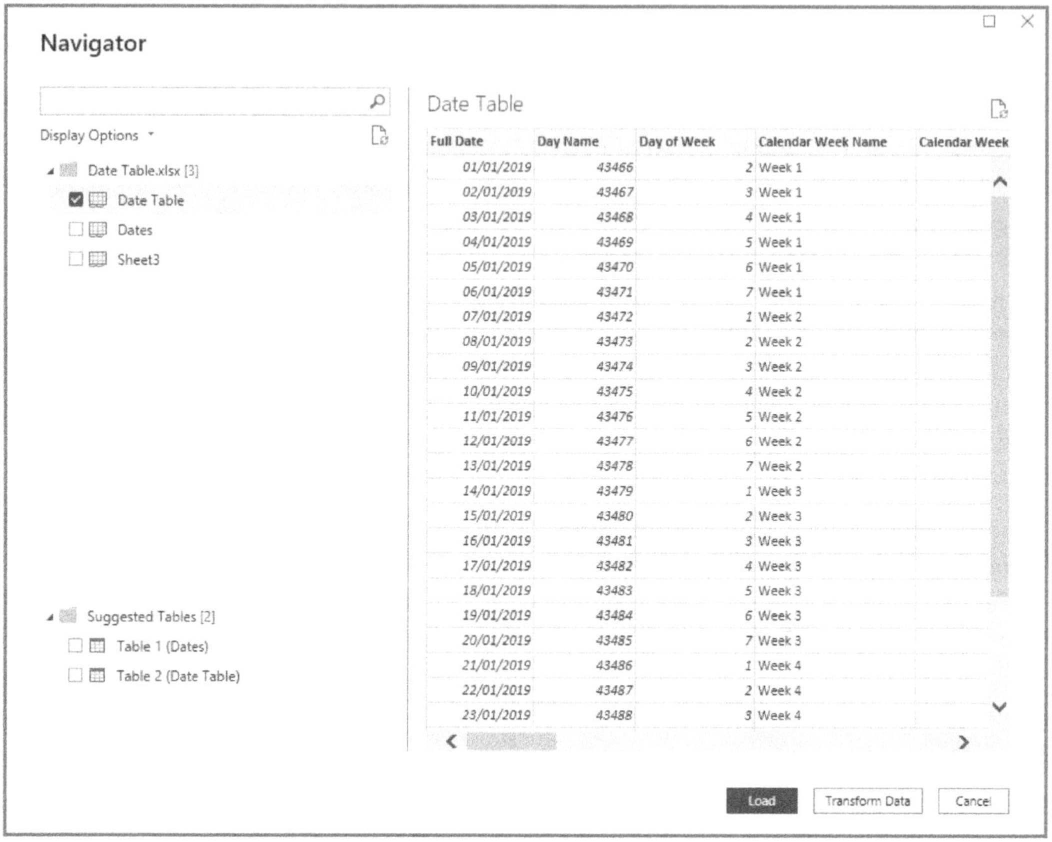

Figure 6.2: Launching Power Query from the Import Data navigator

Because this chapter covers Power Query, we asked you to click on **Transform Data** rather than **Load**. As mentioned, clicking **Transform Data** takes you directly into Power Query. For most people, the normal operation is to click **Load**, especially as it has a green background and white font, so the user interface design makes us think this is the obvious option.

When clicking **Load**, you'll be taken directly to Power BI, and you could easily think the data is loaded directly to Power BI. This is not necessarily the case, as your data will pass through Power Query before it ends up in Power BI. You may not see this step, but it happens.

This leads us to the subject of connection modes, which provide different methods to connect to data sources. We'll cover this briefly and encourage you to research the subject separately.

For the examples in this book, we've used Excel as a data source, which works using **Import** mode. In Import mode, data is loaded, or imported, into your Power BI file and stored locally.

This provides a great user experience as Power BI uses VertiPaq to optimize efficiency, resulting in fast data retrieval and manipulation.

Power BI has other connection modes that you may need to use. Direct Query links to the data source but doesn't import the data to the Power BI semantic model; each time Power BI queries the data, it does so directly to the data source. You'll generally use this option when the dataset is too large to be imported into your semantic model.

Live Connection is similar to DirectQuery and is used when connecting to published semantic models or **SQL Server Analysis Services** (**SSAS**) tabular models.

Finally, Direct Lake is a connection mode specific to Microsoft Fabric, which we cover in *Chapter 12, Financial Reporting in an AI-Driven World*.

With connection modes briefly covered, let's get back to Power Query:

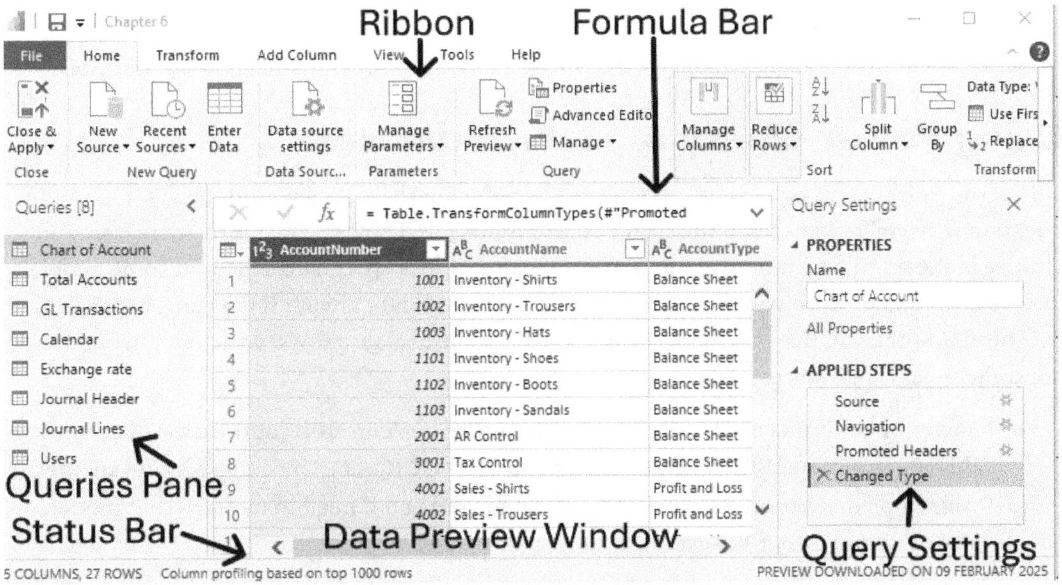

Figure 6.3: Power Query components

The main components of the Power Query user interface are shown in *Figure 6.3* and described next:

1. **Ribbon**: Like most Microsoft products, Power Query has a ribbon user interface where many common functions are available.
2. **Queries pane**: Your data sources are contained within the queries pane. This is where you select which data source to work with, also having a right-clickable menu when selecting a data source.

3. **Formula Bar**: The Formula Bar contains the M code for the current applied step that's selected.
4. **Data preview window**: The data preview window provides a view of fields within the current data source selected. Here, you can interact with the fields from the drop-down icon and right-click menu. It's important to note that the preview window is based on a maximum of 1,000 rows unless changed in the status bar (described next).
5. **Status bar**: The status bar shows statistics of your selected data source and allows you to change the column profiling from the default 1,000 rows to the entire dataset. Note that this will affect performance.
6. **Query settings**: The query settings display the name of the current data source selected and the applied transformation steps. When you make changes to your data, each step is shown in the applied steps, so you can make subsequent changes or undo transformations.

Now that we know the basics, let's put that into action and start transforming our datasets.

Using Power Query to reduce datasets

One of the most useful aspects of Power Query is reducing the size of your datasets. You might question why you'd want to do this; after all, computational power constantly increases, and storage is cheap, so why not just store everything? You certainly can do that, and some people do. We are going to warn you that processing unnecessary data always has a computational overhead. At first, you may not notice this, but over time, as data grows, you may start to. Here are some specific reasons to manage your model size:

- Power BI has limits on the size of the data model you can store; at the time of authoring this book, a Power BI Pro license limits you to a 1 GB model. Once these limits are met, your implementation gets more complicated, and you'll need to manage that model size or upgrade your license.
- Larger data models will mean slower response times to users. This can be a major barrier to user engagement, as users often become frustrated.
- Large datasets are more difficult to work with, especially when sifting through large numbers of columns to locate useful data.

So, what can we do about it? We generally begin with three steps to reduce new datasets:

1. Only import the required tables or entities.
2. Remove columns you don't need.
3. Remove rows you don't need.

Let's explore each step in more detail.

Only importing the required tables or entities

The first step is to consider whether you need every table available to you. It's tempting to import everything "just in case," but this will slow things down, increase complexity, and ultimately be counterproductive. So, the first step is to only import the data you'll need. Building a model in Power Query and Power BI is usually an iterative process of importing essential tables, then adding/removing tables as you discover the structure of the dataset. Importing everything at the start will give you a verbose and unwieldy model, becoming exponentially harder to find the information you need as there's too much superfluous data to work with.

If you don't think you'll need it, don't import it. You can come back for it later.

Removing columns you don't need

Database tables come loaded with columns you don't need. Remember – software applications are built for many different uses, so there'll be many functions you don't need; think how many Excel functions you use compared to how many are available. To extrapolate further, your finance application has many database tables and columns to store data you don't use. It's normal as applications need to cater to many use cases, not just yours.

Taking an example, a standard Microsoft Dataverse environment has a table called `account`, which is used to store organizations you may interact with, whether they're customers, suppliers, or any other category. It's used to store the name, address, and other details of those organizations, and at the time of writing, the `account` entity has 263 columns. In some Power BI semantic models, we only require two of those columns (ID and name), but in general, we'll need approximately 20 columns if we include address and categorization. That's a reduction of over 90%.

Using the `Opening Balances.pbix` dataset let's remove the line description from the **Journal Lines** table since it's free text, and we don't want to analyze it. To do this, we simply select the column we want to remove and click **Choose Columns** from the ribbon (if we later decide we need this column back, we can remove this step from Power Query and reverse the action), shown in *Figure 6.4*:

Figure 6.4: Using Choose Columns to remove a column in Power Query

After selecting **Choose Columns** from the ribbon, deselect the **Line Description** column and click **OK**.

In general, the columns you will want to remove tend to be the following:

- **Free text**: These tend to be large and of limited analytical value.
- **System columns**: Useful for the system, but have no analytical value.
- **Binary data**: It is sometimes the case that systems store images, and so on, in the database. We can't use this in Power BI, and it tends to be very large indeed.
- Any other columns you will not analyze.

Removing rows you don't need

The second approach to make datasets smaller is to remove rows. The most common way of doing this is by date. Let's suppose we want to retain the past 3 years and the current financial year. If the current financial year is 2026, then we're going to remove all data prior to the start of 2023.

We need to consider how much historical data we need, and there's often an urge to retain more than we need. In most cases, users only work with the current year. In some cases, users will need to look at trends from the past 1 or 2 years. In very few cases, users will need to go back further. If you want to maintain a long history, we advise a separate model that is used for that specific purpose, while keeping daily use models limited by date.

To do this, you'll need to find the best date column to use. Data tables typically have many date columns: as a minimum, **Created Date** and **Modified Date**, which refer to the date the transaction was created and the date of the last modification or update to the transaction. You should also see a posting date when the transaction was posted to the general ledger. This is the date we normally want to use. It's important to select the correct date to ensure your transactions appear in the correct period and your TI calculations are correct. Choose the wrong field, and transactions will appear in the wrong month, and your Power BI report won't match the standard transactional report within your financial application. The easiest way to check is to run a transactional summary report by month from your finance application, then match back to a Power BI report. You may need to try using a few different dates until you get a match, and don't forget to check for time zones, as different time zones can place transactions in different months if the time of posting is important. Working with dates is generally more complex than most people think.

When you've found the correct date column, use the date filters in Power Query by clicking the drop-down icon on the column header and using the **Date Filters** option, shown in *Figure 6.5*.

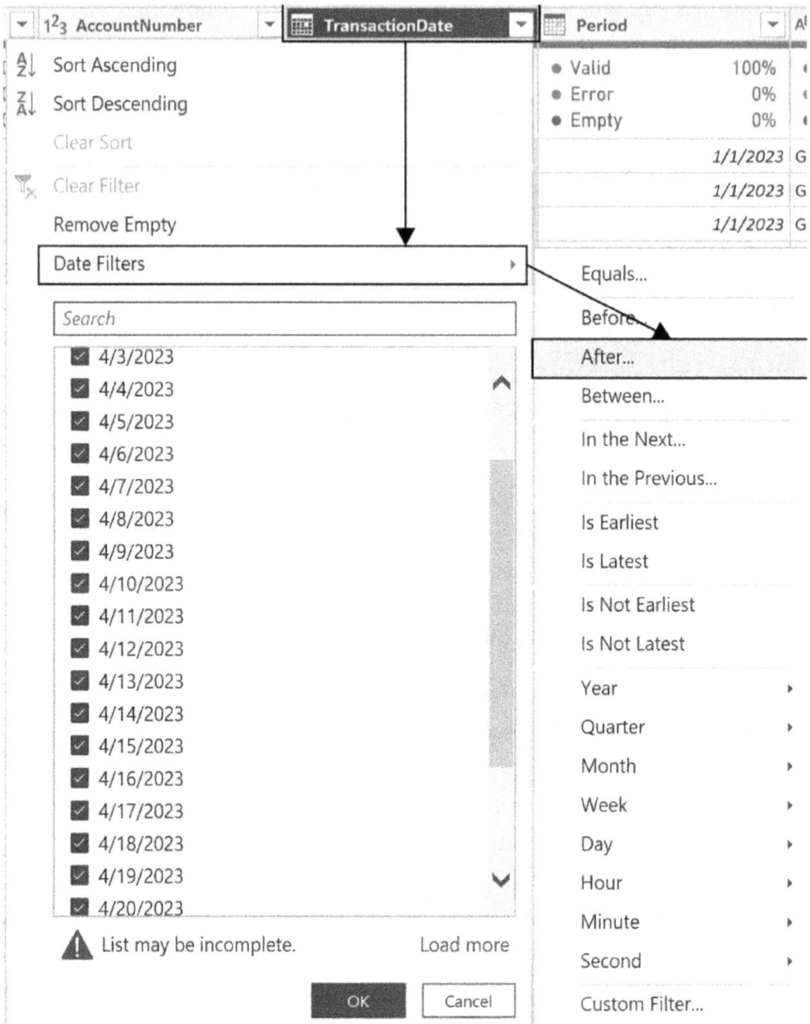

Figure 6.5: Filtering rows by date in Power Query

Choose the **After...** option, and when you click on it, you'll also see **is after or equal to** as an option. Type the date you want the reporting to start and click **OK**. When you next click **Close and Apply**, Power Query will filter out all transactional data that doesn't meet that criteria.

A more advanced method of removing rows is aggregating your data. The most common method is to aggregate data by day and other categories, such as GL account. Therefore, if you have many transactions on a single day, posting to the same GL account, you can aggregate the data to provide a total for that day and that GL account.

Using Power Query to do this, you'll use the **Group By** function, which is under the **Transform** tab (*Figure 6.6*). Using the accompanying dataset, select the **{GL Transactions}** table and then click the **Group By** button. Select the **Advanced** radio button in the **Group By** dialog box and add the **TransactionDate** and **AccountNumber** columns. The next step is to enter the name and aggregation for a new column that Power Query will generate. In our example, we called the new column **Aggregated Amount**, the operation is `[SUM]`, and the column is **Amount**.

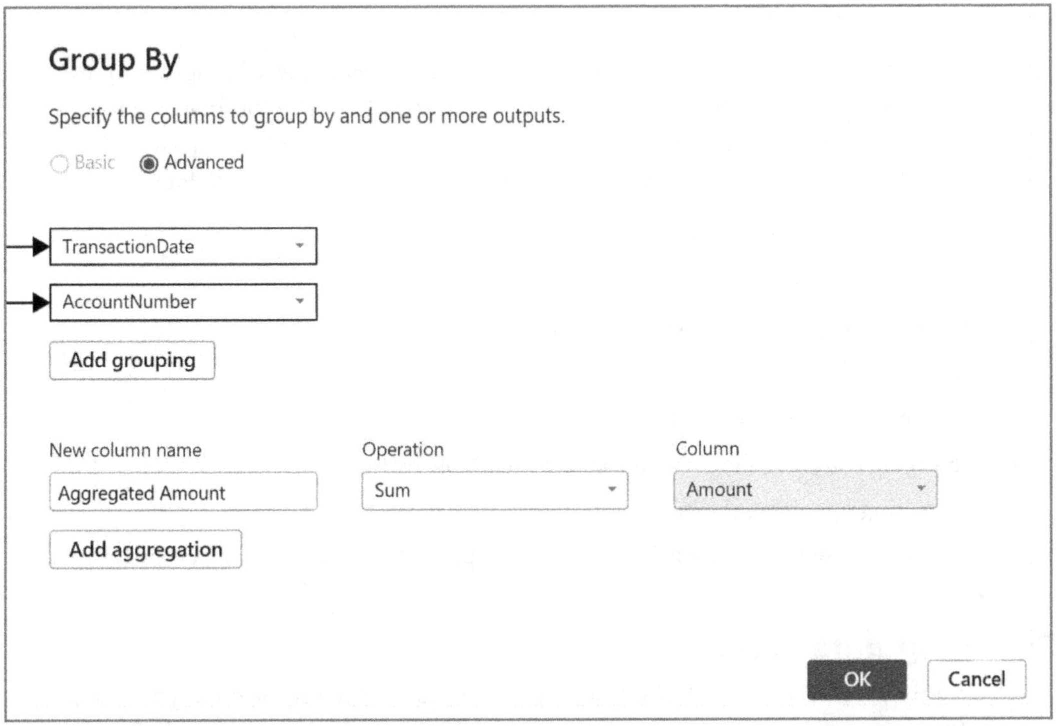

Figure 6.6: Using Group By to reduce dataset size

We're building a new column that'll aggregate the values in the **Amount** column by `TransactionDate` and `AccountNumber`.

When you click **OK** on the dialog box and **Close and Apply** in Power Query, you should see a dramatically reduced row count.

It is possible you'll see an issue with the reporting when it comes to opening balances caused by posting dates. We look at this later in the *Correcting opening balances* section.

Now that you've reduced the size of your dataset, let's look at some other common Power Query transformations.

Common data transformations

In the previous section, we looked at how you can use Power Query to reduce the size of your dataset. In this section, we'll develop those skills with some common data transformations. The lessons from the previous section are also transformations, but we wanted to separate the task of reducing your dataset from the task of transforming your data to make it easier to use and more accurate to work with.

Like the rest of the book, this is far from exhaustive. Power Query is the sole topic in many books, and we have only one chapter, as our core focus here is Power BI for finance, rather than Power Query alone. Our objective is to explain some common methods we employ when working with Power BI and Power Query in the context of modeling financial data.

In this section, we'll explain the following:

- Changing data types
- Adding conditional and custom columns
- Merging data
- Pivoting and unpivoting columns
- Changing column headers using AI to be readable by humans
- Correcting opening balances

Along the way, we'll see some essential Power Query practices we think you'll enjoy for long-term use.

Changing data types

One of the fundamental tasks when building a database table is to set the data types for each column. You've probably entered lots of data into Excel, and as Excel is cell-based, the data type for a column isn't a consideration, as you can enter text, numbers, and dates within a single column. You can't do this within a database, and you can't do this in Power Query or Power BI. Mix up data types in a single column, and Power Query will revert to the lowest standard, which is **Any**, as that'll accommodate every data type. You won't find it very useful, as a date in an **Any** column won't have TI capabilities, and a number will be stored as text.

Setting column types in Power BI is important as it allows the application to treat data according to its type, such as calculations for numbers and TI for dates.

In many cases, you'll find the column type is automatically set as Power Query can read the type from the data source. However, depending on the data source, Power Query may not have this information, so all columns will be imported as text. Fixing this is a simple task and worth your while.

> **Note**
>
> For more details on column types, follow Microsoft's official documentation at `https://learn.microsoft.com/en-us/power-query/data-types`, which lists column types and purposes.

If your data import has a set of columns that are exclusively type **All**, then click on the **ABC123** icon at the top left of the column, and you'll see the different column types you can set. Please use the column type to match the data in the column.

As Power Query generally only samples the top 1,000 rows of data, you may notice errors when your data loads into Power BI. This often relates to row contents that are different from the column type you set, somewhere within the data. If this is the case, you'll need to go back to Power Query and resolve the issue before proceeding. This can be done by removing rows, setting the column back to **Any**, or replacing the errant data. The resolution will depend on how important the rows are.

Adding conditional and custom columns

Here's another Power BI/ Power Query gray area. You can add columns in both, so which should you choose? There's no black and white answer to this one, although we generally try to do as much as we can in Power Query so that the data is in good shape when we use it in Power BI.

There are many reasons to add columns in existing data tables, such as the following:

- Calculations (e.g., *price * quantity*)
- Categorization (grouping of transactions by type or adding text to numeric drop-down values)
- Cleaning (adding flags to rows for data that may need to be cleaned)

You'll find that the ability to extend data tables in Power Query gives you flexibility and options for what you're able to do with your data.

Conditional columns

From Power Query, click the **Add Column** tab and click on **Conditional Column**.

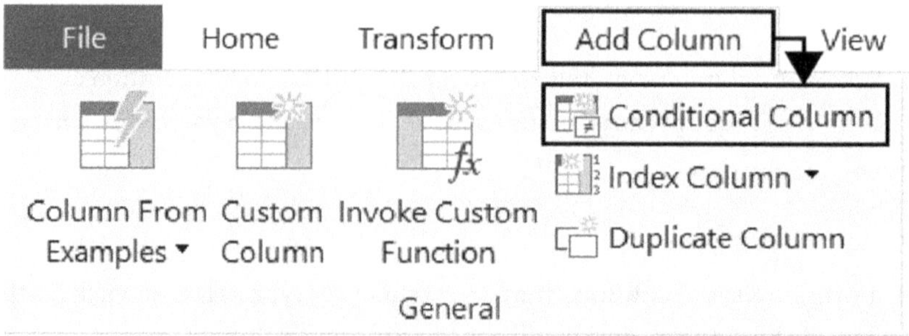

Figure 6.7: The Add Column tab from the ribbon

After clicking on the **Conditional Column** button, you'll see an **Add Conditional Column** dialog:

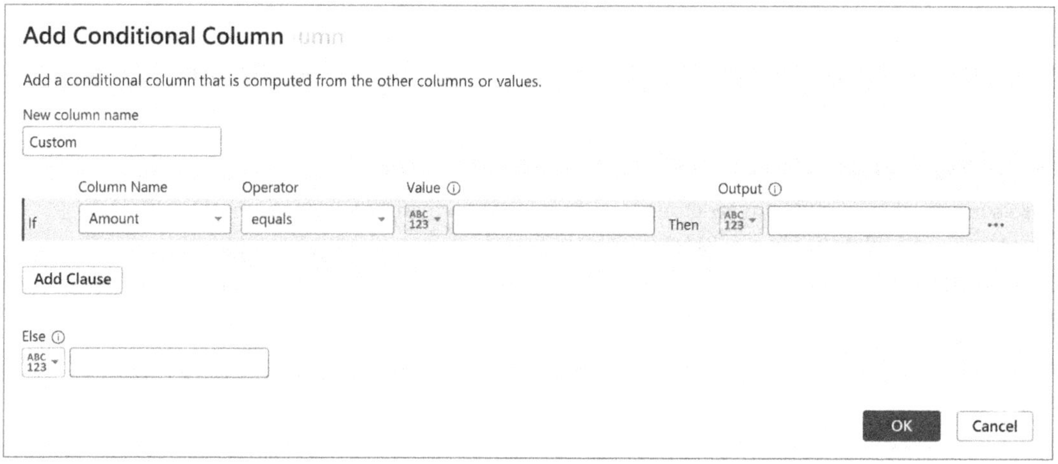

Figure 6.8: Add Conditional Column dialog

The logic of a conditional column is like an `IF` statement in Excel or Power BI (`If`, `Then`, `Else`). You choose a column, then an operator (equals, does not equal, etc.), and a value that could be numeric, text, or another column, then an output. Like a nested `IF` statement, you're able to add many clauses, ending with an `Else` statement. Categorization of transactions is a common example where a transaction type field shows a drop-down list numeric value but not the text label (this happens more often than you'd imagine), so you need to add a conditional column that will say `IF Transaction Type equals 1 Then Output "Credit Note"`. You may also want to categorize amounts as high or low to easily identify transactions that fall outside business norms. Remember that Power Query will evaluate your conditional column in the order you enter conditions, so you may need to adjust the order to make your statement work.

Custom columns

The next common option for adding columns is a custom column. You can do everything from a conditional column in a custom column and much more, which begs the question: *Why use a conditional column?* Conditional columns work with an intuitive point-and-click interface, which makes it easier for users with limited experience to get the result they need. Custom columns require input using Power Query's native scripting language, M. M is relatively straightforward to use, although it's different from DAX, so don't rely on your DAX skills to get the syntax of M incorrect. To continue with the example of an `IF` statement, a conditional column using M could look like this:

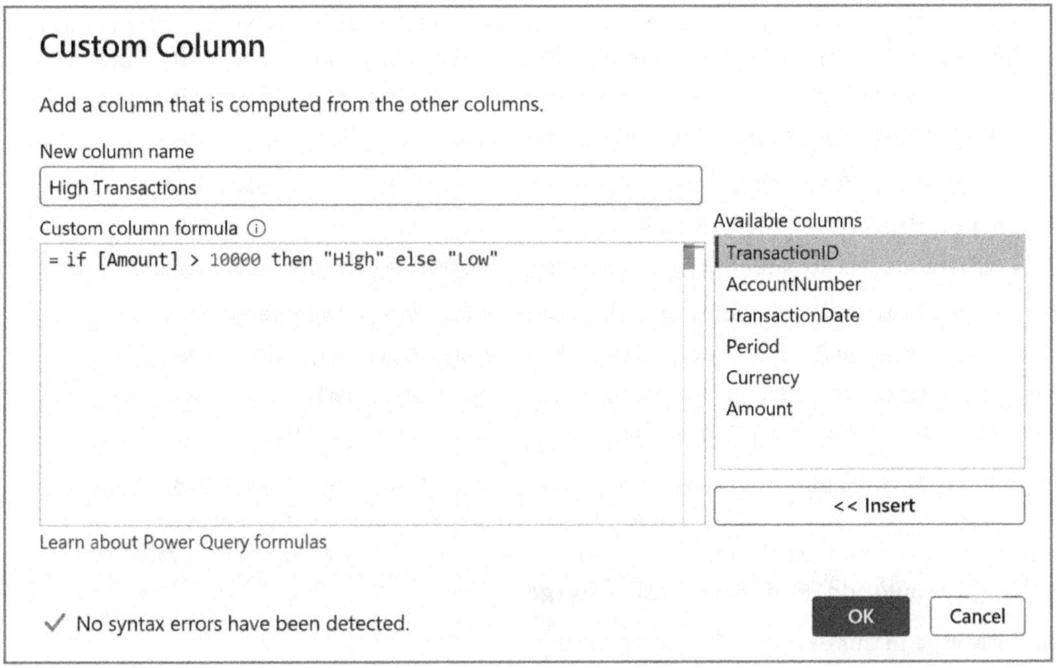

Figure 6.9: Custom Column dialog

If the amount is greater than 10,000, show the word `"High"`; else, show the word `"Low"`. It's a simple example, and M is certainly capable of much more. We use custom columns where the capabilities of conditional columns become a limiting factor. An example could be categorizing transactions based on a value *and* an account type, which you can't do with a conditional column but can do with a custom column.

Now that we have created some simple custom columns, let's have a look at some more complex transformations, starting with merging queries.

Merging data

Merge Queries in Power Query allows us to merge data from separate tables, where we're adding one or many columns from one table to another. When we have a table structure in a database, developers look for efficiency by reducing redundancy or replication of data. For example, the **AccountNumber** column on the **GL Transactions** table may just include the account number, not the account name or other useful attributes. Those attributes will be on the **ChartOfAccount** table that's linked to the **GL Transactions** data via the account ID. This way, we store the **ChartOfAccount** attributes once on the **ChartOfAccount** table, and we don't repeat them on every line item on the **GL Transactions** table.

Merging queries undoes this, which probably seems counterintuitive as we've written about the importance of efficiency within our data model. What works for database efficiency doesn't always work for analytics efficiency; the term we use to describe this is *denormalization*. There are a few reasons why we may choose to do this:

- Queries may run faster with denormalization, as multiple joins between tables have a negative impact on query time
- Data models are simplified and easier to understand and work with for users
- Denormalized tables allow pre-aggregation of data for very large tables

Like many aspects of data, there's a trade-off with **Merge Queries** depending on the complexity of your model, and in most cases, you'll probably use **Merge** to make it easier to work with, unless you're working with very large and complex models.

An example of when and where you may want to do this is for a simple treatment of foreign exchange. Consider the situation where you need daily spot rates for a single currency conversion. We could use the method demonstrated in *Chapter 4, Common DAX Measures*, using DAX, or we could add the daily rate using **Merge**.

To use **Merge** in this example, follow these steps:

1. First, select the **GL Transactions** table in the **Queries** pane with a single click.
2. Then, from the **Home** tab in Power Query, we'll select **Merge**, which will launch the **Merge** dialog box.
3. You'll see the `GL Transactions` table and a dropdown to choose a table that will be merged from, where you'll select the **Exchange rate** table.
4. On the **GL Transactions** table, choose the `TransactionDate` field, and from the **Exchange rate** table, choose the `Date` field (*Figure 6.7*) and click **OK**.
5. The final column of the **GL Transactions** table will now be labeled **Exchange Rate** with an **Expand column** icon to the right of the field header.

6. When you select this, you can choose columns from the **Exchange rate** table to add to the **GL Transactions** table.
7. Select the columns you want to add and click **OK**. The selected columns will then be added to the **GL Transactions** table, matched by date.

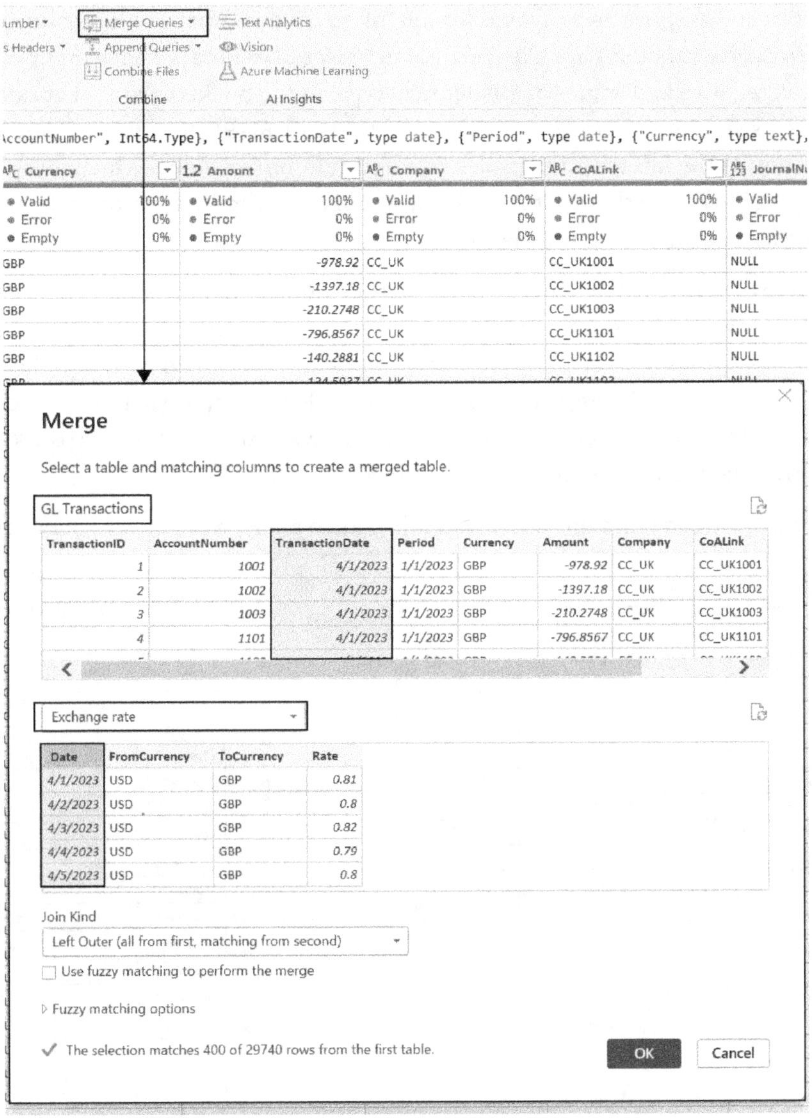

Figure 6.10: Merge dialog

Pivoting and unpivoting columns

Pivoting and unpivoting columns in Excel is a common use, as we frequently use pivot tables as a presentation and analysis method. This section is titled *Pivoting and unpivoting columns*, but more focus will be on unpivoting columns, as it's a frequent transformation. It's common to ingest data into Power Query in a pivoted format, often from standard reports outputted from finance systems. Pivoted tables are like matrices in Power BI, where we have many columns with specific categories and values of an identical type. Aging buckets are a great example where we often see columns categorizing aged debt (31–60, 61–90, 91–120, etc.) and rows with customer names. At the intersection of each row and column is a value, which is the debt value within the aging bucket for that customer. It's a standard method we use to understand the data, as it's quick and easy to identify issues.

When ingesting data into Power Query/Power BI, the temptation is to work with the data in the pivoted form as output from the report. While tempting and often done, it's an ineffective method for the purposes of data analytics, as we limit what we can do with that data. Returning to our example of aging buckets, it's impossible to compare period-on-period changes to aging buckets, as there is no relationship between them when each bucket is a column. For this and many other reasons, we unpivot.

When unpivoted, we can build measures that allow us to analyze the data in detail and make comparisons.

Matrix report generated from finance system

Customer	Period	0-30	31-60	61-90	91-120	121-150	Over 151
Customer A	6	43,618		33,410			
Customer B	6		54,139		17,363		
Customer C	6	18,155			33,922		
Customer D	6	61,892	39,864				
Customer E	6			51,315			
Customer F	6	41,398			64,095		
Customer G	6				34,252	78,200	
Customer H	6	72,220	46,856	78,859			
Customer I	6						30,241

Data unpivoted in Power Query

Customer	Period	Aging Bucket	Amount
Customer A	6	0-30	43,618
Customer A	6	61-90	33,410
Customer B	6	31-60	54,139
Customer B	6	91-120	17,363
Customer C	6	0-30	18,155
Customer C	6	91-120	33,922
Customer D	6	0-30	61,892
Customer D	6	91-120	39,864
Customer E	6	61-90	51,315
Customer F	6	0-30	41,398
Customer F	6	91-120	44,095
Customer G	6	91-120	34,252
Customer G	6	121-150	78,200
Customer H	6	0-30	72,220
Customer H	6	31-60	46,856
Customer H	6	61-90	78,859
Customer I	6	Over 151	30,241

Figure 6.11: The effect of unpivoting data

Our unpivoted table will have many more rows than the original report, but it is more efficient as we can use Power Query to filter out zero or null values from rows in the matrix.

When unpivoted and imported into Power BI, we can connect the **Period** column of the unpivoted table to the **Period** column in our **Date** table for period-on-period calculations using `SUMX` or `CALCULATE` and `FILTER`, discussed earlier.

Changing column names using AI to be readable by humans

This step in our Power Query basics is one that's been made easier by AI tools. It's often the case that column names in your finance application use text that doesn't make sense or is hard to read:

- SAP generally uses five-character field names, derived from German words. For example, the German term for *sales organization* is *Verkaufsorganisation*, and the field name in SAP for *sales organization* is *VKORG*. Even if you're a German speaker, the field name may not be too helpful.
- Dynamics 365 Finance and Operations capitalizes field names and has no spacing between words. For example, *INVOICECUSTOMERACCOUNTNUMBER* is *Invoice Customer Account Number*. From all capitals to mixed case with spacing, the text becomes far easier to read.

Software developers need standards to name fields, so all capitals with no spaces is common and for good reason. However, it doesn't make our data analytics lives easy when we need to interact with it.

Traditionally, we'd find a table that maps the field name to the field label and build a `Rename Columns` command in Power Query. We may even click each column header and rename it. Either way, it's time-consuming but required, so we do it.

The following method is not the most intuitive in terms of the steps you'll follow, but it allows you to use the power of AI to help with column renaming. We do have to warn you first that AI can make mistakes, so if you have any concerns, check the outputs. Despite the accuracy warning, this is a method that can save a lot of time and effort for a basic and necessary task:

1. In Power Query, select a table where you want to change the column names and click on the first column. Press *Ctrl* + *A* to select all columns in the table. Right-click any of the selected column headers and choose **Unpivot Only Selected Columns**.
2. In the Power Query command bar, copy all of the text (*Ctrl* + *A* and *Ctrl* + *C*) and paste it into Notepad.

3. In Notepad, delete the text `['=Table.Unpivot('` from the start of the pasted text and `'"Attribute", "Value")]'` from the end of the pasted text. You'll be left with the table name and all of the fields in quotation marks, separated by commas.
4. In Notepad, add the following text:

```
"Please generate a Power Query rename.columns statement using this table
[tablename] and the following fields. Please make the fields mixed case
with spaces and easily readable by humans: {all of the fieldnames in
quotation marks, separated by spaces}
```

5. Copy and paste the query into a **generative AI** (**GenAI**) tool such as **Copilot**, **ChatGPT,** or **Claude**.
6. Back in Power Query, delete the **Unpivoted Only Selected Columns** step, right-click on **Navigation step**, and select **Insert Step After**. Copy the `RenameColumns` statement generated in your GenAI tool into the command bar, making sure it starts with the = symbol. Press *enter*, and all your columns should be successfully renamed.

A few things can go wrong, such as minor syntax errors; for example, missing the `"="` symbol at the start or missing parentheses, although you should be able to get your GenAI tool to correct this. You may see repeated field texts from the tool, which can be resolved by adding a request to make all new field names unique or editing them manually yourself.

While this method may initially feel like a lot of steps, we're sure you'll find the effort worth it unless your column names are easy to read when loaded into Power Query.

Correcting opening balances

We've just looked at filtering datasets and mentioned a potential problem when filtering GL transaction data. The problem arises when filtering rows of our dataset by date. As we're excluding previous years' data, we won't have opening balances from the prior year, and our balances may therefore be incorrect. If, for example, the filter is only ever applied at the start of a financial year, and the system posts opening balances for the year into a special period (such as **Period 0**), then there should not be a problem. If, however, the system does not store opening balances (for example, the system calculates reports at runtime) or there is a need to filter partway through a financial year, we need to deal with creating opening balances.

The first step is to create a dataset to create opening balances by filtering GL transactions to only show those *BEFORE* the date we want to view the transactions from:

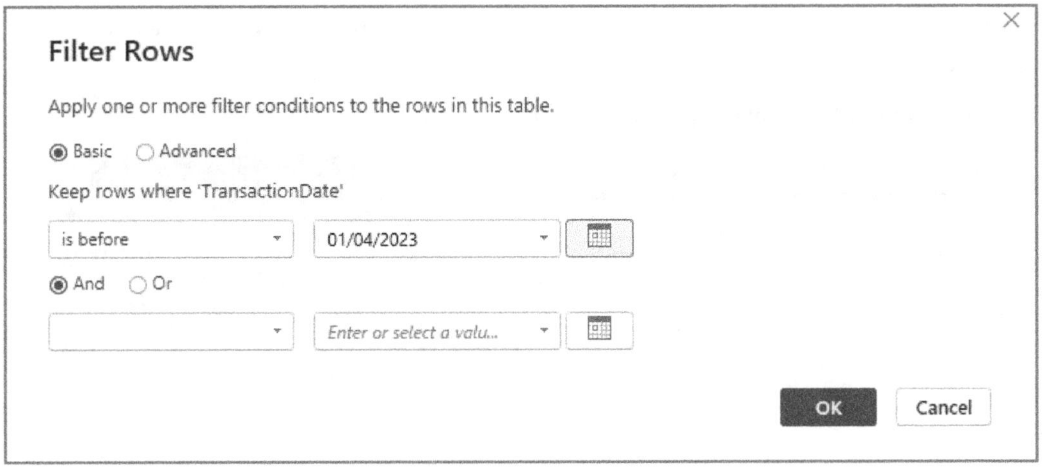

Figure 6.12: Filter Rows dialog

Now, we need to aggregate this dataset to show balances per ledger account:

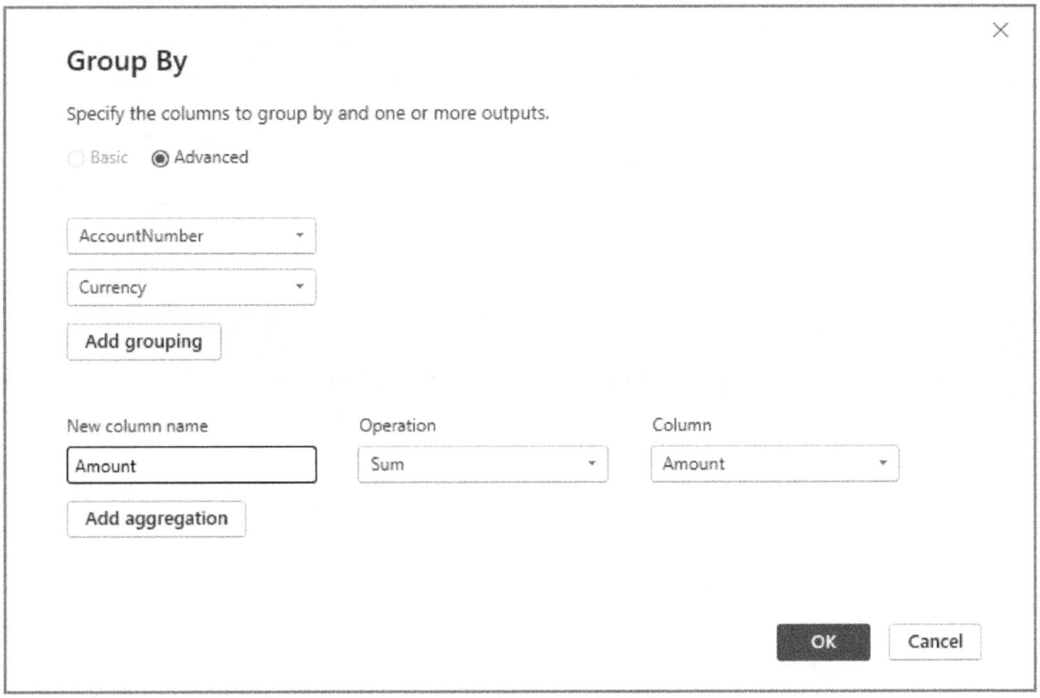

Figure 6.13: Group By dialog

Note that it is important to call the new column **Amount**, as we need column names in the opening balances to match column names in transactions in order to combine the two successfully.

This will result in a basic set of opening balances like this:

	AccountNumber	Currency	Amount
1	1001	GBP	-150239.09
2	4001	GBP	-308017.45
3	5001	GBP	150219.09
4	1003	GBP	-100013.5
5	4003	GBP	-275535.79
6	5003	GBP	100013.5
7	1103	GBP	-101698.31
8	4103	GBP	-210945.71
9	5103	GBP	101698.31
10	1102	GBP	-28088.24
11	4102	GBP	-49079.07
12	5102	GBP	28088.24
13	1002	GBP	-57403.46
14	4002	GBP	-107552.22
15	5002	GBP	57353.46
16	1101	GBP	-22222.55
17	4101	GBP	-56830.07
18	5101	GBP	22222.55
19	3001	GBP	-201592.062

Figure 6.14: Output from grouping by columns

The problem now is that this will not join our model correctly. For a start, it lacks a transaction date as opening balances are aggregated over many different dates. We therefore have to decide where we want to recognize the balance. In this example, we would either want to choose the first day of the financial year we wish to start picking up details in, or the last day of the previous year. Using the first day of the current year will skew any year-to-date calculations, so we will use the last day of the prior year and add a transaction date of March 31, 2023.

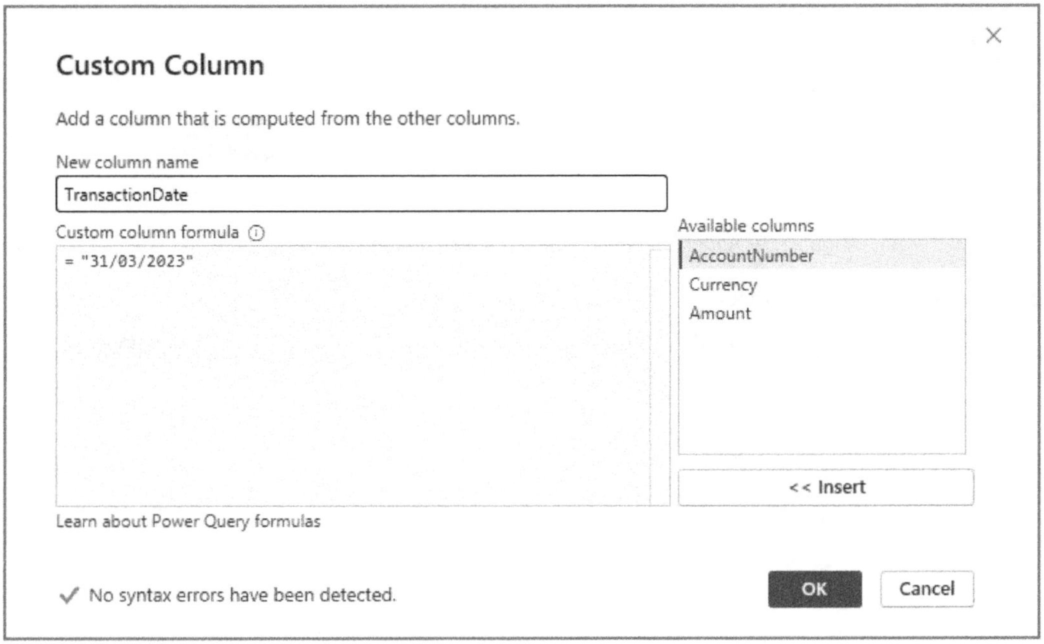

Figure 6.15: Adding a transaction date

Similarly, we will create columns for transaction ID, journal number, and period.

Now, we need to load the GL transactions and filter them to just show details from April 1, 2024, onward, where we use **GL Transactions**.

We can now append the two queries together:

Figure 6.16: Appending the opening balance and the GL transactions

This results in our final dataset:

	AccountNumber	Currency	Amount	TransactionDate	TransactionID	Journal Number	Period
1	1001	GBP	-150239.09	31/03/2023	0		0
2	4001	GBP	-308017.45	31/03/2023	0		0
3	5001	GBP	150219.09	31/03/2023	0		0
4	1003	GBP	-100013.5	31/03/2023	0		0
5	4003	GBP	-275535.79	31/03/2023	0		0
6	5003	GBP	100013.5	31/03/2023	0		0
7	1103	GBP	-101698.31	31/03/2023	0		0
8	4103	GBP	-210945.71	31/03/2023	0		0
9	5103	GBP	101698.31	31/03/2023	0		0
10	1102	GBP	-28068.24	31/03/2023	0		0
11	4102	GBP	-49079.07	31/03/2023	0		0
12	5102	GBP	28068.24	31/03/2023	0		0
13	1002	GBP	-57403.46	31/03/2023	0		0
14	4002	GBP	-107552.22	31/03/2023	0		0
15	5002	GBP	57353.46	31/03/2023	0		0
16	1101	GBP	-22222.55	31/03/2023	0		0
17	4101	GBP	-56830.07	31/03/2023	0		0
18	5101	GBP	22222.55	31/03/2023	0		0
19	3001	GBP	-201592.062	31/03/2023	0		0
20	2001	GBP	1209622.372	31/03/2023	0		0
21	6001	GBP	60000	31/03/2023	0		0
22	6002	GBP	18000	31/03/2023	0		0
23	6003	GBP	24000	31/03/2023	0		0
24	6101	GBP	20000	31/03/2023	0		0
25	3101	GBP	-102000	31/03/2023	0		0
26	3201	GBP	-20000	31/03/2023	0		0
27	1001	GBP	-853.65	01/04/2023	1033	null	01/01/2024
28	4001	GBP	-7428.09	01/04/2023	1034	null	01/01/2024
29	5001	GBP	853.65	01/04/2023	1035	null	01/01/2024
30	1001	GBP	-1250.16	02/04/2023	1036	null	01/01/2024
31	4001	GBP	-8714.93	02/04/2023	1037	null	01/01/2024

Figure 6.17: The complete dataset

The stechniques used here are a good way to reduce the amount of data that needs to be imported into the data model, and do so in a way that avoids some of the problems that can occur with simply filtering transactions out. This tends to be a more significant problem when dealing with ledger data or inventory transactions (which we will cover in *Chapter 8, Managing Inventory Data*), where overall totals may be tracked across all historical data.

Summary

In this chapter, we introduced basic ideas of data transformation and how they can be applied in Power BI. We looked in detail at some more common and useful transformations and why you would want to use them. Finally, we brought these techniques together into a more complex pattern to create opening balances: a critical component to reduce the size of datasets.

In the next chapter, we will use some of the methods learned here to bring in the next big piece of data that we need to drive effective financial reporting – the budget.

7

Incorporating Budgets and Targets

In the previous chapter, we worked through some of the most important functions you'll use within Power Query to help reduce and shape your data. In this chapter, we'll move back to a topic more focused on finance, which is how to incorporate your budget data into your financial model.

Incorporating budgets is an important part of financial modeling as it provides the basis to measure performance and track and analyze differences between budget and actuals. In this chapter, we'll cover the following topics:

- What you need to join your budget data to your financial model
- How to join the budget table to the financial model
- Writing measures to calculate the differences between budgets and actuals
- Choosing the correct visuals to see high-level differences that can easily be interrogated through expanding a matrix and drill-through

As budgeting processes can vary significantly between organizations, we're following an approach based on an Excel-based budget, tracked monthly against the GL accounts of the financial application. This is a simple and common method, and the techniques should be easy to follow if using different tools.

Technical requirements

To follow the examples in this chapter and beyond, you'll need a Windows PC with an internet connection, and you'll also need to download **Power BI Desktop**.

For more details, we suggest you access the following link, where Microsoft details the download process for Power BI Desktop and the PC hardware requirements:

`https://learn.microsoft.com/en-us/power-bi/fundamentals/desktop-get-the-desktop`.

The examples outlined in this chapter can be tried out in the `Chapter 7.pbix` model. A fully worked example of multiple budget models can be found in the `Chapter 7 - Multiple Models.pbix` file. Both files can be found in the GitHub repository here: `https://github.com/PacktPublishing/Financial-Modeling-with-Power-BI_Packt/tree/main/Chapter7`.

Creating a budget table

We'll start with the assumption that you already have a process for budgetary management and budget data, stored in an Excel spreadsheet.

Most applications for financial management will have some sort of budgeting functionality built in, but they're often unused. The reasons are varied, although most tools within financial management systems don't have the flexibility to manage the specifics of the organizational budgetary processes, so it's easier to use a spreadsheet. While we have a lot to say about Excel as a data source, budgets and Excel work very well together.

If you maintain budgets in your financial management application, most of the guidance in this chapter should also be useful.

If you don't have an existing budget spreadsheet, we've provided an example within the `Budget.xlsx` file in the GitHub repository. The example is typical of the budget tables we work with, in matrix format. It's effective for humans but not as effective for Power BI, as we learned in the previous chapter; therefore, we'll need to unpivot the data in Power Query. The benefit of this approach is that your users can maintain budgets in a friendly way for them, as a matrix, and Power Query will unpivot the data to be friendly to Power BI.

If you're creating a spreadsheet for budgetary management, our example for the exercises will fit most use cases. Any template needs to be capable of the following:

- It must be capable of linking to your date table
- It must be capable of linking to the **Chart of Accounts** (**CoA**)
- It must contain values in the same currency as the accounting currency of the GL

The first point to note is that we don't want to join our budgets directly to individual GL transactions, so we use the `Date` and the `Chart of Account` tables to bridge them and allow us to show budgets against transaction totals for the relevant GL account.

The simplest scenario is a budget value per account, per month:

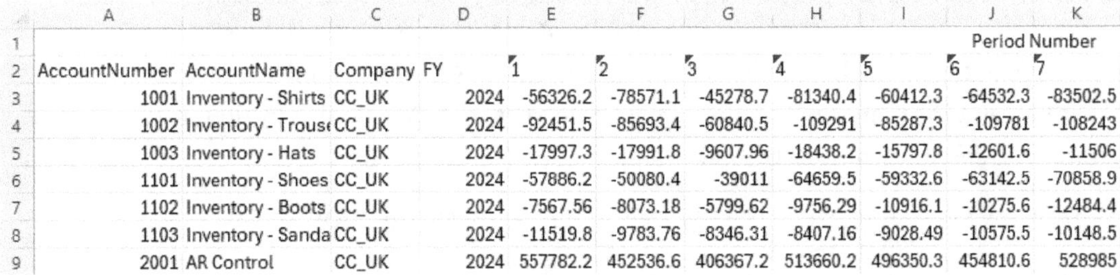

	A	B	C	D	E	F	G	H	I	J	K
1										Period Number	
2	AccountNumber	AccountName	Company	FY	1	2	3	4	5	6	7
3	1001	Inventory - Shirts	CC_UK	2024	-56326.2	-78571.1	-45278.7	-81340.4	-60412.3	-64532.3	-83502.5
4	1002	Inventory - Trous	CC_UK	2024	-92451.5	-85693.4	-60840.5	-109291	-85287.3	-109781	-108243
5	1003	Inventory - Hats	CC_UK	2024	-17997.3	-17991.8	-9607.96	-18438.2	-15797.8	-12601.6	-11506
6	1101	Inventory - Shoes	CC_UK	2024	-57886.2	-50080.4	-39011	-64659.5	-59332.6	-63142.5	-70858.9
7	1102	Inventory - Boots	CC_UK	2024	-7567.56	-8073.18	-5799.62	-9756.29	-10916.1	-10275.6	-12484.4
8	1103	Inventory - Sanda	CC_UK	2024	-11519.8	-9783.76	-8346.31	-8407.16	-9028.49	-10575.5	-10148.5
9	2001	AR Control	CC_UK	2024	557782.2	452536.6	406367.2	513660.2	496350.3	454810.6	528985

Figure 7.1: An example budget spreadsheet

We're going to use our budget spreadsheet for the examples in this chapter, and the first step is to load the data into our Power BI file. On loading, the first thing we note is that the column headers have not been recognized. This is often the case when Excel has treated headers as dates as you can see in *Figure 7.2*. Here, you can see **Column 1**, **Column 2**, and so on as header names and the actual header names in the first row.

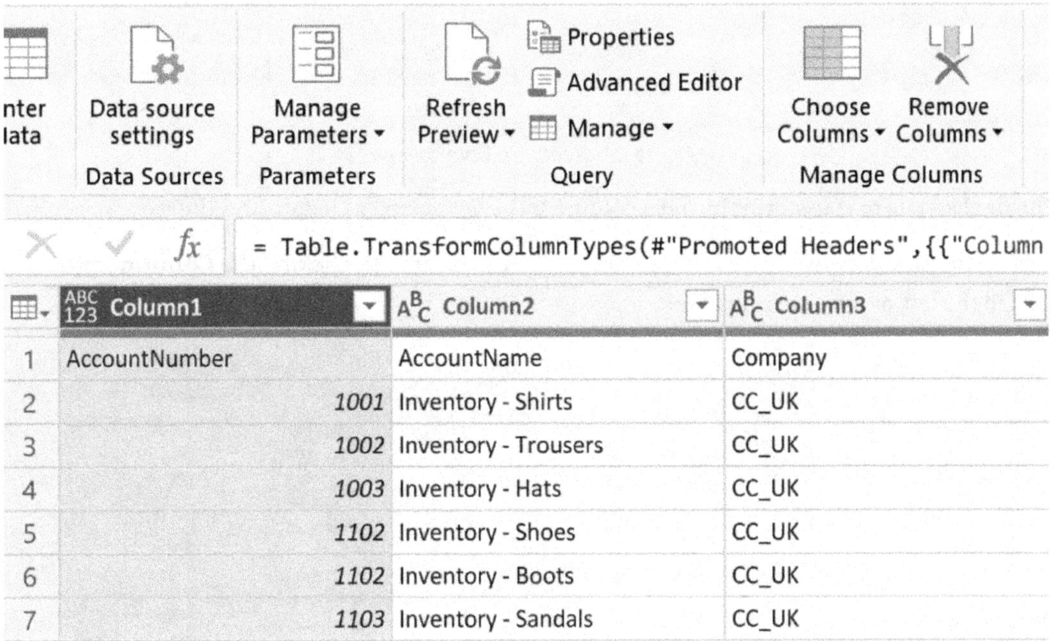

Figure 7.2: Use First Row as Headers

After you click **Use First Row as Headers**, you'll see that Power Query promotes the values in the first row to the headers, so that's fixed.

As discussed in *Chapter 6, Streamlining with Power Query,* we select the date columns with budget values and choose **Unpivot Only Selected Columns** from the right-click menu. We then rename the two columns that Power Query names, `Attribute` and `Value`, to `Month` and `Amount` so that the names reflect the values within the rows. We do this by double-clicking the column header and typing in the new names.

Now, we can create a `Date` column from the period number and the financial year:

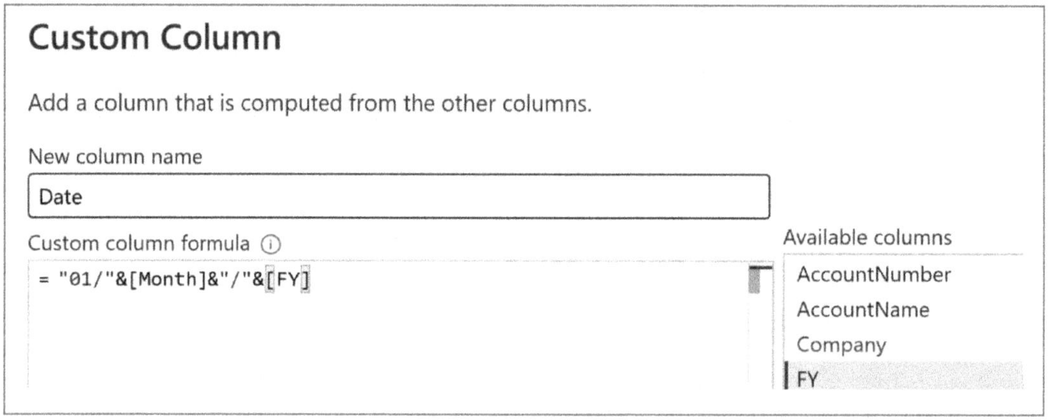

Figure 7.3: Creating a Date column

The final step is to transform the `Date` column to be formatted as a date and the `Amount` column to be formatted as a currency. We can do this by clicking the **Column Type** icon to the left of the column names.

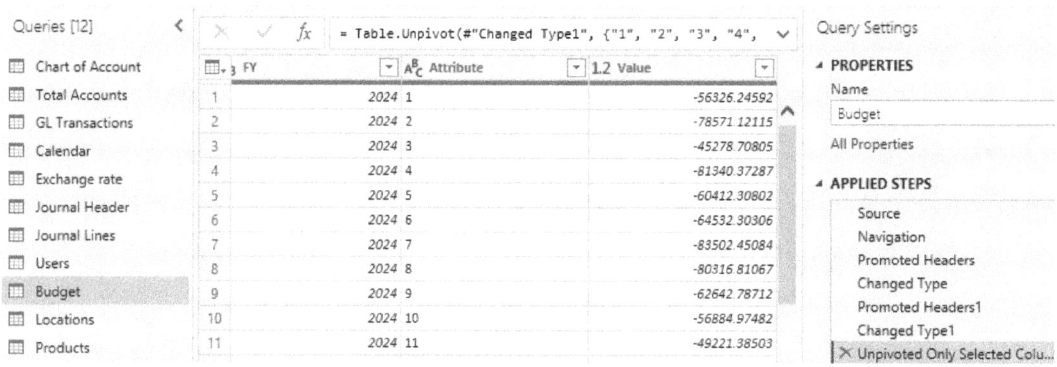

Figure 7.4: Unpivoting the budget data

You'll notice that all budget dates are on the first day of the month. We did this deliberately so that we can utilize the benefits of Power BI's **time intelligence (TI)** functions to make the exercise quicker, as we'll aggregate budgets and actuals by month and year. If Power BI recognizes a full date, it'll make TI functions available. We'll explain this in more detail later.

Once we've done the transformation, it's time to include this in our data model, first by clicking **Close & Apply** in Power Query. We then join the `Chart of Accounts` and `Calendar` tables to the `Budget` table by linking the `date` and `AccountNumber` fields. We made this easier for ourselves in the **Data Model** view by creating a new tab to only see the tables we're working with:

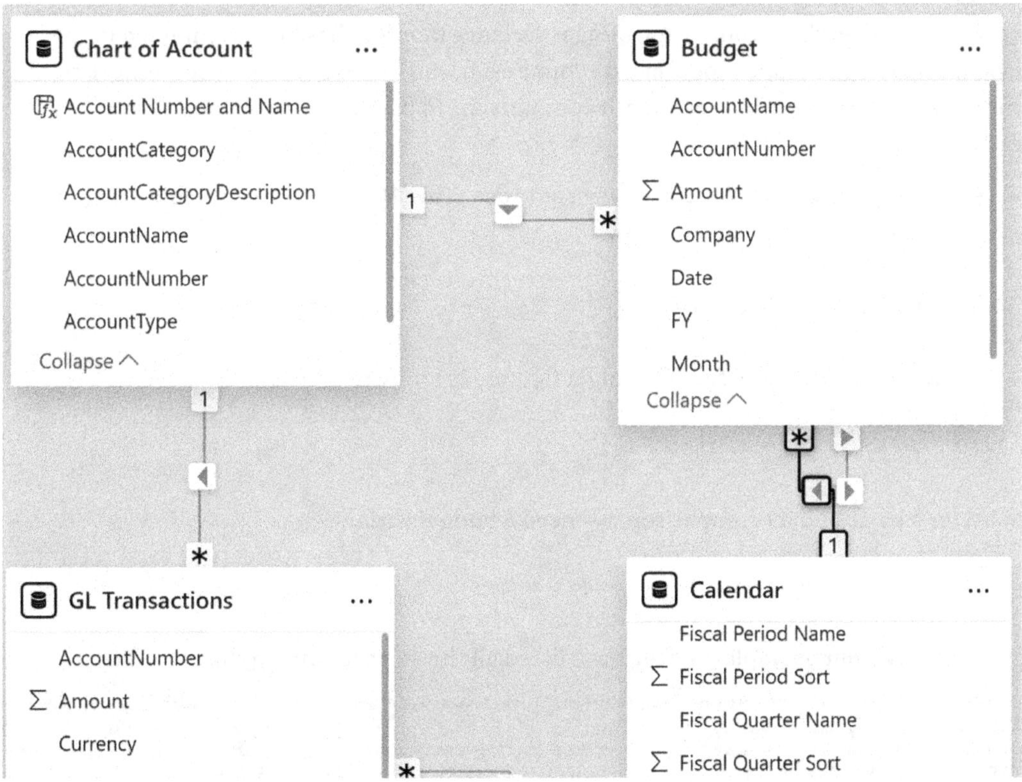

Figure 7.5: Budget data model

We now have the basic data imported, so we're ready to start looking at how we are going to use it. The first step will be to deal with budget data stored by months and transactions stored daily.

Handling differences in granularity

We mentioned previously that budget and GL transactions have a difference in the level at which they store the date. For a start, your monthly budgets are stored on the first day of the month, to utilize TI functions, and your GL transactions are stored based on the transaction date. To deal with this, we'll use the `Calendar` table to aggregate both budget and GL transactions based on month and year values to compare the values correctly.

Comparing values on month and year is the dominant method for reporting, which is what we'll focus on for the rest of the chapter. Some organizations may need to budget daily, and we explain a method for doing that later in the chapter.

Budgeting monthly

Most of the hard work for comparing budget variance monthly has been completed in the previous steps. A good data model can be your best friend, but we still have some work to complete for a basic month-over-month comparison. To begin with, we'll need a few measures.

We'll start with a measure for our `GL Transactions` table. We will create the following measure in our `List of Measures` table:

```
GL Amount = SUM('GL Transactions'[Amount])
```

We then need a `SUM` measure for our budget figures, as follows:

```
Budget Amount = SUM(Budget[Amount])
```

Finally, for a basic budget comparison, we need a budget variance:

```
Budget Variance = [GL Amount] - [Budget Amount]
```

Figure 7.6 shows our example, and we have listed all the steps following this:

AccountNumber	AccountName	AccountCategoryDes	GL Amount	Budget Amount	Budget Variance	GL Amount	Budget Amount	Budget Variance
1001	**Inventory - Shirts**	Inventory	-772,667.08	-776,317.70	3,650.62	-185,436.81	-725,985.64	540,548.84
1001	**Shirts inventory**	Inventory	-797,955.24	-1,575,773.14	777,817.90	-186,629.90		-186,629.99
1002	**Inventory - Trousers**	Inventory	-1,104,130.84	-1,043,962.26	-60,168.58	-264,944.48.48	-1,066,696.20	801,749.72
1002	**trousers inventory**	Inventory	-1,139,720.20	-2,249,657.71	1,109,937.51	-266,190.42		-266,190.42
1003	**hats inventory**	Inventory	-171,582.26	-338,463.03	166,880.77	-39,545.23		-39,545.23
1003	**Inventory - Hats**	Inventory	-166,255.02	-178,320.23	12,065.21	-39,183.40	-157,084.31	117,900.91
1101	**Inventory - Shoes**	Inventory	-1,279,766.92	-1,966,009.66	686,242.74	-301,083.14	-623,863.44	322,781.28
1102	**Inventory - Boots**	Inventory	-224,180.82	-337,652.89	113,472.07	-53,665.55	-109,020.54	55,355.20

Figure 7.6: Month budget report

Here are the detailed steps:

1. We started with a **Matrix** visual that has the following rows:
   - `AccountNumber` from the `Chart of Account` table

    - `AccountName` from the `Chart of Account` table
    - `AccountCategoryDescription` from the `Chart of Account` table
2. Our columns are as follows:
    - `Calendar Year Name`
    - `Calendar Month Name`
3. Our values are as follows:
    - `GL Amount`
    - `Budget Amount`
    - `Budget Variance`
4. We filtered the calendar years 2024 and 2025.
5. From the **Format** options, we chose the **Tabular Layout** option from the **Layout and Style** presets.
6. We then right-clicked one of the `AccountNumber` rows in the visual and chose **Expand | All** to show all levels.
7. Next, we switched off row and column subtotals from the **Format** menu.
8. To build the conditional formatting on the `Budget Variance` columns, we clicked the down chevron icon against the `Budget Variance` values block and chose the following options for font color:

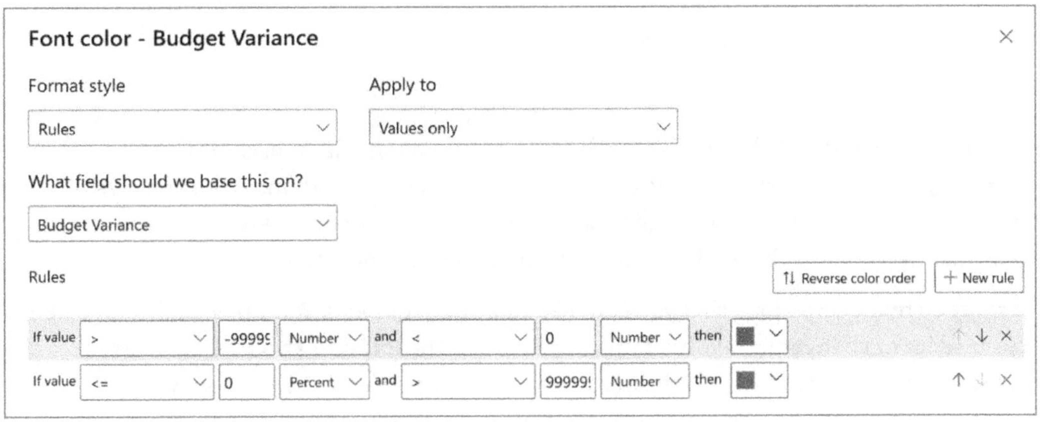

Figure 7.7: Budget Variance font color

9. We also added icon-based conditional formatting to the same field, as follows:

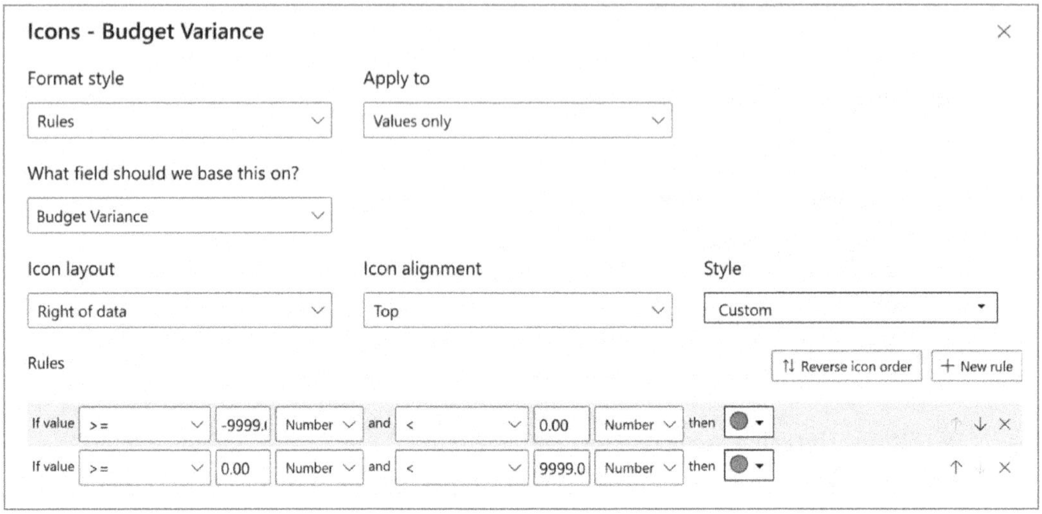

Figure 7.8: Budget Variance icons

Note

A quick note on conditional formatting

We wanted to show anything below zero with a red icon and above zero with a green icon. Therefore, the upper and lower limit values (i.e., the value that the top line must be greater than and the bottom line must be less than) are set to –9999999 and 9999999, respectively, to ensure they are outside the range of possible values that could be reported. It's arbitrary but works.

How you format and calculate variances for monthly budgeting is an organizational preference, so please experiment with the steps we've provided and find formats and styles that work for you. The most important part of the monthly budgeting exercise was to build a model that makes reporting on budgeting variances fast and accurate.

There are so many directions that you can take this budget model. You can add slicers to help focus on data or change the layout of the matrix to use the **Expand and collapse** setting of the hierarchy. Change the conditional formats to help you identify where your budget variance is healthy and where it's an issue for the organization. Whichever direction you choose to pursue, we recommend that you focus more on good modeling techniques to provide accuracy and less on DAX to generate budget comparisons.

Budgeting daily

First, we should consider why we would want to create daily budgets – after all, it would be rare to need to view budgets down to the day level. Broadly speaking, there are two places where this method is useful:

- Where you need to report against budgets at a lower level than monthly, such as weekly, especially since weeks do not neatly fit into months – this is a rare use case but does occasionally show up in some highly seasonal businesses, or where a business's performance can be impacted by events that vary by date between years.
- Where you need to pro-rata the budget to report against month or year-to-date figures, and you may be partway through a month.

Moreover, the techniques covered here can be adapted to other situations where you need to compare datasets stored in different levels of detail.

There are various methods for daily budgeting, and a certain amount will depend on the data you have available and organizational preferences. Based on the demonstration data we've generated, the method we'll use will be to spread the monthly budget sum over the days of the month. If your organization has created daily budgets, please use the monthly method instead of consolidating daily via the date table.

In our example, the budget for each day in April, for example, would be calculated as 1/30 of the total budget for the month:

1. To start, we need to create three calculated columns on our `Budget` table.

   The first is a `Month and Year` column that will be used for the next column we create:

   ```
   Month and Year = FORMAT(Budget[Date], "MMMM")&" "&YEAR(Budget[Date])
   ```

   Similarly, we need to create a column in the `Calendar` table:

   ```
   Month and Year = 'Calendar'[Calendar Month Name ] & " "
   &'Calendar'[Calendar Year Name ]
   ```

   You'll notice that the DAX returns `Month` and `Year` values that are identical to the values in the `Calendar` table.

   The next column uses the preceding column to return a count of days for the given month based on `COUNTROWS` from the `Calendar` table:

   ```
   Days in Month = CALCULATE(
   ```

```
        COUNTROWS('Calendar'),

        FILTER(

            'Calendar',

            Budget[Month and Year] = 'Calendar'[Month and Year])
    )
```

The third column is a simple `DIVIDE` operation of the month budget amount and the days in the month, as follows and shown in *Figure 7.9*:

```
Daily Amount = DIVIDE(Budget[Amount], Budget[Days in Month])
```

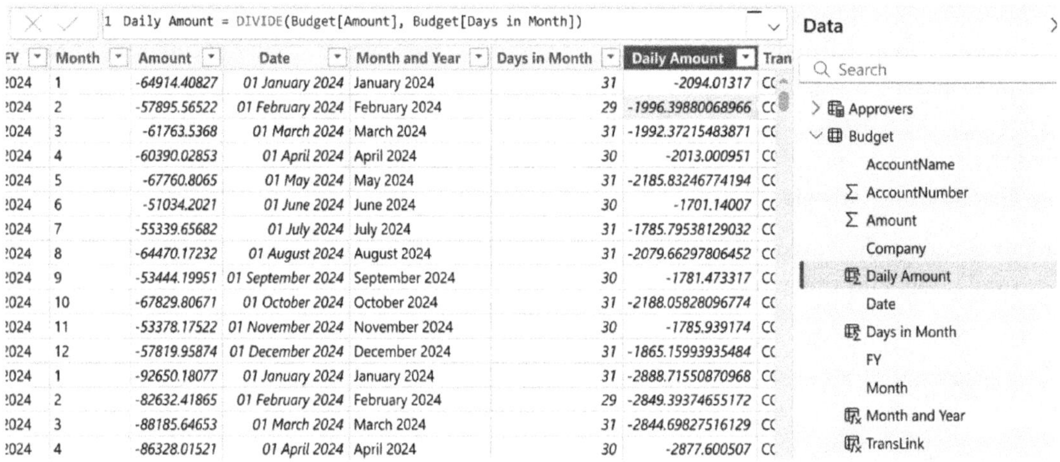

FY	Month	Amount	Date	Month and Year	Days in Month	Daily Amount	Tran
2024	1	-64914.40827	01 January 2024	January 2024	31	-2094.01317	CC
2024	2	-57895.56522	01 February 2024	February 2024	29	-1996.39880068966	CC
2024	3	-61763.5368	01 March 2024	March 2024	31	-1992.37215483871	CC
2024	4	-60390.02853	01 April 2024	April 2024	30	-2013.000951	CC
2024	5	-67760.8065	01 May 2024	May 2024	31	-2185.83246774194	CC
2024	6	-51034.2021	01 June 2024	June 2024	30	-1701.14007	CC
2024	7	-55339.65682	01 July 2024	July 2024	31	-1785.79538129032	CC
2024	8	-64470.17232	01 August 2024	August 2024	31	-2079.66297806452	CC
2024	9	-53444.19951	01 September 2024	September 2024	30	-1781.473317	CC
2024	10	-67829.80671	01 October 2024	October 2024	31	-2188.05828096774	CC
2024	11	-53378.17522	01 November 2024	November 2024	30	-1785.939174	CC
2024	12	-57819.95874	01 December 2024	December 2024	31	-1865.15993935484	CC
2024	1	-92650.18077	01 January 2024	January 2024	31	-2888.71550870968	CC
2024	2	-82632.41865	01 February 2024	February 2024	29	-2849.39374655172	CC
2024	3	-88185.64653	01 March 2024	March 2024	31	-2844.69827516129	CC
2024	4	-86328.01521	01 April 2024	April 2024	30	-2877.600507	CC

Figure 7.9: Extending the Budget table for daily budgets

Figure 7.9 shows a view of how your `Budget` table should look with the additional fields.

2. The next step is to create a daily budget table through a `CROSSJOIN` operation of the `Calendar` table and the `Budget` table. As the `Calendar` table has a row for each day of the year, it provides the basis to populate a new table with daily budget values. To

build this table, we go to **Modeling** | **New Table** when in the **Report** view, or **Home** | **New Table** from the **Table** view.

3. Then, we use the following DAX to create our table:

```
Daily Budget =

FILTER(

    CROSSJOIN(

        SELECTCOLUMNS('Calendar',

        'Calendar'[Full Date],
        'Calendar'[Month and Year]),

        SELECTCOLUMNS(Budget,

            Budget[Daily Amount],
            Budget[Month and Year],
            Budget[AccountNumber],
            Budget[TransLink])
        ),

        'Calendar'[Month and Year] = Budget[Month and Year])
```

The resulting table will look like *Figure 7.10*:

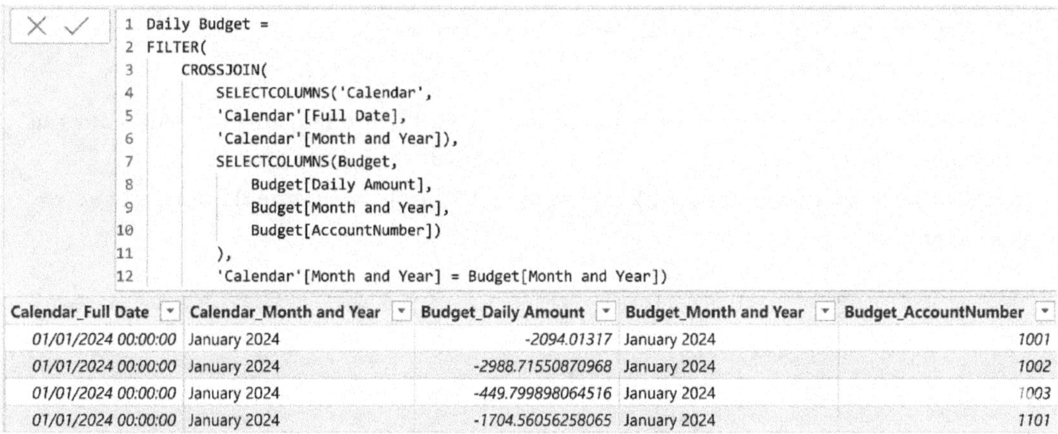

```
Daily Budget =
FILTER(
    CROSSJOIN(
        SELECTCOLUMNS('Calendar',
        'Calendar'[Full Date],
        'Calendar'[Month and Year]),
        SELECTCOLUMNS(Budget,
            Budget[Daily Amount],
            Budget[Month and Year],
            Budget[AccountNumber])
        ),
        'Calendar'[Month and Year] = Budget[Month and Year])
```

Calendar_Full Date	Calendar_Month and Year	Budget_Daily Amount	Budget_Month and Year	Budget_AccountNumber
01/01/2024 00:00:00	January 2024	-2094.01317	January 2024	1001
01/01/2024 00:00:00	January 2024	-2988.71550870968	January 2024	1002
01/01/2024 00:00:00	January 2024	-449.799898064516	January 2024	1003
01/01/2024 00:00:00	January 2024	-1704.56056258065	January 2024	1101

Figure 7.10: Daily Budget table

This can be joined into our model, joining the `Calendar Full Date` values to the `Full Date` values of the `Calendar` table and the `TransLink` values to the `LinkID` values of the `Chart of Account` table.

In the next section, we'll continue our development of budget models by looking at drill-through.

Seeing the details with drill-through

So far, we've created a budget table, joined it to our model, and explained how you can use monthly and daily calculations to compare the budget to actuals from your GL transactions.

Our final step for budgeting is drill-through. Budgeting is an area where the ability to examine underlying transactions is important, so a quick method to go from a calculated summary of data to detail is valued by most users. Drill-through in Power BI is a relatively simple-to-set-up but powerful function that we can add to many reports, not just budgeting.

To add drill-through to your report, start by creating a tab on your canvas by clicking the plus sign next to the current tab. We have called ours `Drill through` so that its purpose is clear.

For our drill-through, we'll start with a table visual, and we'll add the following fields:

- `Chart of Accounts: AccountNumber`
- `Chart of Accounts: AccountName`
- `Chart of Accounts: AccountCategoryDescription`
- `GL Transactions: TransactionDate`
- `GL Transactions: Company`
- `GL Transactions: TransactionID`
- `List of Measures: GL Amount`

The table will provide the data that's returned from the drill-through, but we need to link the `Budget` table to the drill-through. This is done via the drill-through section of the **Visualizations** pane, shown in *Figure 7.11* Here, we add the `GL Amount` field from the `List of Measures` table.

AccountNumber	AccountName	AccountCategoryDescription	TransactionDate	Company	TransactionID	GL Amount +
1001	Inventory - Shirts	Inventory	08 April 2023	CC_UK	281	4,297.41
1001	Inventory - Shirts	Inventory	09 April 2023	CC_UK	321	2,383.53
1001	Inventory - Shirts	Inventory	10 April 2023	CC_UK	361	1,521.70
1001	Inventory - Shirts	Inventory	11 April 2023	CC_UK	401	3,474.75
1001	Inventory - Shirts	Inventory	12 April 2023	CC_UK	441	1,817.25
1001	Inventory - Shirts	Inventory	13 April 2023	CC_UK	481	3,766.82
1001	Inventory - Shirts	Inventory	14 April 2023	CC_UK	521	4,018.40
1001	Inventory - Shirts	Inventory	15 April 2023	CC_UK	561	1,881.23
1001	Inventory - Shirts	Inventory	15 April 2023	CC_UK	561	1,881.23
1001	Inventory - Shirts	Inventory	16 April 2023	CC_UK	641	3,779.88
1001	Inventory - Shirts	Inventory	17 April 2023	CC_UK	641	2,328.25
1001	Inventory - Shirts	Inventory	18 April 2023	CC_UK	681	1,889.94
1001	Inventory - Shirts	Inventory	19 April 2023	CC_UK	721	3,078.66
Total						**0.00**

Figure 7.11: Drill-through table

You'll also notice that when you add the `GL Amount` field to enable the drill-through, Power BI adds a back-arrow icon to the top left of the screen. This is a UI element for the user to return to the original report when they've viewed the drill-through data.

If you return to the **Budget** page and right-click any of the `GL Amount` values, you'll see a **Drill through** option in the right-click menu. Hover over **Drill through**, and you'll see **Budget Drillthrough** appear, indicating that the action will take you to the **Drill through** tab.

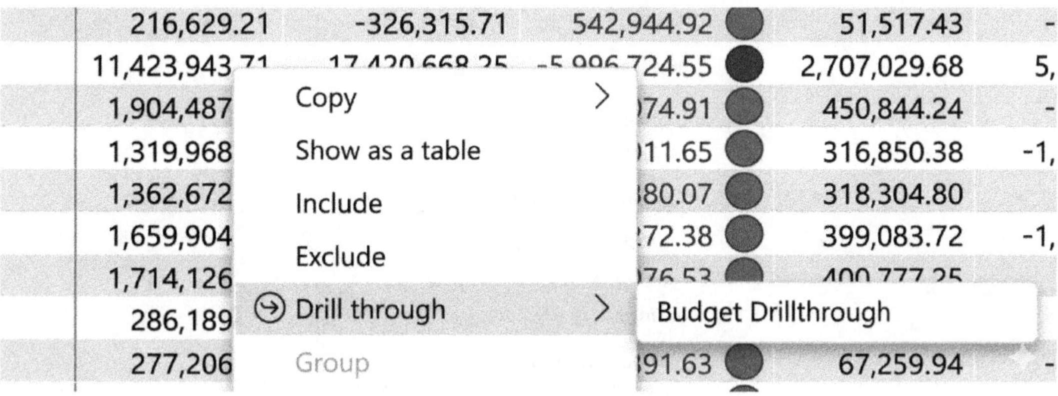

Figure 7.12: Drill through click option

When you click **Drill through**, you'll be taken to the **Drill through** tab, which will be filtered according to the state of the `Budget` table. You can't see from *Figure 7.12* that the value we right-clicked was $216,629.21. The drill-through action took us to *Figure 7.13*:

AccountNumber	AccountName	AccountCategoryDescription	TransationDate	Company	TransacionID	GL Amount
1103	Inventory - Sandals	Inventory	01 January 2024	CC_UK	11179	304.8
1103	Inventory - Sandals	Inventory	01 January 2024	CC_UK	11180	160.68
1103	Inventory - Sandals	Inventory	01 January 2024	CC_US	11217	480.74
1103	Inventory - Sandals	Inventory	01 January 2024	CC_US	11218	52.61
1103	Inventory - Sandals	Inventory	02 January 2024	CC_UK	11250	275.47
1103	Inventory - Sandals	Inventory	02 January 2024	CC_US	11270	330.17
1103	Inventory - Sandals	Inventory	03 January 2024	CC_UK	11290	11.31
1103	Inventory - Sandals	Inventory	03 January 2024	CC_US	11310	915.51
1103	Inventory - Sandals	Inventory	04 January 2024	CC_UK	11330	423.9
1103	Inventory - Sandals	Inventory	04 January 2024	CC_US	11350	177.8
1103	Inventory - Sandals	Inventory	05 January 2024	CC_UK	11370	561.7
1103	Inventory - Sandals	Inventory	05 January 2024	CC_US	11390	140.6
Total						**216,629.2**

Figure 7.13: Drill-through complete

You'll notice that drill-through filters are displayed on the right-hand side of the screen, where you will be able to change them – an action that can be useful when investigating the data.

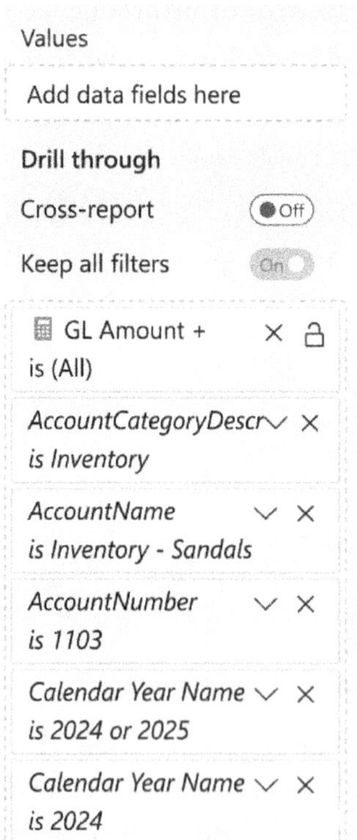

Figure 7.14: Drill-through filters

To return to the `Budget` screen (or the source of the drill-through), click the back-arrow icon in the top left of the screen. Please note that you can move the back-arrow icon anywhere on the screen.

Drill-through is very common for financial and transactional reporting. Most users, when seeing a variance or an issue, will want to view the underlying transactions; drill-through enables this. It has the benefit of being quick to set up, and you can incorporate many drill-throughs against a dataset for different scenarios.

Visuals to consider for analyzing budgets

We used a matrix and drill-through for our examples, which is often the default for highlighting the difference between the budget and actuals, as conditional formatting can be used effectively to highlight differences, and users can see numerical totals. However, depending on user preferences, here are some alternatives you may like to consider:

- **Clustered column or bar charts** with side-by-side measures that show budgets and actuals are very effective, as users can quickly spot differences between the height or length of columns/bars to identify issues. This is particularly effective in seeing the magnitude of differences through relative size.

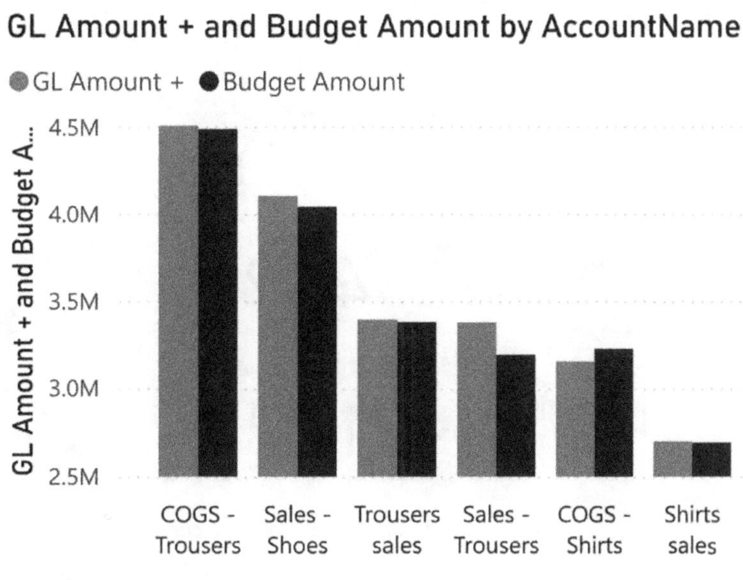

Figure 7.15: Budget as a column chart

- The **Gauge** visual shows an effective high-level view of differences through a classic speedometer style, showing how the budget compares to the actuals or vice versa. The

Gauge visual is effectively used in dashboards where users want to see performance at a glance.

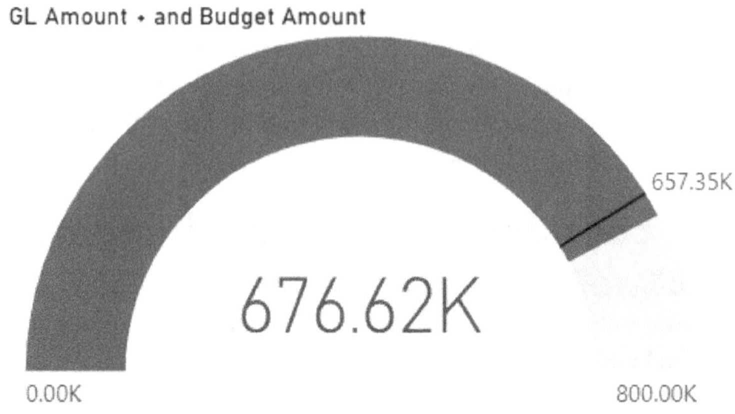

Figure 7.16: Budget as a gauge

- The **New Card** visual (still **Card (new)** in the UI at the time of writing) has great methods to show comparisons of values at a high level. Like the **Gauge** visual, the **New Card** visual is effective for at-a-glance dashboards.

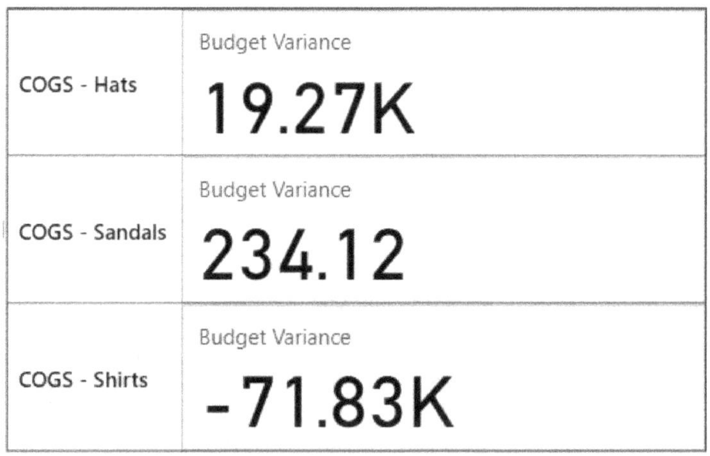

Figure 7.17: Budget as a card

- Less used for financial budgets, but still worth consideration, is the **Waterfall Chart** visual, which shows a step-by-step view of positive and negative variances.

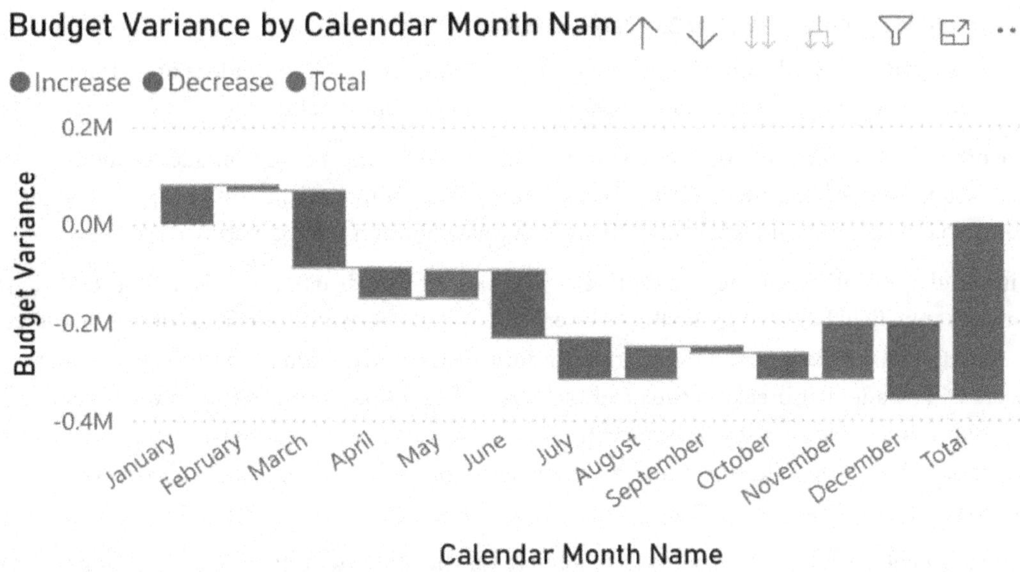

Figure 7.18: Budget as a waterfall

We encourage you to experiment and work with your users on the best visuals for your budgeting needs. There is no right or wrong answer to most areas of analytics; whatever best serves your users or business case should be the visual you use. As we mentioned, we chose the **Matrix** visual with conditional formatting for this chapter as it's the visual we most often deploy, but as you can see from the preceding content, there are many options.

For many organizations, this is everything required for budgeting. However, in some cases, there's a need for a more complex model that includes different scenarios or models. We cover this advanced topic in the final section of this chapter.

Working with multiple budget models or scenarios

So far, we've presented a reasonably simple budget model: one company and one budget. Of course, in reality, you'll probably manage budgets for multiple companies and then manage revisions to those multiple budgets. And let's not forget multiple budgeting methods. Budgets can be complex, so in this section, we have a few tips and tricks to help you deal with that complexity.

We'll start with the most important part, which is why common data structures enable easy consolidation of budgets, then move on to techniques in Power BI that'll allow you to manage multiple budget versions and revisions.

Maintaining a common structure

Unapologetically, we'll labor the point that the best advice we can provide is one of the fundamentals of data management: *maintain a common data structure.*

We often deal with the issues that result from not maintaining a common data structure, so we have a lot of experience here. As you've seen from the examples within this chapter, budget comparisons are not inherently complicated, with a common data structure.

Financial applications are good at enforcing data structures, as users are given little choice; you can't change field labels in QuickBooks or enter `TBD` into a SAP numeric field. However, we've deliberately used Excel as the foundation for budgeting, and experience tells us that some users will be adept at breaking the nicely structured workbook you carefully built – changing a few column headers, adding in some extra rows, or adding `"N/A"` to a cell where a number was required. Sure, Excel will continue to function with these changes, but it'll break Power BI when the data is loaded.

Keeping a common structure can be a challenge for the aforementioned reasons, but it's essential for consolidation if you want to work with multiple budgets and manage change over the long term. We don't have too many technical solutions for this one, other than using everything in Excel's arsenal for worksheet protection and data validations to stop users from having free rein over the worksheet. If you get defeated here, Canvas Power Apps can be built to give an Excel look and feel, where users can't make those tiny changes that break the model. It can be a battle, but it's a battle you need to win if you want to easily consolidate any Excel data.

Using Power Query to incorporate your budgets into one table

Let's start by assuming you've won the battle for a common template that users can't or just don't break. With multiple companies, organizations, or departments, you'll then have to manage multiple files, delivered at multiple times from multiple people. Power Query and some standard Microsoft tools can come to your assistance.

If your budget files are in a common SharePoint folder (which can include sub-folders), you can easily combine files by connecting to the folder from Power BI, then using Power Query to extract the data from the separate files into a common table. When selecting your data source from Power BI or Power Query, choose the option for a SharePoint folder. When you import the data, this option will allow you to append the files into a single table. A pro tip here is to add details to the Excel filename as you can also include that as a column in the data, and it'll help you classify your data.

If your files are in many locations but you can access them from Power BI, you can use the **Append** feature in Power Query to incorporate the separate files into a single table. Similar to what was mentioned in the preceding paragraph, it's a good idea to add a reference to each file so that you can classify them later. This may include the year, organization, and revision, and will be useful for slicing the data when comparing budgets.

As budgets are live and being changed frequently, you'll be able to refresh the data with any changes. As time rolls by, it's advisable to think about long-term storage of those spreadsheets beyond Excel, such as a Dataflow, Dataverse, or a SQL database.

Managing multiple budgeting methods

If you use different budgeting methods within companies or departments, you'll have to consider how you report that information in a unified manner. For example, you may use both incremental and zero-based budgeting methods within the organization, so you'll need to normalize how budgets are presented for consolidated reporting. When we say *normalized*, we refer to a method of providing a common basis for the budgets so that they can be compared. You may choose to use your incremental budget as it stands, then normalize your zero-based budget by calculating the minimum run rate to maintain the organizational plan for the year.

Exactly how you do that is up to the organization, but for our purposes, it's essential that you follow the principles from the previous section, which is to use a common data structure.

With the budgets normalized, you can work with the data on the basis of a common model, using the same fields on both. For all reporting entities, it's important to identify the budgeting method for later reference. The methods described previously can be used to import data from SharePoint or to append within Power Query and compare it back to actual business performance.

Managing budget revisions

It's a common requirement for budgets to be revised within a financial year. The business requirement may have changed, you may have seen a new competitor, or a business strategy may be so successful that you need to find ways to capitalize on or deal with the environment. Whatever has happened, your initial budget has changed, and you need to accommodate that change.

We know we're repeating ourselves, but again, common data structures will be your best friend.

After data structures, the first consideration is not to overwrite the original budget; otherwise, you'll lose history and assumptions about how and why the budget was set. When looking back, the starting assumptions may seem crazy, but they were valid assumptions at the time; you had no idea what was going to change. Revised budgets should always be new versions, separate from the original and comparable. You can do this by copying the original version and adding the version so that you can use DAX and slicers for comparison. Although you may not immediately compare the original and revised budgets, it's often a good exercise to measure the variations between actuals-to-budget versions and budget-to-budget versions. It's a good test of your budgeting processes.

If you plan to revise budgets at some point in the year, make sure you have fields that track budget versions, dates, and free-text notes for concise descriptions to describe the reasons for the change. If you didn't plan to revise your budget and subsequently revise your budget, add a field with the revision version.

Managing multiple budgets in your model

When you have multiple budgets in your model, it's important to make sure your comparisons are clearly defined and the calculations are correct. The comparative calculations we've described in this chapter will work for comparisons of multiple budgets, but you'll need to make sure the calculations are specific to the requirement.

In the case of budget complexity, we generally prefer to use DAX to "hardcode" our comparisons with clear explanations of the comparisons; the alternative is using on-screen slicers and visual or page filters. The purpose of this is that when users work with the measures, they can't change the filter context and accidentally report something that is misleading or incorrect. The explanations should be in the form of clear measure labels and the use of inline descriptions within the DAX. For anyone unsure, a well-written DAX measure with an inline description follows:

```
Budget Variance USA $ = [GL Amount USA +] - [Budget Amount USA]
// takes the absolute value of the GL and deducts from the budget amount for a
direct comparison of budget to actual values
```

In this case, we're referring to measures that calculate and filter budget values for the US, separate from other countries. We've clearly labeled the country and the currency in the measure and included a description of the purpose of the measure.

Please note that starting a new line with "//" in Power BI tells IntelliSense to ignore the text that follows as part of the calculation. We use this to document the calculation inline with the actual calculation statement.

We also like to use display folders within our `List of Measures` table to make the organization of the measures easier for us and our users.

The key to managing multiple budgets is clear organization. The calculations are rarely complicated, but you're dealing with many versions of similar data, so it's important to plan around the risks of duplication and users working with the wrong version, which is very real. In some instances, it may be the best option to use Power Query to filter out previous revisions so that the data is retained but not presented to the user. If you plan around what can go wrong with multiple versions of similar data, you should be in a good position.

In this section, we discussed the potential complexity of dealing with multiple budgets. We started by discussing the need for a consistent data structure as a foundation for success. Then, we moved on to incorporating and managing multiple methods and revisions, and how to stay on top of the process of budgeting. With some careful organization and planning, the process is manageable, and Power BI will deliver some excellent analysis for your users.

Summary

This chapter covered budgets and how you can incorporate and interrogate budgets into your data. Along the way, we also introduced some new functions in calculated tables and drill-through, both of which we're sure you'll find immensely useful across many of your Power BI reports. We ended the chapter by considering some of the options you may like to consider for visually displaying budget-to-actual variances.

In the next chapter, we turn our attention to another applied finance topic, which is inventory.

8

Managing Inventory Data

In the previous chapter, we looked at how to incorporate budgets into your financial model. We'll stay financially focused in this chapter and turn our attention to inventory, discussing how to manage inventory valuations within Power BI.

In many organizations, inventory contributes significantly to cost and value; therefore, accurate representation of inventory within reporting is important.

By the end of the chapter, you will be able to do the following:

- Grasp the differences between financial applications that provide daily snapshots and detailed inventory movement transactions
- Understand important inventory terminology
- Appreciate the measures you can use for inventory valuations

Technical requirements

To follow the worked examples in this chapter and beyond, you'll need a Windows PC with an internet connection, and you'll also need to download Power BI Desktop.

For more details, we suggest you access the following link, where Microsoft details the download process for Power BI Desktop and the PC hardware requirements:

`https://learn.microsoft.com/en-us/power-bi/fundamentals/desktop-get-the-desktop`

An example of how to handle inventory transactions in detail can be found in the `Chapter 8.pbix` file, along with the data that we used in the GitHub repository here: `https://github.com/PacktPublishing/Financial-Modeling-with-Power-BI_Packt/tree/main/Chapter8`.

Introducing inventory data

Within your financial application, inventory valuations will be handled by the General Ledger control accounts on the balance sheet. We find this generally doesn't provide enough detail, so we look to manage inventory through detailed transactional data, writing DAX calculations for items such as slow-moving stock or stock turns. As a result, we'll import transactional inventory movement data to supplement the GL data.

There are two main ways that inventory data will be recorded:

- A daily/weekly/monthly snapshot of quantities
- Detailed movements, inserting one row for every stock movement

Which option is chosen will depend on your inventory management system, although organizations that manage large volumes of inventory will generally have the latter, as the ERP system will support their inventory operations, and transactional records of each move are necessary.

In this chapter, we'll discuss how to approach both scenarios, but we'll include more detail on the latter scenario as it's more common.

Let's start with snapshot data.

Working with inventory snapshot data

The first possibility is the periodic snapshot, where inventory balances are taken at a point in time. Snapshot data may be required from applications where the underlying transactions may change, thus taking a snapshot will preserve the data history. This is easier for report generation as it requires the creation of fewer measures, as the snapshot is already in the form of a report. The basic premise is that your inventory management system will have a table that looks something like this:

Date	01-04-2023	01-04-2023	01-04-2023	01-04-2023
SKU	SH-W-L	BT-Bl-6	SH-W-L	BT-Bl-6
Location	NY1	LON1	WH-UK	WH-US
Physical Stock	10	5	50	30

Reserved	0	0	0	0
Ordered	0	0	20	20
Unit Cost	10	15	10	15

Table 8.1 – Example of inventory snapshot data

The specific columns you'll see will depend on the inventory management system and the complexity of the process in use. That said, for this table to be of any practical use, you should ensure it has at least the following values:

- Date
- Product or **Stock Keeping Unit** (**SKU**)
- Location
- Quantity, broken down by status
- Cost (total or unit cost)

For every date, product, and location, you can calculate a quantity and cost, which is a simple `SUMX` of the quantity and cost columns that we've used in previous chapters.

When working with snapshot data, you'll need to consider how often you're using the snapshot reports and how much, if any, historical data you'll need to report.

How often refers to daily/weekly/monthly/and so on snapshots. In most cases, the frequency will likely be monthly, usually on the final day of the month. That said, the nature of your business may require snapshots to monitor inventory more frequently, so weekly could be preferred. If you need daily snapshots, you're probably using a transactional inventory system. We will cover this in detail in the *Working with transactional inventory data* section.

The next decision to consider is how many snapshot reports to store, if any. In most cases, we see clients store a certain amount of history data to do period-on-period analysis of inventory trends and to manage metrics such as inventory turns. The time period may be the current financial year or rolling 3/6/12 months; again, it depends on the need within the business. Whenever you're working with historical snapshot data, you'll need to consider how to store and consolidate the data.

As each snapshot report from your financial application should have an identical column structure, one potential headache is avoided, as all of the snapshots can easily be appended in Power Query in some manner.

In terms of storage and management of the snapshots for easy reporting, here are some common options:

- Save the individual files as Excel spreadsheets to a SharePoint Online document folder, making sure each snapshot has the report date as a column. From here, you can use a SharePoint folder as a data source option within Power BI and consolidate the data using Power Query. The benefit of this approach is the ease of refreshing data when new files are added, as Power BI will use the new files that have been added upon each refresh. For performance, we recommend periodically clearing out old files that are no longer used for reporting.
- Upload the snapshot files to a SharePoint list for longer-term storage and sharing within the organization. Power Automate can help automate this process. Again, we suggest that you employ a method of limiting or purging older files for performance.
- The snapshot reports can be uploaded to a database table, such as SQL, Dataverse, or a lakehouse, which can be automated using a tool such as Power Automate or data pipelines. Using this method, you can store many years of data without concern about scale or speed of retrieval. You may want to limit the amount of data Power BI is retrieving for performance. Users often like to have the option for many years of data, but it will slow down report performance.

Here, we list three methods to store your snapshot data, and there are many more options, depending on your data architectures.

Measures for snapshot reporting

With some options for how and where to store your inventory snapshots, let's look at some common measures for inventory calculations.

SUM or SUMX

Depending on whether your source snapshot reports have totals or not, you'll certainly need a `SUM` of the total amount or a `SUMX` of amount * cost. This will be the basis of the other measures that follow. `SUM` aggregates values within the current filter context, while `SUMX` iterates row by row through a table to calculate and then sum expressions for each row.

CALCULATE

Reporting on inventory by status, you'll certainly need a number of `CALCULATE` statements, which will be similar to the following:

```
Total Qty Unrestricted =

CALCULATE(
```

```
        [Stock Qty],

        'Stock Snapshot'[Status]="Unrestricted")
```

In this case, we used stock quantity, but the measure could easily be switched to stock value. For usability, we often use field parameters to allow users to easily switch between financial values or quantities. The idea is to have a number of measures that can be used for quantities by inventory status. In this example, we're using the `Unrestricted` status as the most common status, but a `CALCULATE` statement for each status will be useful, allowing you to add and subtract the status for various analyses. We discuss this in the next section.

Period-on-period calculations

Period-on-period calculations are very common to analyze how inventory quantities and valuations are changing over time.

To start, you'll need a current inventory calculation, as follows:

```
Current Inventory =

CALCULATE(

    [Stock Qty],

    FILTER(

        ALL('Calendar'),
        'Calendar'[Date] = MAX('Calendar'[Date])
    )
)
```

The next step is a calculation that provides a quantity for last month. This will also work for inventory value if you change the quantity measure:

```
Inventory Prior Month =

CALCULATE(

    [Stock Qty],
```

```
    DATEADD('Calendar'[Date], -1, MONTH)
)
```

Here, we use the `DATEADD DAX` function to subtract one month, using `-1` and `MONTH` in the formula. Some of you may prefer tighter inventory control and use a week on week based comparison model. To do this, the preceding `Inventory Prior Month` statement can easily be changed to `Inventory Prior Week`, as follows:

```
Inventory Prior Week =

CALCULATE(

    [Stock Qty],

    DATEADD('Calendar'[Date], -7, DAY)
)
```

Within the `DATEADD` function, we do not have the option of `WEEK`, so we use `DAY` and set the increment to `-7`.

The next two measures are a simple subtraction and `DIVIDE` for the period-on-period value and percentage changes:

```
MoM Inventory Change =
[Current Inventory] - [Inventory Last Month]

MoM Inventory Change % =
DIVIDE(
    [MoM Inventory Change],
    [Inventory Last Month],
    0
)
```

By taking these DAX examples and extending based on quantities, values, and status, you'll be able to perform most essential inventory calculations we see in use with our customers.

Now that we've looked at how you can use snapshot data, let's move on to how you can use transactional data.

Working with transactional inventory data

The second model for inventory is to import stock movement transactions. This will involve more work than the snapshot example that we saw earlier, but it will yield more detail for your reporting. By its nature, transactional inventory data is generally composed of large tables, so please use the techniques from *Chapter 6, Streamlining with Power Query*, to optimize your tables by removing unnecessary columns and rows so your users will experience the fastest possible response times. In our example, we're going to start with a lean dataset, and as it is example data, it's not big enough to need optimization.

The dataset should, at a minimum, have these fields:

Date	SKU	Location	Status	Qty Change	Unit Cost
01/04/2023	SH-W-L	NY1	Purchased	10	10
01/04/2023	BT-Bl-6	LON1	Purchased	5	15
01/04/2023	SH-W-L	WH-UK	Purchased	50	10
01/04/2023	BT-Bl-6	WH-US	Purchased	30	15
01/04/2023	SH-W-L	WH-UK	Ordered	20	10
01/04/2023	BT-Bl-6	WH-US	Ordered	20	15
02/04/2023	SH-W-L	NY1	Sold	-2	10
02/04/2023	BT-Bl-6	LON1	Sold	-1	15
02/04/2023	SH-W-L	NY1	Ordered	20	10
02/04/2023	BT-Bl-6	LON1	Ordered	20	15
02/04/2023	SH-W-L	WH-UK	Transferred	-20	10
02/04/2023	BT-Bl-6	WH-US	Transferred	-20	15

Table 8.2 – Example of transactional inventory data

In our example data, we have a **Status** column. It's important to note that statuses for inventory systems will vary widely, so we're going to use some common terms we see. Your wording will probably be different, but the concepts will be similar:

- **Purchased**: Inventory that has been purchased and is available for use and in stock.
- **Ordered**: Inventory that has been ordered by a purchase order but has not arrived in stock.
- **Sold**: Inventory that has been sold to a customer and is no longer in stock. This could also be called **Completed** or **Posted**.
- **Transferred**: Stock that has been physically moved between locations.

There can be many other statuses, such as blocked or in quality control, but for the sake of simplicity, we'll just use the statuses listed.

Please note that we have positive and negative signs on our inventory. This is to show stock receipts, which are positive, and stock issues, which are negative.

Like our prior example with snapshot data, after loading the data into our model, Power BI connects the **Date** column of our inventory data to the **Date** column of our calendar table. Again, to make viewing the model easier, we've added a tab to the Model view called **Inventory** to separate the table we'll work with.

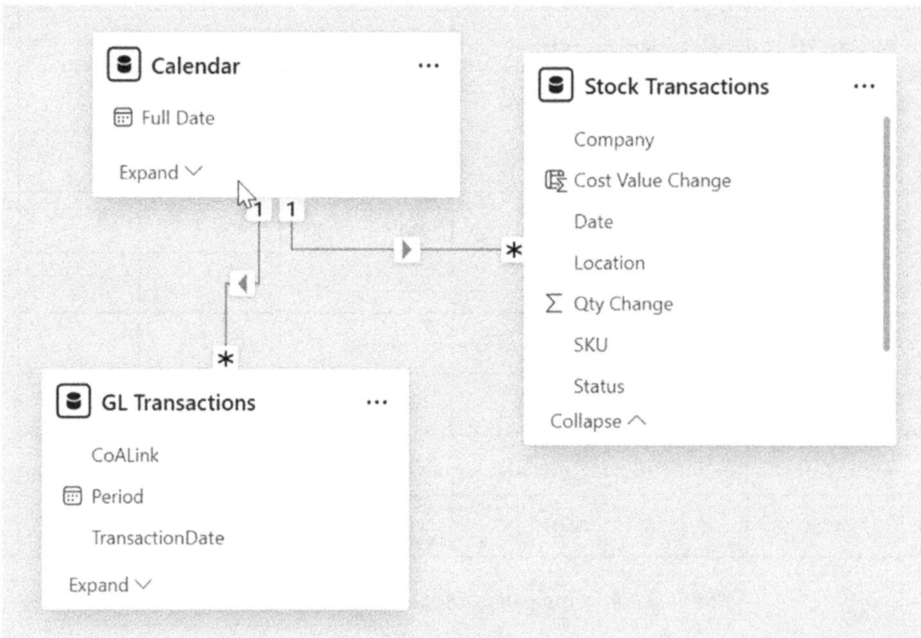

Figure 8.1: Inventory Model view

For similar reasons as before, the automatic connection of **Date** columns is expected behavior; the date is the only common field amongst our other data tables.

Now we've loaded our data, we need to add some additional dimension data to support our report requirements – in this case, **Locations** and **Products**.

Inventory-specific dimensions

When we add more context to our inventory data through dimensions such as location and products, we're able to provide a greater depth of analytics to our users, such as the following:

- Product sales performance
- Stock coverage
- How we're storing products near the sale location

These are important as they allow us to optimize our inventory for maximum efficiency; after all, stock represents a significant investment.

You'll see we already have **Locations** and **Products** columns with our **Inventory** transactions. But on closer examination, you'll notice the data only has **Location** and **Product** codes, which won't be enough for analysis, so we're also going to add the `Location` and `Product` tables to provide ourselves with more data to help with analysis.

When we add the `Product` table, we have much more detail about our inventory for detailed analysis.

After **Product**, we add the location data. The location data represents where the inventory is actually stored. In many instances, this can be at a detailed level, such as warehouse, aisle, bay, shelf, and bin. To simplify our model, we've only included the warehouse name in the `Location` table, but the principle remains the same.

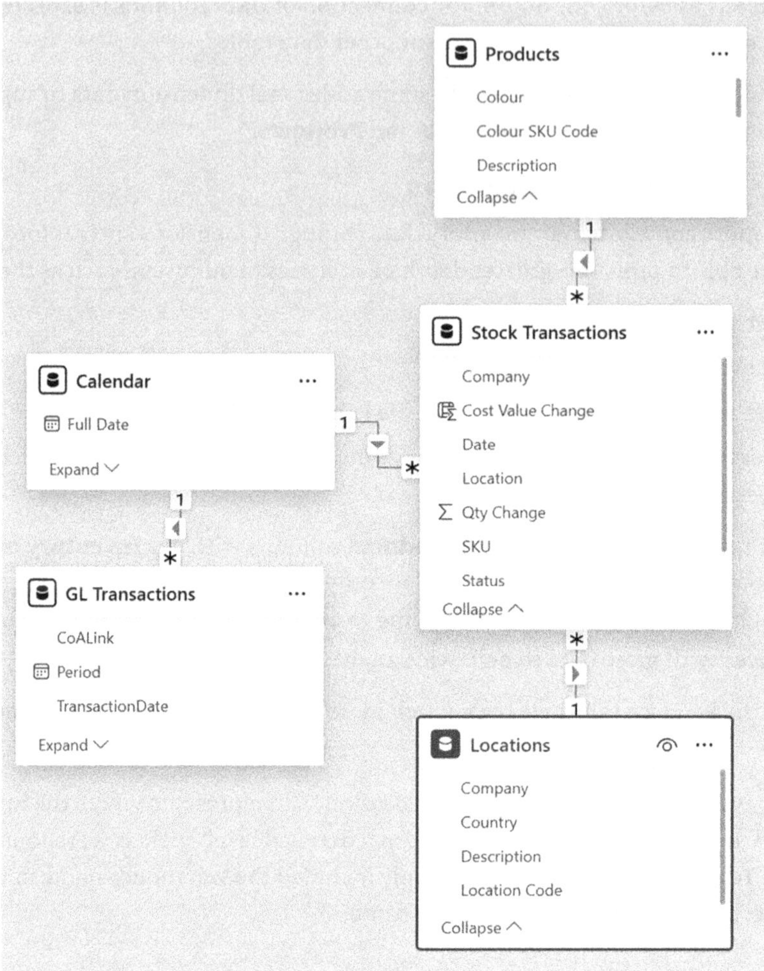

Figure 8.2: Inventory model with Locations and Products

Creating inventory measures

Now that we have our inventory data imported, we can create our measures to analyze the data.

The basics

When we have stock transactions, we need to sum the stock transactions to get the current total quantity and value. These may be further filtered by transaction type and status to create other measures to show what stock is available, ordered, reserved, and so on.

Calculating stock quantities is based on summing all stock movements in the inventory transaction table back to the earliest date from our transactional table. Our starting measure is calculated as follows:

```
Stock Qty =
CALCULATE(
    SUM('Stock Transactions'[Qty Change]),
    FILTER(
        ALL(Calendar),
        Calendar[Full Date] <= MAX('Calendar'[Full Date])
    )
)
```

As this measure sums all stock movements, regardless of the type of move, we'll only use it as the basis of other measures that will be filtered to provide the calculations we need.

There are four initial calculations we can derive from this, since we have four statuses in our stock transactions:

```
Total Qty Unrestricted =

CALCULATE(

    [Stock Qty],

    'Stock Transactions'[Status]="Unrestricted")

Total Qty Sold =

CALCULATE(

    [Stock Qty],

    'Stock Transactions'[Status]="Sold")


Total Qty Purchased =

CALCULATE(

    [Stock Qty],
```

```
    'Stock Transactions'[Status]="Purchased")

Total Qty Reserved =

CALCULATE(

    [Stock Qty],

    'Stock Transactions'[Status]="Reserved")
```

From these measures, we can start to derive additional measures, such as on-hand stock – typically defined as the total amount of the product in stock at present, whether it has been allocated to an order or not:

```
On hand stock = [Total Qty Unrestricted] + [Total Qty Reserved]
```

We can then calculate how much stock is available by including stock ordered for delivery. Please note that your organization may have rules about how it treats the availability of ordered stock based on the forecast delivery date.

```
Available to Sales Order = [Total Qty Unrestricted] - [Total Qty Reserved] +
[Total Qty Purchased]
```

Stock value calculations will, in general, follow the same pattern as the quantity calculations above, although if the total value for a specific product is not stored, we'll need to calculate it. In our dataset, the quantity and unit value are shown, so we multiply the unit value by the quantity to get the total product value based on status. There are two approaches here. The first is to create a calculated column (not a measure) in the stock transactions table, like this:

```
Cost Value Change = 'Stock Transactions'[Qty Change]*'Stock Transactions'[Unit
Cost]
```

From this, we can now create a value column of the on-hand and quantity calculations we have already done:

```
Stock Value =
CALCULATE(
    SUM('Stock Transactions'[Cost Value Change]),
    FILTER(
        ALL(Calendar),
```

```
        Calendar [Full Date] <= MAX('Calendar'[Full Date])
    )
)

Total Value Purchased =
CALCULATE(
    'Stock Transactions'[Stock Value],
    'Stock Transactions'[Status] = "Purchased"
)

Total Value Sold =
CALCULATE(
    'Stock Transactions'[Stock Value],
    'Stock Transactions'[Status] = "Sold"
)
```

The second approach is to calculate the value dynamically, using the `SUMX()` function:

```
Stock Value =
CALCULATE(
    SUMX(
        'Stock Transactions',
        'Stock Transactions'[Qty Change] * 'Stock Transactions'[Unit Cost]
    ),
    FILTER(
        ALL(Calendar),
        Calendar [Full Date] <= MAX(Calendar[Full Date])
    )
)
```

Once again, the rest of the value measures are approached in the same way. The choice of which approach will be based on your specific business needs. On the one hand, the second approach has slightly more complicated code, but it also keeps everything calculated in measures. The first approach might be easier to read, but could produce a slightly larger model. In most cases, the choice comes down to personal preference; only rarely will it really impact performance – and in that case, only testing will give a definite route to take.

The final key measure that we need to create for inventory is stock turn. This is the main measure used to assess the health of the inventory – the higher the number, the higher the overall throughput over the period. What good or bad looks like will depend entirely on the industry – a fast fashion brand may want to see inventory turned over every 2-3 months, where a luxury car retailer may be happy with once or twice a year. In any case, the calculation is the same:

```
Stock Turn = COGS/Average Inventory
```

Where:

```
Average Inventory = (Opening Stock - Closing Stock)/2
```

In our model, we already have the closing stock, but we still need to create the opening stock position:

```
Opening Stock Value =
CALCULATE(
    SUMX(
        'Stock Transactions',
        'Stock Transactions'[Qty Change] * 'Stock Transactions'[Unit Cost]
    ),
    FILTER(
        ALL(Calendar),
        Calendar [Full Date] <= MIN(Calendar[Full Date])
    )
)
```

Now we can create our average inventory:

```
Average Inventory = ([Opening Stock Value] - [Stock Value])/2
```

Then, using the COGS measure from *Chapter 4*, *Common DAX measures*, we get the following:

```
Stock Turn = [COGS]/[Average Inventory]
```

At this point, we can create some basic visuals. We will start by adding some slicers to the page for color, size, and stock location:

Figure 8.3: Slicers for the inventory on hand

Notice that the location slicer is titled **Description**. This is because it takes the title from the name of the field, rather than the table. This is easily fixed in the **Field** section of the slicer by double-clicking and changing the name:

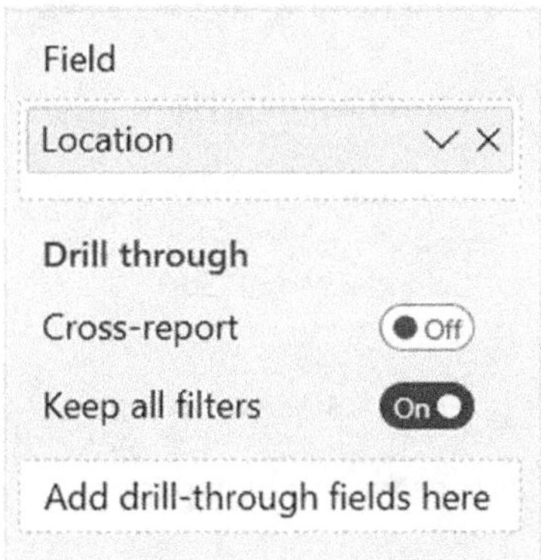

Figure 8.4: Updated field name

Now we can add a column chart, placing calendar year name and calendar month name on the *x* axis and on-hand stock on the *y* axis:

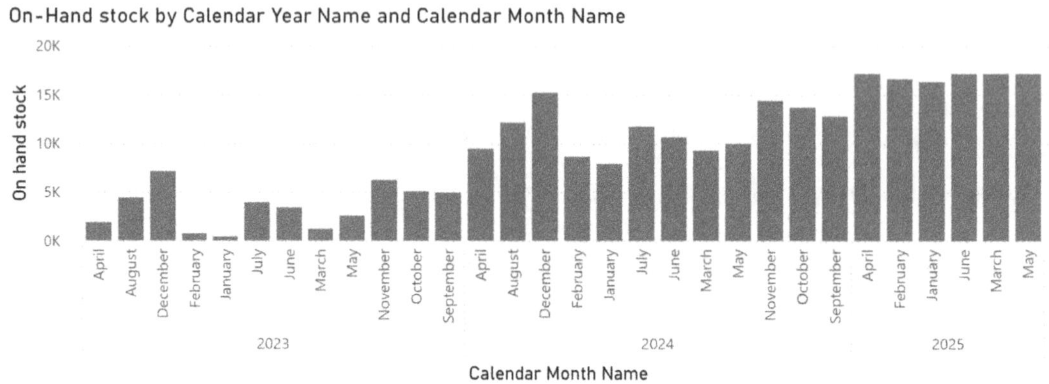

Figure 8.5: Column chart showing on-hand stock

You will notice that when sorted by month, the months are sorted alphabetically. This is easily fixed by going to the **Data** view and setting **Sort by column** as **Calendar Month Sort**:

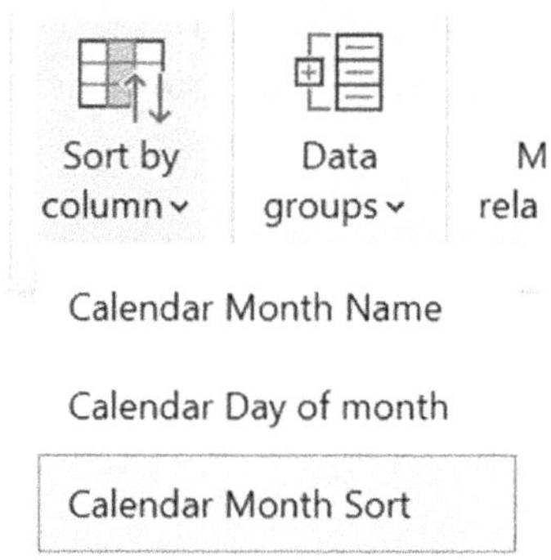

Figure 8.6: Sort by column

Now we can see that everything sorts as we might expect:

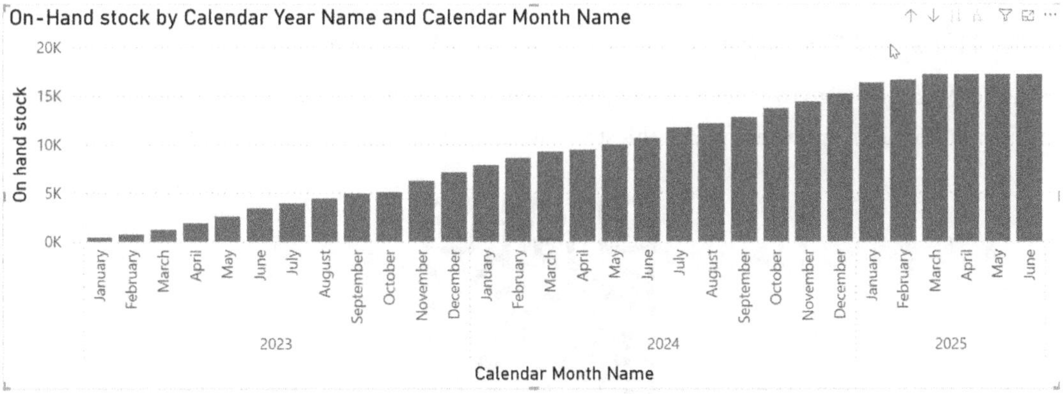

Figure 8.7: Correctly sorted chart

Of course, there will be many more analyses that you will want to do with the various measures we have created in this chapter, but the on-hand stock tends to be the most ubiquitous starting point for any inventory analysis.

Summary

In this chapter, we learned how to bring in inventory data in a couple of different ways. We covered how to add new dimensions to the model that relate only to the inventory data, and why we need to use these to add context to our measures. Finally, we created some inventory measures and created some basic visualizations of our inventory data. This is the last new dataset we will be using in this book, but in the real world, it is likely you will want to add more datasets to answer the questions you are asking of your financial data.

Get this book's PDF version and more

Scan the QR code (or go to `https://www.packtpub.com/unlock`). Search for this book by name, confirm the edition, and then follow the steps on the page.

UNLOCK NOW

Note: Keep your invoice handy. Purchases made directly from Packt don't require an invoice.

9

Creating a Suite of Financial Reports

In the previous chapter, we explained how to add inventory data to your financial model. In that chapter and throughout, we've been adding visuals to our model to view our data, although we've done very little to format the visuals or consider how the visuals become an overall report for our users. In this chapter, we will focus on some best practices for building compelling visuals in Power BI.

By the end of this chapter, you will do the following:

- Understand the need for good report design
- Appreciate why responsiveness matters
- Be confident in designing reports to user specifications
- Understand how to use different visuals for different use cases

Technical requirements

To follow the worked examples in this chapter and beyond, you'll need a Windows PC with an internet connection, and you'll also need to download Power BI Desktop.

For more details, we suggest you access the following link, where Microsoft details the download process for Power BI Desktop and the PC hardware requirements:

`https://learn.microsoft.com/en-us/power-bi/fundamentals/desktop-get-the-desktop`.

The examples outlined in this chapter can be found in the `Chapter 9.pbix` file in the GitHub repository here: `https://github.com/PacktPublishing/Financial-Modeling-with-Power-BI_Packt/tree/main/Chapter9`.

Designing a suite of reports

In *Chapter 1, Understanding Your Needs and Data Sources*, we discussed the five essential considerations when building a Power BI report. To recap, those are the following:

1. Your numbers are accurate.
2. Data is secure and appropriate for the user.
3. The reports are responsive.
4. The report has a clear purpose or answers a defined question.
5. The report layout and design are consistent, clean, and well considered.

In the preceding chapters, we covered points *1* and *2* through data management and modeling best practices. If you work with these standards, your reports should be accurate and secure, but please always check. To some extent, we covered point *3*, as a well-built model should provide responsive visuals. To be clear, when we say *responsive*, we mean fast. Reports that take time to load often lapse into disuse as users become frustrated. Time the load speed for your reports; if you're over 10 seconds, you'll need to reduce that time. While 10 seconds sounds like an incredibly short period of time, most people in a work environment are not known for their patience.

In this chapter, we'll cover the essential tips and tricks we use in every implementation to meet requirements *1* to *5* in the preceding list. Points *1* to *3* will be covered briefly, and we'll cover *4* and *5* in detail. The "rules" around the design of your reports aren't hard and fast; reporting is part art, part science.

We always endeavor to ensure users are happy with their reports, even if we're not. A good example is pie charts, which the data community tends to frown upon, an attitude we generally share. However, if a user insists on pie charts to visualize their data, the user will get pie charts to visualize their data. It's our job to advise, not to tell the user what to do. We will cover pie charts later in this chapter.

Starting with a blank canvas in Power BI can be daunting, so there are methods to avoid this from becoming a problem. Report authoring is a skill, so if you find this challenging, your skills will improve over time with practice. There are certainly some people who have a flair for report authoring, but with a few simple guidelines, anyone should be able to produce visually appealing, compelling reports. Now you know where we're heading, let's work through those five principles.

Your numbers are accurate

We're not going to dwell much on this one, as most of the previous chapters provide guidance on how to model your data, especially *Chapter 2, The Basic Model for Financial Reporting*, where we introduced data modeling techniques. The next chapter will discuss testing techniques to ensure that your numbers are accurate, along with some of the common causes of incorrect numbers. We mention it now as the first principle of successful report authoring because it's the first box to check. If your numbers aren't accurate, please don't move on to the next steps, as you'll run into the danger of producing visually appealing reports that are wrong. When this happens, users lose confidence very quickly. Getting your numbers correct can be an iterative and lengthy process, depending on the complexity of the calculations, the data sources, and the quality of the specification you're working with, but please take time to do this first. And as work progresses, check repeatedly. You've got the message, so let's move on to data security and appropriateness.

Data is secure and appropriate for the user

As with the previous section, we'll keep this one short as it's important for the context of the chapter but not an area we intend to cover in detail. We build reports around data to ensure that the visuals are correct for the data and the purpose of the report. We write reports for users or audiences when we group them. Therefore, it's important to consider your audience when building a report, ensure that the data contained within the report is appropriate for the audience, and that we're not creating an unintended security risk. Financial data can be particularly sensitive, so please consider any ramifications of users having access to data they shouldn't have access to, or don't need. In most cases, we recommend deploying Power BI reports in apps that have great tools for profiling a group of reports against an intended audience. If using workspaces for those users who need access to edit or create reports, then please review the data that can be accessed by the users. We're not going to labor this point as it's not the real subject matter for this chapter, but it's impossible to properly cover report writing without thinking about who's accessing the data and the security risks associated with it.

The reports are responsive

When talking about responsive reports, we mean the speed at which the data loads when the user clicks on the report from the app or the workspace. Your data structure, amount of data, and measures will be the primary drivers that govern this, but the choice of visuals will also have an effect. Some visuals are more demanding on Power BI than others. This doesn't mean don't use them, but you may choose to limit the use of certain visuals. We can't talk to custom visuals here, but from the standard visuals, maps and cards can be demanding, with the net effect of slowing down responsiveness. A report with 30–40 cards will certainly be slow compared to using a more efficient visual, such as a table. And yes, we've seen reports with 30–40 individual cards. Even visuals such as tables and matrices will be demanding when using large datasets, so you may need to limit the amount of data if this is an issue. Techniques such as pre-aggregation can help here, where you aggregate daily amounts using the Power Query

`GroupBy` function we described in *Chapter 6, Streamlining with Power Query*. If your reports are slow, it will generally affect usage as users become impatient. If this is the case, please don't worry, as there's generally a fix for the issue, whether that's simplifying a complex calculation, such as filtering your data, or making smarter choices with your visuals. We've experienced reports that have taken minutes to load, that was reduced to seconds with some relatively simple changes. We will speak more about this in *Chapter 10, Testing and Fine-Tuning your Data*.

This section and the previous section have been largely structural; in the next section, we'll look at the purpose of your report.

The report has a clear purpose or answers a defined question

We've seen many reports where we've struggled to understand the purpose. Maybe there was one when the report was built, but it's been lost over time, and no one can figure out why it's needed now. When planning a report, we ask the users what question they need answered or what the specific purpose is. A simple sales report showing sales revenue with time on the *X* axis and revenue on the *Y* axis may answer the question of how we are performing. Overlay a year-on-year comparison and attainment against planned revenue, and you have more meaningful data points that help users understand the nuance behind current business performance. Asking users about the purpose of a report often helps refine their thought processes about what they want and why they want it. In many instances, you may find yourself replicating an old, well-used report, but in many cases, Power BI is capable of producing much more. So, you may need to raise the expectations of your users, allowing Power BI to truly shine. Here are some questions you may like to ask:

- What is the main objective of this report?
- Who will be using this report, and how often?
- What decisions will this report help you make?
- Are there any existing reports, and what's missing in them?
- What specific business questions should this report answer?
- What are the **key performance indicators** (**KPIs**) or metrics you need?
- Are there any benchmarks or targets to compare against?

Getting practice in having friendly, open-ended conversations with users about what and why they need something is an important skill for a report author. You should be comfortable with respectfully challenging a user about their needs. We often tell users to expect to be challenged; it's our day job, and we're good at this, so our questions come from experience. With practice, you'll also become good at this. We can generally provide some input that the user wouldn't have previously considered. And if they say no, then there's no harm. More harm comes from not challenging a poorly considered report request, where you could have made a significant difference to the capability of a user to make an informed decision. We have, at times, built speculative versions of a report that we feel improve on the requirement from a user if we genuinely believe we could make a significant difference. In many cases, the users will see one or more elements they hadn't considered. They just needed someone to show them the art of the possible.

As business requirements change over time, you may need to reevaluate the questions the report is expected to answer and alter and retire reports accordingly. Regular reviews of reports are important to ensure they continue to be relevant. Many people resist retiring old reports just in case they're required again, so an archive workspace may help in removing them from daily view without deleting them. Users like the safety net that it's still there if they need it. Clutter has the general effect of overwhelming users, and if you move the report to an archive, you can easily move it back.

In the next section, we'll look at some fundamental design principles you'll want to think about when building your reports.

Report layout and design are consistent, clean, and well considered

There are a lot of vague words in that title, so what do they really mean? Let's start with *report layout and design* and *consistent*. We're going to cover the basics of report design next, but the principle here is to be consistent with how your reports look. When approaching a new report, a user shouldn't be confused by the overall appearance. Fundamentally, it needs to look broadly the same as the other reports. That means reports are instantly familiar, and users know where to look for data and have expectations about UI elements such as slicers and buttons. *Steve Krug* wrote a famous book about the usability of websites called *Don't Make Me Think*. The point was to make a website's UI so intuitive that the user doesn't have to think; they navigate to where they need to go with minimal mental effort.

To paraphrase Steve Krug, don't make your users think. Or at least, minimize how much they need to think.

We try to structure reports based on three sections, which are the following:

- Title, logo, and remove filters/slicers
- Slicers and cards
- Main report visuals

An example is shown in *Figure 9.1*:

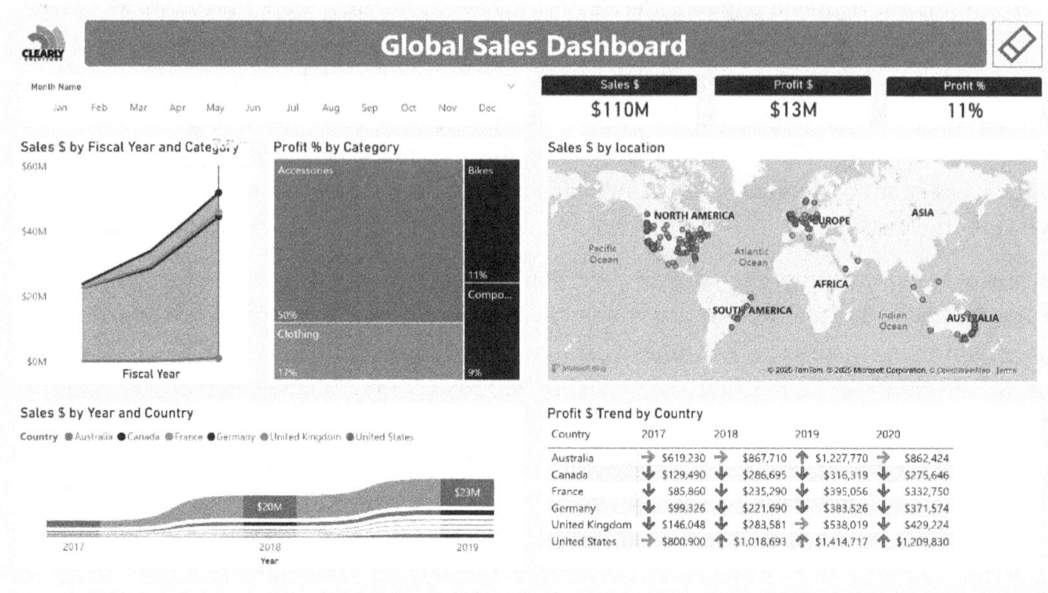

Figure 9.1: Sample dashboard structure

Consistency comes from agreeing to fundamental design principles early in the project and applying them. As we've mentioned before, they don't have to be hard and fast; you can bend a few rules, just make sure they're not abused.

Let's tackle another part of this section title, *clean*. This means making sure the lines around your visuals line up and look neat. A report shouldn't be a patchwork quilt; it should be clean and with a sense of order to the visuals that line up well and don't look like they've been victim to a scattergun approach of report design. Please refer to *Figure 9.1*, where we've used the capabilities in Power BI to line up the boxes of the visuals. It's quick and easy, so there's no excuse for a messy report. In *Figure 9.2*, we added some thicker black borders to the visuals, adjusted the alignment, changed the colors, and largely removed the negative space. What do you think?

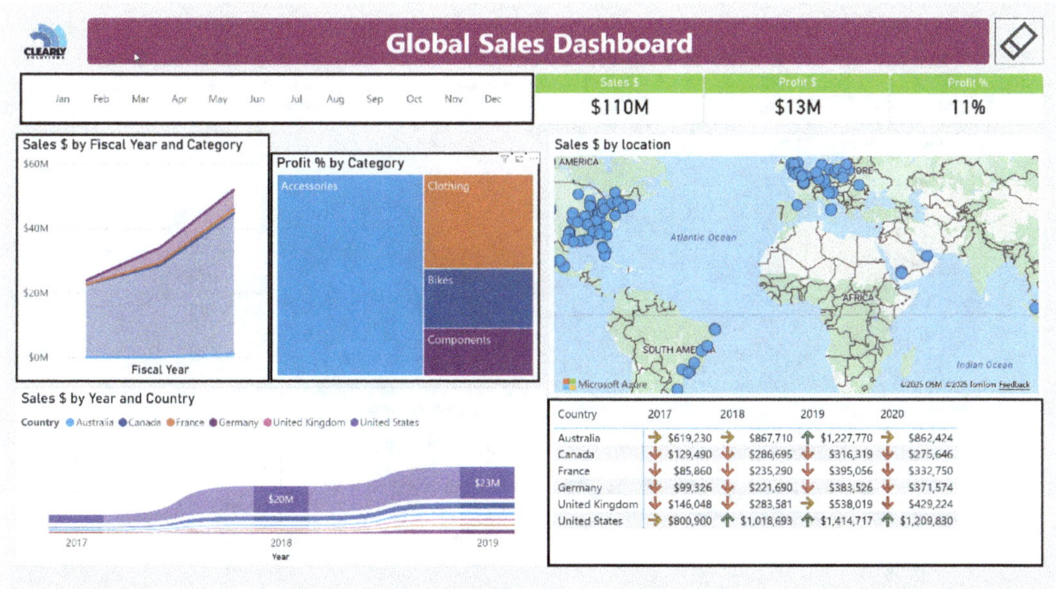

Figure 9.2: Our report with a bad design

OK, we made these changes to prove a point, but we see this on a regular basis, so the changes are a fair reflection of reality for many users.

Next, we'll look at some basics that make a difference.

Avoid garish colors

A report doesn't need to be high visibility in the event of an emergency. *Figure 9.3*, for example, has some garish colors.

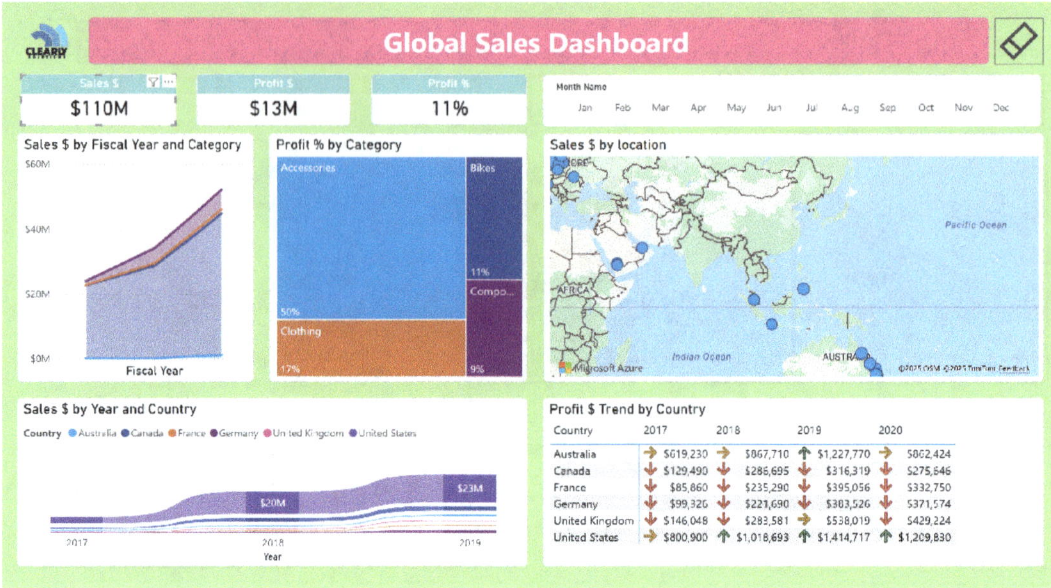

Figure 9.3: Garish colors

Garish colors introduce a lot of negatives into your reports:

- They distract from the data. Users can either be distracted from the purpose of the report or, in the worst case, fixated on why the report author decided on the use of a specific color or color scheme. We know that if we see garish colors, we'll spend a few minutes trying to work out what the author intended.
- Garish colors cause visual fatigue, especially when viewed for an extended period of time. And many reports are viewed for extended periods of time, especially when used as the basis of a meeting.
- Garish colors can be problematic for reading text when used as a background.
- Overall, they make a report look unprofessional.

Garish colors are generally excessively bright or vivid, causing the effect of clashing with other colors and dominating the report. They often have no purpose in the report, other than to indicate a poor choice by the author. Corporate color schemes are generally a good remedy to garish colors. If they're not on the list of allowed choices, they're not to be used.

Subtle, rounded boundaries

Subtle, rounded boundaries create a welcoming and friendly basis for a report that highlights the data, rather than distracting. Be careful with the use of high contrast elements within your visuals. Hard black lines around a white background visual can look dramatic, making the user focus more on the harsh contrast than the data. *Figure 9.4* has two examples, one with a light border and the other with a black border. For us, the lighter border with rounded corners is subtle and allows the user to focus on the substance of the visual, whereas the solid black border competes for attention with the visual.

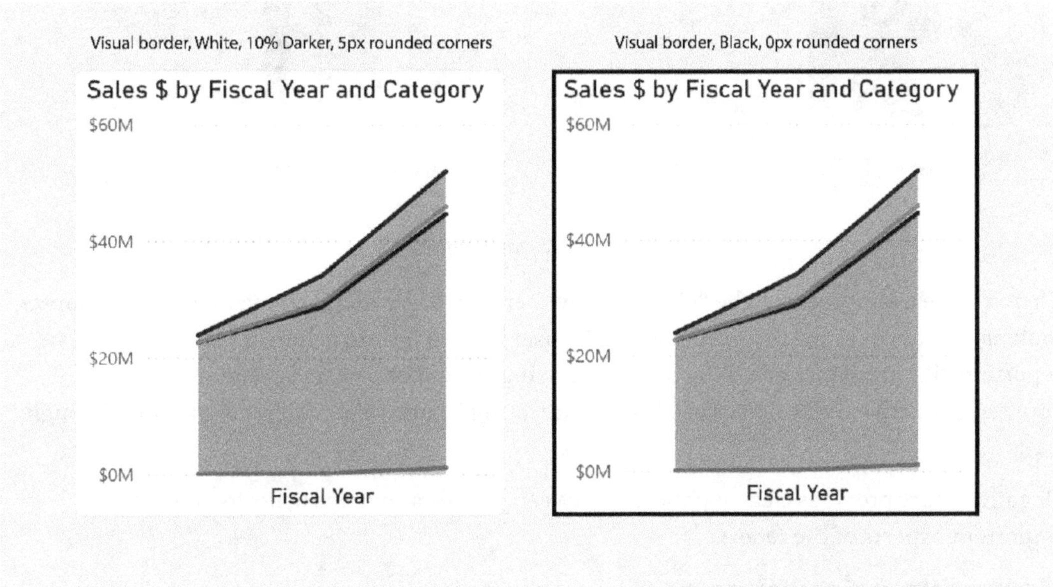

Figure 9.4: Visual border differences

To expand on a point, rounded corners are quick to implement in Power BI and have a positive effect of softening the image, often making the overall aesthetic more friendly. Rounded corners are also a hallmark of modern design, which can be more engaging for users. If you look at the user interface of most applications on your desktop, you'll see rounded corners throughout; in fact, it can be hard to spot a hard edge in a user interface.

Use negative space

Use negative space as it helps users make sense of what's in front of them. Negative space is the space not being used, which is important as it helps users focus on the individual visuals due to the clear separation between them. Close or connecting visuals make it more difficult to delineate between the separate visuals. *Figure 9.4* shows an example.

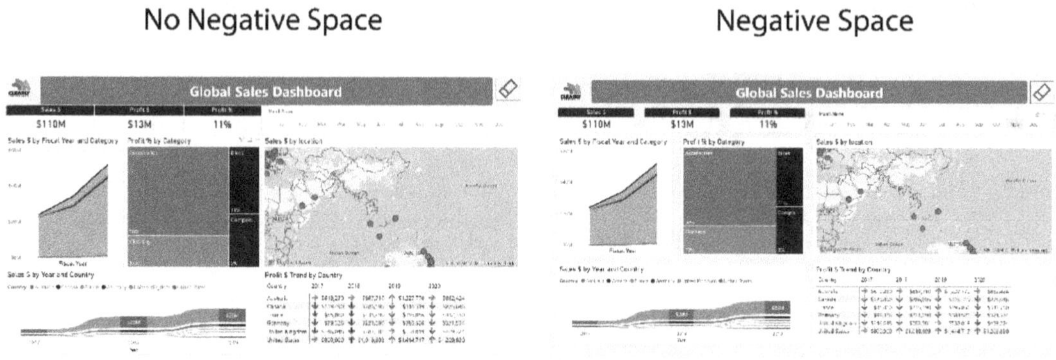

Figure 9.5: Negative space

There can be a temptation to be "efficient," deliberately using all pixels available in the canvas, looking to cram in as much as possible so the user has maximum value on a single screen. In reporting, like art, less is generally more, and using the entire canvas is generally counterproductive to the objective of communicating information and telling a story through data.

Negative space provides clear separation between visuals and helps users focus on the important aspects of the report.

Corporate color schemes

When talking to customers, we generally advise corporate color schemes. There are several reasons to do this:

- Corporate color schemes will be familiar to users and welcoming, helping to acclimate new users to reports.
- Corporate color schemes are (hopefully) well considered and pleasing in balance and tone.
- Set color schemes limit the ability of users to stray from the beaten path and experiment with their own color choices. Some will try, but it's easier to stop this behavior when there's an agreed standard.
- Corporate colors should be defined for UI elements, so the application of colors is also uniform. Again, limiting bad choices and providing a better experience to users, as they're able to digest new reports quickly due to common UI elements and colors.

Conversely, there may be reasons not to use corporate colors as the basis of the design of reports. Most commonly, this will be because the corporate identity does not offer enough contrasting shades to create meaningful, accessible reports.

If corporate colors aren't agreed upon, a logo and website are a good starting point. If these provide too few color options, there are many websites that provide color swatches based on a single choice that are complementary with hex codes, so they can be easily replicated. Good color choices are surprisingly easy.

If you need help with choosing colors, there are some great websites where you can enter a starting color, which may be from a logo, and then the website will provide options for complementary colors. Check out `https://coolors.co` or `https://imagecolorpicker.com`, where you can start with a hex code, and the sites will provide many options for attractive complementary colors. Producing attractive and professional reports isn't that difficult; you only need to remember a few key principles to make the difference between a messy and inconsistent set of reports and a clean, neat, and compelling set of reports. If you remember that the priority is the needs of the users rather than the needs of the report author, then you'll start ahead of most implementations.

In the next section, we're going to apply everything we've discussed to some of the specific requirements of financial reporting.

Key visuals for financial reporting

Now that you have a good idea of the most important aspects of report design, we're going to focus on specific visuals for financial reporting.

Before starting to build your visualizations, it's a good idea to consider the types of visuals you want to use for particular use cases. For example, if you have a single figure that you need to display, a bar chart is unlikely to be the right choice. Equally, if you are trying to see how a measure is evolving over time, then a line chart will highlight the trend far better than a table of numbers. The main use cases we will have in financial reporting will be the following:

- Magnitude
- Change over time
- Rank
- Part-to-whole

Magnitude

Visuals that use magnitude use relative size to display differences. The most common are bar and column charts, which are commonly grouped into a common category of bar charts. *Figure 9.6* shows the difference between a column chart and a bar chart.

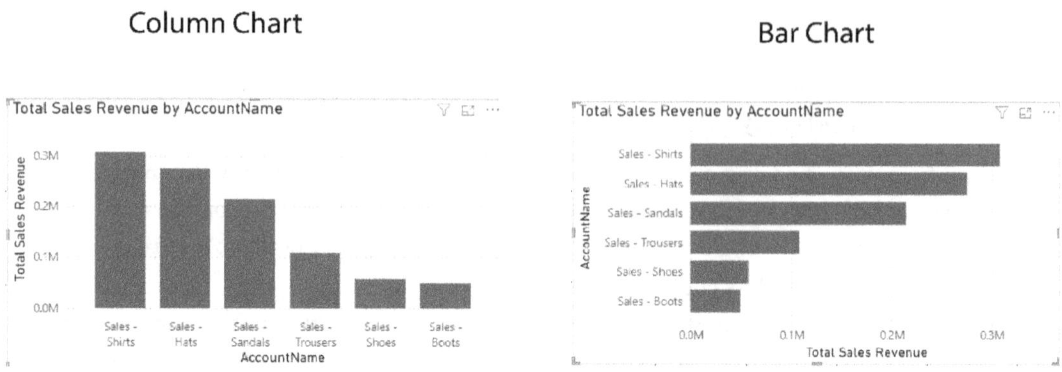

Figure 9.6: Column and bar charts

Bar and column charts are axis-based categorical visuals that use visual proportion to show the relative difference between categories. Although both bar and column charts are generally referred to as *bar charts* in daily vernacular, the distinction is that bars are horizontal and columns are vertical. The column chart is more frequently used but generally referred to as a bar chart.

In usage, both have different applications. Column charts work well to show trends over time, such as revenue by month, with time on the *X* axis and revenue amount on the *Y* axis. Bar charts are useful when you have many categories or when category names are long. Time doesn't work well on bar charts.

The variants in Power BI are stacked, 100% stacked, and clustered. In most cases, you'll see clustered column charts as the typical time-based series. If you want to break down the columns into categories, you'll use a stacked column chart that breaks down each column by category. If you want to show categories in proportion to each other, then you'll want to use a 100% stacked column chart where each column is an identical size; the difference will be in the individual category size.

All of these work for bars and columns. As we mentioned, the difference is one of specific application.

Both bars and columns use proportion to highlight the difference in categories or time periods and are highly effective visual indicators of financial patterns. Column charts are particularly effective in financial reporting, where time-focused views tend to dominate. With drill-down capabilities, it's quick to see data by years, then quarters, then months and days, effortlessly moving from high level to detail.

Beware of bars and columns when you have many categories that total similarly, as you won't benefit from the visual, unless all categories having a similar total is an important trend to identify. Conversely, when you have one category far bigger than the others, bars will be less effective as the proportions between all of the other categories will look very similar, and the chart becomes something that states we have one huge category and many smaller categories and not much else. In this instance, a snakeplot visual is ideal, although that's sadly missing from Power BI.

Change over time

Bar and column charts can be used to show change over time. This is effective when you have a restricted number of points that you want to show due to the difficulty of fitting a significant number of bars or columns on a visual. If you wanted to see a daily trend or just more granularity, you'd need to use a line chart.

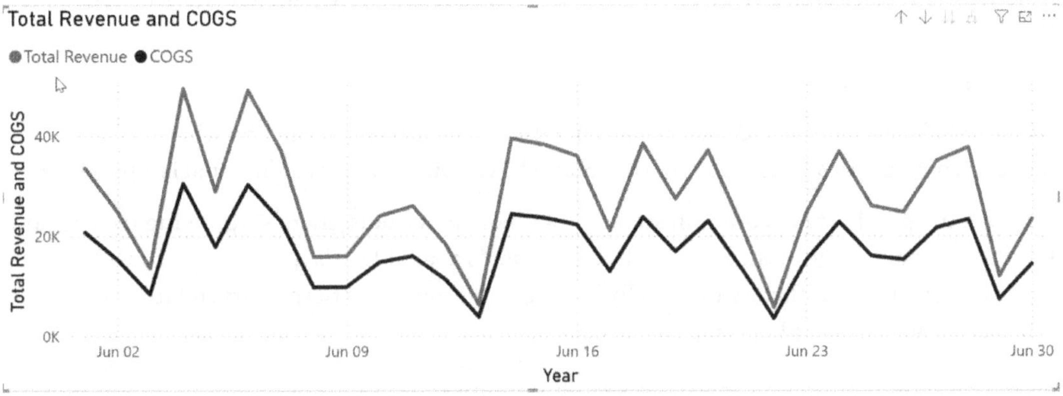

Figure 9.7: Example of a line chart

Even though the profile here is very spiky, it is still easier to comprehend the trend compared to a column chart.

When discussing line charts, we can expand the discussion to include area charts as they generally serve a similar purpose, although with a few differences. Line charts show trends and differ from columns as the trend is unbroken. Where columns and bars show differences through relative proportion, lines show trends through continuous data. Lines can be used to show multiple series on a single chart, where columns may struggle to do this as effectively. Think of how commonly they're used to show the relative performance of stock prices over time.

Lines and areas can be angular, as in *Figure 9.7*, where data points have straight connecting lines. They can also be smoothed, where Power BI applies a smoothing algorithm so data spikes aren't a distraction. Many people prefer a continuous, smooth-flowing line as a more natural reflection of a trend instead of a jagged straight-line connection of data points. Power BI allows both, so please test with your users.

Lines may be more effective than bars for showing budget versus actuals, as the relative intersections of the lines may be more explicit to the user when looking to identify issues or trends. A line chart will work well for anything showing financial trends over time, especially where multiple measures are being tracked. Areas also work well for trends, but are particularly effective when there is a cumulative nature to the data being presented. Product cost and margins over time work well with area charts, as there's an obvious relationship between them.

Part to whole

Part-to-whole shows how individual components contribute to a total. The whole is 100%, and the parts contribute to equal 100% of the total. The classic part-to-whole visual is a pie chart.

Although the pie chart is a common stalwart of reporting visuals, there's a growing recognition that the pie chart is one of the more ineffective visuals available. It's increasingly considered ineffective due to the difficulty of visually judging the proportion of the parts relative to each other. Consider this simple example:

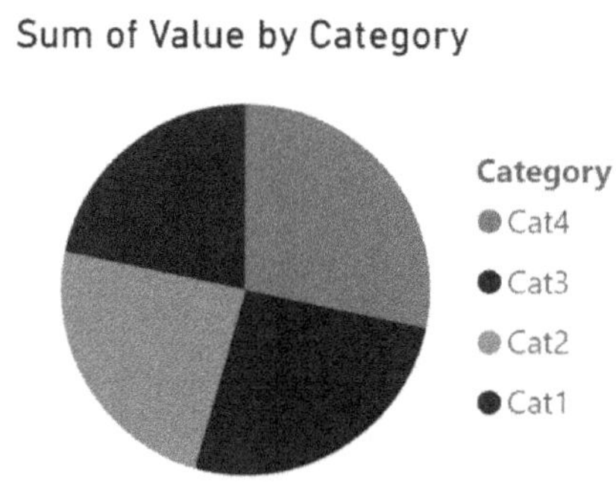

Figure 9.8: Pie chart where the difference is unclear

It is clear that **Cat3** + **Cat4** is larger than **Cat1** + **Cat2**, but is **Cat2** bigger than **Cat3**? In the absence of labels, it's difficult to tell. If we change the visual to a column chart, you can see the differences clearly:

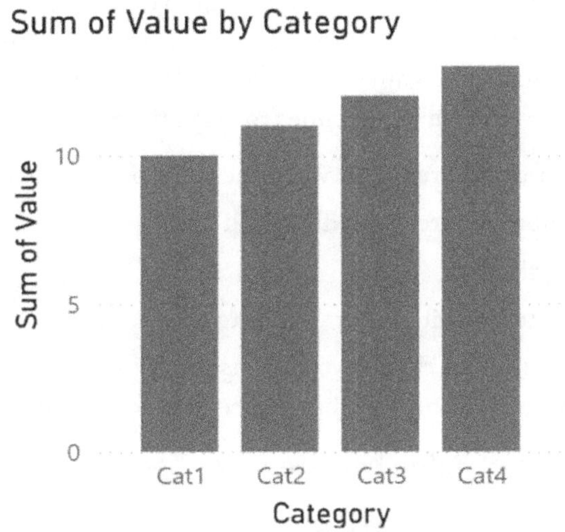

Figure 9.9: Column chart showing clear differences

And suddenly the differences are obvious. The second big problem is when there are many slices:

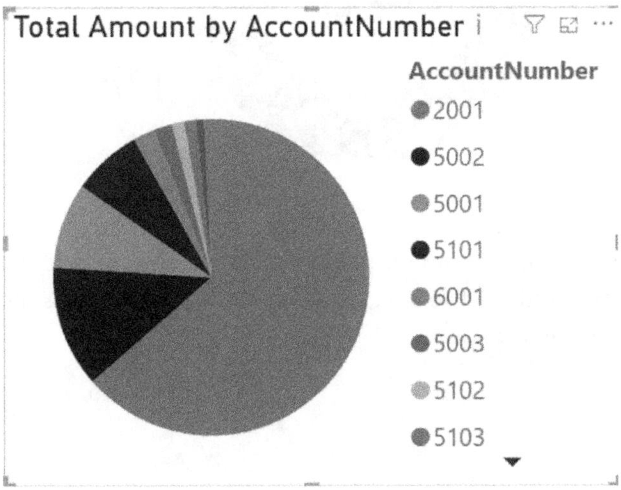

Figure 9.10: Pie chart with many sections

This example has 13 categories, and the chart is ineffective, other than highlighting that account number 2001 is far larger than the others.

The final problem is that the pie chart does not show the overall magnitude, so there will almost always be a need to use additional screen real estate to show the overall size that these are contributing to.

So, is there ever a time to use a pie chart? The first thing to note is that there is always an alternative. If you have to use one (for example, pressure from user demands to make a report look a certain way, or because the organization is so used to using them), the change may be hard to push through. There are some guidelines to make them effective:

- Ensure there is a large difference between the sizes of the categories chosen
- Minimize the number of categories displayed
- Avoid subdividing slices
- Consider how to interact with other visuals to show the magnitude

The closest relative to the pie chart that is worth consideration is the donut. This has the advantage of having a space in the middle that can be used for showing the overall total:

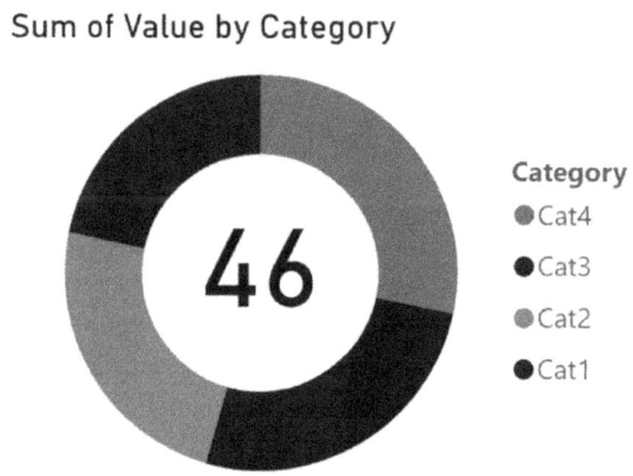

Figure 9.11: Donut chart

This addresses the third concern, but fails to deal with the issue of clarity and how easy it is to see the difference between slices. The next possibility that helps address the issue of a large number of categories is the tree map:

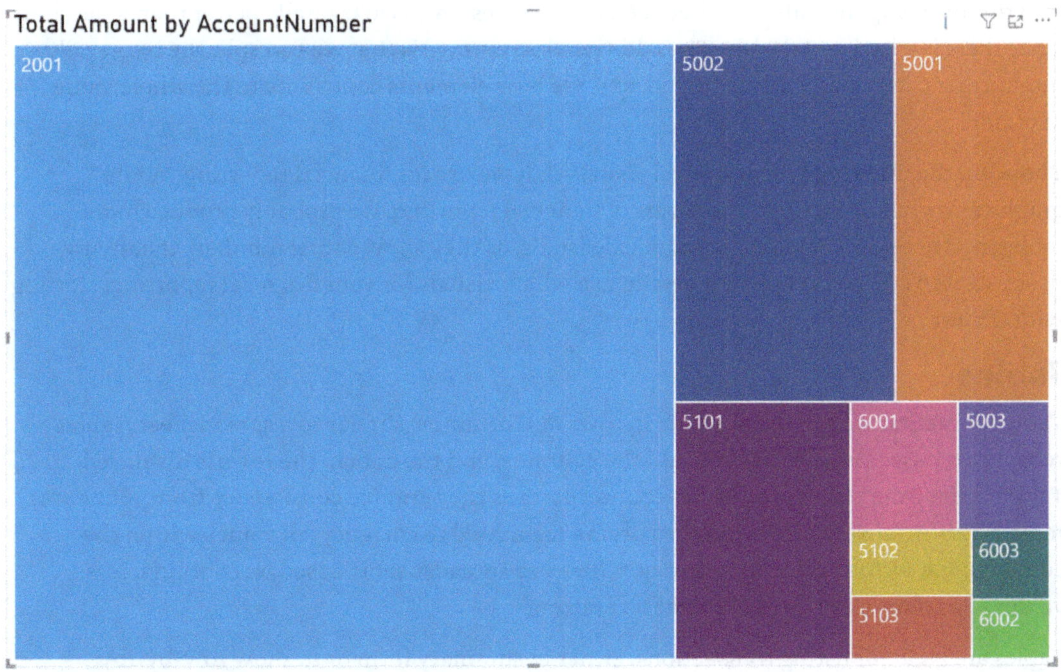

Figure 9.12: Tree map

Here, we can see that a lot of categories can be displayed easily, more clearly than can be displayed in a pie chart. That said, care still needs to be taken not to create too many categories, as the color contrast will still start to become a problem; if the smallest category is significantly smaller than the largest, it will easily be lost.

The final option we can use to visualize part-to-whole is the stacked bar or column.

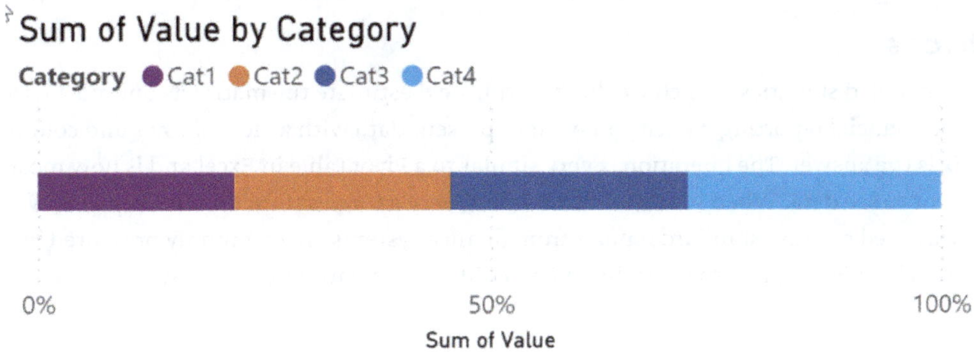

Figure 9.13: Stacked bar with differences still unclear

In terms of seeing the difference between close values, this is marginally better than a pie chart since there is a horizontal scale. The additional advantage is that we can split the bars easily into further categories, such as period, and see how elements contribute to the whole value over time.

Those are the main types of graphical visuals that we use for financial reporting. While graphical visuals are an important part of financial reporting, we probably produce more tables, matrices, and cards than graphical visuals, as they show actual numbers that many users want to see. Let's explain where to use which visuals for your financial reporting, starting with tables.

Tables

Tables or tabular visuals display data in rows and columns, similar to a spreadsheet. Tables reflect database tables in that you add the columns, and the data in the rows is displayed. Tables differ from their spreadsheet counterparts as they enforce consistency from your data model. This means that if you have a column formatted to currency, all values within the column must be formatted to currency, whereas a spreadsheet is based on coordinates, so values in a column can have different formatting.

Tables are great for listing transactions, either in summary form or to show row-by-row transactions in drill-throughs. It may be the case that you use a matrix view (explained next) as the main visual, but you'll then drill through to a table to see transactional detail when looking to interrogate the data.

You can use measures and calculated columns in tables, so there's a lot of flexibility, especially when being used for budget versus actual comparisons.

When using tables for transactions, we recommend that you filter or summarize the transactions to enable the visual to be responsive and useful to users.

Matrices

Without detailed statistics (which we don't have), we'd estimate the matrix as our most used visual for financial reporting. When you want to present data with a view of rows and columns, a matrix is the answer. The operation is very similar to a PivotTable in Excel and is how most users want to see data. When we discussed Power Query's *Unpivot* function in *Chapter 6*, we said it was used because standard reports from finance systems are commonly presented in matrices, which we unpivot to be useful in Power BI for calculations on the data.

When using the matrix visual, you have immense flexibility in how you present data, as follows:

- Row and column groupings, allowing you to align important data
- Totals and subtotals within your report
- Use of hierarchies to form data structures using expand and collapse to navigate into deeper layers of data
- Conditional formatting using colors and symbols to show important data, exceptions, and trends
- Drill-through capability, allowing users to easily navigate to underlying transactional detail within a dataset

When building your matrix, you can easily add multiple measures to view different calculations at once. Matrices combine well with field parameters, a feature that allows you to quickly change the fields used in an analysis, and a favorite feature for many users.

Most financial reports work well; the following are particularly well suited:

1. Income Statements (Profit and Loss):
    - Power BI's capability to break data down into hierarchies means you can easily group revenues, expenses, and net income by categories (e.g., product lines and regions)
    - Drillthrough means users can expand expense categories to see detailed costs and quickly identify trends or issues
2. Balance Sheets:
    - Organize assets, liabilities, and equity into clear subcategories (such as current vs. non-current)
    - The matrix visual automatically calculates and displays totals and subtotals, allowing users to identify issues and spot trends

3. Cash Flow Statements:
    - Display operating, investing, and financing cash flows in distinct sections
    - Drill down into each section to explore the sources and uses of cash in more detail
4. Budget vs. Actual Reports:
    - Set up side-by-side comparisons to highlight variances between budgets and actuals
    - Use visual cues through conditional formatting to quickly spot significant deviations

Overall, matrices provide a great way to analyze multi-dimensional data and are generally the go-to visual for most financial reporting.

Cards

The final visual we're going to call out in this section is the card. Cards are great to show anything as a big, bold part of your report. Cards are generally used for numbers, in particular KPIs, and conditional formatting options mean you can use color and text to highlight the good and the bad. The new card visual introduced in November 2023 added many options for sub-measures, helping to add more context to the main measure.

Now that we've given you an overview of the main points to consider when building your financial reports, let's work through some specific examples.

Building reports

We looked at the basic principles and the types of visuals you want to consider. Let's move on to concrete examples of some of the reports we will need.

Profit and Loss report

Now, we will look at building a **Profit and Loss** (**P&L**) report within Power BI using our financial data model.

The first element to building a P&L report is to identify the account categories we'll use to analyze our data.

Within our model, we have an **AccountCategory** field with **AR**, **COGS**, **INV**, **PROPEXP**, **SALES**, **SALEXP**, and **TAX** categories. We also have an **AccountType** field that separates *Profit and Loss* and *Balance Sheet*. To provide more flexibility with our reporting, we'll start by using a feature in Power BI called **groups**.

Step 1: Creating the category groups

To analyze our P&L by revenue and expenses, we can use the **AccountCategory** field, but we want to group the categories in a more logical manner. To do this, we'll use Groups in Power BI:

1. Right-click on the **AccountCategory** field in the data pane and select **New group**, as shown in *Figure 9.14*.

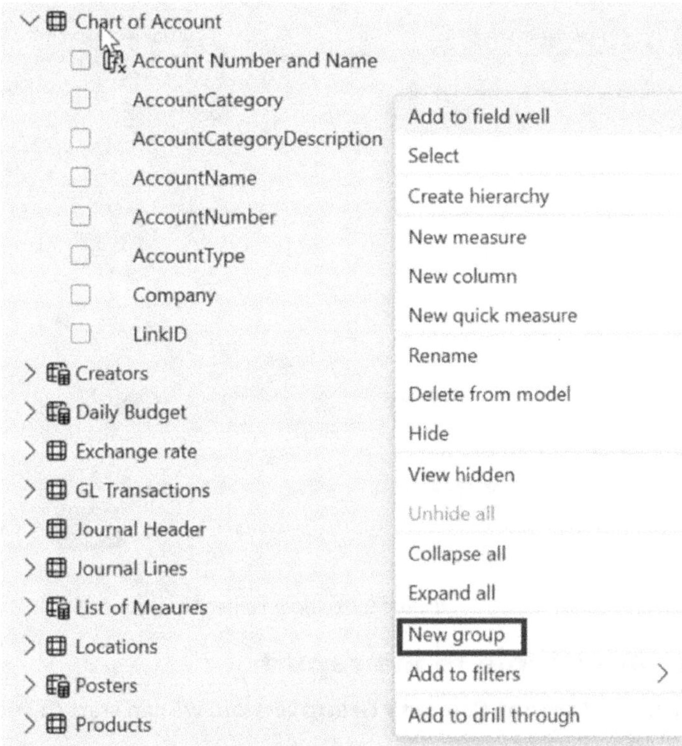

Figure 9.14: Adding a new group

2. Holding down the *Ctrl* key, select **AR** and **INV**.
3. Click **Groups**.
4. In the right-hand pane, double-click the new group name you just created, which will be called **AR & INV**. Update the group name to `Asset`.
5. Now, repeat this for **Expense**, **Liability**, and **Revenue** using the categorization shown in *Figure 9.15*.

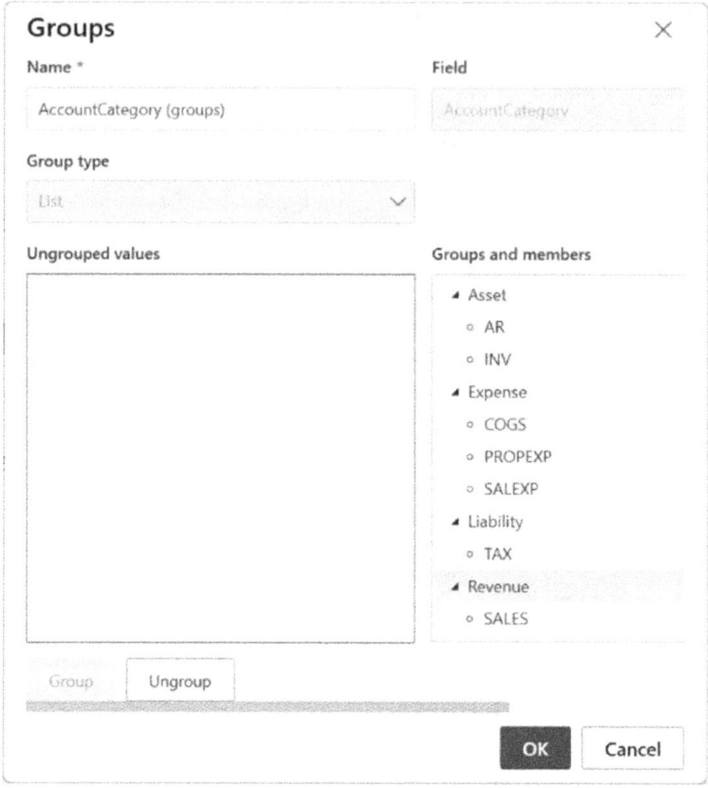

Figure 9.15: Adding category groups

Step 2: Adding a table to the report

Now that we have our **Account Category Group** section, we can start to build our report, focused on revenue and expense:

1. Add a table visual to the design pane.
2. Drag **Account Category Group** to the columns of the table, shown in *Figure 9.16*.

AccountCategory (groups)
Asset
Expense
Liability
Revenue

Figure 9.16: Category groups in the table visual

3. Now, add **Closing Balance** from the list of measures to the table:

Account Category Group	Closing Balance
Asset	11,145,786.25
Expense	13,154,458.10
Liability	-5,190,114.86
Revenue	-19,110,129.48
Total	**0.00**

Figure 9.17: Balance by category group

Step 3: Filtering the page for only P&L items

As this is a P&L report and we are interested in revenue and expense, we'll place a filter on the page to show only those categories:

1. Navigate to the **Filters** pane.
2. Drag **Account Category Group** to the section labeled **Filters on this page**.
3. Select **Revenue** and **Expense**. The page filter is shown in *Figure 9.18*.

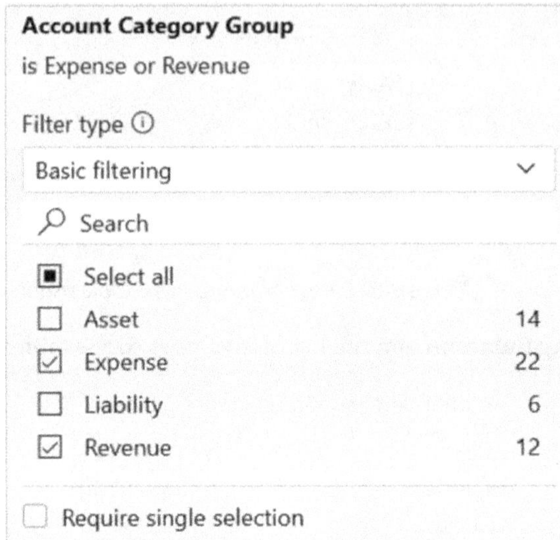

Figure 9.18: Filtering for Expense and Revenue

We now have a new report page within Power BI (*Figure 9.19*), with the page filtered to only show values for the **Expense** and **Revenue** categories, and we have a table chart that shows the closing balance for each category.

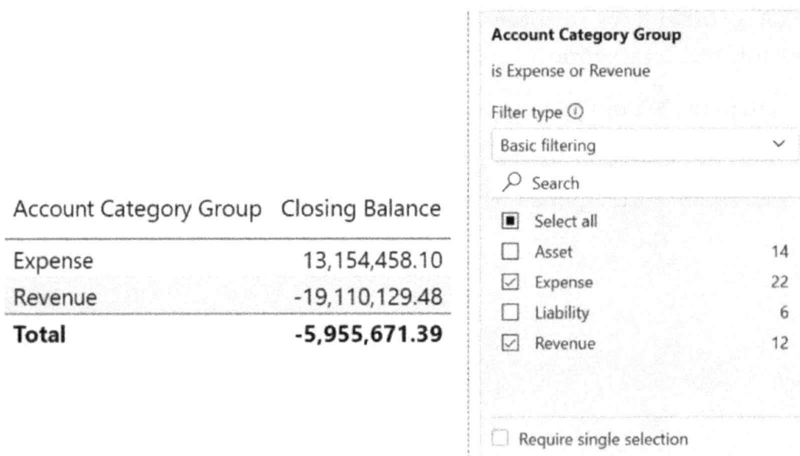

Figure 9.19: P&L report page

Step 4: Adding a column chart

We've started with a simple table on our report page; let's continue with further visuals and expansion of our P&L report:

1. Add a clustered column visual to the report page.
2. Add **Total Expenses** and **Total Revenue** to the *Y* axis on the chart.

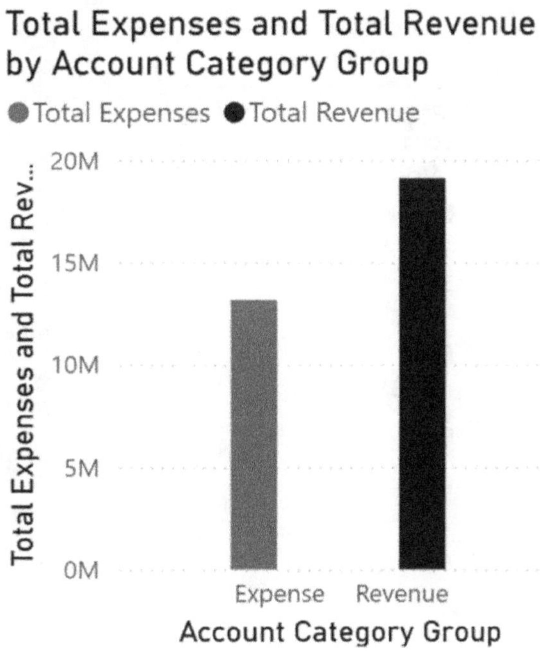

Figure 9.20: Adding a clustered column chart

Step 5: Adding the details in a matrix

A hierarchy within visuals is a powerful feature that allows us to drill down to further information. A natural hierarchy we commonly use is a date hierarchy, such as **Year**, **Quarter**, **Month**, and **Day**.

Follow these steps for our first hierarchy:

1. Start with a matrix visual.
2. Add **AccountCategory (groups)** to the rows of the matrix, then add **AccountNumber** and **AccountName** below it. This'll allow us to view groups with corresponding account numbers beneath and automatically create a hierarchy, as shown in *Figure 9.21*.

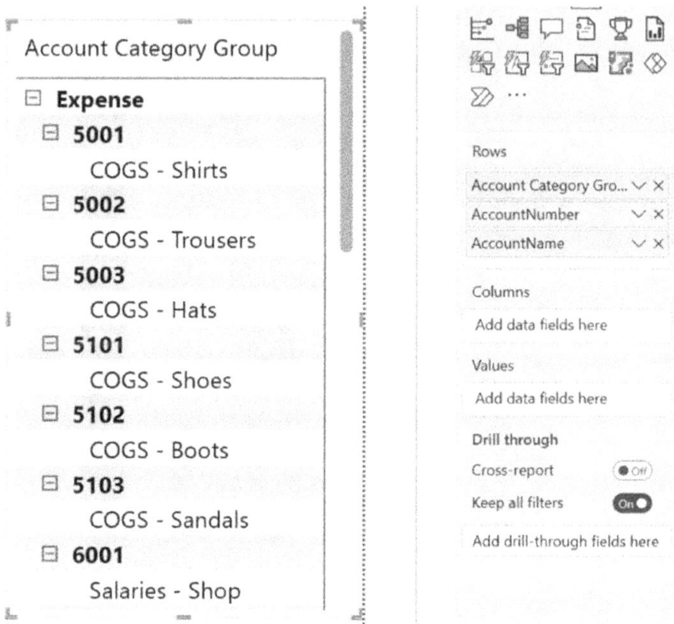

Figure 9.21: Matrix chart with account categories

We now need some columns for our matrix, and for this, we'll use the `Full Date` column from the `Calendar` table.

To do this, add the full date to the columns on the matrix within the **Visualizations** pane.

Within our matrix, we have rows and columns, so we need to add values, which we place in the value box of the matrix. From our data pane, we'll use the **Closing Balance** measure as the values. By dragging this measure as the values for the matrix, we're now able to visualize closing balance values by account category groups, with account numbers and names, over a full date period. See *Figure 9.22* for how your matrix will look.

Account Category Group	2023	2024	2025	**Total**
⊟ **Expense**	**4,957,271.10**	**11,525,352.62**	**13,154,458.10**	**13,154,458.10**
⊟ **5001**	**1,204,102.21**	**2,777,720.06**	**3,153,241.06**	**3,153,241.06**
COGS - Shirts	1,204,102.21	2,777,720.06	3,153,241.06	**3,153,241.06**
⊟ **5002**	**1,719,689.47**	**3,967,815.91**	**4,503,883.02**	**4,503,883.02**
COGS - Trousers	1,719,689.47	3,967,815.91	4,503,883.02	**4,503,883.02**
⊟ **5003**	**258,665.06**	**597,145.78**	**676,616.40**	**676,616.40**
COGS - Hats	258,665.06	597,145.78	676,616.40	**676,616.40**
⊟ **5101**	**980,379.81**	**2,262,585.14**	**2,566,479.15**	**2,566,479.15**
COGS - Shoes	980,379.81	2,262,585.14	2,566,479.15	**2,566,479.15**
⊟ **5102**	**173,093.39**	**397,703.49**	**451,863.86**	**451,863.86**
COGS - Boots	173,093.39	397,703.49	451,863.86	**451,863.86**
⊟ **5103**	**165,341.16**	**382,382.23**	**434,374.60**	**434,374.60**
COGS - Sandals	165,341.16	382,382.23	434,374.60	**434,374.60**
⊟ **6001**	**264,000.00**	**660,000.00**	**792,000.00**	**792,000.00**
Salaries - Shop	264,000.00	660,000.00	792,000.00	**792,000.00**
⊟ **6002**	**88,000.00**	**220,000.00**	**264,000.00**	**264,000.00**
Salaries - Warehouse	88,000.00	220,000.00	264,000.00	**264,000.00**
⊟ **6003**	**104,000.00**	**260,000.00**	**312,000.00**	**312,000.00**
Salaries - Office	104,000.00	260,000.00	312,000.00	**312,000.00**
⊟ **Revenue**	**-7,295,422.99**	**-16,833,022.41**	**-19,110,129.48**	**-19,110,129.48**
⊟ **4001**	**-2,056,571.13**	**-4,744,324.27**	**-5,385,374.38**	**-5,385,374.38**
Sales - Shirts	-1,044,680.42	-2,368,207.56	-2,685,460.55	**-2,685,460.55**
Shirts sales	-1,011,890.71	-2,376,116.70	-2,699,913.83	**-2,699,913.83**
Total	**-2,338,151.88**	**-5,307,669.79**	**-5,955,671.39**	**-5,955,671.39**

Figure 9.22: Fields in the matrix

A matrix visual will automatically add row and column totals to our P&L report page, which we don't need. To remove the column totals from the **Visualization** pane, select the *format* icon at the top, and toggle the **Column subtotals** switch to **Off**.

Account Category Group	2023	2024	2025
⊞ Expense	4,957,271.10	11,525,352.62	13,154,458.10
⊞ Revenue	-7,295,422.99	-16,833,022.41	-19,110,129.48
Total	**-2,338,151.88**	**-5,307,669.79**	**-5,955,671.39**

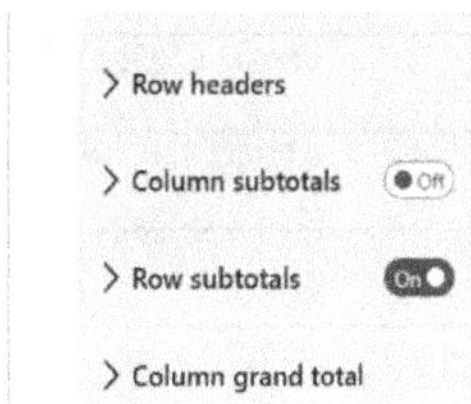

Figure 9.23: Matrix chart without column subtotals

To interact and drill down by columns or rows, these can be selected from the top of the matrix visual shown in *Figure 9.24*.

Year	2023			2024		
Account Category Group	Qtr 2	Qtr 3	Qtr 4	Qtr 1	Qtr 2	Qtr 3
⊟ **Expense**	**1,604,858.92**	**3,274,220.32**	**4,957,271.10**	**6,585,367.61**	**8,260,834.04**	**9,911,604.36**
⊟ **5001**	**398,949.16**	**799,538.71**	**1,204,102.21**	**1,594,063.09**	**1,996,498.28**	**2,392,409.46**
COGS - Shirts	398,949.16	799,538.71	1,204,102.21	1,594,063.09	1,996,498.28	2,392,409.46
⊟ **5002**	**569,464.58**	**1,141,861.49**	**1,719,689.47**	**2,276,214.14**	**2,850,851.88**	**3,416,485.85**
COGS - Trousers	569,464.58	1,141,861.49	1,719,689.47	2,276,214.14	2,850,851.88	3,416,485.85
⊟ **5003**	**85,691.03**	**171,746.91**	**258,665.06**	**342,413.62**	**428,920.38**	**514,088.65**
COGS - Hats	85,691.03	171,746.91	258,665.06	342,413.62	428,920.38	514,088.65
⊟ **5101**	**324,734.51**	**651,078.09**	**980,379.81**	**1,297,647.77**	**1,625,369.53**	**1,947,923.74**
COGS - Shoes	324,734.51	651,078.09	980,379.81	1,297,647.77	1,625,369.53	1,947,923.74
⊟ **5102**	**57,170.12**	**115,215.79**	**173,093.39**	**228,883.52**	**286,417.99**	**342,741.77**
COGS - Boots	57,170.12	115,215.79	173,093.39	228,883.52	286,417.99	342,741.77
⊟ **5103**	**54,849.52**	**109,779.32**	**165,341.16**	**219,145.46**	**274,775.98**	**328,954.88**
COGS - Sandals	54,849.52	109,779.32	165,341.16	219,145.46	274,775.98	328,954.88
⊟ **6001**	**66,000.00**	**165,000.00**	**264,000.00**	**363,000.00**	**462,000.00**	**561,000.00**
Salaries - Shop	66,000.00	165,000.00	264,000.00	363,000.00	462,000.00	561,000.00
⊟ **6002**	**22,000.00**	**55,000.00**	**88,000.00**	**121,000.00**	**154,000.00**	**187,000.00**
Salaries - Warehouse	22,000.00	55,000.00	88,000.00	121,000.00	154,000.00	187,000.00
⊟ **6003**	**26,000.00**	**65,000.00**	**104,000.00**	**143,000.00**	**182,000.00**	**221,000.00**
Total	**-811,333.53**	**-1,571,110.56**	**-2,338,151.88**	**-3,071,067.98**	**-3,832,347.83**	**-4,580,462.80**

Figure 9.24: Interacting with the matrix drilldown

Our matrix chart is now complete. We have the main visualizations within our P&L. We will now focus on adding some prominent numbers, slicers to allow filtering, and a label for the report name.

Step 6: Adding the gross margin

Our next visual will be to show **Gross Margin %** over financial years and months. A line chart is a great way to visualize percentage change over time. To do this, follow these steps:

1. Add a line chart to the report.
2. Drag **Gross Margin %** onto the *Y* axis.
3. Drag **Calendar Year** and **Calendar Quarter** onto the *X* axis.
4. From the ellipsis in the top-right corner, go to **Sort axis** and select the year and quarter, then select **Sort ascending**.

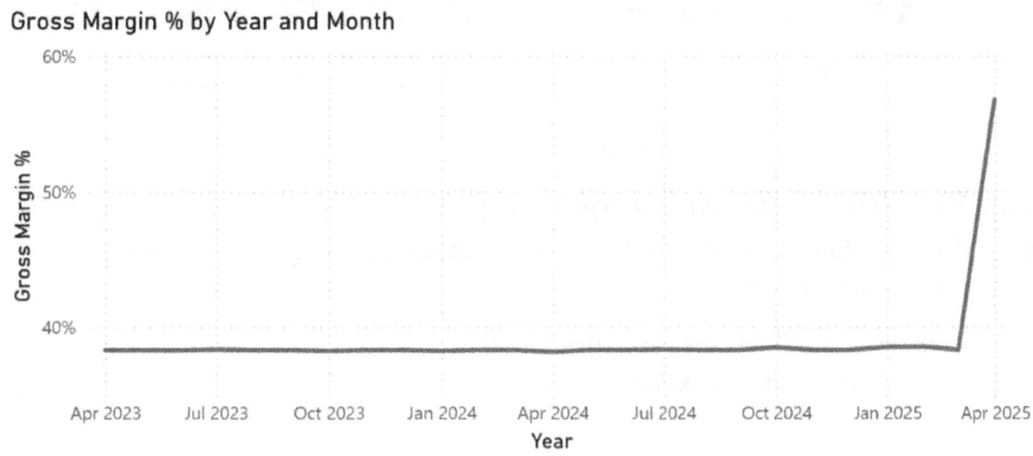

Figure 9.25: Gross Margin % over time

Step 7: The headline figures

Our next set of visuals on our P&L report page will be to present prominent figures so our users can quickly see the most important data they need. We'll use Power BI cards to display these numbers:

1. Create a new measure for `Gross Profit`:

```
Gross Profit = ([Total Revenue]-[Total Expenses])
```

2. Drag a card visual into the report canvas.
3. Drag the new **Gross Profit** measure onto the **Fields** area of the card.
4. From the **Format** tab, choose the **Visual** option, then turn **Category Label** off.
5. On the **Format** tab, go to **General** and turn on the title.
6. Add a title: `Gross Profit`.
7. Set the text color to white.
8. Set the background to dark blue.
9. On the **Visual** tab, turn off the category label.
10. Repeat this procedure for total revenue, total expense, and gross margin:

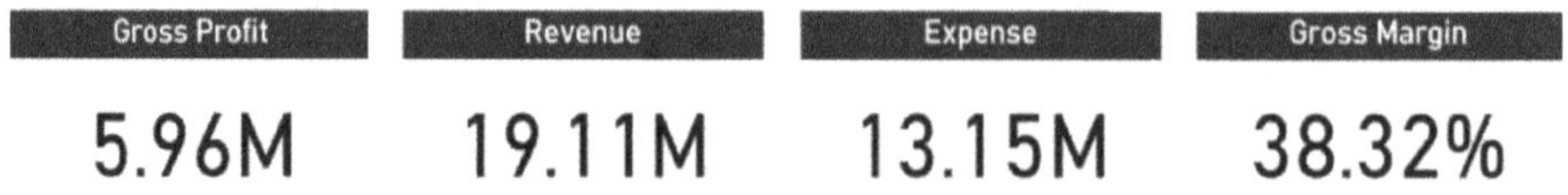

Figure 9.26: Cards to display figures

Step 8: Adding a gross margin gauge

Our final visual before slicers and headings will be a gauge; this is a great visual to show percentages and target values:

1. Drag the gauge visual onto the report design.
2. Now, add **Gross Margin %** as the value.

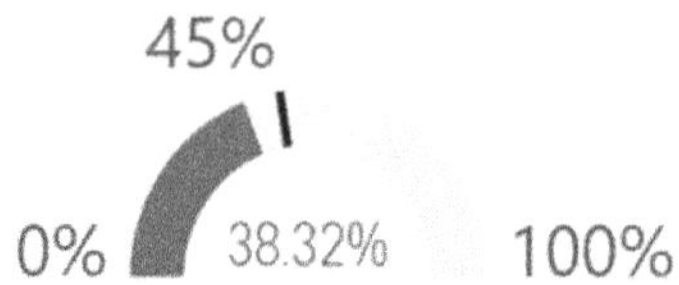

Figure 9.27: Gross margin gauge

3. Go to the **Format** tab.
4. Expand the **Gauge axis** dropdown and set the target to **0.45** (i.e., 45%).

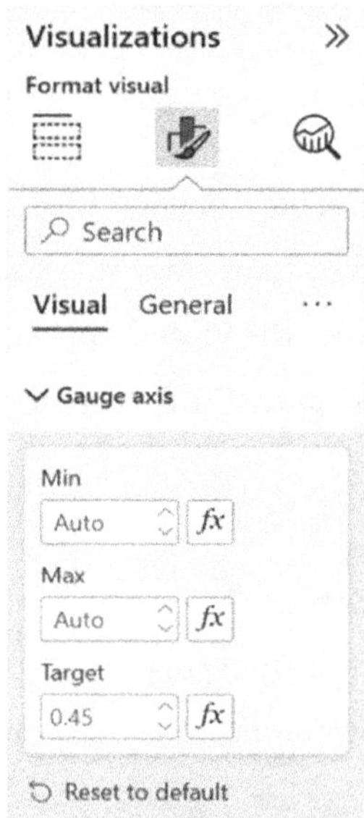

Figure 9.28: Gross margin gauge format

5. Under the **General** tab, make sure the title is switched on and set the title to **Gross Margin %**.
6. Under **Data labels**, select **Value decimal places** and enter `0` to not show decimal places.
7. Format the background as dark blue and the text as white.

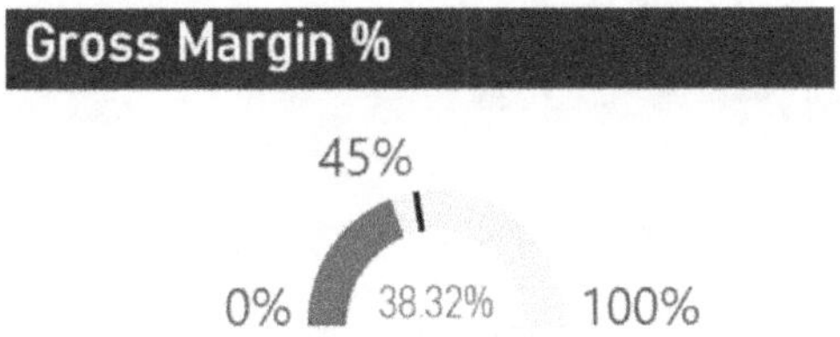

Figure 9.29: The finished gauge

Step 9: Adding slicers

Slicers offer flexibility to reports within Power BI; they can filter visuals on a report page, across all tabs on a report, and they can be synchronized to show selected values or ranges, such as financial year, quarter, or month. In our P&L report, we'll add slicers for **Account Name**, **Account Number**, and the financial date hierarchy:

1. Drag a slicer visual onto the report canvas.
2. Add the calendar year, quarter, and month fields from the calendar to the values of the slicer.
3. Go to the **Format** tab and the **Slicer** settings.
4. Change **Style** to **Dropdown**.
5. Go to the **General** tab.
6. Turn on the title.
7. Set the title to **Year**, **Quarter**, and **Month**.
8. Set the background to dark blue and the text to white.

Repeat this to create a second slicer for **Account Number and Name**. The finished date slicer is shown in *Figure 9.30*.

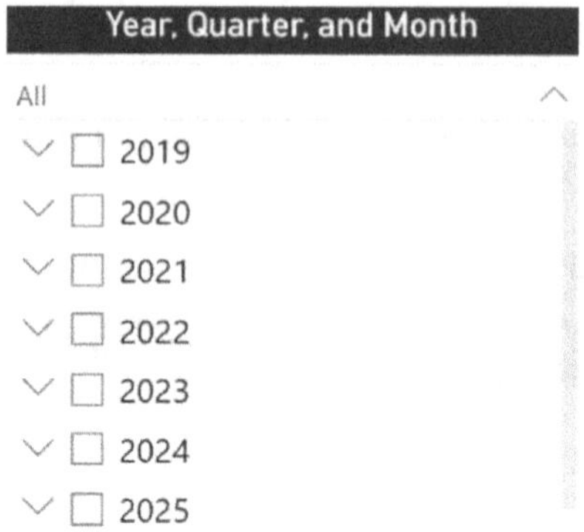

Figure 9.30: Date slicer

Step 10: Adding a title

The next step is to add a title to our report:

1. From the ribbon, go to **Insert**.
2. Choose **Text box** and add this to the report.
3. Add a title: `Profit and Loss`.
4. Set the font to bold and the size to 28.
5. Position this at the top left of the page.

Figure 9.31: Inserting elements, Text box, and logo

6. Finally, from the **Insert** tab, go to **Shapes** and choose a *line*.
7. Draw that across the page under the title.
8. On the **Format** tab for the line, go to **Shape,** then **Style,** and set the color to blue.

The report we have built now helps us answer key questions in the business, such as gross profit, gross profit %, revenue, expense by account category groups, account numbers, and over financial periods such as year, quarter, and month.

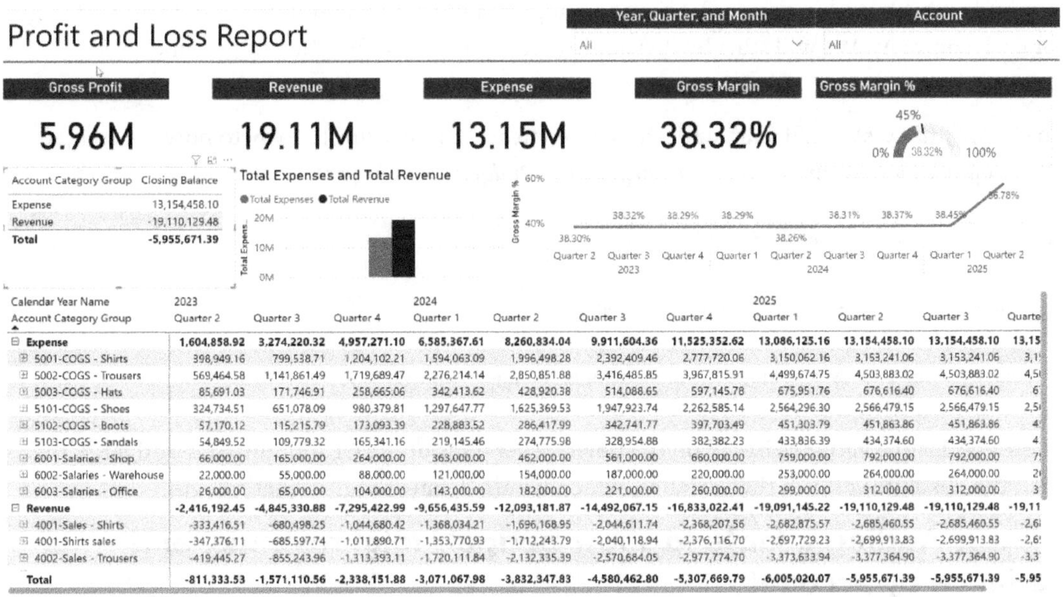

Figure 9.32: Completed P&L report

In a similar way, we can create a Balance Sheet report. While we have included an example of a balance sheet in the Power BI download, we have not gone into detail on how to create it, since the process is almost identical to what we have done for P&L, but with some different measures and filters.

Now that we have a detailed analysis of the actuals, we must turn our attention to business performance. A profit of $1 million would be amazing for a "mom and pop" grocery store, but a drop in the ocean for the likes of Amazon. To really assess the performance of the business, you need to look at how the actuals compare to the budget. We created a basic budget report in *Chapter 7, Incorporating Budgets and Targets*, and we'll now add a more detailed analysis to our report.

Budget variance report

A budget variance report is a beneficial key report, one that can be developed in Power BI with relative ease, as the data can be modeled with Power BI. Now that we have budget information and actuals within our Power BI, we can create a budget variance report.

Our budget table within the model has the budget amount by account number, by period, and for each company. We will start by developing a report that shows the budget amount by account number.

To simplify the task, we'll start with three new measures (in a similar way to how we created a *GL Amount + measure* in *Chapter 7, Incorporating Budgets and Targets*):

```
Budget Amount + = ABS([Budget Amount])

Budget Variance + = [GL Amount +]-[Budget Amount +]

Budget Variance % = [Budget Variance +]/[Budget Amount +]
```

The second is the variance based on the positive versions of the GL amount and budget, rather than the absolute value of the variance, which would be meaningless. Let's begin.

Step 1: Adding a table to show budget, total revenue, and variance by account

1. Add a new page to the Power BI file.
2. Drag a table visual onto the page.
3. From **Chart of Accounts**, drag **Account Number and Name** to the table fields.
4. Now, from **Measures**, add **Budget Amount + as shown in figure 9.33**.

Account Number and Name ▲	Budget Amount +
1001-Inventory - Shirts	1,502,303.35
1001-Shirts inventory	1,575,773.14
1002-Inventory - Trousers	2,110,658.46
1002-trousers inventory	2,249,657.71
1003-hats inventory	338,463.03
1003-Inventory - Hats	335,404.54
1101-Inventory - Shoes	2,589,873.10
1102-Inventory - Boots	446,673.43
1103-Inventory - Sandals	430,879.05
Total	**930,824.07**

Figure 9.33: Budget by account

5. As we want to show this against revenue, we will add page-level filters on the account category.

6. Drag **AccountCategoryGroup** from **Chart of Accounts** to the page filters.
7. Select **Revenue**.

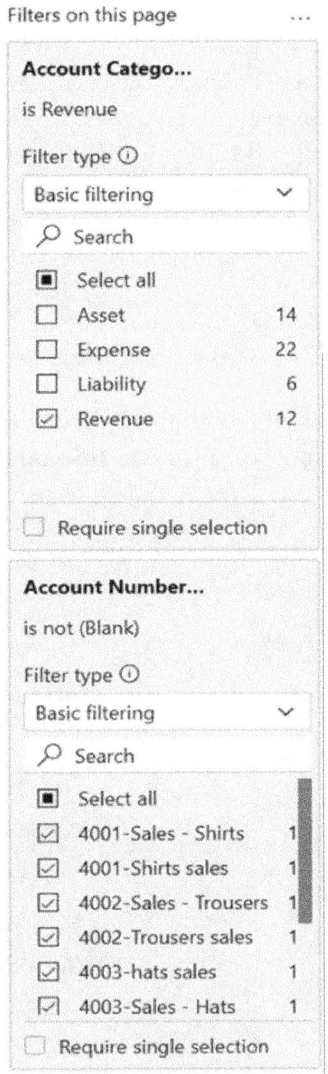

Figure 9.34: Adding page filters

8. Now, drag the **Revenue** amount next to **Budget Amount** in a table to present the following:

Account Number and Name	Budget Amount +	Total Revenue
4001-Sales - Shirts	2,568,926.08	1,636,818.73
4001-Shirts sales	2,690,207.29	1,680,977.58
4002-Sales - Trousers	3,191,647.10	2,05[illegible]988.26
4002-Trousers sales	3,382,950.44	2,114,903.34
4003-hats sales	564,810.14	353,595.63
4003-Sales - Hats	543,159.22	344,466.79
4101-Sales - Shoes	4,037,098.84	2,525,648.91
4102-Sales - Boots	663,078.04	413,769.11
4103-Sales - Sandals	1,030,693.28	646,473.54
Total	**18,672,570.43**	**11,775,641.89**

Figure 9.35: Budget vs. Revenue table

9. Now add the *Budget Variance + measure* to the table.
10. From the **Variance** dropdown, go to **Conditional formatting** and select **Icons**.

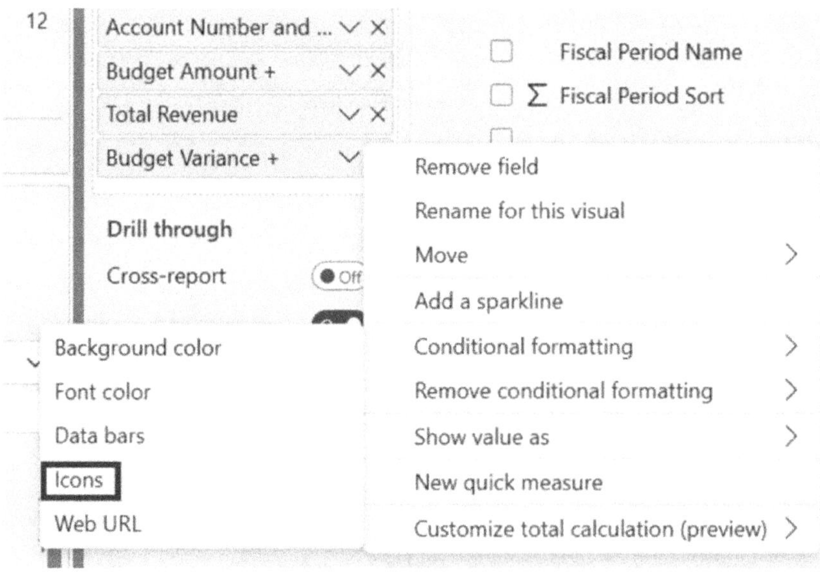

Figure 9.36: Conditional formatting

11. In the **Format style** option, choose **Rules**, and in **Apply to**, choose **Values only**.

12. Now, select the new measure, **Budget Variance %**, as the field to base this on.
13. Finally, set up the rules. Since the value we are working with is a percentage, we can reasonably assume that 1 to +1 is a sensible range, and we will set `0` as the boundary between red and yellow, and `0.03` as the boundary between yellow and green.

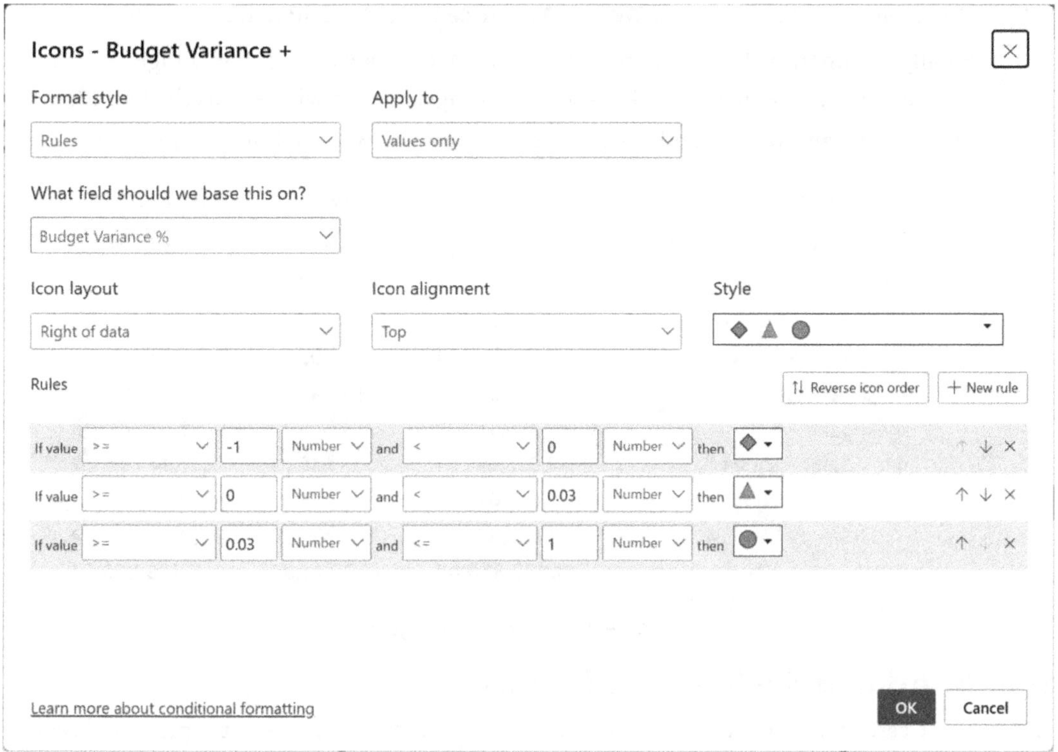

Figure 9.37: Adding the conditional format

In this way, we can have a conditional format based on a value that is not, in fact, shown in the table itself.

Step 2: Adding a matrix

Now that we have created a table showing budget, revenue, and variance with a conditional icon format, we will move on to our next visual on our page. As we have budgets by periods, a great standard visual with Power BI is a matrix:

1. Add a matrix to the design.
2. Drag **Account Number** and **Name** to the rows.
3. Now, add **Calendar Year**, **Calendar Quarter**, and **Calendar Month** to the columns.

4. Next, add **Total Revenue**, **Budget Amount +**, and **Budget Variance +** to the values.
5. Once again, go to the dropdown on **Budget Variance +** and select **Conditional formatting**, and then **Icons**.
6. In the **Format** style, choose **Rules**, and in **Apply to**, choose **Values**.
7. Now, select the new measure, **Budget Variance %**, as the field to base this on.
8. Finally, set up the rules. Since the value we are working with is a percentage, we can reasonably assume that -1 to +1 is a sensible range, and we will set `0` as the boundary between red and yellow, and `0.03` as the boundary between yellow and green.

Account Number and Name	Budget Amount +	Total Revenue	Budget Variance +
4001-Sales - Shirts	2,568,926.08	1,636,818.73	-932,107.35
4001-Shirts sales	2,690,207.29	1,680,977.58	-1,009,229.71
4002-Sales - Trousers	3,191,647.10	2,058,988.26	-1,132,658.85
4002-Trousers sales	3,382,950.44	2,114,903.34	-1,268,047.10
4003-hats sales	564,810.14	353,595.63	-211,214.50
4003-Sales - Hats	543,159.22	344,466.79	-198,692.43
4101-Sales - Shoes	4,037,098.84	2,525,648.91	-1,511,449.92
4102-Sales - Boots	663,078.04	413,769.11	-249,308.93
4103-Sales - Sandals	1,030,693.28	646,473.54	-384,219.74
Total	**18,672,570.43**	**11,775,641.89**	**-6,896,928.54**

Figure 9.38: Formatted budget matrix

Step 3: Adding the headline figures

As a variance can be displayed as either a figure or as a percentage value, multiple visuals can be used to best represent the data. The absolute values can be shown as cards, the percentage as a gauge:

1. Add a card to the report page.
2. Now drag **Budget +** into the card.
3. Go to **Format visual**.
4. On the **Visual** tab, turn off **Category label**.
5. In the **General** tab, switch on **Title**.
6. Add the title as `Budget`, and set the background to blue and text color to white.
7. Repeat this for **Total Revenue** and **Budget Variance +**. It is a good idea to use different colors for different aspects – here, we use dark blue for **Revenue** and orange for **Variance**.

8. Now, add a gauge.
9. Add **Budget Variance %**.
10. Go to **Format visual** and in the **Visual** tab, go to **Gauge axis**.
11. Set the min to `-0.5`, and max to `0.5` (i.e., +/- 50%)
12. Set the target to `0` (i.e., on budget).
13. On the **General** tab, turn on the title, add the title, set the background to orange, and the text to white.

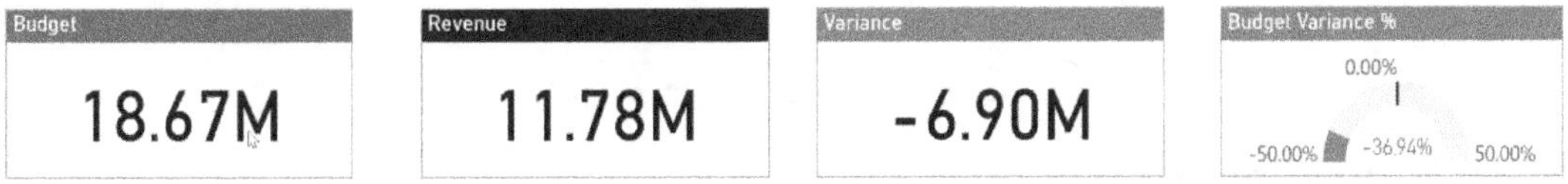

Figure 9.39: Headline cards

Step 4: Showing change over time

To show the measure over time, a bar, column, or line chart is a good visual to display such information. In our **Budget Variance** report, we will utilize the column and line chart visuals:

1. Add a line and a clustered column to the page.
2. Drag **Calendar year** to the *X* axis.
3. Now, add **Budget Amount+** and **Total Revenue** to the **Column** *Y* axis.
4. Add **Budget Variance +** to the **Line** *Y* axis.
5. Go to **Visual Format**, then under **Columns**, select **Budget amount +**, and set the color to light blue.
6. In the same area, select **Total Revenue** and set the color to dark blue.
7. Finally, under **Lines**, set the color to orange – this ensures that colors are consistent across the page.

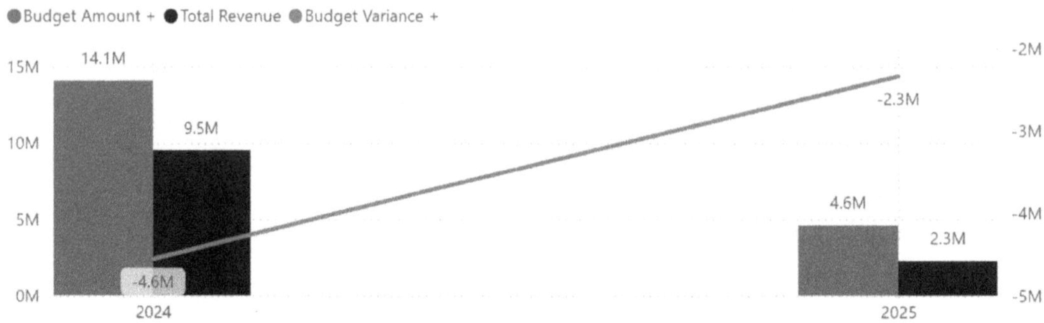

Figure 9.40: Budget vs. actual column chart

Step 5: Adding slicers

We want the same slicers on **Budget Variance** as on **Profit and Loss**, so we can simply copy and paste between pages:

1. Go to the **Profit and Loss** page.
2. Either right-click and select **Copy**, or use the keyboard shortcut *Ctrl* + *C*.
3. Now, go to the **Budget** page.
4. Hit *Ctrl* + *V* on your keyboard (there is no right-click option here).
5. You will be asked whether you want to sync the visuals.
6. Select **Sync**.
7. If we need to change the synchronization behavior later, select **Sync slicers** from the **View** tab of the ribbon.

Figure 9.41: Sync slicers button

8. Now, select the slicer you want to sync.
9. You can now choose which pages the slicer will apply to.

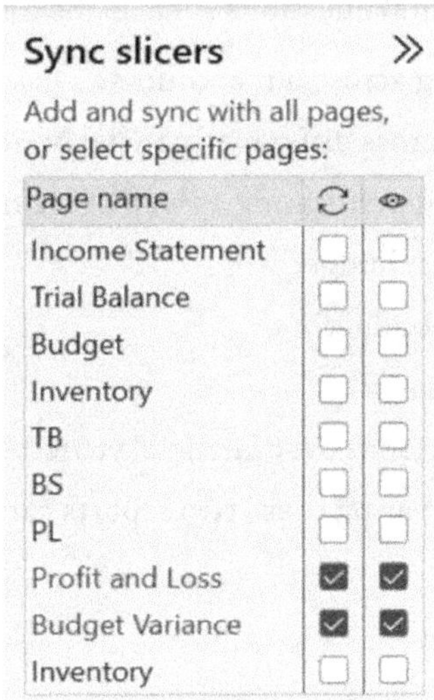

Figure 9.42: Configuring Sync slicers between P&L and Budget Variance

10. Note that there is a second column with an eye at the top – this can be used to hide the synced slicer on a given page. While this can gain back some screen real estate, you should use this with extreme caution, as it can confuse users.

Our final budget variance report is shown here:

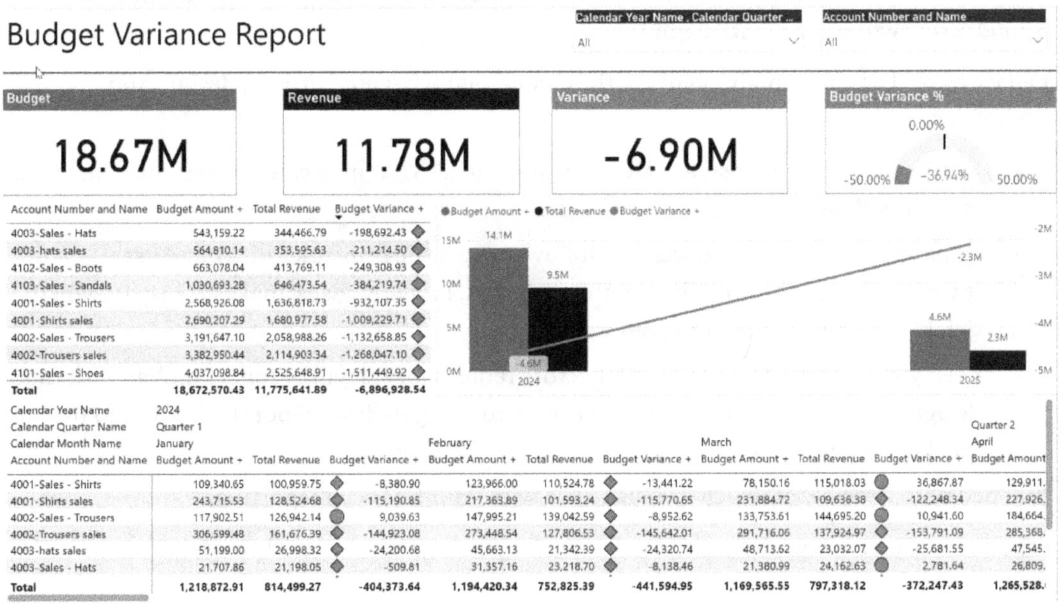

Figure 9.43: Final detailed budget page

We can now answer fundamental questions such as the following:

- How are we performing across our accounts?
- What is the variance across different financial periods?
- Which accounts are not performing as well as we need to take action on?
- How far are we from our budget?
- Have we exceeded our budget?
- Can we see any exceptions?
- What is our budget variance over financial years?

The techniques described in creating these two reports can now be applied to any dataset that you need to report on.

Summary

In this chapter, we discussed effective report design. We started by revisiting our five principles of effective reports, which are accuracy, security, speed, purpose, and design.

To start, focus on accuracy and security. If your numbers are wrong or for the wrong audience, fix this first.

Then, if your reports are slow to respond, examine your semantic model schema and measures. There will be some issues you need to fix, but please don't release reports that are slow to respond; users will cease using them.

Then we moved on to the main points of the chapter, which were purpose, design, and consistency:

- Every report should answer a clear business need. That may change over time, and your reports will need to change accordingly.
- Deploy well-designed reports that follow some basic principles of art and user interface design. Power BI has all the tools and, in many cases, makes it easy for you to quickly produce professional reports.
- Keep your report design consistent across reports. Users will become familiar with that design and layout, making it easy for them to navigate from report to report and to quickly train new users.

We ended with a review of which visuals to use with your financial reporting.

In the next chapter, we go deep into an aspect of reporting that we briefly covered here, which is testing and fine-tuning your data.

Get this book's PDF version and more

Scan the QR code (or go to `https://www.packtpub.com/unlock`). Search for this book by name, confirm the edition, and then follow the steps on the page.

UNLOCK NOW

Note: Keep your invoice handy. Purchases made directly from Packt don't require an invoice.

10

Testing and Fine-Tuning Your Data

The previous chapter explained how to build your suite of financial reports. One of the foundations of that chapter was the importance of making sure your data is correct. This chapter describes a core skill of a good data analyst: testing and fine-tuning your data, which can be difficult and time-consuming. Why is that?

Data from financial systems is complex, and it's often the case that the data you see onscreen has been manipulated, filtered, and calculated to provide the result based on data within the database.

Data tables from finance applications are complicated. For example, they'll include voided and cancelled transactions, so straight sums of data will also include everything. Ensuring your data is correct is an essential task that'll become an ever-present skill throughout your time developing Power BI reports. Reports that were correct one day can be incorrect the next, and understanding this and how to fix it will serve you well.

In this chapter, we'll look at some common methods to check data accuracy, how to reconcile that data back to the source at a transaction level, and techniques to deal with differences in that reconciliation. Finally, we'll take a look at why cleansing data within Power Query and Power BI is a bad idea, what to do instead, and when there might be no choice but to do so.

By the end of this chapter, you will do the following:

- Understand how to get accurate data in your Power BI reports
- Grasp how the trial balance from *Chapter 3, Creating a Trial Balance and Income Statement*, can help you check data

- Learn how to create a transaction-level reconciliation
- Appreciate the dangers of cleansing data within Power Query and Power BI

Technical requirements

To view the example that goes with this chapter, you will need an internet-connected device and access to Microsoft Excel. In this book's GitHub repository, there is an example of a test script that you can use to help you methodically test your reports: `https://github.com/PacktPublishing/Financial-Modeling-with-Power-BI_Packt/tree/main/Chapter10`.

What is incorrect data?

What does correct or incorrect mean anyway, and why is data "incorrect"?

Let's begin with the idea that your application isn't generating "incorrect" data. It's generating data you don't need for reporting, so you need to filter it out.

You need a starting point to find out what you need to filter out. We generally judge reporting to be correct or incorrect based on a comparison to transactions and reports generated directly from the source system, and we will ask users for copies of those reports. With this, we have a good idea of where we're heading.

This asks why there's a difference between the data you've extracted *directly* from the database of your financial application and the reports run *directly* from the same financial application.

The reason, generally, is that postings exist in the database that you don't see in the reports from the financial application. A common example is a cancelled or void transaction. Transactions are often cancelled or voided due to user error or a supplier/customer change. When this happens, you won't see the transaction in the application or within reporting, as it's considered reversed or even deleted. But, apart from rare circumstances, those transactions are still recorded on the database with a status of cancelled or similar; they're just filtered out when reports are run.

When you extract data from the database, you'll see those transactions and likely many more. Build a simple `SUM` measure on the **Amount** field, and those transactions will be included, and your `SUM` will be incorrect.

Date/time fields are another common reason for incorrect data when compared to your finance application. Transactions often have many dates; a sales order can have dates for initial order entry, delivery, customer request, and financial posting. Pick the wrong date, and transactions will fall into different periods from the finance application and will be considered incorrect. We've seen time zone issues place transactions into different periods because of a single hour. It happens more frequently than you may think.

The first part of this chapter is to understand that the data extracted from the source is likely to be incorrect when compared to a system report. In fact, we expect it to be incorrect and have to work on it to match the system report. If you start with that expectation, you'll be ready for anything. To begin, we'll move on to some common techniques to test and fine-tune your data.

Using the trial balance to test your data

In *Chapter 3, Creating a Trial Balance and Income Statement,* we created a basic trial balance, which is a great starting point to check your data model. The first and simplest approach to testing the data integrity of our reports is to compare the trial balance we created with the trial balance from the source system. But even before we get that far, there are a number of checks we can quickly carry out on our Power BI trial balance:

1. Is the total zero?
2. On the rows of the trial balance, does **Opening Balance** – **Total Credit** + **Total Debit** = **Closing Balance**?
3. Do the columns total correctly?

If the answer to any of these is *no*, then there is a problem either with the semantic model or with one of the calculations.

Common checks for the trial balance

The first check is the structure of the semantic model. Start with the `GL Transactions` table and trace the related tables. Make sure every relationship has the cardinality you expect. In general, the relationship from `Chart of Account` to `GL Transactions` and `Calendar` to `Transactions` should both be one-to-many. There will be one `GL account` on the `Chart of Account` table for many accounts on the `GL Transactions` table. If you have a many-to-many relationship, you've got duplicated data in the `Chart of Account` table, or you've linked the wrong fields. If you've linked the correct fields but have a many-to-many relationship, you probably have duplicated values in your `Chart of Account` table and need to ensure you only have unique values using Power Query. If you've connected the wrong fields, use the `Manage Relationships` function in the model view to link the correct fields.

Another common issue you may have to check is how positive and negative numbers are imported, and whether the sign is correct. For example, if your revenue is imported as a positive, you'll need to correct that in Power Query.

The next step is to work through the calculations to make sure they're correct. Spelling errors in the filter of a `CALCULATE` statement will stop the measure from calculating the desired result.

Here's an example from *Chapter 4, Common DAX measures*. The first DAX statement is correct, the second is incorrect:

```
Total Revenue = CALCULATE(
    [Total amount],
    FILTER(
       'Chart of Account',
       'Chart of Account' [AccountCategory]="SALES" ||
            'Chart of Account' [AccountCategory]="OTHERINC"
    )
)*-1

Total Revenue = CALCULATE(
    [Total amount],
    FILTER(
       'Chart of Account',
       'Chart of Account' [AccountCategory]="SALE" ||
            'Chart of Account' [AccountCategory]="OTHER1NC"
    )
)*-1
```

Although the changes are minor spelling errors, the second statement will return zero as "SALES" and "OTHERINC" are incorrect. DAX and M are precise, and the most innocuous error will return an error or zero.

Finding these errors can be time-consuming since the calculations are likely to be detailed. Most commonly, the problems in calculations will relate to a sign or a filter.

To help locate calculation errors, create a table in the canvas view and add the measures. If any rows equal zero, you've probably found your error.

If you are confident that the semantic model is correct and there are no calculation errors, that leaves two broad possibilities:

1. There is an error in the data transformation from Power Query
2. There is an error in the source system

The most likely problem is an issue with the data load. This is especially true if the data doesn't come directly from the source (e.g., your semantic model is working from a system report that has been output to Excel) or if you're performing transformations during the Power Query data load. In the latter case, start by making a copy of the semantic model and, in Power Query, remove the transformations one by one and check the effect on the data. Remember, Power Query transformations are applied from top to bottom, and it's often the case that the order is incorrect. If the trial balance now balances, you've proved the issue is in the transformation, and you can fix it.

If the transformations are good, the next step is to ensure that the source data is correct – if your data is sourced via an Excel export, check if the spreadsheet has the correct, latest data, that the format is correct, and that you're not hitting the row limit for the sheet. Using an out-of-date spreadsheet is also a very common error.

If those things are fine, check whether there's an issue with the trial balance in the source system. This would be an exceptionally rare occurrence, and an error in the trial balance in Power BI is almost always something that arises either in the data model or in the transformation steps. If the source system's trial balance still doesn't match yours, there's an error you've missed, so you'll need to restart the troubleshooting process.

The trial balance adds up, so we're done, right?

Generally, no. All we've done so far is verify the internal consistency of the semantic model. While that's important and a necessary minimum step, it's only the first step to prove that our data model is correct. As we've previously mentioned, the data in our model must match the data in our source systems.

The next step is to check the subtotals from the trial balance. If the source and Power BI don't match, there is a problem. If they do, look at whether the two reports match at an account level.

Depending on the size of your *chart of accounts*, you may choose to reconcile every account, checking the opening balance, debit, credit, and closing balance for each one. More likely, you will have a large chart of accounts, and you may not reconcile to that level. In this case, the approach to take is to reconcile a sample of accounts, rather than all of them. The rationale is that if a sample of accounts is correct, and the model is internally consistent, there's little space for errors.

When choosing accounts to check, you should aim for at least 10% coverage of the overall set of accounts. The accounts should also be representative of your main business processes, spread across the balance sheet and P&L, and indicate whether the expected transaction is a credit or debit.

Applying this, you might choose some accounts to test, such as the following:

- AR Control account
- Tax Payable Control account
- An Inventory account
- A Revenue account
- A COGS account
- Another cost account

This will cover different transaction types, different business processes, and different parts of the chart of accounts. Obviously, if you have more than 60 accounts or you have more business processes, such as manufacturing, you'll need to expand that list.

If everything matches at this stage, we can be reasonably assured the data is correct. If not, the next step is to look at a transaction-level reconciliation.

Creating a transaction-level reconciliation

Typically, transaction-level reconciliation is required when a higher-level reconciliation has failed. The implication is that something is wrong with the data flow, and only a detailed examination of the individual transactions will allow for diagnosing the problem. The most common tool for this reconciliation is Excel.

Before you start

Consider whether you need to download all transactions. Can you, for example, identify a single account where the issue is occurring? Alternatively, is the issue in a single month? If that's the case, then you only need to export the subset that's exhibiting a problem. Whatever the case, unless your dataset is very small, it's sensible to start by downloading a subset of the data and reconciling first, as this is often enough to identify a systematic issue, and it's faster to deal with small datasets than large ones.

What to do

To carry out a line-level reconciliation, you need datasets from your accounting system and from your Power BI model that have the same columns. It's also important to avoid additional manipulation of the data when downloading it from Power BI, since this creates an opportunity for new errors to enter the system and obfuscate the issue you're trying to diagnose. How you export the data from your source system to reconcile to the Power BI data will depend on the exact accounting system you are using, but almost all modern accounting systems offer some means of exporting data into Excel. Once you have this, you need a dataset from your Power BI model to match it. For the purposes of demonstration, we'll assume the download from the source system contains the following columns, so we'll generate a table in Power BI with identical columns as the basis for a data extract:

- Transaction ID
- Account number
- Date
- Amount

We'll now create a new page in our report and create a simple table containing these columns:

Structure Formatting

Count of TransactionID	AccountNumber	TransactionDate	Sum of Amount
1	1001	30 September 2022	-853.65
1	2001	30 September 2022	8,913.71
1	3001	30 September 2022	-1,485.62
1	4001	30 September 2022	-7,428.09
1	5001	30 September 2022	853.65
1	1001	01 October 2022	-1,250.16
1	2001	01 October 2022	10,457.92
1	3001	01 October 2022	-1,742.99
1	4001	01 October 2022	-8,714.93
1	5001	01 October 2022	1,250.16
1	1003	02 October 2022	-654.40
2064			**0.00**

Figure 10.1 – Table showing transactions

It's important to double-check the settings on the fields. In our example, Power BI has defaulted to counting `TransactionID`, which is not useful, so we need to set this to **Don't summarize**:

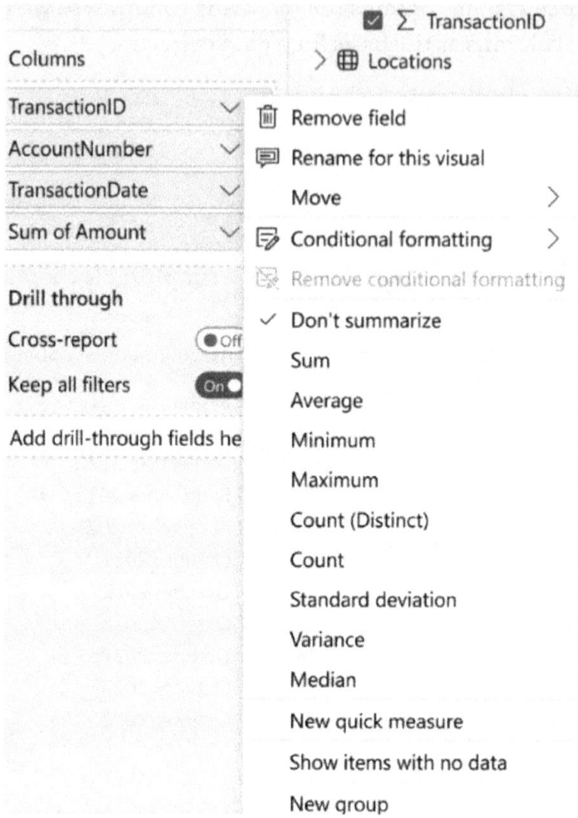

Figure 10.2 – Dropdown of column settings and options

Now that we have the table in the desired format, we can export the data for our reconciliation by clicking the ellipsis on the table and choosing **Export data**:

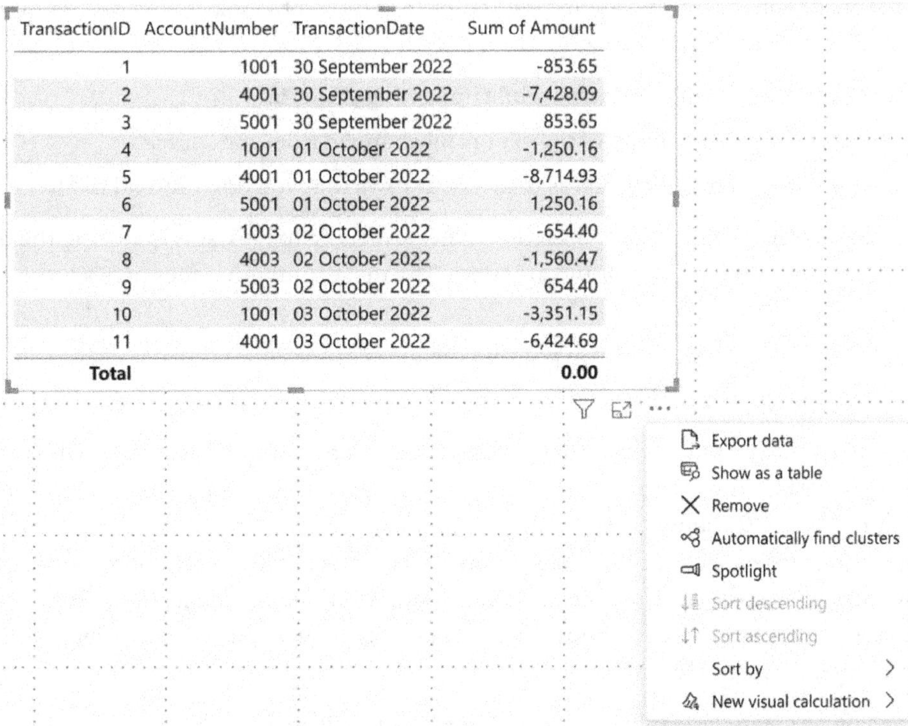

TransactionID	AccountNumber	TransactionDate	Sum of Amount
1	1001	30 September 2022	-853.65
2	4001	30 September 2022	-7,428.09
3	5001	30 September 2022	853.65
4	1001	01 October 2022	-1,250.16
5	4001	01 October 2022	-8,714.93
6	5001	01 October 2022	1,250.16
7	1003	02 October 2022	-654.40
8	4003	02 October 2022	-1,560.47
9	5003	02 October 2022	654.40
10	1001	03 October 2022	-3,351.15
11	4001	03 October 2022	-6,424.69
Total			**0.00**

Figure 10.3 – Dropdown of options from the table visual

This will download the data from this table as a CSV that can be interrogated in Excel. Remember, Power BI Desktop limits CSV export to 30,000 rows. If you need to export more data, publish the report to the Power BI service, where you can export up to 150,000 rows. We should add that a 30,000-row reconciliation is beyond anything we'd recommend.

What to do, and what to look out for

First, start by checking the row counts – assuming the two datasets have the same scope, then the row counts should match. If they don't, you know the Power BI report is getting either more or less data than expected (usually less, but if there is an issue relating to dates and date formatting, it may show more because the data is being assigned to the wrong dates).

The next step is to match the two datasets by `TransactionID`, the unique ID for each transaction. You can do this by creating a relationship between the two tables in Power BI and building a table with the transaction IDs side by side. If transactions in the Power BI table are either missing or you have extra, identify the culprits and start to look at why this might be occurring. The most likely root causes are as follows:

- Errors in the Power Query steps while importing the data
- Errors in the configuration of the export mechanism from the source

The most common Power Query error is to filter out rows that you don't intend to filter out.

If both datasets contain the same transactions, the next thing to look at is matching the details. Check the account numbers, dates, and amounts. The most common issues here are the following:

- Mis-matching amounts due to rounding
- Issues with date formats

This list is, of course, not exhaustive, but date issues are very common, especially when working across systems configured for the common date formats in different countries (e.g., MM/DD/YYYY in the US, and DD/MM/YYYY, common across Europe). Most of these issues can typically be addressed by making changes in the Power Query steps that import the data in the first place. Issues are common in a single country with multiple time zones, such as the United States. We've seen instances where transactions in Power BI were placed in a different financial year due to an incorrect time zone conversion.

Assuming you've created the table using the "raw" column from the table, meaning no measures or calculated columns, this points to one of two possible issues. Either there's an issue in the measures that have gone into the trial balance, or there is a problem with the source system. Again, the latter option is highly unlikely, but not impossible.

While the sort of error that would cause reconciliation issues from the source system is exceptionally rare, it's likely that any reconciliation will highlight data quality issues. So, if we find those, what do we do about them?

This takes us to the next section, where we discuss data cleansing in Power Query and Power BI.

Cleansing data in Power Query and Power BI

By cleansing data in Power Query and Power BI, we mean changes to fix data quality issues, either while importing data into the reporting system or creating calculations that remove certain data quality issues. In many ways, this should be the shortest section in the book: don't do it, as it generally causes more problems than it solves. Our advice is to fix data issues in the source system, not Power Query or Power BI. That said, there is value in a discussion of why it's a bad practice, and when it can be done acceptably.

Let's first consider why it's a bad practice. First and foremost, cleansing data in Power Query / Power BI means creating data that's different from the source system, which is a fundamental data integrity issue, raising the question of how you test it. Moreover, there needs to be consideration given to how to document the changes so future users aren't confused by the difference between the source system and Power BI.

The next problem in fixing the data in Power Query / Power BI is removing the incentive to fix the data at the source. We can also say with confidence that once you've fixed source data in Power Query / Power BI, you'll be asked to do it again and again.

Looking further into the future, what happens if there's a need to change the reporting system? That'll require a major clean-up of the historical data, or the new implementation needs to replicate the cleansing that has been done.

So, now you know why this is a bad idea. What do you do when there's no choice? First of all, this should be seen as a Band-Aid, a temporary measure that needs to be communicated to stakeholders. Another term we might use is *technical debt*. Like any other debt, when we incur it, we need a repayment plan. In this case, by fixing the source data and removing the cleansing from the reports.

Non-functional testing

So far, our tests have been concentrated on whether or not the data is correct, or "functional" testing, as it is also known. Almost as important, although often neglected, is non-functional testing.

Non-functional testing refers to the aspects of a report outside the calculations and measures used within the report and looks to examine aspects such as load times, security, and adherence to design standards.

We've already touched on some of these ideas – two in particular, in the form of responsiveness and accessibility. Let's start with responsiveness.

One of the problems of non-functional tests is that they're often subjective. Let's start with how long is too long for a visual to refresh.

As a general rule of thumb, if you're hitting 3 seconds for all the visuals on a page to update after a control is clicked or a slicer is updated, that's too long. For some edge cases and complex scenarios, more time may be allowed, but in general, anything slower than 3 seconds becomes a frustration to the user. This will lead to a perception by the user that the report is slow and, in turn, lead to them seeking other avenues to get the data they need. You'll possibly see low usage of the reporting suite as a result.

> **Tip**
>
> A detailed treatment of how to handle poor report performance is beyond the scope of this book, but we would recommend you check out this book:
>
> `https://www.packtpub.com/en-gb/product/microsoft-power-bi-performance-best-practices-9781801071390`

The next item is accessibility. Some elements of this are more objective than others and sometimes need to be tailored to your specific user base.

In general, you should consider how a report works for people with reduced vision or impaired color vision. Make sure font sizes are large enough, try not to go below 12 point, and only below 10 point if the information conveyed is not critical. Also, think about contrast; there are online tools that can check the contrast ratios between different colors. Similarly, there are tools that you can use to ensure color palettes are readable for those with impaired color vision.

Accessibility is different between users, so focus on specific users and work with them to ensure the report is legible.

Visual clutter is also an accessibility issue. We discussed this in *Chapter 9*, *Creating a Suite of Financial Reports*, when talking about good design, and this should be covered in the testing phase of the project, not simply be assumed to be done.

Another non-functional test you should consider is the refresh time of the dataset. This may be less obvious than the tests we have discussed so far, but it can be just as important. If a report takes too long to refresh, then the data may not be up to date when the end user needs it.

This depends a lot on the needs of the organization, and in finance reporting, an overnight refresh is generally enough, where you have many hours for that to run. That said, the longer the refresh takes to run, the higher the chance of a timeout, so make sure the refresh is fast and efficient. Again, as a rule of thumb, for an overnight refresh, a 1-hour refresh would be considered slow.

The final main non-function test to consider is security – is the report accessible only to those users who are authorized to see it? To do this, there are a number of approaches, either by working with trusted users to see if they can access a restricted report or restricted data if you're using row-level security.

Having completed both functional and non-functional testing, we can be reasonably assured that the report is ready for release to end users.

Summary

In this chapter, we covered some common methods for testing and fine-tuning your data. This is an important topic and a set of skills we'd encourage anyone working with data to become proficient in. If something doesn't calculate correctly, you'll need to find out why. This is work that demands patience and time, and a task you'll improve at over time, as you become better at spotting the issues and develop your own methods for fixing them.

Don't forget the importance of non-functional testing by making sure your test plans include both functional and non-functional tests. A perfectly calculated report that takes minutes to load will likely not be used.

In the next chapter, we move on to a very different topic, although another important one in the world of financial reporting. That is, paginated reports.

11

Printable Financial Statements with Power BI Paginated

In the previous chapter, we looked at testing and fine-tuning your data and reports. In this chapter, we return to the creation of reports and focus on how to print your reports. Although this is seen less often these days, printing financial reports remains important.

Most of the visuals you'll design in Power BI are not designed to be static prints. Power BI is an interactive business intelligence tool where fresh data is never far away, and visuals can be expanded, collapsed, and scrolled. But in the financial world, printed, static documents that portray a financial report based on a specific period are occasionally required. So, how do we get something not designed for printing static reports to print static reports?

The answer is **Power BI Report Builder**, a companion application to Power BI that, as you may have guessed by now, is the tool we use to build paginated, pixel-perfect reports.

Just to dissect what that means, paginated means separating report data into pages that can be printed, instead of a long vertical scroll, and pixel-perfect means the printed report will be accurate and consistent based on a specific size of paper. A paginated report can be one or many pages, but it will fit on the printed page correctly, and it'll break at the correct point when there is a need for many pages. We're used to the term "responsive" when referring to applications and web pages, meaning a design will work equally on a PC screen, a tablet, and a phone. Pixel-perfect is the opposite of this. It produces a design and format that is always faithful to the intention of the designer on the printed page. By page, we mean a paper page.

It's important to note that Power BI Report Builder *is not* Power BI. It's a separate tool and behaves differently from Power BI. Please don't assume that your Power BI skills will serve you well for working with Power BI Report Builder. Unfortunately, they won't, and our best advice is to treat them as different applications in terms of use and navigation.

In this chapter, we will look at how to build paginated reports. We will then look at how we can go about using Power BI Report Builder and how it uses data from the Power BI data model that we created in *Chapter 3, Creating a Trial Balance and Income Statement*. Finally, we will go through a worked example of creating an income statement as a paginated report and consider why this may be a better option than the reports created in *Chapter 3, Creating a Trial Balance and Income Statement*.

By the end of this chapter, you will be able to do the following:

- Appreciate why printable reports are useful
- Understand the tools available for creating printable reports
- Be confident in creating a printable income statement

Technical requirements

To follow the examples in this chapter and beyond, you'll need a Windows PC with an internet connection and Power BI Report Builder, which can be downloaded using the following link: `https://www.microsoft.com/en-us/download/details.aspx?id=105942`.

As with all of our examples, you'll need Power BI Desktop, which can be downloaded using the following link: `https://www.microsoft.com/en-us/download/details.aspx?id=58494`.

You'll also need a Power BI PBIX file. For the examples in this chapter, we use `Chapter 3 - Final.pbix`, which can be found in the `Chapter 3` folder of this book's GitHub repository: `https://github.com/PacktPublishing/Financial-Modeling-with-Power-BI_Packt/tree/main/Chapter3`.

The GitHub repository for this chapter contains an example of a PDF export of the final report.

Understanding when paginated reports are useful

Paginated reports are useful when there's a need to display data in a fixed format. This is generally intended for printing but can equally be used to create electronic documents such as reporting packs. While paginated reports can be used onscreen, they are not generally intended for this purpose. There are ways of creating some interaction in paginated reports, but if your use case is a screen-readable, interactive report, the right tool for the job will be a regular Power BI visual.

Paginated reports work best where there are tables of figures with a limit on the number of columns displayed to help control the overall look and feel of the reports, and to ensure the columns fit within the boundaries of the page. Remember, paper doesn't have a scroll option, so columns that are too wide for the page will cause extra pages to be printed. The following is a list of questions to consider when deciding whether to use a paginated report:

- Is there a requirement for a report that has fixed dimensions?
- Is there a limited need for charts?
- Do you need to print the report?

If you answer yes to 2 or 3 of these, then paginated reports are worth considering.

Using Power BI Report Builder

Power BI Report Builder is available as a free download from Microsoft. You'll notice that in comparison to Power BI, Report Builder may feel a little old-fashioned. Essentially, it's a tool that was originally built for developers rather than those more familiar with the modern look of Office applications. So, for an Office user, the learning curve will be steeper.

On creating a blank report, you will be greeted with this screen:

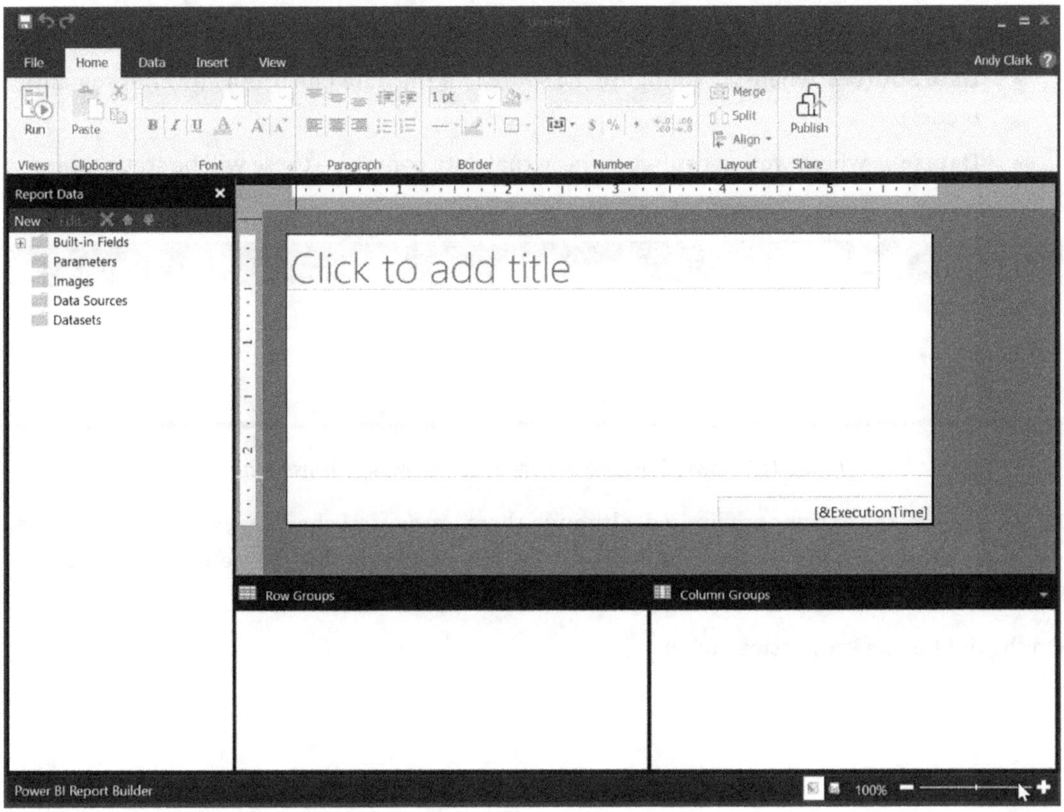

Figure 11.1: Power BI Report Builder

On the left, we see the area where we configure the report data:

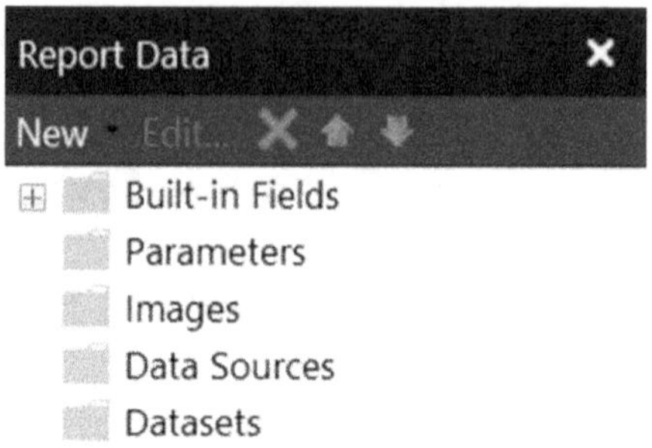

Figure 11.2: Power BI Report Builder folders

We have several folders here:

- **Built-in Fields**, where we can find such things as page number or report name
- **Parameters**, where we can configure drop-down options to filter the report data
- **Images**, where we can add static images (such as logos) to the reports
- **Data Sources**, where we configure the source for the data (such as a Power BI semantic model)
- **Datasets**, where we can configure the actual data content—these will be static tables

On the ribbon, if we go to **Insert**, we can see the visualizations available:

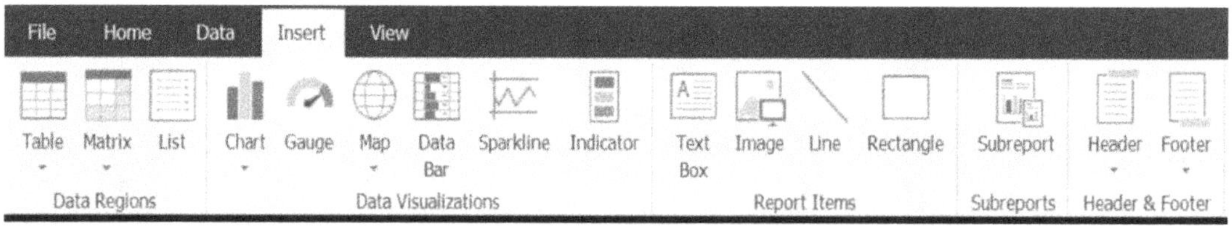

Figure 11.3: Power BI Report Builder ribbon showing the Insert tab

As you can see, the options are limited, although there are several chart types. Most of the time, you'll use a table or a matrix (such as Power BI Desktop, a matrix that is essentially a pivot table).

On the right is the **Properties** panel:

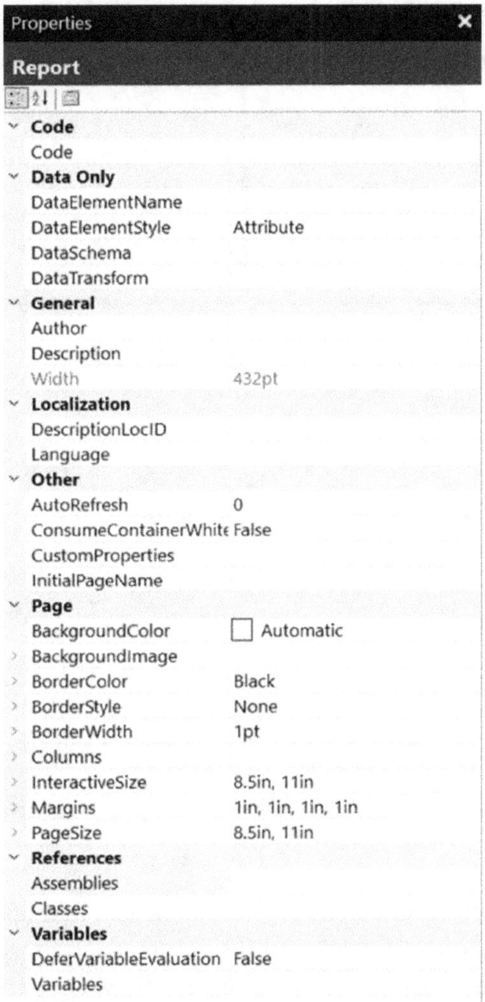

Figure 11.4: The Properties panel

There is a **Properties** panel for every element on the report. Here, you can precisely configure the properties of each report item, such as colour and position on the page. The **Properties** panel is an important part of the application to configure your reports and changes based on where you've clicked on the screen.

At the bottom, we can configure the grouping of rows and columns in a table or matrix:

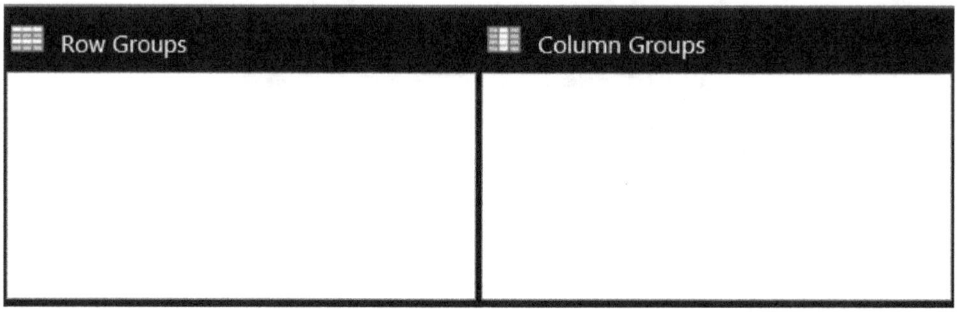

Figure 11.5: Row and column groups

Finally, we have the design area:

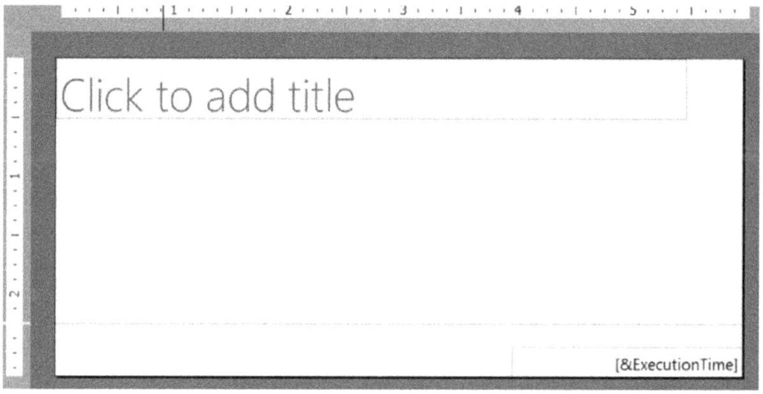

Figure 11.6: The design area

This is where we work on the layout of the report. Please note that unlike Power BI, when you add items, it does not immediately populate the data; the report must be run to get a preview of the data. This makes the report development process slower and less flexible, so please set your expectations accordingly.

Now that we can navigate around Power BI Report Builder, we can start to create a report.

Creating a printable income statement

We have seen the basic navigation and features of the paginated report builder. Let's use it to create a printable income statement.

To start, we need to make data available to Power BI Report Builder. This does not come directly from the PBIX file within Power BI Desktop; it comes from a PBIX file that has been published to the Power BI service. We do this by publishing our semantic model to the Power

BI service from Power BI Desktop. We'll cover the publishing process briefly here. We also cover publishing reports in *Chapter 13, Evolving and Maintaining Your Reports.*

For our data source, we'll use the model that we completed in *Chapter 3, Creating a Trial Balance and Income Statement.*

To be able to publish a Power BI PBIX file, you'll need a free or paid Microsoft Fabric account. If you don't have one, please follow the instructions at the following link to obtain an account: `https://www.microsoft.com/en-us/power-platform/products/power-bi/getting-started-with-power-bi`.

Once you have your free or paid Microsoft Fabric account, you'll need to log in and create a workspace, the instructions for which are explained in the following Microsoft online guide: `https://learn.microsoft.com/en-us/power-bi/collaborate-share/service-create-the-new-workspaces`.

Once you've got your Microsoft Fabric account and created your workspace, make sure you're logged in to Power BI Desktop using your Microsoft Fabric account, open the `Chapter 3 - Final.pbix` file, and click **Publish**. When you do that, a dialog box will open where you can confirm the workspace that you'll use to publish the model. The dialog box will look similar to *Figure 11.7*:

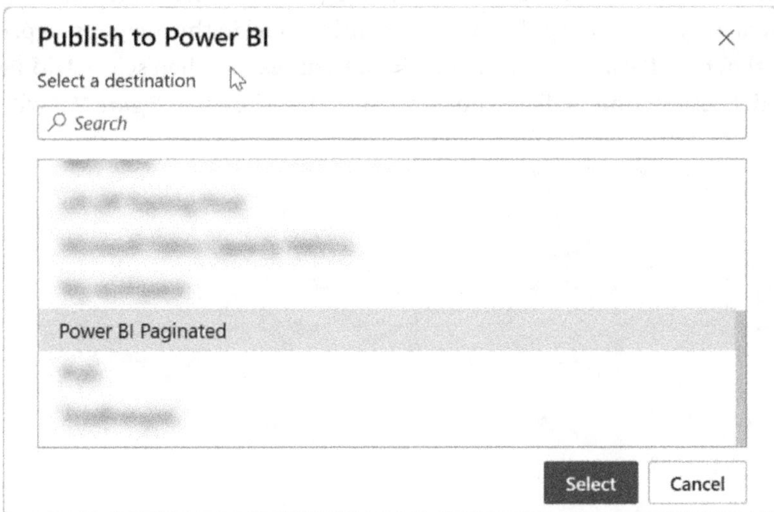

Figure 11.7: Publish to Power BI from Power BI Desktop

After publishing to the Power BI service, the model underpinning our report will be available as a data source for Power BI Report Builder.

Now open Power BI Report Builder, where we'll start with a blank report. Use **File** | **New** to launch the **New Report** window, as shown in *Figure 11.8*. From this menu, click **Blank Report**.

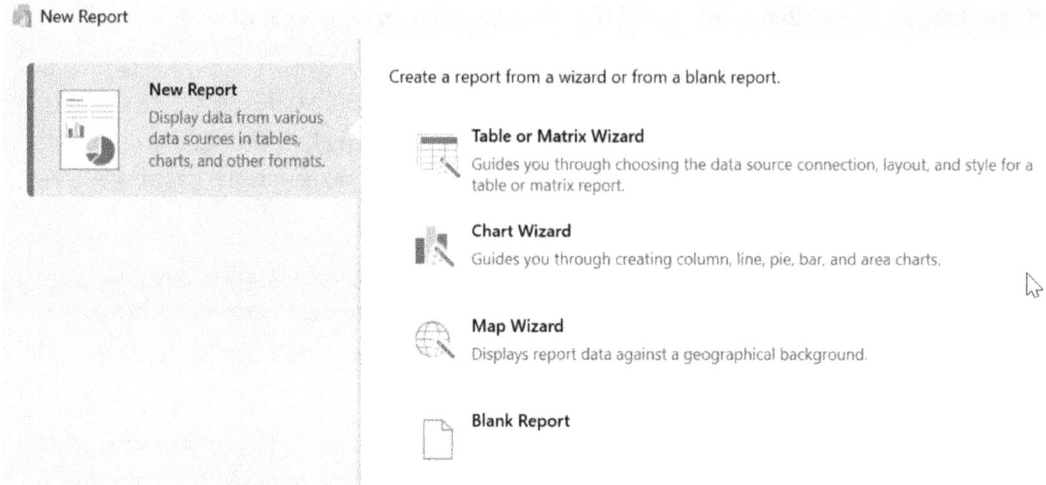

Figure 11.8: Creating a new report

With our blank report created, we need to connect to the data we're going to use for our income statement. To start, make sure you're also logged in to Power BI Report Builder using the same credentials you used to publish the semantic model in the previous step. From the report folders shown in *Figure 11.2*, right-click **Data Sources** and then select **Add Power BI Semantic Model connection**. A dialog box similar to that shown in *Figure 11.9* will appear.

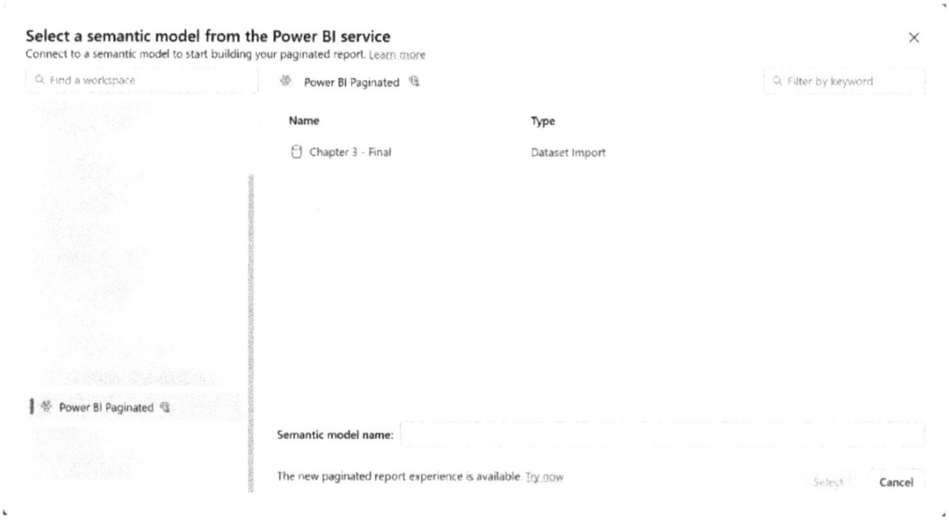

Figure 11.9: Selecting your data source

From the workspace you used to publish the semantic model, you can then choose the semantic model as the data source for the paginated report.

When you see the semantic model under **Data Sources** in the folders, right-click on the new data source and select **Add Dataset**. You'll see the dialog box that appears in *Figure 11.10*.'

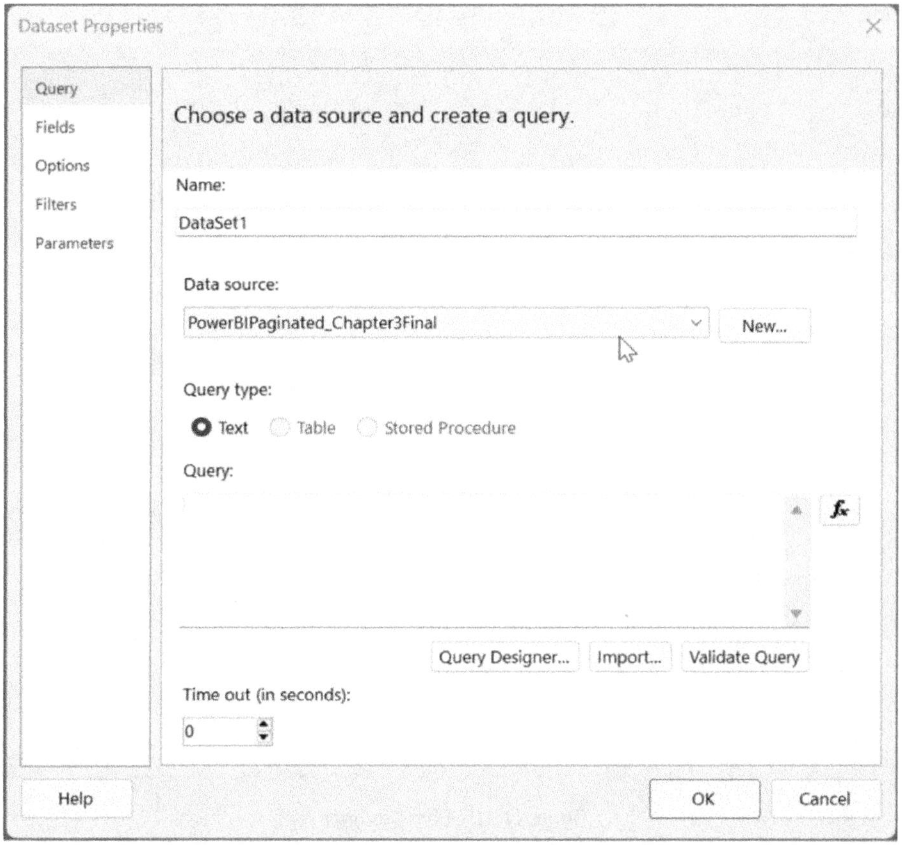

Figure 11.10: Dataset Properties

At this point, we can edit some of the dataset properties, such as the name, and define the query that will deliver data to our report using **Query Designer**, which is the next step. Click **OK** to accept the settings in the **Dataset Properties** dialog box.

Query Designer is the standard way to generate a query. To access **Query Designer**, right-click the newly created dataset and select **Query**.

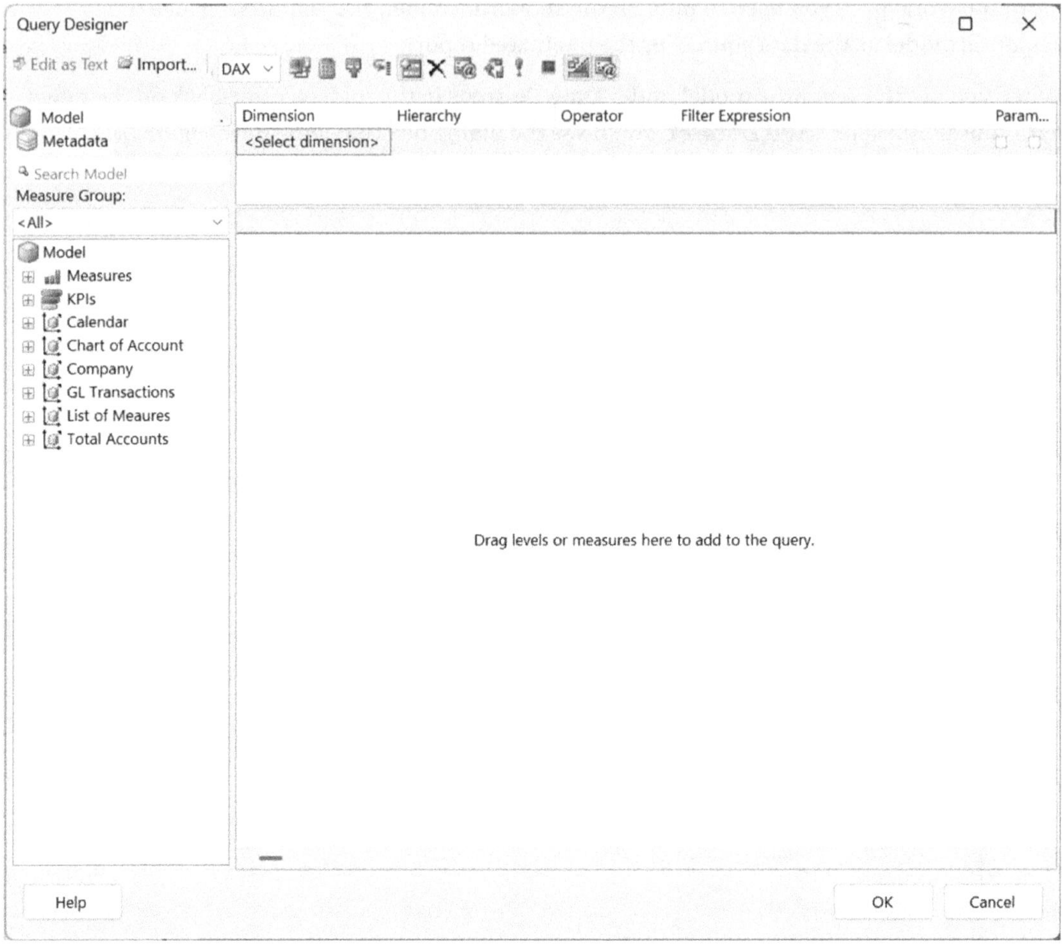

Figure 11.11: Query Designer

From here, we can select the measures and columns we need for our income statement. We do this by dragging the columns and measures from the left to the area where it says **Drag levels or measures here to add to the query**. Don't you love it when they make it obvious for you?

Typically, it's easier to start with the measures and add columns after. Note that the measures are listed under the **Measures** node, not the **List of Measures** node, where you would expect to see them within Power BI Desktop. We'll start by adding the measures for **COGS**, **Net Revenue**, **Rent Expense**, **Salary Expenses**, **Total Revenue**, and **Sales Revenue**, as shown in *Figure 11.12*. You'll need to click where it says **Click to execute the query** to see the data.

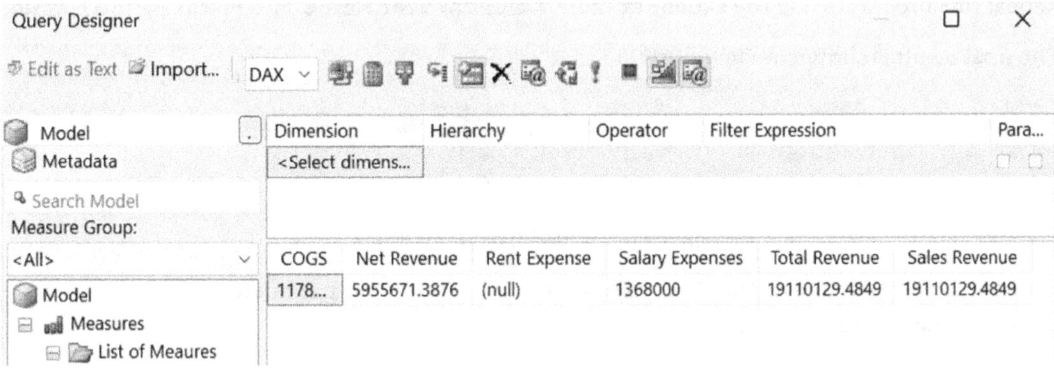

Figure 11.12: Report structure in Query Designer

Now we can add the descriptive columns that we'll need—in this case, we will use **Fiscal Year Name**, **Fiscal Period Name**, and **Company Name** as we will want to use these for our filters. Drag those fields to the query view, as shown in *Figure 11.13*. Again, you'll need to click **Click to execute the query** to see the data.

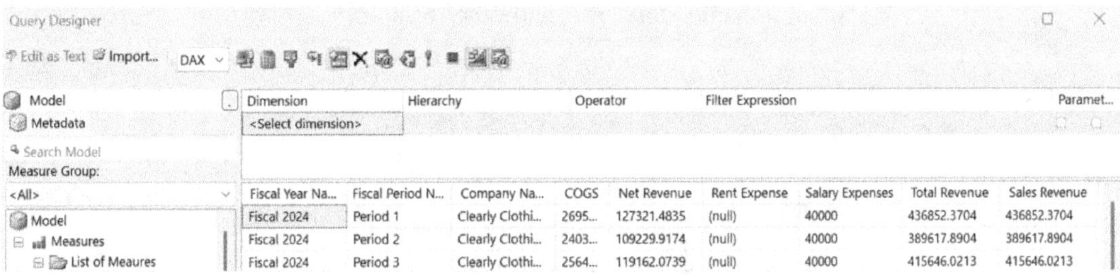

Figure 11.13: Running our report in Query Designer

Note the **(null)** values under **Rent Expense**—in our dataset, the rent transactions have been posted quarterly, so only periods in which rental expense is actually posted will we see an actual value.

Still in **Query Designer**, look to the top window, which has the **Dimension**, **Hierarchy**, **Operator**, **Filter Expression**, and **Parameters** column headings.

Under the **Dimension** header, click **<Select dimension>** and select **Company**. Under the next column header, which is **Hierarchy**, click **<Select hierarchy>**, where you'll see a drop-down field, and choose the company name.

The next column is **Operator**, where you'll choose **Equals**.

Under **Filter Expression, use the dropdown control and select All for each parameter,** then check the first checkbox under **Parameters**.

Repeat this process to add the **Calendar** table, **Calendar Year Name**, and **Fiscal Period Name**.

The final result is shown in *Figure 11.14*.

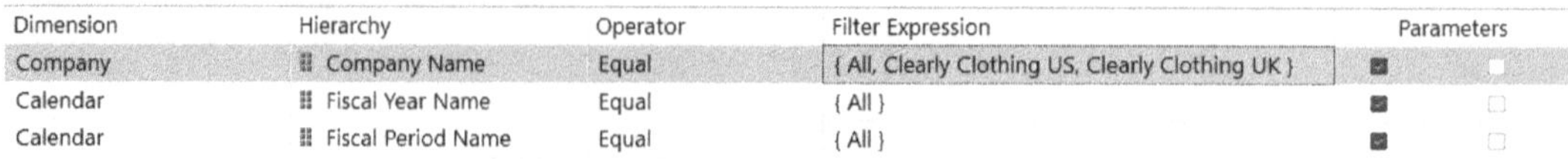

Figure 11.14: Adding query parameters

When you click **OK** to close the **Query Designer** dialog box, your parameters will be created under the **Parameters** folder.

You can now double-click on each parameter to change the prompt to something easier for users, such as **Select Company**. Remember, we use parameters the same way we use slicers in Power BI Desktop.

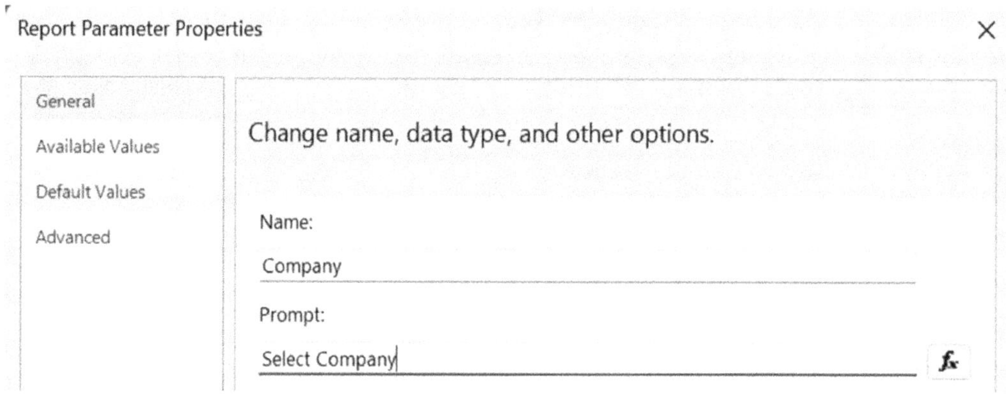

Figure 11.15: Adding a report parameter

Now repeat this procedure for the fiscal year and fiscal period. With this, we are ready to use the parameters to filter our main dataset. Right-click your dataset, choose **Dataset Properties**, and then click **Filters** in the **Dataset Properties** dialog box.

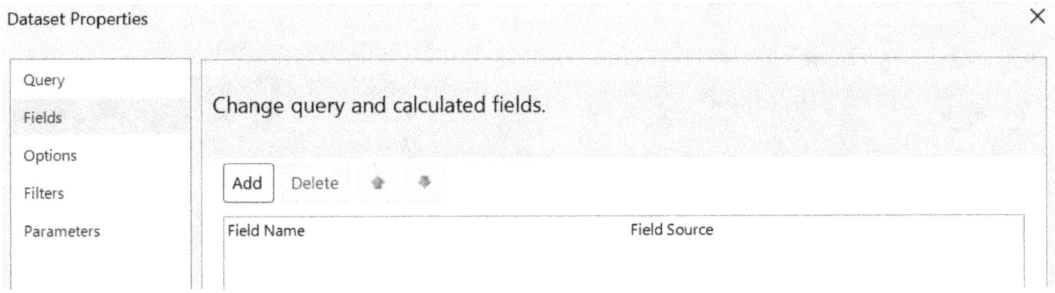

Figure 11.16: Adding a filter to a dataset

Click **Add** and configure the first filter. Select `Company_Name_` as the expression and then click the **fx** button beside the value so we can set up an expression.

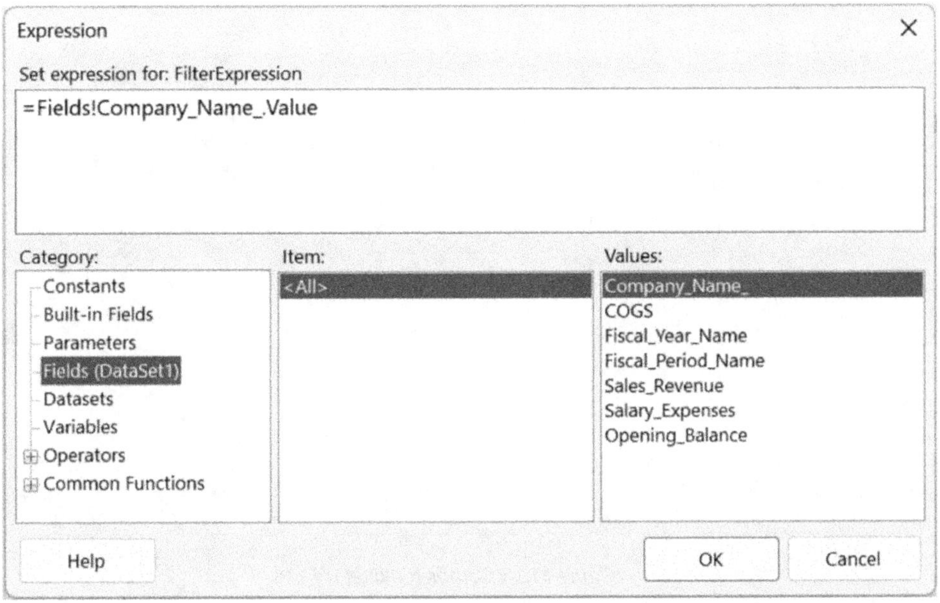

Figure 11.17: Configuring the value to use a report parameter

Now, click **OK** on the dialog box and repeat the procedure for the fiscal year and fiscal month.

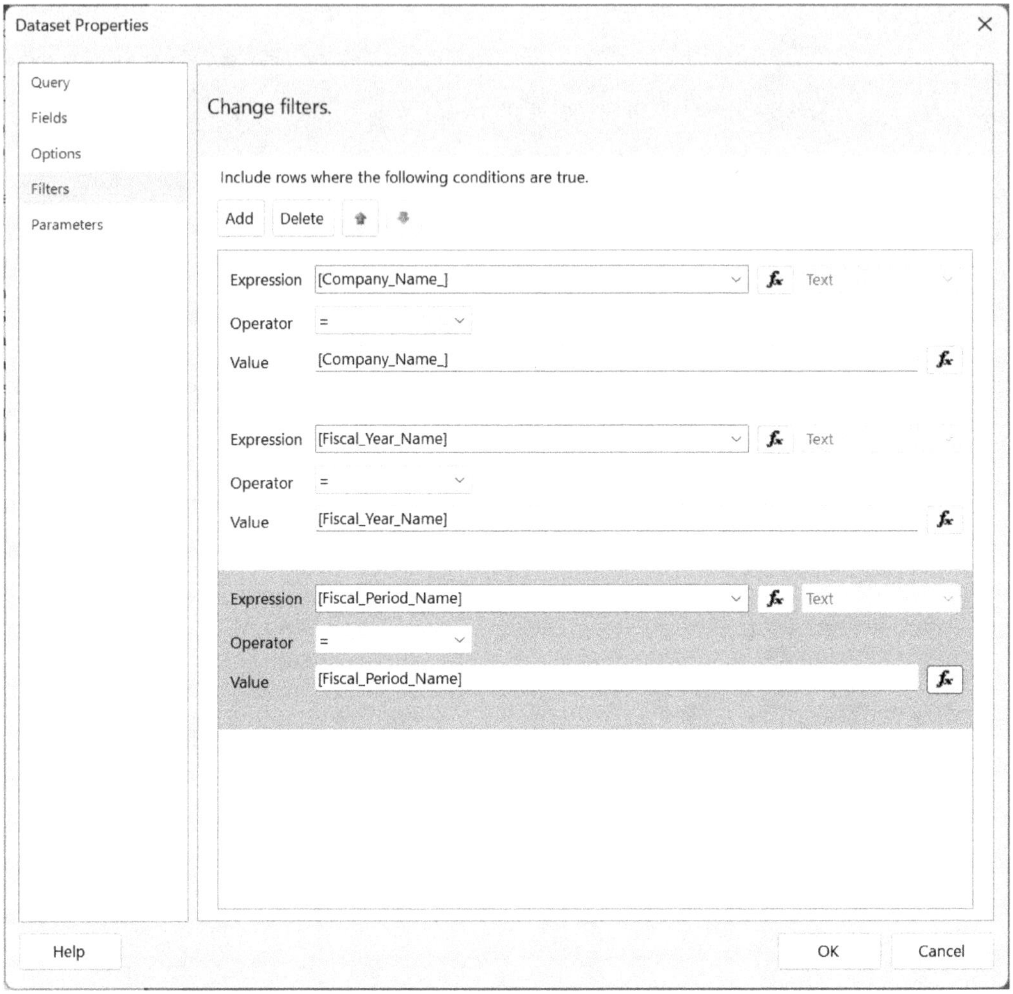

Figure 11.18: Completed filters

Now, click **OK**, and we are ready to lay out our actual report. There are numerous approaches that can be taken here, but for the sake of flexibility, we will be using text boxes. We need to add two text boxes: one for the value and the other for the label. The text box for the value can be added by simply dragging and dropping the value from the dataset onto the design surface. The text box for the label will need to be drawn using the text box tool, which can be found under the **Insert** tab of the ribbon:

Figure 11.19: Adding fields to the report

A word of caution here: in certain versions of Power BI Report Builder, the preview only works correctly for text boxes where the font size is smaller than 11pt.

Now, we need to finish the report by adding the remaining fields, formatting them, and adding some lines to break up the report visually.

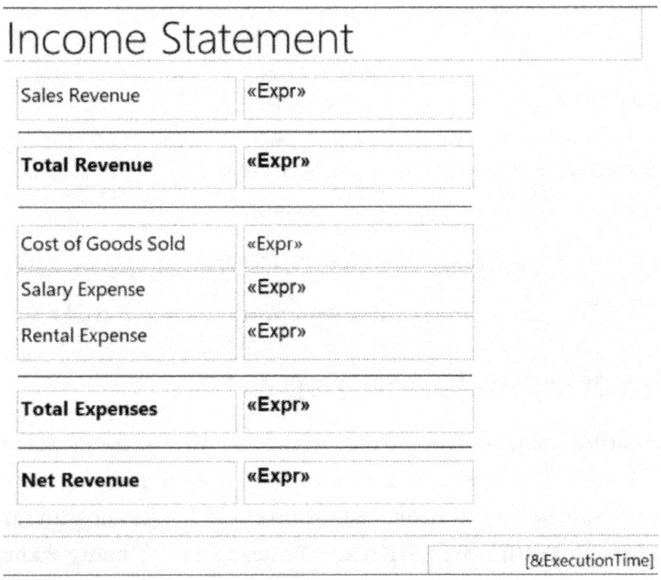

Figure 11.20: The completed report design

Finally, we can drag and drop the parameter values into the report so we can see what company, year, and period the report has been run for. When we preview this, we can see our final report.

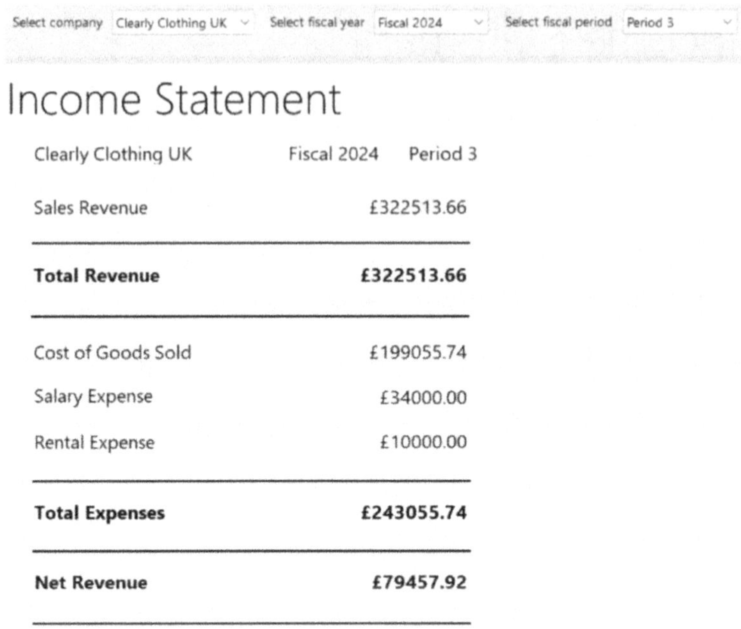

Figure 11.21: Running the report

We can also use this tool to create other printable reports, such as a trial balance report.

Creating the trial balance report

The core steps for creating the trial balance report are the same as for creating the income statement report. The key differences are the contents of the dataset and the details of the layout. The dataset in this case will contain data from every single account, and use the measures for **Total Credit**, **Total Debit**, **Opening Balance**, and **Closing Balance**. These would typically be formatted in a matrix with accounts on the rows and the various measures on the columns.

Reports created in this way are much more suited to fixed formats and printing, since although Power BI Report Builder is a lot more complicated to use and has a much steeper learning curve than the rest of the tool, it allows much more fine-grained control of report layouts.

Summary

In this chapter, we looked in detail at how to create a printable report. While in the modern workplace, this may seem obsolete, it remains an important tool for us to have available. In the next chapter, we move to a current hot topic which is how we may use AI to drive financial decisions.

Get this book's PDF version and more

Scan the QR code (or go to `https://www.packtpub.com/unlock`). Search for this book by name, confirm the edition, and then follow the steps on the page.

UNLOCK NOW

Note: Keep your invoice handy. Purchases made directly from Packt don't require an invoice.

12

Financial Reporting in an AI-Driven World

Writing any book on a technical subject can be a nerve-racking experience. You wonder how current your words and screenshots will remain. Will there be a major UI refresh, rendering every screen-clip outdated? Will the product name change? Will there be a major technical breakthrough rendering most of the book instantly outdated?

While writing this book, this is the chapter we worried about the most. For every other chapter, we know the technical accuracy of the content, and for the majority of the book, we know the techniques will be relevant for many years to come.

The three of us have been in technology long enough to have witnessed the birth of modern computing and the rise of the internet, so we're experienced in managing change. In all cases, we endeavor to be at the forefront; that's our business.

That also applies to **Artificial Intelligence** (**AI**). But our fears for this chapter are *how* wrong we're going to get it, because we *will* get some of this wrong. Not wrong as we write it, but wrong in months and years to come. Maybe we're being hard on ourselves, and "outdated" is a better word. Sadly, we're not in possession of a crystal ball.

By the end of this chapter, you will understand the following:

- What AI is
- How to use generative AI tools to aid in report creation
- How Microsoft Fabric fits into AI and Power BI
- How to store data to enable AI insights
- The dangers and risks of using AI tools

We will start by looking at what AI actually is and what it can do.

What is AI?

Before we dive into how we can use AI, we should make it clear what we actually *mean* by AI.

Foundations of AI

AI refers to a broad set of technologies that perform tasks requiring human-like intelligence. These include the following:

- **Machine learning**, where systems learn patterns from data
- **Deep learning** and **neural networks**, which power more complex recognition and prediction
- **Natural language processing** (**NLP**), which allows machines to understand and generate human language
- **Computer vision**, which enables the interpretation of images and video

Together, these areas form the backbone of AI as it has developed during recent decades.

Looking at the current trends

More recently, our focus has shifted toward generative AI and AI agents. These approaches use **Large Language Models** (**LLMs**) that can respond to user prompts, generate content, and perform multi-step tasks.

Those are short explanations for complex topics, and we advise you to undertake your own research into AI to develop further understanding, beyond this chapter.

Our stance on this chapter is to equip you with general advice, based on principles rather than specifics. Those principles should last you longer than a "use function A to achieve result B" approach.

Therefore, in this chapter, we've set out to do the following:

- Show you where to start with an AI project based on an immediate requirement
- Explain how to organize your data in the short and long term for the AI projects you've planned and haven't planned
- Help you think about the development of AI within your organization

We're going to work through this chapter in the order of the preceding bullets, starting with where to start with an AI project. That may seem counterintuitive, as organization of data and understanding should be the foundations before you start. But we're seeing many instances of AI projects starting immediately, so we're trying to be as pragmatic as possible. To many who read this chapter, starting with long data management and storage projects may not be realistic in the face of organizational pressure. We believe you should still do the data management and storage projects, but we appreciate that it may not be an option.

OK, that's all the caveats over. If you're reading this as part of a data history project in 2040, just upload the entire book via your cerebral cortex interface and remember to leave the house at least once this month.

For everyone else, let's look at where to start an AI project.

Where do you start with an AI project?

We're going to start with where many organizations are currently starting.

Leaders in many organizations appear to be in the following modes:

- Excited about AI
- Confused about AI
- In self-protection mode and need to be seen within the organization to be working on internal AI initiatives

It's probably fair to say that many of the same leaders move between all three on a daily basis.

What's going on?

AI is a transformative technology and is being heavily marketed as such. Many people in many organizations are under immense pressure to adopt the technology so the organization doesn't fall behind. This is leading, in many cases, to a "throw spaghetti against the wall to see what sticks" approach. Inevitably, that leads to failed projects and wasted money.

There's a simple and effective (although not foolproof) method to deal with this problem.

Start with the business problem, not the technology.

Wherever you or your organization are, the pressure to use AI is driving emotions and probably a few questionable decisions. As many organizations are experiencing similar patterns of behavior, now is the time to stay calm and focus on some basics to start an AI project.

We'd start with two requirements:

- A problem that can benefit from the application of AI
- A technical method to solve the problem (or a data science team to build it for you)

Start with a business need

There's an important distinction in comprehending where AI works well, so you can use it to solve problems that'll benefit from the technology. It's certainly not the answer to every problem, despite what a few people may want you to believe.

So, what does AI do well right now?

Above all, AI is good at taking a mass of information, summarizing it, and/or detecting patterns based on data.

Conversely, AI is not a good solution for issues involving human emotion, creativity, or strategic vision, not to mention pretty much all tasks that require a human body. I'm not using AI to fix my air conditioner, and I'd rather use AI to analyze sales trends to spot anomalies, as opposed to building a rebranding exercise with an accompanying strategic marketing plan.

In a finance function, you may want to start by applying AI to a cash flow forecast or error detection to speed up the month-end process. Whatever you choose to do, you'll need access to an AI model to help with the analysis, which we will discuss next.

A technical method to solve the problem

So, how do we get access to AI to help us solve these problems?

If you work in a very large organization, you may have the benefit of a data science team to build a solution.

If you don't, then you may need to look at off-the-shelf options you can configure to use. In most cases, we expect the latter to be the case.

Off-the-shelf options may come from the software vendor that built your application, or they may come from elsewhere. In all cases, it should have a relatively user-friendly method of building capability against your data.

As this is a Power BI book, let's start with the following scenario: *I'm a Power BI user and want to use AI to help analyze my data.*

Using Power BI and AI together

In starting to discuss Power BI and AI, let's be clear about what we're talking about and what we're not talking about.

What we *are* talking about is using generative AI to help analyze your data and produce visuals and insights using natural language prompts (hereafter, "prompts").

What we're *not* talking about is using AI to help write DAX, which we don't cover in this book, as our intention is to teach you the basics of DAX applied to finance. We've found that AI tools do a so-so job of writing DAX, which can sometimes be incorrect. If you want to analyze the data in your Power BI semantic model(s) using AI, you'll also need a **Fabric** subscription. Fabric is Microsoft's end-to-end analytics platform, and Power BI is a component of Fabric. We will describe Fabric later in this chapter.

Fabric is a subscription-based service from Microsoft, although a different subscription type from Power BI. With Fabric, you purchase a subscription for compute capacity, not a $/user/month license. The subscription is consumption-based, meaning you pay while it runs.

Fabric and Power BI give you access to Copilot, which is Microsoft's product term for its AI offerings. For the sake of clarity, "Copilot" is used broadly within the Microsoft product portfolio, and the Copilot offering in, say, Excel, is different from the Copilot offering in Power BI and Fabric. It's also licensed differently, and a Copilot license that gives you AI features in the Office suite is a different license from the Fabric subscription license we're explaining here. If you're unclear, we'd advise getting clarification from your IT function or whoever buys licenses in your organization. Licensing can be as complex as data, so we'll leave this with your experts.

Needless to say, Power BI combined with a Fabric capacity provides you with the capability to use a ChatGPT LLM against one or more semantic models that reside in a workspace that has Fabric capacity assigned to it. For a Power BI user, it's probably the easiest way to use AI against the data in a semantic model.

The most important step, for this scenario and any scenario involving the use of semantic models and AI, is to ensure that your model is a simple star schema and you remove columns that aren't required for the purpose of the project. Simplification is an essential step to successfully using Copilot with Power BI.

Why is this, and why isn't AI clever enough to just figure out the complexity?

You can, of course, publish a semantic model with complex relationships and all columns from the source tables. But when you start using the Copilot prompt in Power BI, you'll see some strange responses that'll be difficult to track back to the data. The reason is that Copilot needs to be told what data to use, or at least, that data needs to be restricted as much as possible.

To take an example, we've mentioned the challenges of using dates in your financial models, and especially the correct dates for the intended calculation. Sales reports that use the *created* date instead of the *invoice* date will place the transactions in the wrong date buckets, and your reporting will be incorrect. Therefore, if you give Copilot multiple dates, how does it know which one to pick? It doesn't, and you need to provide clear instructions or, even better, restrict the options it has.

To be successful with any data and AI project, make it easy for AI.

To start using Copilot with a semantic model, you'll need a Fabric licensed workspace in Power BI. To see whether a workspace has Fabric capability, check **Workspace settings** and choose the **Workspace type** option:

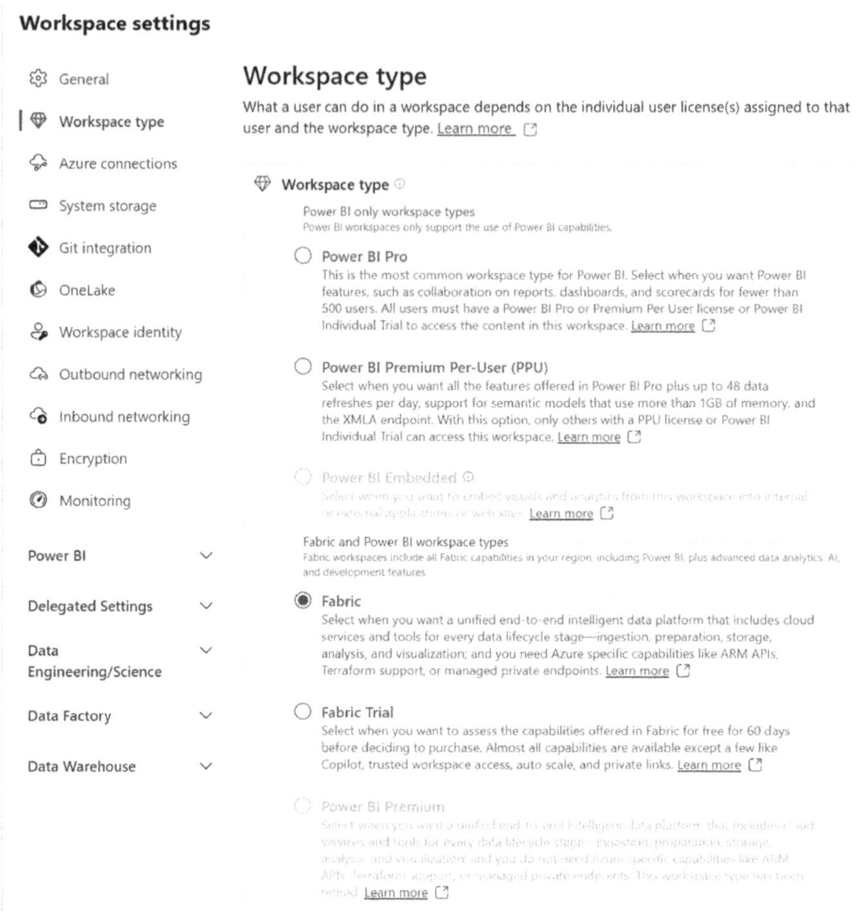

Figure 12.1: Workspace settings

You can see from *Figure 12.1* that the workspace has Fabric capacity. The **Fabric** option may be grayed out, which means you don't have a Fabric subscription. As of writing, Fabric trials are available, so you may be able to test the capability with a free trial.

Once you have a workspace with Fabric capacity, publish a semantic model from Power BI Desktop. In our example, we used `Core Data Model.pbix`. When you've done this, you'll be able to use the **Prep data for AI** button in Power BI Desktop. On clicking that button, you'll see the following dialog:

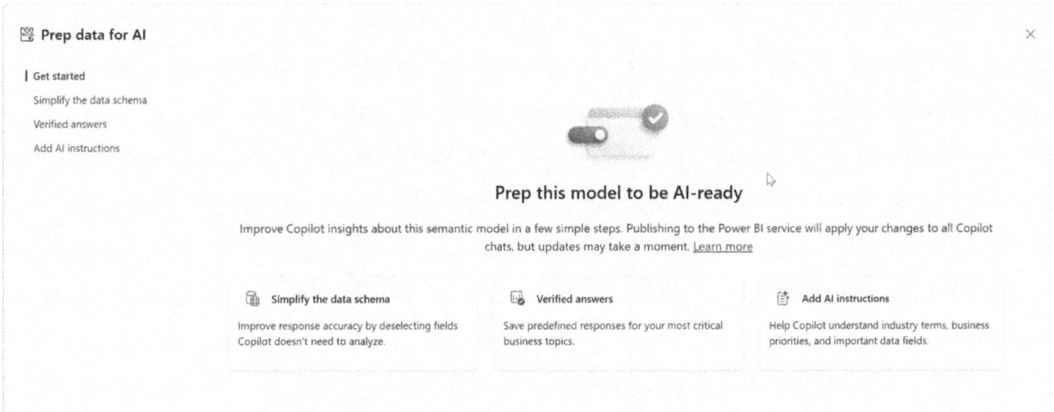

Figure 12.2: Prep data for AI

This provides three options:

- **Simplify the data schema**
- **Verified answers**
- **Add AI instructions**

It's important you follow each option as described next.

Simplify the data schema

An important task when using Copilot is to remove the fields you don't want Copilot to use. We do this to limit the options Copilot has when trying to formulate an option against a user prompt. We'll certainly remove IDs and indexes, text fields, and superfluous date fields. When using the **Simplify the data schema** option, we uncheck those fields, as shown in *Figure 12.3*:

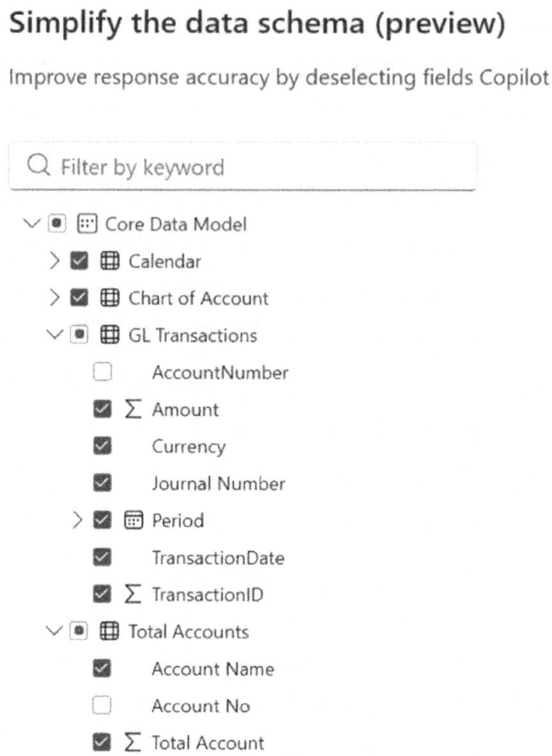

Figure 12.3: Simplify the data schema

You can see from *Figure 12.3* that we've removed the ID fields for **AccountNumber** and **Account No**, as we don't want Copilot to use these. Remember, you can repeat this exercise many times, and you'll likely need to add/remove fields as you test how Copilot responds to user prompts.

The next task is to set up **Verified answers**.

Verified answers

The purpose of a verified answer is to tell Copilot how you want AI to respond when certain questions are answered. It may be the case that your users want to use prompting to interrogate the data, but, in reality, they're going to ask similar questions, such as *What were our property expenses in 202x?*. With **Verified answers**, you can give Copilot a number of questions and instruct it to use a certain visual when the question is asked, to respond.

When setting up **Verified answers**, you do this using the ellipses on the visual. To show an example, we have a visual of GL transactions over time, split by account category, shown in *Figure 12.4*.

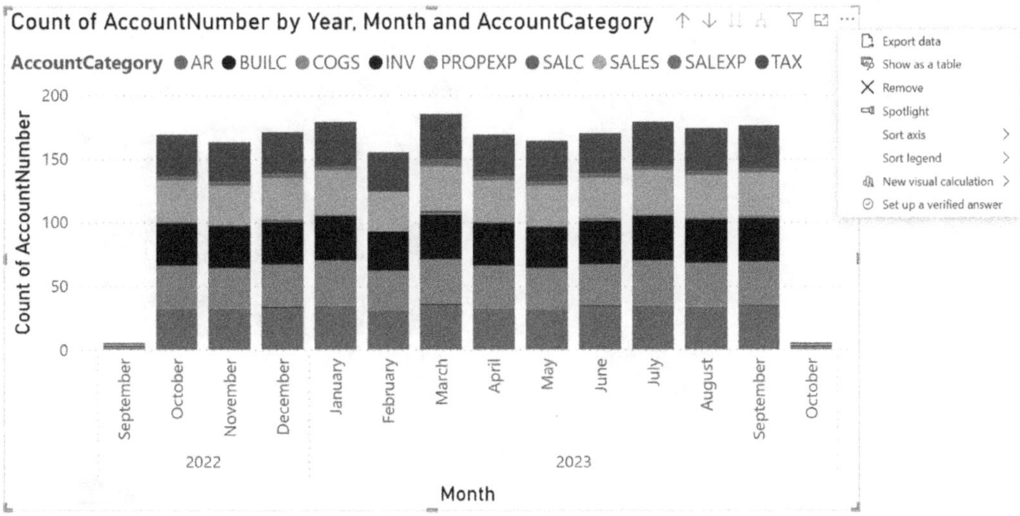

Figure 12.4: Setting up a verified answer

From the ellipses menu, select **Set up a verified answer**. After doing this, you'll see the dialog shown in *Figure 12.5*. Copilot will suggest questions, but it's important you provide your own. In our example, we've provided `What are the property expenses based on X year` and `What is our Sales Revenue for X year`. We also accepted **How many transactions are there each month?**, which was suggested by Copilot. The intention is that when users ask similar questions (they don't need to be exact), the visual will be returned with the answer to the prompt.

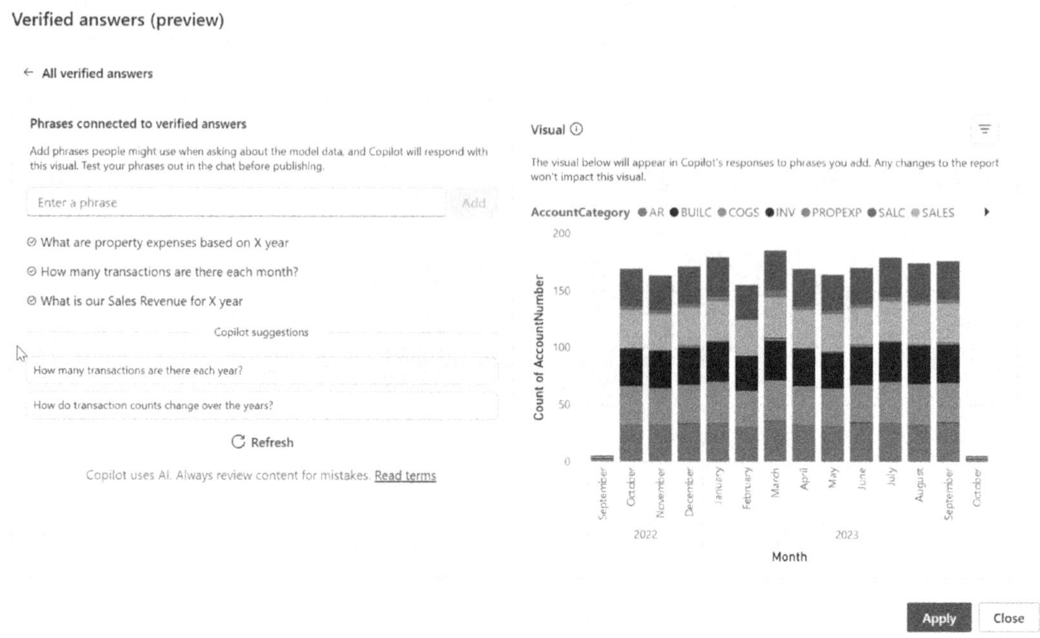

Figure 12.5: Setting up Verified answers

The final option to instruct Copilot is to add AI instructions.

Add AI instructions

AI instructions allow you to enter anything you think may help Copilot in responding to a user prompt. This is probably the most important option of the three options to guide and fine-tune Copilot, and experience has told us, the most iterative of the three based on a test and refine cycle. You should plan to test prompting and use AI instructions to tell the model where to correct behavior based on errors when responding to prompts. Here's an example of AI instructions we may choose to use for this example to start the process:

- This model contains general ledger financial data. Use it to analyze account balances, transaction activity, and spending trends over time. The primary fact table is `GL Transactions`, which links to the `Calendar` table for time intelligence and a `Chart of Account` table for grouping accounts by type (e.g., `Revenue`, `Expenses`, and `Assets`).
- Standard `Calendar` dimension. Use this table for all time-based filtering and comparisons. Fields such as `Month`, `Quarter`, and `Fiscal Year` control how data is sliced across time. This is the only table that should drive date filters.

- `GL Transactions` is a fact table containing one row per journal entry line. Each row has an amount (credit/debit), posting date, account number, and reference keys to the `Account Categories` and `Date` tables. Positive amounts represent debits; negative amounts represent credits (or adjust per your convention).
- `Chart of Account` is a dimension table that maps individual GL accounts to broader groupings such as `Revenue`, `Cost of Goods Sold`, and `Operating Expenses`. Use this table to roll up transactions by financial statement category.

Figure 12.6 shows these instructions entered into **Add AI instructions**:

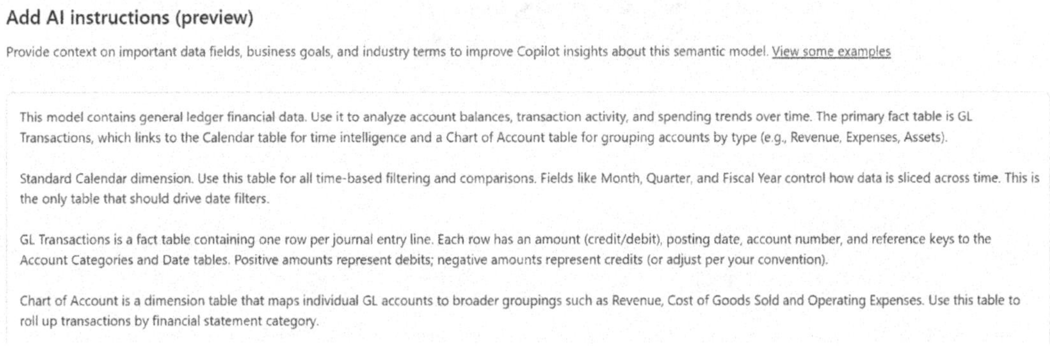

Figure 12.6: Add AI instructions

Once you've followed these three steps, you can start testing prompts either in Power BI Desktop or within the Power BI service. If using the service, make sure you republish your model. To test in Desktop, click on the **Copilot** button under the **Home** tab. When you do so, the Copilot sidebar will open, and a prompt will appear.

In *Figure 12.7*, we asked Copilot, `what is the PROPEXP amount for year 2023?`. This is very specific to the model, as we know the *Property Expenses* category is called `PROPEXP`. Copilot got this correct:

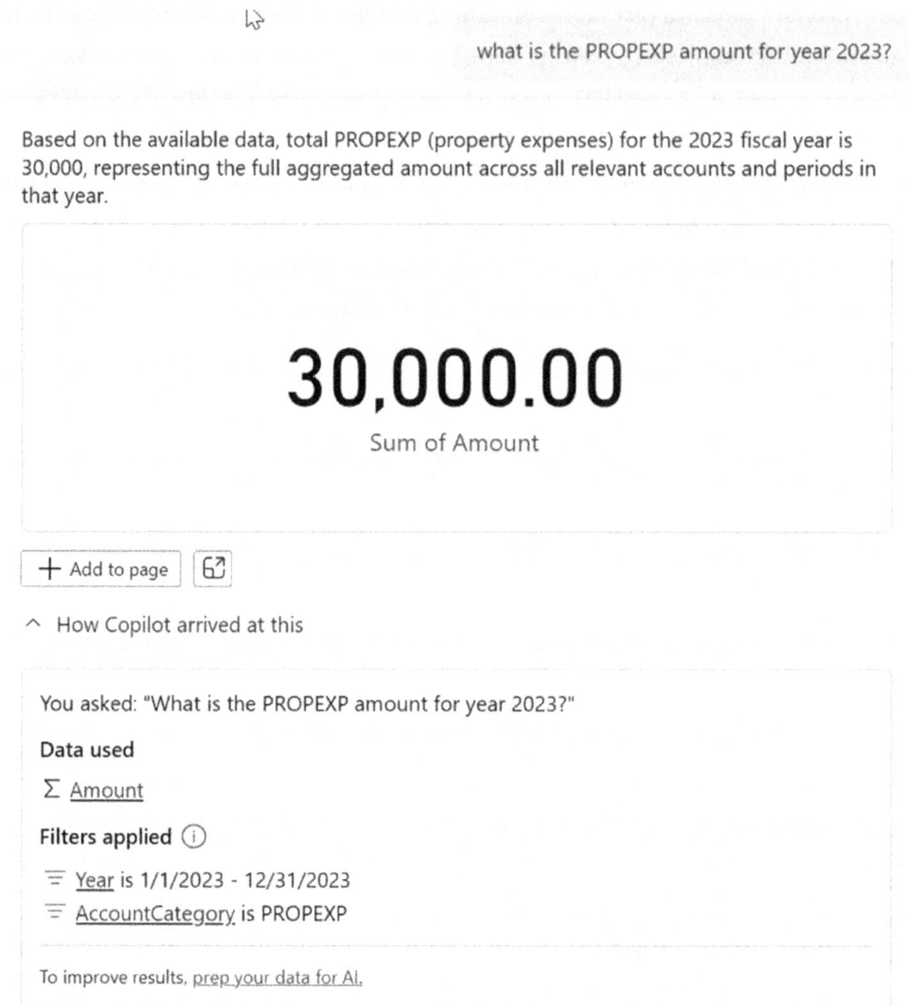

Figure 12.7: Prompting on PROPEXP

Also note that Copilot tells you how it gets to $30,000.

We then tested with a similar question, using different terminology, which was `what were our property costs for June 2023?`, and we got the response in *Figure 12.8*:

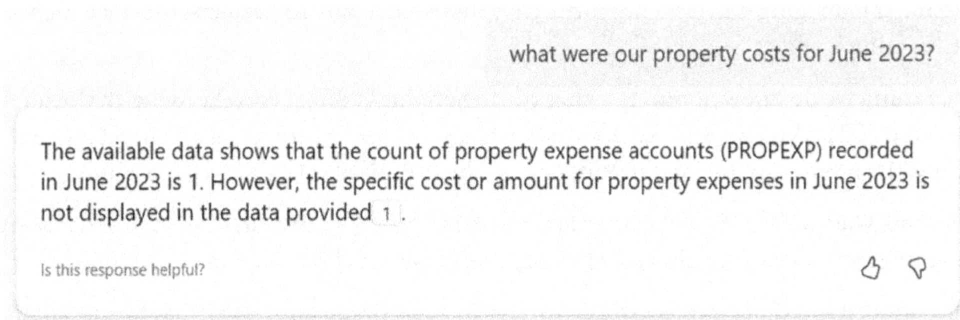

Figure 12.8: Further prompting

In this example, Copilot wasn't able to determine the meaning of the word *costs* in the prompt, returning a count instead of a fiscal amount. When starting to use Copilot, these issues are common.

In addition to preparing your semantic model for AI, we advise exhaustive testing by providing prompts to your model and testing that the results are in line with expectations. This will help you discover how AI interprets your semantic model and whether any unintended fields are being used. The examples we provided about date and index fields are exactly the issues to look for.

Ask the model realistic questions and check the results. In some instances, you may not immediately understand the basis of the response if it's not in line with expectations, and you'll need to understand why Copilot responded the way it did and, therefore, the changes you'll need to make to the semantic model to deliver the results you expected.

We ask users the kind of questions they'd ask the model, so we have a realistic sample of likely questions. User questions are often imprecise, such as "Who is my biggest customer?" Does that mean the biggest customer by sales or quantity, and what's the time period? All time, last year, this year, or this month? Ask vague and imprecise questions to understand the assumptions Copilot will make.

When Copilot doesn't respond in a manner you expected, you'll need to make changes to the model and/or any instructions you've given to Copilot about how to respond to certain questions. This can be a lengthy and iterative process, but essential to ensure responses are in line with expectations.

Short and medium-term data planning and storage

AI needs data. While that may be obvious, the role of data in AI projects cannot be understated, so if you're managing data within your organization, you have a pivotal role in making AI successful. If managing data and not intricately involved in any AI projects, there's a high chance of failure.

Another thing we do know about AI is that the benefit has a direct correlation with the quality and volume of data you have to work with. To be effective, AI needs good-quality data, and generally, the more data, the better. But if your data is limited, AI can still have value.

Conversely, what we also know about AI is that using poor-quality data is a very bad strategy. The common misconception that AI will just fix it is, well, a common misconception.

We also understand that a project to get all data in good shape for AI is probably unrealistic for most organizations, so we suggest not starting there. It's too much to take on and will randomize the organization, missing some quick wins. But that project needs to start somewhere, and it's far better to start the data project in parallel with the immediate need AI projects, as opposed to not at all.

Let's consider a different starting point, that you've not begun to plan how AI will benefit you, or have just started considering how AI *may* benefit you. What do you do with your data?

There are a few defining characteristics:

- Your data is clean. To test, you may want to clean a subset of your data, which will be quicker and give you more control over outcomes. You can introduce more data over time.
- Table and column labels use commonly understood business language, not cryptic developer labels.
- Tables and columns that aren't required are removed from the model, or the AI is instructed to ignore them. Columns such as IDs and system data that don't support the purpose aren't going to help AI analyze your data and, in some instances, may be incorrectly used by AI. We had a recent example where data in a numeric ID column was used to answer a generative question for a specific sales result.
- If many columns have similar data, only use the column(s) you need. Dates are a great example. If you have multiple date columns, which is very common, remove the columns you don't need. Otherwise, you give AI the opportunity to use the wrong column.

If you've taken the right steps now, you'll be ready when you start AI projects, and we're 100% certain that good quality data, in abundance, will benefit you. It may not ensure project success, but your project certainly won't fail due to data.

As you work with AI, plan to evolve your data structures as you go through test cycles to ground your data. If your model isn't delivering desired or consistent results, you may need to revisit your data to make changes. Test again and see whether that improves the results.

Remember that testing your AI model is a critical task, and the process of testing has to be a priority for a successful project and deployment.

We've just discussed some short-term tactics for using your data to support AI projects, so what are the longer-term actions you can take to help make your AI projects successful?

Long-term considerations for AI projects

Short-term tactical data plans are useful to help your organization learn about how to be effective with AI, but that needs to be paired with some long-term systemic data policies so your data is ready for whatever strategies the business wants to follow.

That means that we need to think about how to store data to make it readily available for AI tasks in the future, rather than for the purpose of reporting. Depending on how you want to process your data, the Power BI semantic model is not a good place to store your data if you want to process it for AI workloads. In fact, a semantic model shouldn't be considered as a data storage mechanism.

Add to that, it's often not easy to directly access the data in a Power BI model, other than via Power BI, and we need to consider ways to store our data outside of Power BI to help you manage AI projects in the future. There are several approaches we can take to this.

The first, and simplest, is to leave the data in the source system. We're considering financial data, so we can assume that at least seven years of history will be preserved at source, and in most cases, this should be enough. If your source financial application is mainstream, the data structures should be well designed by the developers. It's also worth considering how much historical data you'll need. In many cases, when you go too far back in time, the structure of the business was different, so, for example, 15-year-old data has little relevance to today.

The preferred method of handling this data is to move it out of the source system and put it somewhere else for later processing. To understand the specifics of how to do this and the choice of tools, please refer to any of the great texts on data lakes, lakehouses, and data warehouses. A detailed explanation of these concepts is outside the scope of this book, but we'll cover the basics.

There are many choices for how to store data, but they generally come down to whether it makes more sense to store the data in a structured form, such as a SQL database, or unstructured, such as a data lake. Or something in between, such as a lakehouse.

The general considerations are how much data you're storing and the cost implications. Typically, storing data in a data lake can be more cost-effective, especially for larger datasets. Since the data will generally be used in bulk, the advantages of storing the data in a SQL database may not transpire. Normally, this option would be considered if and only if there is an additional need to process the data in smaller subsets than would be typical for AI.

The other decision is how to move the data into the data store for AI. Leaving aside specific tools, there are two main approaches: a regular trickle or a periodic bulk load of all the data. While the bulk load pattern is certainly easier to design and implement, the trickle feed (for example, created and modified rows each day) will mean you're constantly up to date.

There is no right or wrong approach to this, just considerations when planning for an AI future.

Think about how you develop AI capabilities

You have many choices about how you develop your AI capabilities, and those choices are growing almost monthly as new services are launched.

It may be the case that your financial application provider is already beginning to provide AI capabilities in the application you use, so you may get some quick wins by deploying those.

In lieu of some off-the-shelf capabilities, to start planning for how AI could help your business, you'll need to consider the following:

- What are the use cases within the finance function, and what impact should you expect to see? Examples could be accelerating the close process, automating reconciliations, or detecting anomalies.
- What resources and skills do we need to develop the strategy and begin the initial projects? In general composition, the roles you'll need will resemble the roles we proposed in *Chapter 1, Identifying Your Reporting Needs and Data Sources*, for your Power BI project team. Naturally, you'll also need some data science, machine learning, and data engineering skills. That doesn't need to be in the form of full-time employees; you may choose to employ external consultants as you ramp up, then employ personnel as your use becomes widespread.
- What technical platforms will you need to support this initiative?
- What data will you need to support the scenarios?
- What is the organizational readiness to adopt these technologies and the change management processes to take your current workforce on this journey?

Few organizations will or should transition from no AI to lots of AI overnight; there are steps we recommend to help you understand the technology and assist in the transition.

There may be a question, and we do hear it, which is "Why not just go all-in?".

You certainly can, but that approach involves risk, like any major organizational change project, so the ultimate arbiter is how much risk you're willing to accept. As with other technical initiatives, there may be unintended consequences to the use of AI that you'll want to manage. We'll discuss this later in the chapter.

When considering the projects that will benefit the business, it's useful to have a framework to assess current organization capabilities, allowing you to make an objective judgement of your current capability. A mess of Excel spreadsheets isn't going to be the foundation for a successful AI project, so it's important to be objective about your current level of data maturity before investing in an AI project that could fail.

We use the following model (*Figure 12.9*), which is common within data circles. It has four levels of data capability that are developed based on the difficulty of deploying them, and then the value you generate from the work to deploy. The levels are shown in *Figure 12.9*.

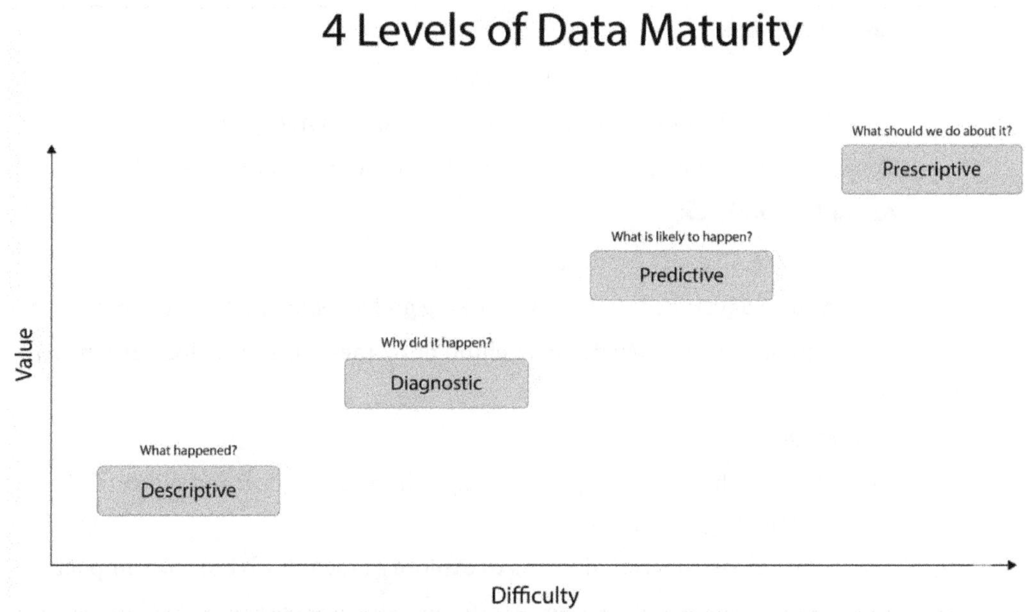

Figure 12.9: The level of data maturity

The levels are described as follows:

- **Descriptive**:
  - **Characteristics**:
    - Standard reports, dashboards, and KPIs
    - Focus on historical performance (e.g., sales last quarter)
  - **Tools**: Excel, Power BI/Tableau dashboards

  - **AI readiness check**:
    - The organization is not AI-ready yet
    - Organization is likely still data-reactive
    - You're capturing data, but not analyzing cause or forecasting trends
  - **Next steps**:
    - Improve data quality, governance, and accessibility
    - Start instrumenting systems to capture richer, real-time data
    - Begin centralizing data sources for consistency
- **Diagnostic**:
  - **Characteristics**:
    - Root cause analysis and correlation tracking
    - Use of drill-downs, statistical analysis, and ad hoc queries
  - **Tools**: SQL, R/Python for basic stats, and more advanced BI tools
  - **AI readiness check**:
    - You are AI-ready for narrow use cases
    - You've developed analytical thinking and are starting to test hypotheses
    - You understand key drivers behind outcomes—essential for building AI models
  - **Next steps**:
    - Pilot machine learning models (e.g., churn prediction and demand forecasting)
    - Build cross-functional teams to explore AI ideas with business impact
    - Ensure proper data lineage and feature documentation
- **Predictive**:
  - **Characteristics**:
    - Forecasting models, regression, and classification
    - Using historical patterns to predict future outcomes
  - **Tools**: Python/R, Azure ML, AutoML, DataRobot, and so on
  - **AI readiness check**:
    - You have solid ground for AI expansion

        - Models are likely already in use—time to focus on scaling, accuracy, and governance
        - You can start exploring advanced AI, such as deep learning and NLP
    - **Next steps**:
        - Move toward MLOps: versioning, retraining, and monitoring models
        - Integrate predictions into business workflows or apps (e.g., through Power Platform or APIs)
        - Evaluate model bias and explainability frameworks
- **Prescriptive**:
    - **Characteristics**:
        - Optimization models, AI recommendations, and simulations
        - Suggested actions based on predictions
        - Use of reinforcement learning, decision intelligence, and automation
    - **Tools**: Currently, this is chiefly delivered via custom-developed applications
    - **AI readiness check**:
        - Highly competent, ready for transformative AI
        - Capable of creating closed-loop systems where AI doesn't just inform but acts (e.g., robotic process automation and AI co-pilots)
    - **Next steps**:
        - Implement real-time decision-making and AI-assisted operations
        - Use generative AI to explore and test decision scenarios
        - Prioritize governance, human oversight, and audit trails for AI actions

Your AI readiness is very dependent on where you sit, from descriptive to prescriptive, so objectively placing yourself within one of the categories is a good starting point. At least you're in a good place to move forward, understanding the road ahead. This should also reduce the risk that a project is aborted or fails.

Working with Microsoft Fabric

We mentioned Fabric earlier in the chapter; here, we provide some more detail.

While Power BI continues to thrive as a standalone product, it also forms one of the core components of Microsoft Fabric. Fabric is Microsoft's unified, cloud-hosted data analytics platform. Power BI represents the data visualization engine within Fabric and continues to have all the same functionality that we have come to know in the standalone product, but, used within Fabric, the capability of the platform goes beyond what Power BI can do on its own.

The Fabric platform itself is built on top of **OneLake**, a data lake solution designed to hold all an organization's data. From this base, it provides capabilities for data engineering, data science, data warehousing, and business intelligence. As of late 2025, traditional databases are also being introduced into the platform, which will make Fabric a one-stop shop for almost any data analytics need an organization might have.

Throughout the platform, Copilot provides built-in AI capabilities to help the user produce analyses quickly and easily. This means that generative AI is available across the platform's capabilities.

We've already discussed a number of considerations around how to store data for AI workloads, such as using a data lake or database to store raw data, and Fabric provides a platform in OneLake. It also provides the means to get the data there. One of the key capabilities in Fabric is the ability to create data pipelines in much the same way as you can in Azure Data Factory to import data at scale into the OneLake storage.

The data engineering and data warehousing capabilities allow organizations to create complete analytical solutions and work with ad hoc analyses.

Storage

The OneLake storage built into Fabric is designed to reduce the amount of data that needs to be moved around an organization. As a data lake, it is capable of storing almost any kind of data, from financial to data gleaned from social media, such as videos and photographs. For the most part, we are interested in more structured data, as this is generally the nature of financial data. Here, we need to get the data into OneLake since it is highly unlikely that the financial management system will be using OneLake natively (although, of course, tighter integration from Microsoft products is likely to be coming in the future). We also need to consider the data formats to use: for smaller datasets, something simple such as CSV may be suitable, whereas for larger datasets, a more advanced format such as Parquet might be the right choice.

Data warehouse and data lakehouse

Fabric allows managing data in both warehouses and lakehouses. Typically, the warehouse is going to be more suitable for structured and semi-structured data, where tools such as **SQL** will be the main means of interacting with the data. Lakehouses are better suited for less structured data sources and highly heterogeneous data, and interacting with that data using tools such as **Spark**. While financial data in itself will tend toward being a better use case for warehousing, if the overall needs of the organization require the processing of a lot of unstructured data, then a lakehouse might be the better option.

In either case, and especially where we are looking toward leveraging AI, the medallion architecture will serve an organization well. Typically, this will involve creating three layers of data:

- **Bronze**: Typically holding the raw data as exported from the source
- **Silver**: Holding cleansed and augmented data (although see *Chapter 10, Testing and Fine-Tuning Your Data*, for why to be careful in cleansing)
- **Gold**: Data that is structured for analysis

The gold layer would be best suited to creating the sorts of Power BI reports we've been discussing throughout this book. This sort of data is streamlined for reporting and may lose some of the details that we need for AI workloads. This is where the silver layer comes in. This layer preserves the details and is therefore well-suited to training AI models and inferring conclusions using such a model.

Whether you are using a data warehouse or a data lakehouse, typically, the data will still be stored in OneLake. This means that large amounts of ingested data can be persisted in the bronze layer and allow for historical reloads or retrospective changes to business logic without bringing that data into expensive database storage.

Data factory and data engineering

One of the main use cases for the data factory capability in Fabric is for the ingestion and transformation of data. Data used in the preceding medallion architecture example will need to be ingested from the source system and landed into the bronze layer, from here it will be de-deduplicated, enriched, and cleansed into the silver layer, and finally, transformed and aggregated to create the gold layer. This work is generally all done by the data factory capability, but more interactive tools, such as notebooks, are also available. Notebooks can be a powerful tool for data analysts to carry out ad hoc and exploratory work using organizational data. They can be a good starting point for too for experimenting with AI.

Data science

As with all areas of AI, the data science capability in Fabric represents a fast-changing landscape, and some of the features we describe here are in preview and therefore subject to change. At its heart, it integrates data science and machine learning right into the Fabric platform, and consequently, right into Power BI, too. Fabric data science is a collection of tools for data science and machine learning, incorporating both low-code/no-code tooling and full pro-code tooling to create, train, and consume machine learning models. These outputs can then be consumed directly into Power BI reports.

The notebook function in Fabric data science facilitates data exploration by data scientists and can be used to aid the ingestion of data into OneLake. If we have data already structured into a medallion architecture, the silver layer would likely be the prime source of data for machine learning experiments.

On the pro-code side, there is integration with Python and Apache Spark for processing data at scale. Python is one of the most popular languages for machine learning due to the large number of libraries available that lend themselves to machine learning workloads. For more "traditional" statistical workloads, there is also the **R** language. R is popular among statisticians due to the specialized libraries available for statistical analysis. Both of these languages can be used within notebooks.

For teams that lack direct expertise in AI and machine learning, there is **AI Services**. Formerly Azure Cognitive Services, this offers prebuilt AI models for workloads such as text analytics and translation services.

Throughout all of Fabric data science, there is Copilot. Whether you are just starting out with data science or are a seasoned professional, Copilot is able to assist in working with data and data science. It will have access to the datasets you are working on and be able to take a bigger overview of the data than any human can reasonably expect to. As a result, it can help with questions on how to cleanse and prepare data, and even suggest code that you can use within your data science experiments. As ever, though, be careful that any code it suggests works and doesn't expose you to any security breaches. We tackle these risks in more detail in the *Understanding the risks of AI* section.

Real-time intelligence

In most financial use cases, loading data daily is close enough to real time not to need any special tools to do it, especially if there are overnight batch processes to post to the GL from other subledgers. There are related topics, however, that may ask for much more up-to-the-minute approaches. We discussed in *Chapter 8, Managing Inventory Data*, how to manage inventory data, but what if we could monitor stock levels in real time? Fabric has built-in tools for streaming and transforming data from source into reports and dashboards in near-real time.

Power BI

If you are publishing Power BI reports to be shared, this is the Fabric capability you will most likely already be using. Power BI is the visualization engine for Fabric and is tightly integrated across all of the other Fabric workloads. For example, if you create a data warehouse in Fabric, you can immediately create a new report from that without leaving your browser. And the same applies across other areas of Fabric.

Understanding the risks of AI

"Garbage in, garbage out." This has never been truer than in our modern AI-driven world, but what does it mean? Essentially, anything misprogrammed or fed with the wrong data can rapidly generate an incorrect response and will do it consistently.

In non-AI systems, it's easier to test these and ensure that these errors do not get through to the final production code, although by no means guaranteed.

When we start working with AI, we have a more complex problem. AI algorithms will change the output based on learning from the data they've been trained on, and herein lies the key problem: how good is that data? Since we cannot be certain of what data the AI is using, we need to ensure that the data being used to train the AI model is good, comprehensive, and unbiased.

One of the risks of AI is the risk of **hallucination**. That is to say that the algorithm can come up with spurious results, not based on reality. An example of this can be found in the field of image recognition and classification. An example given in *When will AI misclassify? Intuiting failures on natural images – PMC* (`https://pmc.ncbi.nlm.nih.gov/articles/PMC10082388/`) shows that a bird casting a shadow may be misidentified by an AI image classification algorithm as a sundial.

And this is the crux of what we have to remember. AI is not actually intelligent. In the preceding example, the algorithm has no idea what a sundial is or what a bird is, but a sundial is a shadow-casting object, and so is the bird. A human intelligence will bring more context and identify that this is more likely a bird, but you cannot guarantee an AI system will do that.

So, when you want to start working with AI, you need to look carefully at your data and understand whether it is good enough to train an AI model. If your data is of poor quality, AI is not a magic bullet that will fix the problem. Any intelligence, artificial or real, will make bad decisions when those decisions are made on bad data. As such, it is vital to ensure that the data you are training a predictive model on is the best it can be. And in these circumstances, it can be acceptable to start processing data to remove outliers.

But what if you don't want to train your own model? What about using pretrained models? While they may have been trained on bigger datasets, and this can reduce the impact of outliers, they come with their own risks.

Most of these models will come from commercial providers, and these providers are reluctant to share the specific data they are using to train their models. Therefore, these models can start producing unexpected results, so care must be taken to keep validating the outputs from these predictions.

It's also worth considering when not to use AI predictive models. AI is typically non-deterministic, that is to say, given the same set of inputs, there is no guarantee the output will always be the same.

Rather, predictions made by AI are probabilistic; they're based on the probability of outcomes. This poses a problem when you use AI to predict things that are broadly deterministic. The outcome, for example, of a small price increase will typically have a fairly linear impact on the gross margin. This is especially true for non-elective purchases such as groceries as there's a limit beyond which the consumer can reduce their overall spend. That said, there are areas around pricing where AI could be valuable since it can factor in the impact of price change on the customer's chances of making the purchase at all.

Finally, we must consider the risks of generative AI in creating reports and writing code. There has been a trend in recent years for the use of generative AI by non-professionals to create code to build everything from small utility scripts right the way up to full-blown applications. To be clear, there is nothing inherently wrong with using AI tools to produce code. Where the problems begin, however, is when nobody in the organization knows what the code produced actually does. This will raise numerous issues from maintainability to data security. Let's look at some of these in detail.

Maintainability

If nobody knows how the code works, how will you fix it if it goes wrong? The obvious answer here is to go back to the AI that generated the code, but to what extent can you now trust it? After all, it got the code wrong in the first place. It might be that the original prompt was wrong, but just as likely is the possibility that the model was trained too long ago and is working off old information, or else it has been improperly grounded and is repeating information that was wrong in the first place. After all, it is not uncommon to see responses on internet forums that are just false.

Accuracy

If you have used AI to generate code, how sure are you that the output is accurate? This can be mainly covered by comprehensive testing. AI is not necessarily any more error-prone than a human developer, but a human developer having an understanding of how the code relates to the data is better positioned to understand the edge cases that testing can miss.

Security

This is the big one. If you truly do not understand the code, how sure are you that it is not sending your data to bad actors or otherwise leaking it on the internet? In a Power BI context, it is very unlikely that this will happen with DAX calculations. But of course, Power BI is more than DAX. You can add Python scripts, and Power Query can make calls to web APIs, so it is vital to understand what the code is doing and protect your data assets.

So, does all of this mean we should be avoiding AI? Clearly, that is not practical. But the risks need to be managed.

Managing and mitigating the risk

The risks posed by AI can be fairly easily managed by the imposition of a strong governance process. This is an area that needs to be considered from the perspective of policy, rather than technological controls. As an organization, it is important that there is a clear, enforceable, and enforced policy framework for the use of AI tools.

That framework should consider the following:

- Acceptable use of generative AI
- Peer review process for code built by AI (although this should apply to all code, no matter what)
- Appropriate use cases for AI-driven predictive analytics
- Review process for the accuracy of predictions
- Data loss prevention procedures
- Response protocols in the case of data leaks or other issues detected in AI usage

Such a framework should also be reviewed on a regular basis to ensure that it remains in compliance with the regulations of the day.

Summary

In this chapter, we learned what AI is and how it can be used in finance reporting and business intelligence projects. We considered how generative AI can be leveraged to increase productivity and help create new reports. We looked at how we can store data for AI and the steps we need to take to ensure that the organization is ready for AI. In the context of Power BI, we saw how it fits into Microsoft Fabric and, finally, looked at the dangers and risks associated with AI and how we can create a governance framework to mitigate them.

Get this book's PDF version and more

Scan the QR code (or go to `https://www.packtpub.com/unlock`). Search for this book by name, confirm the edition, and then follow the steps on the page.

UNLOCK NOW

Note: Keep your invoice handy. Purchases made directly from Packt don't require an invoice.

13

Evolving and Maintaining Your Reports

Having built our reports, we will now turn our attention to sharing reports with our users and managing those reports over the long term.

Throughout this book, we've worked in Power BI Desktop, which is the developer environment for Power BI. As this is a file-based application, it's not ideal for sharing reports with users. Emailing PBIX files to users will result in version issues and duplication. We've all been there with Excel and other files that have been distributed via email, where everyone is confused about which version is the latest.

So, it's important to have robust practices to secure and share your reports, ensuring the right users have the right reports in a secure manner. This chapter will cover that.

Beyond that, we need to consider how to keep the data current. If the data becomes old, the report will have limited use. This should be automatic, to minimize the manual handling of data and the possibility of data refresh being forgotten or being missed because the person responsible for it is off work.

The next step in the life cycle of a report is to make provision for change. Organizations evolve over time, and unless the reporting suite also evolves, it will quickly become out of date and fall out of use. There needs to be consideration of how new requirements are captured, validated, and implemented.

The final step is to retire old reports. This requires a process of identifying reports that are no longer used, identifying candidates for deletion, and deleting them from the Power BI tenant.

By the end of this chapter, you will understand the following:

- The core features of the administration portal

- The importance of life cycle management
- The basic principles of security
- How to ensure that data is kept up to date in published reports

There's a lot of important information to cover in this chapter, so please grab a drink, sit back, and take it all in.

User access and publishing to the web

To make our reports useful, we have to make them available to our users. We will start by looking at how to get everything set up.

Admin portal and publishing to the web

In this section, we discuss one of the most important settings in the Fabric admin portal for security. Please note that the admin portal for Power BI is also called the Fabric admin portal and is an important component of Power BI to be aware of. As an aside, we recommend working through the settings to check what may be enabled by default, as there may be some settings that you want to change.

The first step toward securing organizational data is to identify and classify the data being managed. Consideration should be given to who the intended audience is and the consequences if the data is lost or transmitted to unauthorized people inside or outside of the organization. Data leaks are very serious and happen more frequently than you may think.

For the most part, when dealing with purely financial data, the risk will be commercial. If, however, there is personally identifying data, additional consideration should be given to securing this data, as there are likely more stringent regulations with regard to personal data than commercial data.

It's important to note that there are no failsafe methods to prevent data loss. You can't guarantee that there won't be a malicious actor within an organization, or, as is more likely, human error, which causes data leakage.

One key setting to check for the organization is whether or not the **Publish to web** function is enabled in the admin portal. When this feature is enabled, users can publish reports openly to anyone on the internet.

While this can be useful for publishing information from an organization into the public domain, if used incorrectly, it can expose confidential data to anyone with the correct link.

The admin portal can be found by selecting the cog wheel icon in Power BI (or Fabric), which is in the top right of the screen:

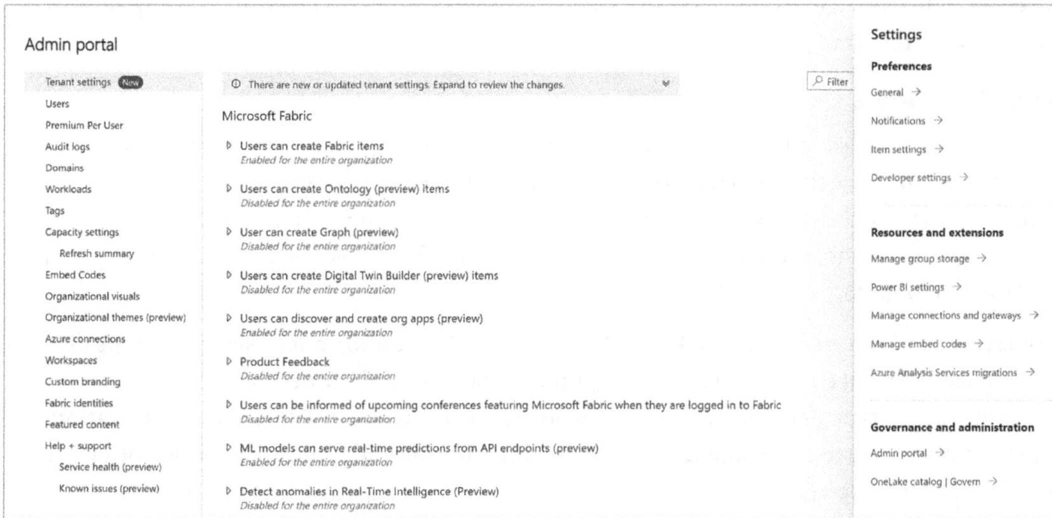

Figure 13.1: The Fabric admin portal

Here, admin users can access organization-wide settings—a number of which are useful for preventing the download and sharing of data, such as the following:

- **Publish to Web** (this should always be disabled unless there is a need for it)
- **Download to CSV**
- **Download to Excel**
- **Download report**

Restricting these can reduce the risk of data loss, since it makes it harder to extract data from a report and then send it out via email or save it to a USB drive. Conversely, restricting these can make the reporting suite less flexible and frustrate users, who may start creating their own ways around it, such as building reports in Excel. There are always trade-offs with decisions around security.

The Fabric admin portal has a comprehensive list of settings that we recommend you review and assess how they affect your organization in terms of security and daily usage.

Next, we will explain workspaces in the Power BI service and how they can be set up to help manage your reports.

Workspaces

Workspaces behave similarly to folders on a computer, storing reports and associated objects such as the data model. When a report is published from Power BI Desktop, there are two components loaded to a workspace: the data model and the report. Please note that a workspace cannot store other information, such as Excel files or Word documents; it's solely for Power BI objects.

You create workspaces within the Power BI service, and it's important to select the type of workspace; this will control the license required for accessing the workspace. The options available for the type of workspace will depend on the licenses owned by your organization and the licenses currently available from Microsoft, but this will typically include options such as **Pro** or **Fabric Capacity**.

Whichever license mode is assigned, it will determine which license the user will require when accessing the reports within that workspace.

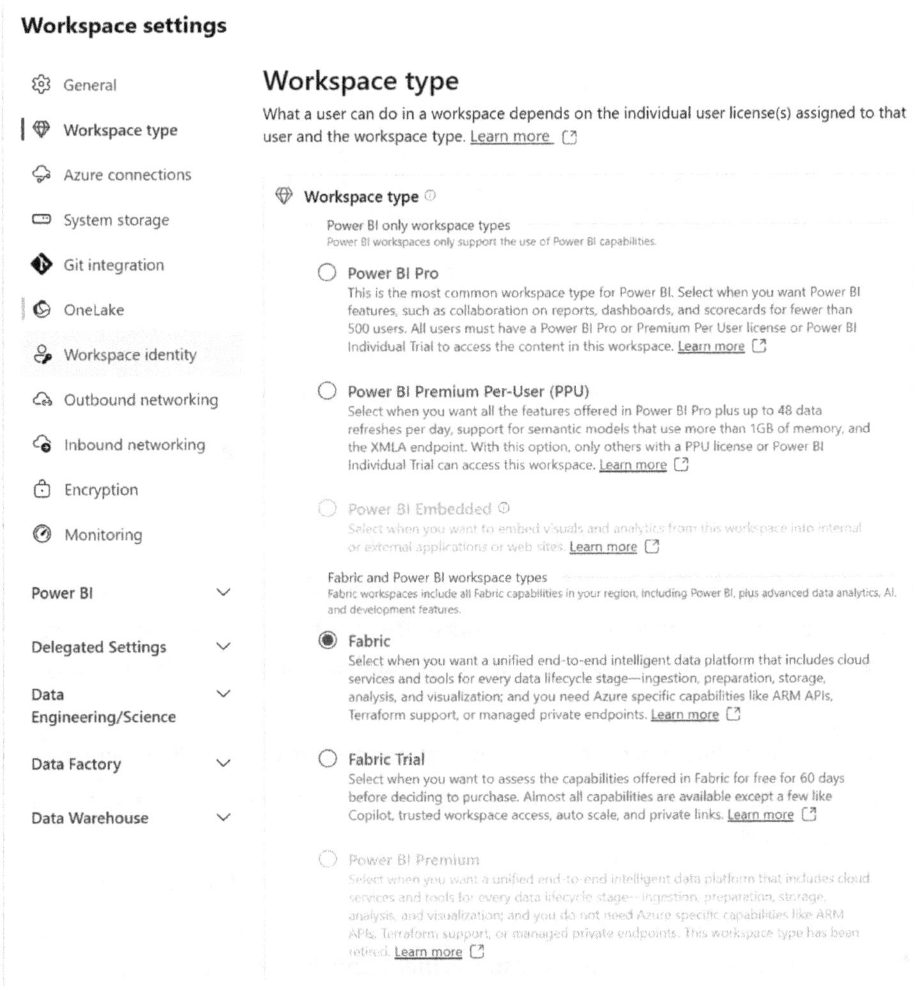

Figure 13.2: Applying a licence to a workspace

Once a workspace has been created, it can be shared with other users.

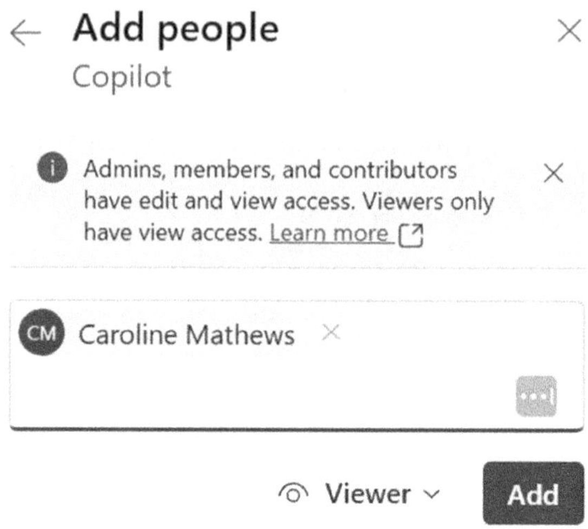

Figure 13.3: Adding users to a workspace

Controlling access to data and reports via workspace permissions is one method to manage security for Power BI. In granting access to the workspace, you grant access to the reports and the data contained within that workspace. There are a number of access levels that can be applied:

- **Viewer**: Can view the reports and data, but cannot modify or create new reports
- **Contributor**: Can view reports and data, and can create new reports based on data stored in the workspace
- **Member**: Can do all that a contributor can, but can also control some permissions and update apps
- **Admin**: Has full control over the workspace, including deleting the workspace

Most users will typically be viewers or contributors, with only a few admins or members.

The downside of securing data only in workspaces, however, is that it is a very blunt tool; either the user sees everything in the report or they see nothing. Sometimes a more nuanced approach is required, and that calls for row-level security, which we discuss later in this chapter.

Now that individuals can access the workspace, we need to consider the processes of publishing reports to the workspace.

Publishing reports

Now that we have our workspaces with the correct security established, we can publish reports to them.

From Power BI Desktop

From Power BI Desktop, it's a straightforward process: the user must ensure they have logged in to the service from Power BI Desktop, and then select the **Publish** button in the home ribbon bar. This will launch a new window, where the user is presented with the workspaces that they have access to, and they can then select and publish the report. It's a straightforward process to publish a report to a Power BI service workspace from Power BI Desktop.

Within the service

You can directly import semantic models and paginated reports from within the Power BI service using the **Import** button within a workspace. This is less commonly used than publishing from Power BI Desktop, but the capability exists.

Workspace planning

You have many choices when planning your workspaces, and it's easy for workspaces, like computer folders, to get out of control. We recommend limiting the number of people creating workspaces to maintain control, as well as planning workspaces with specific purposes.

A common deployment method is to create workspaces based on typical software development practices, using a development, test, and production structure. This means a base of three workspaces:

- Development (or dev)
- Test (which can be called test or UAT for user acceptance testing)
- Production (or prod)

Once development work reaches a stable milestone, we move the content from development to a test environment for validation and quality assurance. The test environment should be accessed by users who will test the reports before they're published to a production environment. The test workspace would normally mirror the production environment in terms of its configuration and security settings, allowing users to review functionality, validate data accuracy, and conduct user acceptance testing. This testing phase ensures that all reports meet business requirements and perform optimally before reaching end users. Once testing has been completed, we promote the report content to the production environment.

This production workspace represents the live business environment with formal governance controls, monitored refresh schedules, and established support procedures. The maintenance phase encompasses ongoing activities such as data refresh monitoring, performance optimization, user access reviews, and content updates to ensure continued business value delivery across all environments.

Successful workspace life cycle management requires the implementation of automated governance frameworks, regular audit processes, and clear escalation procedures to address issues promptly. We know many organizations don't follow these practices, but we recommend that you review what would help your organization.

Deployment pipelines

Deployment pipelines are a Power BI capability that allows the cloning of content from one workspace to another. For example, in our scenario, we can clone and deploy from **development** to **test** and from **test** to **production**.

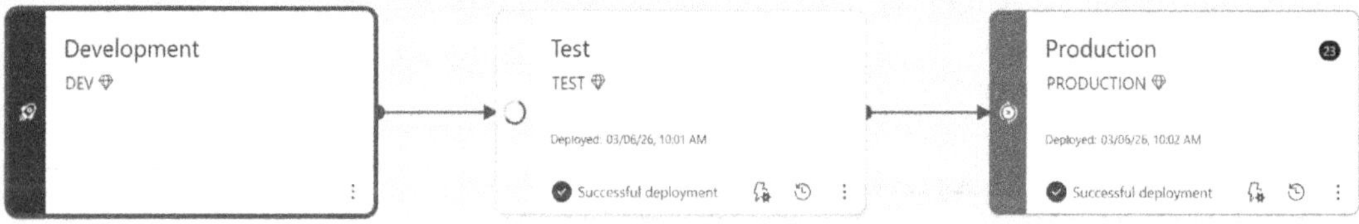

Figure 13.4: Creating a deployment pipeline

When cloning an environment, the components are as follows:

- Datasets
- Reports
- Data flows
- Dashboards
- Paginated reports

Once the pipeline has been created and content assigned, the pipeline can be deployed.

We should note that deployment pipelines in Power BI are a Premium license feature, requiring a Premium Per User or Fabric license. They make the process of moving reports through the development cycle far easier, largely removing the risk of uploading the wrong semantic model and report.

Sharing reports

When a user within the organization requires a report, it can be shared from within the workspace either directly or as a Power BI app. We will discuss both and the use cases for each.

Workspace versus app sharing

You can share reports with users directly from the production workspace. This is done by adding users via the **Manage Access** button. As mentioned earlier, there are different access options, and **Viewer** should be the default for most users. **Contributor** and **Member** allow users to change reports, which should only be done when planned. Having certain users make changes to reports on a whim can be very frustrating for other users.

We advise against sharing the production workspace, and workspaces in general, with anything other than a very limited number of users. Workspaces, in general, don't provide the best user experience for navigating between reports, as users need to click in and out of reports to navigate between them. This is where Power BI apps have become the default sharing method for most deployments.

Power BI apps allow you to build a collection of reports in an easy-to-navigate package for groups of users. Users can easily navigate between reports within the app, and folder structures can be built that mirror organizational structure. Within your Power BI environment, you can build one or many apps that users can download. When we say download, they only download to their own app workspace.

After adding the content to the app, you'll need to add an **audience**. An audience is a list of users who can access the app, and you can add one or many audiences who can see different reports within a single app. As you can see, there is a lot of flexibility and decisions to make with Power BI apps. Do you choose one app and multiple audiences or many apps and single audiences? Or multiple apps with multiple audiences? In reality, you would go with whatever suits your user base.

Apps are a view-only experience for your users, although they can manipulate slicers and use buttons within the reports. With a list of multiple reports, users can quickly click in and out of reports with ease when accessing an app.

When deploying apps, it's best to avoid giving users access to workspaces. There still needs to be a method for users to access the underlying data: the **Manage Permissions** option, which you'll find when clicking on the ellipses against the semantic model that's linked to the reports. For most users, we recommend that they just have read access to the semantic model. The benefit of this deployment method is that users don't see the workspaces, just the apps.

That then raises the question of when users should have workspace access. The main use of workspaces for users is self-service reporting, where users can build reports against semantic models. For this use case, we recommend a separate workspace from production, as users will have the permissions to change production reports.

As you can see, there are a lot of choices and options for deploying reports to users, and many of those choices will depend on your needs. If you want a robust basic model, we recommend the following:

- Workspaces for development, testing, and production. If you have Premium licenses, use deployment pipelines. Your testers will need access to the test workspace.
- Apps for the majority of users to interact with reports.
- If you have a self-service model, separate workspaces for those users so they don't break production reports.

Row-level security

Row-level security is, as the name suggests, a way of controlling access to data at the level of a row. What do we mean by that? In the context of finance reporting, let's consider the position of the sales manager. The sales manager is likely to need access to certain data held within the suite of reports, but not all the data. For example, they would expect to be able to access data on sales revenue, costs, and so forth, but the organization might not want them to be able to interrogate data on the salary overheads or building maintenance costs. In this case, row-level security can be used to restrict which accounts or account categories are visible to a user.

The starting point for setting up row-level security is to identify the account categories (for example) that they are permitted to see, and create a role in the Power BI file (**Modeling** | **Manage Roles**) to which can be attached rules that filter the data:

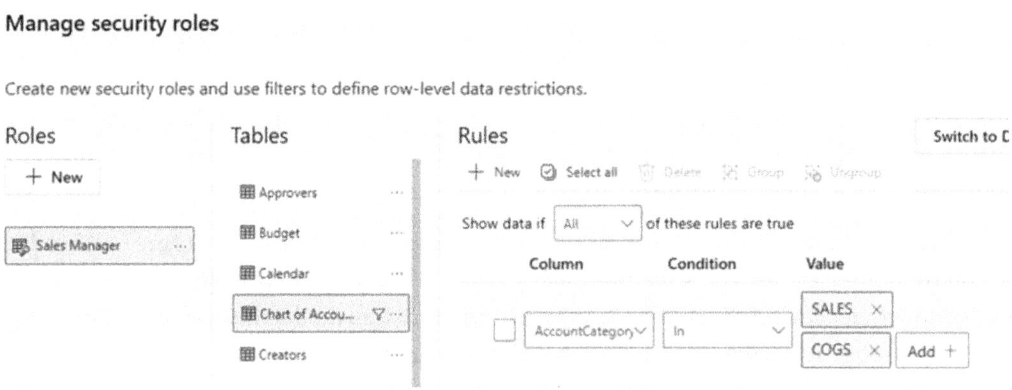

Figure 13.5: Setting up row-level security roles

Now, once the report is published to a workspace, we can assign users to the role. To do this, navigate to the semantic model, click the ellipsis, and select **Security**.

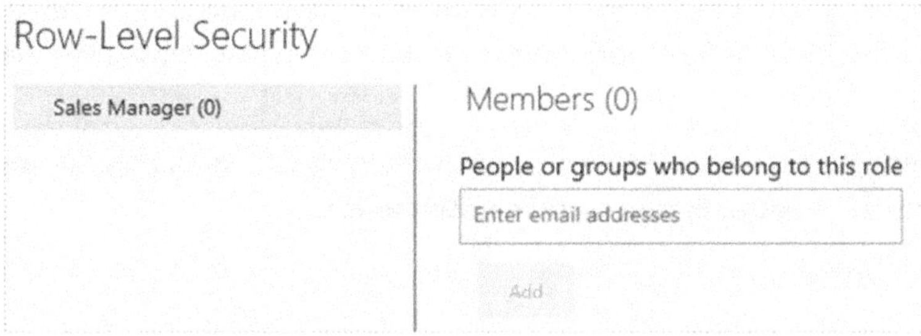

Figure 13.6: Adding users to row-level security roles

Most of the time, however, row-level security needs to be much more complex and dynamic than this simple example, and requires a level of DAX coding beyond the scope of this book. There are also pitfalls associated with row-level security that must be considered. First, it will impact report performance as it increases the amount of processing to be done. Second, it can create some inconsistent results. The preceding example does not include all the relevant offset accounts, and therefore, the report will not fully balance. Finally, if done incorrectly, it could lead to unauthorized data access. We therefore recommend taking expert advice before embarking on any project that will require row-level security.

Data refreshes

Refreshing data once the Power BI report has been published within the service is achieved within the service. If the data source is on-premises, a gateway will be required that allows the Power BI service to securely access data on-premises.

The gateway handles authentication, encrypts data during transfer, and can be configured to refresh datasets on a schedule, ensuring your Power BI reports always display current information while maintaining your organization's security requirements and keeping sensitive data within your premises.

The gateway is a software component installed on an on-premises server with access to the data required by the report. Typically, the gateway should be installed on a server that remains available 24/7. If installed on a normal desktop PC or laptop, the gateway would become inaccessible if the machine is turned off. For security reasons, the gateway only requires outbound communications. It "watches" for a signal from the Power BI service that tells it when to send data. That means that no internet services need to reach into your local corporate network.

When a data source is an online service such as Microsoft Dynamics 365 or Office 365, the data connection to Power BI can refresh without the need for a gateway. This makes refreshing data a lot simpler and easier to maintain.

The gateway settings are configured within the Power BI service, under the settings of the semantic data model's **Gateway and cloud connections** tab.

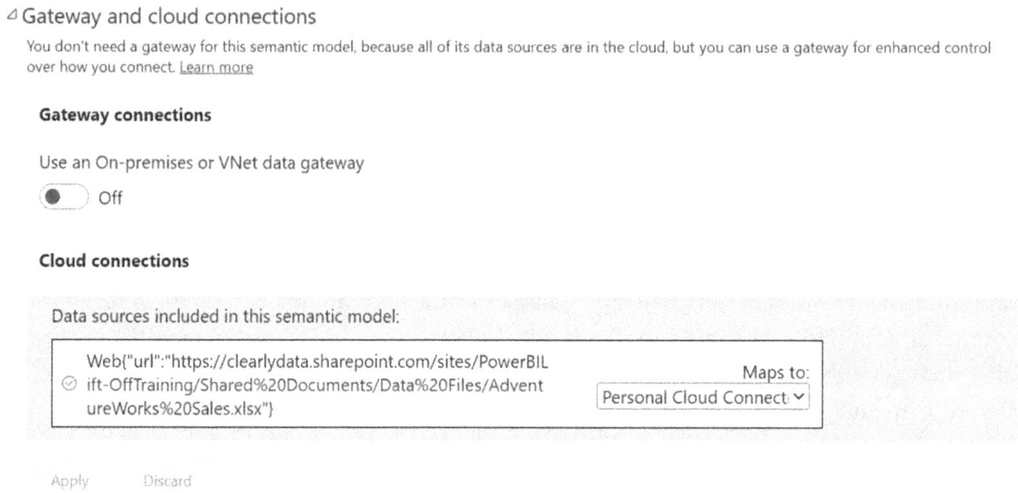

Figure 13.7: Configuring a gateway connection

If the data model is an import data model, the limitation of refreshing data is governed by your Power BI license; for example, the Pro license allows up to eight refreshes a day.

Scheduling refreshes is configured within the Power BI service, under the settings of the semantic model, and can be set up for daily or weekly refreshes of the data.

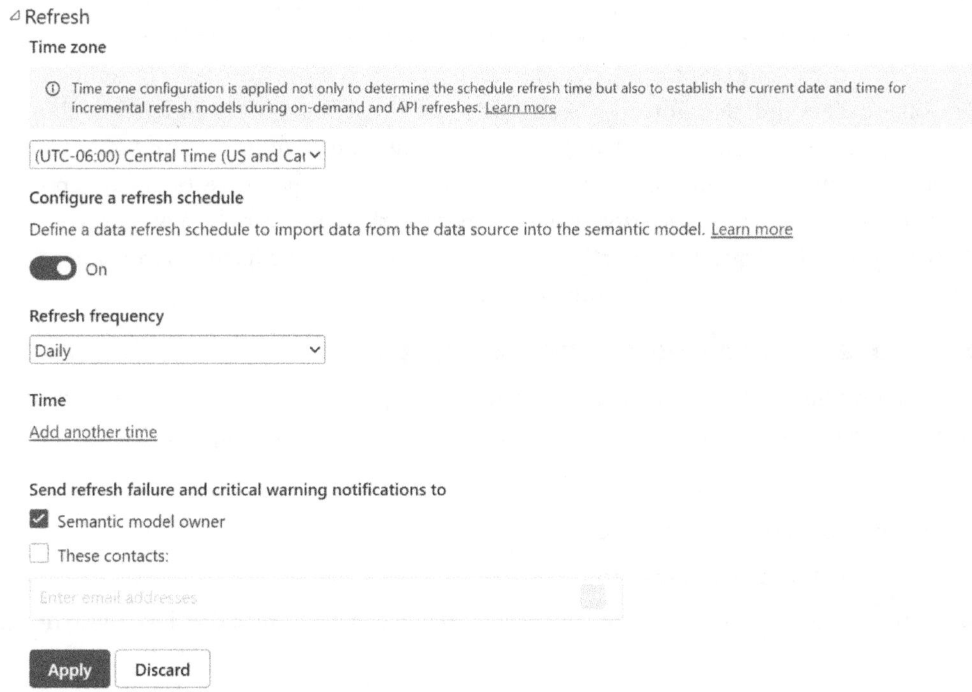

Figure 13.8: Setting up data refreshes

As mentioned, Pro licensing allows for 8 refreshes in a 24-hour period, whereas Premium licenses allow for 48 refreshes in the same period.

Change control

Once reports are released, refreshes are set up, and users have access, there's still work to do. Businesses evolve, and reporting requirements change. In order to remain relevant, the suite of financial reports must change with the business. It's therefore important that there is a process in place to capture changing user requirements and prioritize those changes. Depending on the size of the organization, this might be as simple as taking in requests via email. In larger organizations, these requests may come in via the IT helpdesk or be submitted to a project management tool such as Jira.

Bug or change

When users have issues, a system for enabling support requests will help your deployment. It's useful to divide the requests into bugs and changes, as you may want to resolve bugs quickly and plan changes more deliberately based on organizational need and available resources.

Whether a request is a bug or a change can sometimes be a hard question to answer. Many requests for change are submitted in the form of a bug report, such as "This report doesn't include sales orders." The reality, in this example, is that the report was never designed to include sales orders and, therefore, is a change request, not a bug. This is understandable, as the user may not have been involved in the original requirements gathering and may not know the original specification. Sometimes, users may word their change requests as bug reports, thinking that resolution may get prioritized. In any case, there needs to be a process to establish whether the request is reporting a bug that will need to be fixed or requesting a change that may or may not require immediate action.

Planning and implementation changes

Once new requirements have been captured, the next step is to plan which will be worked on and when. This will depend on a number of factors. Here are some examples:

- The number of users requesting the change
- The cost of making the change
- The business value of the change

Once the next set of changes is selected and planned, we can move into the development phase.

The implementation of changes is very similar to the initial implementation of a Power BI project, with one important difference: it's vital that you don't break what's already there.

That means regression testing is required. It's not sufficient to just test the new features that are being added to a report. You must also test the existing features to ensure that they continue to work as expected. Typically, this can be done with the set of tests carried out when the report was first created. Usually, regression tests don't need to be as comprehensive as initial testing, but they must never be missed.

Once implemented, tested, and ready to publish, the last step before release is communication. It is important to communicate with your users that a change is coming, and how that change affects the reports. Nothing bogs down an IT helpdesk like calls about a change in a report that nobody was expecting. It's often assumed that any such change represents a problem in the application.

Beyond keeping our reports up to date and relevant with new features, the final steps in the reporting life cycle are monitoring and retirement.

Let's start with monitoring the use of our Power BI reports.

Monitoring

Usage metrics are available for reports within the Power BI service. Clicking on the ellipses next to a report name will present a **View usage metrics report** option. Once selected, this will open a usage report about the selected reports.

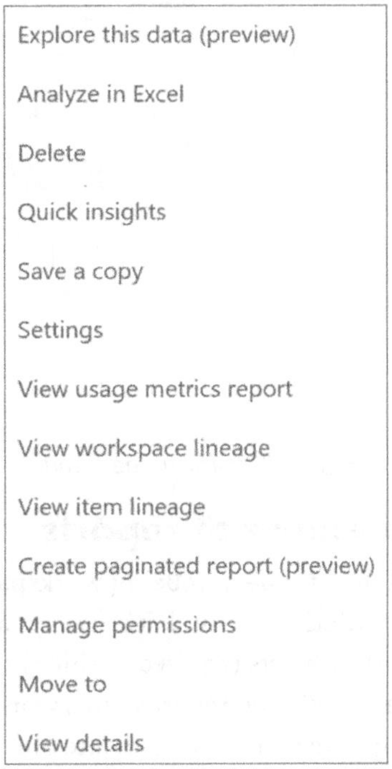

Figure 13.9: Accessing the usage metrics

The usage report will show information such as access, views, and viewers. There is also a **Report performance** page. Note that only a month of history is stored within the service.

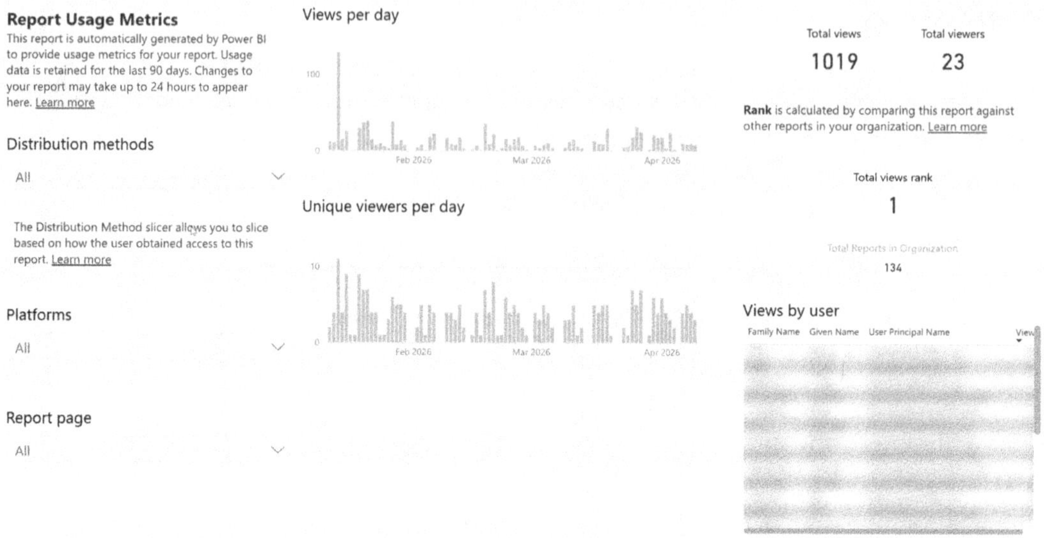

Figure 13.10: The usage report

Maintenance and retirement of reports

Within the service, there are no limits to the number of workspaces or the number of semantic models, reports, or dashboards. With that in mind, it is always a good idea to keep the environment lean and only have the reports required within the service. For example, there is little point in having report v1, report v2, and report v3 in a workspace when users will only access report v3. A general tidy-up is recommended; delete unnecessary reports, semantic models, and workspaces if they are not used or required.

It's important to work with users and communicate these plans, especially plans to delete reports. An alternative method to straight deletion may be a retirement process where reports are moved to an archive workspace and deleted if not required after a set period, say, six months.

Summary

This chapter has covered a lot of ground. We started by describing security and the admin portal, and the importance of restricting publishing to the web.

We then moved on to setting up workspaces, publishing reports, and methods of managing the development process with your workspaces. From there, we explained the importance of using Power BI apps as the main delivery mechanism of reports to your users.

We explained data refresh and the difference between on-premises gateways and cloud apps that may not require the gateway.

Along the way, we expanded on security by briefly explaining row-level security as a method to filter your dataset according to user needs and responsibilities.

We ended the chapter on the importance of longer-term maintenance and retirement of reports to ensure your reports are current and old reports are not lingering within your environment.

With this, we have reached the end of this book. By now, you should have a good appreciation of how you can leverage Power BI to deliver high-quality, maintainable financial reporting to your users, from sourcing data through to how to use DAX and Power Query to ensure calculations are done robustly and data models are efficient. You will have an appreciation of how you can go about enriching your financial data with additional datasets, and how best to visualize the data. Finally, we have covered how to ensure that everything works as expected and more abstract topics around how to leverage AI and how to manage your reports into the future. We would like to thank you for reading, and wish you an enjoyable future developing financial reports in Power BI.

14

Unlock Your Exclusive Benefits

Your copy of this book includes the following exclusive benefits:

DRM-Free PDF Version

Download DRM-free PDF and ePub copies of this book.

7-Day Packt Library Access

Get 7-day unlimited access to 8,000+ books and videos. No credit card required.

Available for first-time Packt+ trial users only.

Next-Gen Reader Access

Read this book on Packt Reader with progress sync, dark mode and note-taking.

Follow the guide below to unlock them. The process takes only a few minutes and needs to be completed once.

Unlock this book's free benefits in 3 easy steps

Step 1

Keep your purchase invoice ready for *Step 3*. If you have a physical copy, scan it using your phone and save it as a PDF, JPG, or PNG.

For more help on finding your invoice, visit `https://www.packtpub.com/en-us/unlock?step=1`.

> Note
>
> **Note**: If you bought this book directly from Packt, no invoice is required. After *Step 2*, you can access your exclusive content right away.

Step 2

Scan the QR code or go to `https://www.packtpub.com/unlock`.

On the page that opens (similar to *Figure 14.1* on desktop), search for this book by name and select the correct edition.

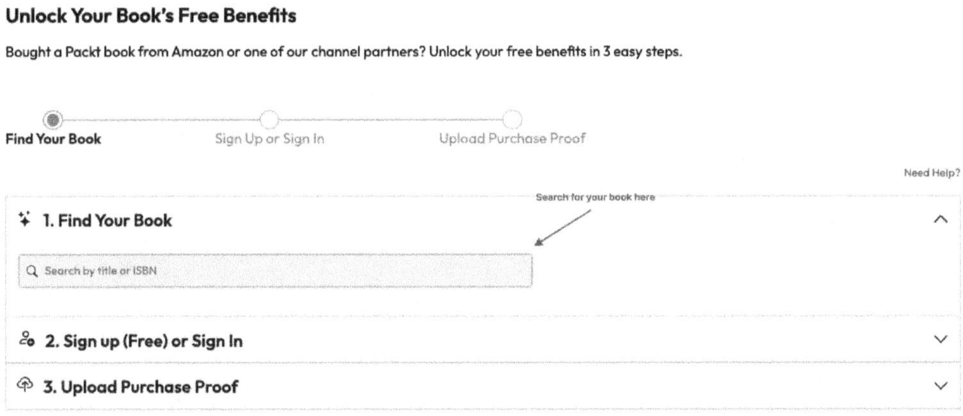

Figure 14.1: Packt unlock landing page on desktop

Step 3

After selecting your book, sign in to your Packt account or create one for free. Then upload your invoice (PDF, PNG, or JPG, up to 10 MB). Follow the on-screen instructions to finish the process.

Need help

If you get stuck and need help, visit `https://www.packtpub.com/unlock-benefits/help` for a detailed FAQ on how to find your invoices and more. This QR code will take you to the help page.

Note

Note: If you are still facing issues, reach out to `customercare@packt.com`.

https://www.packtpub.com

Subscribe to our online digital library for full access to over 7,000 books and videos, as well as industry leading tools to help you plan your personal development and advance your career. For more information, please visit our website.

Why subscribe?

- Spend less time learning and more time coding with practical eBooks and Videos from over 4,000 industry professionals
- Improve your learning with Skill Plans built especially for you
- Get a free eBook or video every month
- Fully searchable for easy access to vital information
- Copy and paste, print, and bookmark content

At https://www.packtpub.com, you can also read a collection of free technical articles, sign up for a range of free newsletters, and receive exclusive discounts and offers on Packt books and eBooks.

Other Books You May Enjoy

If you enjoyed this book, you may be interested in these other books by Packt:

Power BI for Finance

Martin Kratky

ISBN: 978-1-83763-501-6

- Apply multi-currency handling and group consolidation techniques in Power BI
- Model discounted cash flow and company valuation scenarios
- Design and manage write-back workflows with Dynamics BPP and Acterys
- Integrate Excel and Power BI using live connections and cube formulas
- Utilize AI, Copilot, and LLMs to enhance automation and insight generation
- Create complete finance-focused dashboards for sales and operations planning

Learn Microsoft Power BI

Greg Deckler

ISBN: 978-1-83664-741-6

- Understand the fundamentals of Microsoft Fabric and Copilot
- Plan and manage your business intelligence projects
- Connect to and transform data using Power Query
- Create semantic models and DAX calculations optimized for analysis and reporting
- Uncover business insights and design professional reports
- Deploy and govern Power BI, with a focus on gateways and deployment pipelines

Packt is searching for authors like you

If you're interested in becoming an author for Packt, please visit `https://authors.packt.com` and apply today. We have worked with thousands of developers and tech professionals, just like you, to help them share their insight with the global tech community. You can make a general application, apply for a specific hot topic that we are recruiting an author for, or submit your own idea.

Share your thoughts

Now you've finished *Financial Modeling and Reporting with Microsoft Power BI*, we'd love to hear your thoughts! Scan the QR code below to go straight to the Amazon review page for this book and share your feedback or leave a review on the site that you purchased it from.

`https://packt.link/r/1835880274`

Your review is important to us and the tech community and will help us make sure we're delivering excellent quality content.

Index

A

AI Services 286

AI projects
- AI capabilities, developing 281
- capabilities, developing 280 – 283
- long-term considerations 279

AI risks 287, 288
- accuracy 288
- maintainability 288
- managing 289
- mitigating 289
- security 288

AVERAGE function 58 - 61

Agile methodology 11

Artificial Intelligence (AI) 266
- AI project 267
- business need 267, 268
- combining, with Power BI 268 – 271
- current trends 266
- Foundations 266
- technical method, for solving issues 268

Artificial Intelligence (AI), with Power BI
- data schema, simplifying 271, 272
- instructions, adding 274 – 277
- short and medium-term data 277, 278
- planning and storage
- verified answers 272 – 274

audience 299

B

budget data handling 153
- daily, budgeting 157 – 160
- monthly, budgeting 154 – 156

budget table
- creating 150 – 153
- incorporating, with Power Query 166

budget variance report 221
- headline figures, adding 226
- matrix, adding 225, 226
- over time change, displaying 227
- slicers, adding 228 – 230
- table, adding 222 – 225

budgets analyzing 163 - 165

C

CALCULATE function 84 - 86

Calendar table 34 - 36

Chart of Accounts (CoA) 36, 150
- hierarchy 38
- totaling account 38 – 40

ChatGPT 142

Claude 142

Copilot 142

Cost of Goods Sold (COGS) 15, 65

calculated columns 57, 58

change
- bugs 304
- controlling 303
- implementation 304
- maintenance retirement of reports 306
- monitoring 305
- planning 304

common data transformations 134
- column names, changing with AI 141, 142
- conditional columns, adding 135, 136
- custom columns, adding 137
- data merging 138
- data types, changing 134, 135
- opening balances, correcting 142 – 146
- pivoting columns 140
- unpivoting columns 140

credit and debit totals
- adding 64 – 68

D

DAX calculations 56
- calculated columns 57, 58
- measures 57, 58

Data Analysis eXpressions (DAX) **55, 56**
Data Analysis eXtensions (DAX) **16**
data cleansing
in Power BI 243
in Power Query 243
data model
credit and debit totals, adding 64 – 68
measures, adding 61 – 64
data refreshes
setting up 301, 302
data sources
considerations 18, 19
identifying 18 – 21
database **26**
denormalization **32**
dimension table **30, 31**
drill-through **160 - 163**

E

Enterprise Resource Planning (ERP) **101**
Extract, Transform, and Load (ETL) **104, 123**
entity **27, 28**

F

Fabric subscription **268**
fact table **30, 31**
financial application, terminology
database 26
entity 27, 28
facts and dimensions 30
relationships 29
schema 31, 32
table 27
financial reporting, core entities
Calendar table 34 – 36
Chart of Accounts (CoA) 36 – 38
common terminology 26
creating 26
financial application structure 33
transactions 41
financial reporting, key visuals **199**
cards 208
magnitude 199, 200
matrices 206, 207
over time change 201, 202
part-to-whole 202 – 206
tables 206
foreign exchange **93 - 98**
considerations 51, 52
pitfalls, of calculating in data model 52

G

General Ledger (GL) **101**
Generally Accepted Accounting Principles (GAAP) **103**
generative AI (GenAI) tool **142**
groups **208**

H

hallucination **287**

I

International Financial Reporting Standards (IFRS) **103**
income statement
creating 69 – 76
incorrect data **234**
inventory data **172**
inventory measures
basics 180 – 187
creating 180
inventory snapshot data
working with 172 – 174
inventory snapshot data, measures **174**
CALCULATE 174, 175
period-on-period calculations 175, 176
SUM or SUMX 174

K

key performance indicators (KPIs) **192**

L

Large Language Models (LLMs) **266**

M

MAX function **58 - 60**
MIN function **58 - 60**
Microsoft Fabric
data engineering 285

data factory 285
data lakehouse 284, 285
data science 285, 286
data warehouse 284, 285
Power BI 286
real-time intelligence 286
storage 284
working with 283, 284

MoSCoW method 6

manual journal entries 103 - 105
facts and dimensions, deriving 109 – 111
linking, to GL transaction 111 – 120
structure, exploring 105 – 108

measures 57, 58
adding, to data model 61 – 64

modeling, via multiple companies or legal entities 46
approaches 47
company, linking to Chart of Accounts (CoA) 47, 48
company, linking to transaction 49 – 51

multiple budget models or scenarios
common structure, maintaining 166
working with 165

N

natural language processing (NLP) 266

non-functional testing 243, 244

O

OneLake 284

P

Power BI
data cleansing 242, 243

Power BI Desktop 102, 149

Power BI Report Builder 247
using 249 – 252

Power BI file (PBIX) 2

Power BI report
accurate numbers 190
designing 190
layout and design 193 – 195
purpose 192
responsive reports 191, 192
secure data 191

Power BI report, layout and design
corporate color schemes 198, 199
garish colors, avoiding 195, 196
negative space, using 197, 198
Subtle, rounded boundaries 196, 197

Power BI user types
administrators 17
consumers 16
creators 17
developers 17

Power Query 123 - 126
budget revisions, managing 167
columns, removing 129, 130
common data transformations 134
components 127, 128
data cleansing 242, 243
datasets, reducing with 128
multiple budgeting methods, managing 167
multiple budgets, managing 168
required tables or entities, importing 129
rows, removing 131 – 133
using, to incorporate into budget table 166

Profit and Loss (P&L) report 208

Proof of Concept (POC) 19

paginated reports
usage 248

percentages 87 - 89

printable income statement
creating 252 – 262

project scope
change control process 11
communication plan 13, 14
data sources 8, 9
detailed scoping 4 – 6
documentation and sign-off 14
goals and objectives, setting 4
resource planning and time management 10, 11
risk management 10
security and access 8
setting 2, 3
stakeholder identification and engagement 9, 10
standard reports 7
test plan 12
training plan 13

Q

QuickBooks **38**

R

R language **286**

relationships **29**
- many-to-many 29
- one-to-many 29
- one-to-one 29

relationships, in Power BI
- active, versus inactive relationships 46
- filter direction 46
- managing 42 – 45

report sharing **298**
- row-level security 300, 301
- workspace, versus app sharing 299

reports
- admin portal 292 – 294
- budget variance report 221
- building 208
- category groups, creating 209
- column chart, adding 213
- gross margin %, adding 216
- gross margin gauge, adding 218, 219
- headline figures 217
- matrix details, adding 213 – 216
- need for 14 – 16
- page, filtering for P&L items 211
- Profit and Loss (P&L) report 208
- publishing 297
- publishing, from Power BI Desktop 297
- publishing, to web 292 – 294
- publishing, within service 297
- slicers, adding 219
- table, adding 210
- title, adding 220, 221
- user access, granting 292
- workspaces 294 – 296

revenue **86**

S

SQL Server Analysis Services (SSAS) tabular models **127**

SUM function **58 - 60**

Spark **284**

Stock Keeping Unit (SKU) **173**

schema **31**
- star schema example 32

self-service business intelligence
- planning 21 – 23

sprints **11**

T

table **27**

time intelligence (TI) **89, 152**
- calculations 124
- period to date, easy way 89
- period to date, hard way 90 – 93

totaling account **38 - 40**

transaction-level reconciliation
- creating 238
- datasets, matching 241, 242
- line-level reconciliation 238 – 240
- row counts, checking 241, 242
- transactions, downloading 238

transactional inventory data
- inventory-specific dimensions 179
- working with 177, 178

transactions **41**

trial balance **77**
- common checks 235 – 237
- creating 78 – 82
- purpose 77
- report, creating 262
- using, to test data 235

W

Waterfall methodology **11**

workspace planning **297**
- deployment pipelines 298

www.ingramcontent.com/pod-product-compliance
Lightning Source LLC
LaVergne TN
LVHW060024210926
848481LV00013B/3786

* 9 7 8 1 8 3 5 8 8 0 2 6 5 *